THE CASE
for the
INVESTIGATIVE
JUDGMENT

Also by Marvin Moore

THE CASE
for the
INVESTIGATIVE JUDGMENT

Its Biblical Foundation

Marvin Moore

Pacific Press® Publishing Association
Nampa, Idaho
Oshawa, Ontario, Canada
www.pacificpress.com

Cover design by Steve Lanto
Cover resources from Dreamstime.com
Inside design by Aaron Troia

The author assumes full responsibility for the accuracy of all facts and quotations as cited in this book.

Unless otherwise noted, all Scripture quotations are from the New King James Version, copyright © 1979, 1980, 1982, Thomas Nelson, Inc., Publishers.

Scriptures quoted from KJV are from the King James Version of the Bible.

Scripture quoted from NASB are from *The New American Standard Bible*®, Copyright © 1960, 1962, 1963, 1968, 1971, 1972, 1973, 1975, 1977, 1995 by The Lockman Foundation. Used by permission.

Scripture quotations marked NIV are from the HOLY BIBLE, NEW INTERNATIONAL VERSION®. Copyright © 1973, 1978, 1984 by International Bible Society. Used by permission of Zondervan Publishing House. All rights reserved.

Scriptures quoted from RSV are from the Revised Standard Version of the Bible, copyright © 1946, 1952, 1971 by the Division of Christian Education of the National Council of the Churches of Christ in the U.S.A. Used by permission.

You can obtain additional copies of this book by calling toll-free 1-800-765-6955 or by visiting http://www.adventistbookcenter.com.

Library of Congress Cataloging-in-Publication Data:

Moore, Marvin, 1937-
    The case for the investigative judgment : its biblical foundation / Marvin Moore.
        p. cm.
    Includes bibliographical references.
    ISBN 13: 978-0-8163-2385-2 (pbk.)
    ISBN 10: 0-8163-2385-2 (pbk.)
    1. Seventh-day Adventists—Doctrines. 2. Judgment of God. I. Title.
    BX6154.M6235 2010
    236'.9—dc22

                                                    2010003462

10 11 12 13 14 • 5 4 3 2 1

Acknowledgments

Several individuals have contributed to making this book a success. My dear wife, Lois, put up with an awful lot of neglect so that I could write it. Also, I read each chapter to her as I completed it, and her questions about my meaning contributed to making this book significantly more understandable.

Several Adventist scholars have read parts of the manuscript. Dr. Martin Proebstle, a professor at the Bogenhofen Adventist Seminary in Austria, made his dissertation on Daniel 8:9–14 available to me, and he read the chapters dealing with Daniel. Dr. Felix Cortez, a professor in the religion department of Montemorelos University in Mexico, wrote a doctoral dissertation on Hebrews that he shared with me, and he read the chapters on Hebrews. Dr. Roy Gane, a professor in the Old Testament department at the Theological Seminary at Andrews University did his doctoral studies on the sacrificial system in Leviticus and has written several books on the topic, all of which I have read. He read the chapters in this book that deal with the Levitical rituals. And Dr. Brempong Owusu-Antwi, president of the Adventist University of Africa in Kenya, read the chapters on Daniel 9—the area of his dissertation.

Three individuals read the entire manuscript before it was published: Dr. Richard Davidson, the chair of the Old Testament department at the Seventh-day Adventist Theological Seminary at Andrews University. Dr. William Shea, a former professor of Old Testament at the Andrews University Theological Seminary and a former associate director of the General Conference Biblical Research Institute. And Dr. Desmond Ford, who for many years chaired the religion department at Avondale College in Australia, and who has since become a critic of the Adventist doctrine of the investigative judgment—the doctrine presented in this book. I deeply appreciate the time each of these individuals took from their busy schedules to read my manuscript and to share their comments.

Finally, every author benefits from the services of a good editor, and I have been fortunate to have the skilled touch of David Jarnes on several of my books. I first learned to appreciate David's editing when he was my associate editor at *Signs of the Times*®, and his careful work has made this book more readable for you. I also want to give credit to a group of people who are often overlooked in the editing process—the copy editors and proofreaders. Wendy Marcum, Tammie Knauff, and Amy Scoggins corrected misspelled words, verified facts, called attention to wording that might be misunderstood, and attended to all the many other details that are required to bring a book to the level of accuracy that you will find on the pages that follow.

To each of these experts in their various fields, I wish to say a hearty thank you!

Foreword

This book by Marvin Moore can well be considered the capstone to his long and illustrious writing career. He has published a number of other books as well as many articles on religious subjects. But in this case, he has considered a major biblical teaching—the judgment—from virtually every point of view.

A number of passages in Daniel and Revelation point to the judgment. Moore rightfully places considerable stress upon the great judgment scene in Daniel 7:9–14. This is a major source for the subject, and I believe he evaluates it correctly.

The judgment is "investigative" because it shows heavenly books being opened, and it is "pre-Advent," because it occurs in heaven before Jesus comes to earth the second time. And because this judgment is set in the context of the heavenly sanctuary, it is natural that Moore examines the major biblical texts that refer to the earthly sanctuary in Leviticus and its antitype in Hebrews. In all of this, he shows that the doctrine of the investigative judgment is a sound and solid biblical teaching. Other Seventh-day Adventist interpreters have demonstrated this before him, and Moore is in harmony with those previous interpreters, but he also, at times, gives his own unique interpretation to the biblical evidence.

One topic that has especially needed attention in years past is the individual believer's assurance of salvation in the light of the judgment. As Moore demonstrates so well in several of his early chapters, there is no conflict between judgment and assurance. The gospel itself calls for judgment regarding the way each Christian has responded to Christ's call. The investigative judgment at the end of time doesn't change any of the decisions that Christ has made about individuals through the course of time. Rather, it reveals what the great truth of righteousness by faith has accomplished in the lives of the saints throughout the ages.

When I was teaching at the Seventh-day Adventist Theological Seminary, a student once commented on a research paper I had written. "That was an excellent treatment of the subject," he said. "Now you should translate it into English!" No such translation is needed in Moore's book because his writing is always crystal clear; he doesn't leave the reader in doubt as to what he means.

Marvin Moore has produced a deeply significant study on the subject of the judgment. His treatment is comprehensive and detailed, and the conclusions he adopts are theologically and exegetically sound. I strongly recommend this book to both scholarly and lay readers who wish to be informed on this important biblical topic.

William H. Shea, MD, PhD
Former professor of Old Testament,
Seventh-day Adventist Theological Seminary
Former associate director, Biblical Research Institute
General Conference of Seventh-day Adventists
October 25, 2009

Contents

Chapter 1

Getting Started

Back about 1962, when I was a ministerial intern in the Southern California Conference, a friend brought to my attention a significant problem with our Seventh-day Adventist interpretation of Daniel 8:14 and the investigative judgment. He pointed out that in Daniel 8:9–12, it's the sins of the little horn that defile the sanctuary; therefore, the solution to the problem in Daniel 8:14 should address the sins of the little horn. However, according to the Adventist interpretation, it's the sins of God's people that are resolved in Daniel 8:14, not the sins of the wicked little horn. The criticism seemed reasonable to me then, and I've pondered it from time to time over the years. Since then, I've also become aware of other criticisms of our teaching about the investigative judgment.

Seventh-day Adventists bring together issues from several parts of the Bible to form this doctrine. There's the sanctuary in Leviticus, especially the Day of Atonement in chapter 16. In Daniel, there's the judgment scene in chapter 7; there's the desecrated sanctuary in chapter 8, with its cleansing after 2,300 days/years; and there's the seventy weeks in chapter 9, from which we calculate that the 2,300 years ended in 1844. Then there's the book of Hebrews, which features the sanctuary/temple in heaven and Christ's ministry there. And finally, there's the year-day principle by which we interpret the time prophecies in Daniel and Revelation.

A controversial teaching

The Seventh-day Adventist teaching that in 1844 God began an investigative judgment in heaven has been more controversial than the Sabbath, the state of the dead, and hell. It unquestionably has been our most disputed doctrine. Throughout most of our history, people both from outside our church and from within have challenged this doctrine, and it has caused more defections from the church than have any of our other teachings. Even some people who remain in the church, are loyal Sabbath keepers, and maintain their belief in the Adventist understanding of the state of the dead and hell, nevertheless question our teaching about the investigative judgment. Two of the most prominent of these during the late twentieth century were Raymond F. Cottrell and Desmond Ford.*

The biggest challenge our critics have thrown at us is that the Bible doesn't support the Adventist teaching regarding the investigative judgment. Instead, they say, it's based on the writings of Ellen White and the erroneous biblical interpretations of our uneducated pioneers. On the other hand, Ellen White said that "the correct understanding of [Christ's] ministration in the heavenly sanctuary is the foundation of our faith."[1] By Christ's "ministration," she meant everything associated with His ministry in the heavenly sanctuary, including an investigative judgment that began in 1844. And the church as a whole continues to insist that the investigative judgment doctrine *is* biblical. Our statement of Fun-

damental Beliefs affirms it,[2] and the *Handbook of Seventh-day Adventist Theology* includes at least two chapters that deal with the sanctuary and the investigative judgment.[3]

Why I wrote this book

When I completed the manuscript for my book *Could It* Really *Happen?*[4] I decided that it was time to settle once and for all in my own mind the various questions that have been raised about our teaching on the investigative judgment. My chief interest has been to investigate whether the various aspects of this key doctrine can be defended from the Bible. Hence this book, the production of which has unquestionably been the most complex writing project I have ever attempted.

I decided that I should begin with the best and most recent Adventist thinking on the investigative judgment and related topics. In March 2007, I had a speaking engagement on the campus of Andrews University in Berrien Springs, Michigan, so I decided to spend two or three extra days visiting with professors at the Theological Seminary and doing research at the Center for Adventist Research in the James White Library. I came home with several books and doctoral dissertations by Adventist scholars, all of which had been writ-

---

*Because Desmond Ford has been the most challenging and most well-known critic of recent times, his name appears frequently in this book, as I've responded to his critiques.

ten in the previous twenty years, including several since the year 2000. I have also read the relevant parts of several other recent books on the investigative judgment and related issues, including the seven-volume Daniel and Revelation series published by the Biblical Research Institute of the General Conference.* After spending more than a year of research and a year and a half writing, I have become thoroughly convinced that our historic teaching about an investigative judgment in the heavenly sanctuary that is the antitype of the earthly Day of Atonement is entirely biblical—which explains the title of this book: *The Case for the Investigative Judgment: Its Biblical Foundation.*

You may wonder what qualifies me to write on the various aspects of the investigative judgment since my training and professional experience are more in the line of writer and editor than of biblical scholar. My response is simple. The lay person often finds the technical language of scholars difficult to understand. My task as a writer is to become familiar enough with the work of the scholars that I can make it understandable to the average person. I want to bridge the gap between the scholar and the lay person. Also, most people, even

among those who can easily read and understand the technical language of biblical scholarship, don't have the time to pore through the literature dealing with the various aspects of the subject. That's why, in this book, I bring everything together in one place.

Growing in our understanding

In saying that I've found our historic teaching about the investigative judgment and related topics to be biblical, I don't mean that everything we've ever said about this doctrine is correct. We *have* changed some aspects of our teaching during the years since 1844. In the manuscript that Desmond Ford presented at Glacier View in 1980, he mentioned twenty-two aspects of our doctrine of the investigative judgment that we've modified over the years since 1844. Ford sees this as a problem. I don't. In fact, to the contrary, I believe we should expect such modifications. Ellen White herself said, "There is no excuse for anyone in taking the position . . . that all our expositions of Scripture are without an error."[5] That's why chapters 8 to 31 of this book are almost exclusively an evaluation of the biblical evidence about the investigative judgment and related topics.

*The Daniel and Revelation Committee Series comprises William H. Shea, vol. 1: *Selected Studies on Prophetic Interpretation;* Frank B. Holbrook (editor of volumes 2–7), vol. 2: *Symposium on Daniel;* vol. 3: *Seventy Weeks, Leviticus, Nature of Prophecy;* vol. 4: *Issues in the Book of Hebrews;* vol. 5: *Doctrine of the Sanctuary: A Historical Survey;* vol. 6: *Symposium on Revelation—Book I;* and vol. 7: *Symposium on Revelation—Book II.*

I realize that some of those who hold differing interpretations of the biblical evidence will disagree with me. This is true of nearly every doctrine Christians have ever drawn from the Bible. Some people interpret what the Bible says about a particular topic in one way, while others understand the same biblical evidence in another way, yet all are thoroughly convinced that their biblical interpretation is correct. That's simply how it is and how it always will be, and it's as true of the doctrine of the sanctuary and the investigative judgment as it is of any other doctrine. I don't expect to persuade every reader—especially those who have been critical of our teaching on this topic—that my understanding of the biblical evidence is the correct one. However, I hope that even those who continue to differ with me after they've read this book will agree that I've presented a strong biblical case for our Adventist teaching about the investigative judgment. That's the reason for the subtitle *Its Biblical Foundation*.

I also hope that this book can help to resolve some of the questions that have been nagging some of our pastors and thoughtful lay persons. I hope it can help them to see that our traditional teaching about the sanctuary and the investigative judgment *does* have a firm biblical foundation. If, in addition, one or more critics are persuaded by what I say, I will feel amply rewarded.

And I do expect the critics to respond to what I've written. I'd be disappointed if they didn't, for criticism of each others' thinking is how we all grow in our understanding. We Adventists have refined our doctrine of the investigative judgment over the years largely because of the validity of some of the criticisms that were lodged against it. Therefore, I shall read what the critics have to say in response to this book with interest, and I hope to learn from them.

Getting technical

Now for a few technical details. First, you will discover as you get into the book that I use two kinds of references: footnotes and endnotes. Footnotes are always indicated with the symbols *, †, ‡, etc. Their purpose is to provide information that it seemed to me might be helpful to the reader but that would detract from the flow of thought in the main text. Footnotes always appear at the bottom of the page where the material they contain applies, so the reader can refer to them quickly and get back to the main text. Endnotes provide information about the sources and other information. They are always indicated by numbers, and they appear at the end of the chapter to which they apply, where I've presented them in abbreviated form. The bibliography at the back of this book contains the full bibliographical information—

author, publisher, etc.—about the sources that I refer to or quote from.

Second, in this book I use the New King James Version (NKJV) as the primary translation. While I generally prefer the New International Version, I find it to be a bit too interpretive. The King James Version is quite literal in its translation, but because of the archaic English, I have chosen the New King James Version. I identify by its abbreviation any Bible version other than the New King James Version that I cite in this book. (For the abbreviations, see the copyright page.)

Third, a word about transliteration—spelling the sounds of Greek and Hebrew words using the letters of the English alphabet. Scholars vary somewhat in how they transliterate words, especially from Hebrew to English. In order to maintain consistency, I generally adopt the transliterations of the scholars I quote. And on a related matter, where scholars I've quoted have used Hebrew or Greek script, I've transliterated the words to make them easier to read and pronounce.

Shouldn't it be simple?

One objection to the doctrine of the investigative judgment that I've heard numerous times over the years is that while the gospel should be simple enough for a child to understand, this doctrine is very complex. I agree that the gospel should

be—and is—simple enough for a child to understand and respond to. However, thousands of books that a child couldn't possibly understand have been written about the exegetical and theological intricacies having to do with the gospel: the atonement, righteousness by faith, conversion, justification, and sanctification. In fact, these concepts are far over the heads of many adults!

The gospel and the doctrines of the Trinity, eschatology, inspiration and revelation, and many other doctrines lend themselves to both simple explanation and profound reflection. The same is true of the investigative judgment. You'll find my simple explanation of this doctrine in chapters 2, 3, and 4. Children would no doubt need those chapters adapted to their age level, but I think they could grasp the basic concepts. Most of the rest of this book probes the deeper issues of the judgment and why it's biblical. Much of it is technical and will require you to concentrate, to think hard. It seems to me that complex objections justify complex responses.

I suggest that there are two ways to read what I have written. You can simply read the book through from beginning to end. Or you can read only the chapters that deal with the specific questions you have about the investigative judgment. I have titled the chapters so that readers who are familiar with this doctrine can easily find my comments on the various issues. I believe, however, that even those who are interested primarily in specific issues will also find it helpful to read the book straight through.

Why read this book?

Many people have thanked me for the spiritual blessing they received from some of my previous books, such as *The Crisis of the End Time, Conquering the Dragon Within,* and *Forever His.* Unfortunately, I can't promise you the same with every chapter of this book. As I've already noted, much of it is of necessity quite technical, and it's difficult to make a highly technical discussion be also deeply spiritual. Why then should you even bother to read this book? I'll respond with the words of Ellen White:

The subject of the sanctuary and the investigative judgment should be clearly understood by the people of God. All need a knowledge for themselves of the position and work of their great High Priest. Otherwise it will be impossible for them to exercise the faith which is essential at this time or to occupy the position which God designs them to fill. . . .

. . . It is of the utmost importance that all should thoroughly investigate these subjects and be able to give an answer to everyone that asketh them a reason of the hope that is in them.[6]

That's why this book is important

My purpose in writing this book has been to help you with your study of the sanctuary and the investigative judgment so that you understand it clearly. My prayer is that you will be blessed as you learn more about the biblical foundation for the Seventh-day Adventist understanding of this doctrine.

---

1. White, *Evangelism,* 221.
2. See the *Seventh-day Adventist Church Manual,* 17th ed.
3. See Ángel Manuel Rodríguez, "The Sanctuary," and Gerhard F. Hasel, "Divine Judgment," in *Handbook,* 375–417, 815–856.
4. Moore, *Could It Really Happen?*
5. White, *Counsels to Writers and Editors,* 35.
6. White, *The Great Controversy,* 488, 489.

The Most Critical Issues

Chapter 2

Will There Be an Investigative Judgment?

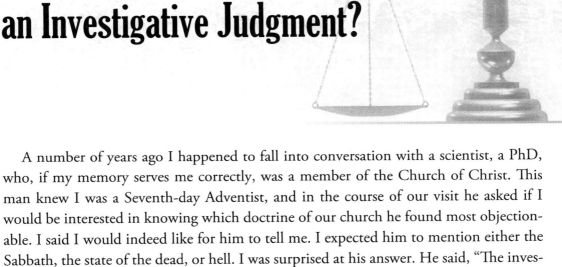

A number of years ago I happened to fall into conversation with a scientist, a PhD, who, if my memory serves me correctly, was a member of the Church of Christ. This man knew I was a Seventh-day Adventist, and in the course of our visit he asked if I would be interested in knowing which doctrine of our church he found most objectionable. I said I would indeed like for him to tell me. I expected him to mention either the Sabbath, the state of the dead, or hell. I was surprised at his answer. He said, "The investigative judgment."

"Why do you find that teaching so objectionable?" I asked.

"Because," he said, "with a doctrine like that, no one can ever have any assurance of salvation."

Since then, I've found that Adventists have indeed been criticized regarding our teaching about the investigative judgment for this very reason, and not just by those who aren't of our faith. Even some Adventists have criticized the investigative judgment because it has kept them in a continual state of anxiety regarding their standing with God. After all, the idea of an *investigative judgment* suggests that God is examining our lives so He can determine whether we are worthy to be saved.

Clifford Goldstein's wife, a lifelong Adventist, provides a good example of this anxiety. Cliff relates what she had been told:

My wife [was taught] . . . "that the judgment is going on in heaven right now, and that our names may come up at any time. We can't know when that happens, but when it does, our names are blotted out of the book of life if we are not absolutely perfect. We are lost. We won't know it, and we may keep on struggling to be perfect, even though probation has closed for us and we have no hope."[1]

Cliff went on to say, "Such teaching is not 'good news,' nor is it an accurate picture of what happens in the investigative judgment. Nevertheless, it is what many Adventists believe, and with such a theology, who can blame people for leaving the church?"[2]

Indeed, some Adventist preachers and evangelists have used the investigative judgment to urge people to live holy lives. "You'll never know when your name may come up in the judgment!" they warn ominously. "Therefore, you must be sure every moment that you're living right!" This view of the judgment is easily dismissed as a contradiction of the biblical truth of righteousness by faith. It keeps people in a constant state of uncertainty over their standing with God.

If this concept of our doctrine of the investigative judgment is correct, then my Church of Christ friend is right. For if God can't be sure of the salvation of His saints till He examines the record of their lives in the investigative judgment, then obviously none of us can have the assurance of our full acceptance by God until He makes up His mind about our worthiness for salvation. And, of course, He can't do that until we've drawn our final breath!

This is the cause of much of the criticism of the investigative judgment both from those outside our church and from people within our own ranks. Many Adventist critics, having experienced this uncertainty over the investigative judgment, have abandoned the entire teaching as a spiritually devastating heresy. And the way they understood this doctrine, that's what it was!

Because of this misunderstanding of the judgment, some Adventists have come to prefer the term *pre-Advent* judgment, which avoids some of the unfortunate theological difficulties that the word *investigative* has created in some people's minds. But is this necessary? Is there something inherently wrong with the idea of an *investigative judgment*?

Will there be an *investigative judgment*?

I propose that the term *investigative* in connection with the final judgment described in the Bible is most appropriate. After all, every judgment in the free world is, by its very nature, *investigative*. Charges are brought by the prosecution. The defense then presents evidence that it hopes will exonerate the defendant or at least get him a more favorable sentence. The jury listens to all the evidence and then retires to deliberate. (Though I should point out that God doesn't give anyone veto power over His decisions.) The whole process constitutes an *investigation* into the charges and countercharges for the purpose of reaching a verdict. Whether the case is criminal or civil, every court session is an *investigative* judgment.

The idea that God will conduct an *investigative judgment* someday is very biblical. In Ecclesiastes 12:14, Solomon said, "God will bring every work into judgment, including every secret thing, whether good or evil." And Jesus said, "men ... will give account of it in the day of judgment. For by your words you will be justified, and by your words you will be condemned" (Matthew 12:36, 37). Thus, our works, our words, and even our very thoughts (the secret things) will be examined in God's final judgment. That's *investigative judgment.*

Daniel 7:9, 10 also suggests an *investigative judgment:*

"I watched till thrones were put in place,
And the Ancient of Days was seated;
His garment was white as snow,
And the hair of His head was like pure wool.
His throne was a fiery flame,
Its wheels a burning fire;

A fiery stream issued
And came forth from before Him.
A thousand thousands ministered to Him;
Ten thousand times ten thousand stood before Him.
The court was seated,
And the books were opened."

The Ancient of Days in these verses is God the Father. He's the One seated on His throne as the supreme Judge. Millions of beings surround the throne, almost certainly angels (see Revelation 5:11). Daniel concludes by saying, "the judgment was set, and the books were opened" (KJV). *This is a judgment scene.*

Notice that this judgment includes the opening of "books." We shouldn't think of these "books" as volumes on library shelves, though. There were no books in Daniel's day. Back then, people wrote on scrolls and clay tablets. Today, we record events, financial accounts, legal agreements, and other information in books, computers, and so forth. Without these records, it would be impossible for us to remember all the information we need to know. But surely heaven's information-storage devices are far more sophisticated than the most modern of our computers. So, we should think of the "books" in Daniel 7:10 as a symbol of heaven's method of record keeping, whatever that may be.

The reason for the books

But why "books" in heaven? Doesn't God know everything? Does He need books to remember anything? Of course not! But the books aren't for His benefit. They're for the benefit of the beings standing around His throne. Notice that Daniel introduced "books" immediately after his description of the angels, not immediately after his description of the Ancient of Days. And for a good reason. Angels aren't omniscient. They need a record of what's happened in the past in order to recall the information when they need it. Even if they remember an event, they, like us, may need a record to refresh their minds about the details. *That's the purpose of the books in this heavenly court scene.*

What kind of information do these books contain? Some fifteen texts throughout the Old and New Testaments mention books in heaven, and we can draw several conclusions from these texts: (1) The books contain a record of the thoughts, words, and actions of God's people (see Psalm 56:8; Malachi 3:16; Philippians 4:3; Revelation 20:12–15; 21:27). (2) They have been prepared for the purpose of judgment (see Daniel 7:10; Revelation 20:12–15). (3) Some names will be retained in these books and some will be removed (see Exodus 32:32, 33; Psalm 69:28)—a process that implies judgments being made.

Let's consider the significance of these books in the judgment. It's reasonable to suppose, as I suggested a moment ago, that God passes His judgment on our thoughts, words, and deeds at the time we think, say, and do them. Since God is omniscient, it's also reasonable to assume that He doesn't need to be reminded of the decisions He's made about us. Thus, whatever judgment will occur prior to Christ's second coming isn't for God's benefit. It's for the benefit of the angels and other created beings. It's true, as the Bible says, that God will "bring every work into judgment" (Ecclesiastes 12:14). But bringing something into judgment doesn't necessarily mean that He Himself will do the judging in this particular "trial." Even in our human court systems, there's a jury as well as a judge, and the jury has to reach a conclusion as to the guilt or innocence of the person on trial.

The objection that "no one can have the assurance of salvation" with a doctrine like the investigative judgment assumes that Adventist theology is the only theology of God's final judgment that poses this problem. But the truth is that *anyone who believes in the Bible's teaching that there is a final judgment has to deal with the issue of assurance.* If God is going to "bring every work into judgment" (Ecclesiastes 12:14), if "we must all appear before the judgment seat of Christ" (2 Corinthians 5:10), and if God is the One who will do this judging in order to make up His mind about our worthiness for salvation, then none of us can have the assurance of salvation until that judgment is concluded regardless of what we call it. And this is true whether you're a Baptist, Pentecostal, Catholic, or Adventist. However, Daniel 7:9, 10 puts God's judgment in a completely different light. *This judgment is for the benefit of the angels, not for God.* God is simply *revealing* to them the reasons for His actions and His judgments in the past so that they can understand and affirm the decisions He has made. (You may wonder why God needs the angels to approve His decisions. I will respond to that question in chapter 4.)

Official Adventist teachings

Two of the most authoritative sources of information about Seventh-day Adventist beliefs make it utterly clear that this is how we understand the judgment today. The *Handbook of Seventh-day Adventist Theology* says, "The investigative judgment . . . does not inform God but reveals His justice."[3] The official statement of Seventh-day Adventist teachings is our twenty-eight Fundamental Beliefs. Fundamental belief number 24 leaves no doubt that the purpose of the investigative judgment is to reveal to the angels the justice of God in His dealings with His people. Here's the relevant part of that fundamental belief:

The investigative judgment *reveals to heavenly intelligences* who among the dead are asleep in Christ and therefore, in Him, are deemed worthy to have part in the first resurrection. It also *makes manifest* who among the living are abiding in Christ, keeping the commandments of God and the faith of Jesus, and in Him, therefore, are ready for translation into His everlasting kingdom. This judgment *vindicates the justice of God* in saving those who believe in Jesus. It *declares* that those who have remained loyal to God shall receive the kingdom.[4]

The italicized words provide a much different view of the judgment than some Adventists have held in the past. The judgment doesn't *decide* who is to be saved and who will be lost. It "*reveals* to the heavenly intelligences"—the angels surrounding God's throne and no doubt other intelligent beings God has created—God's decisions as to the salvation or condemnation of every human being. These are decisions that God and Christ have already made. This revelation "vindicates the justice of God in saving those who believe in Jesus." Satan has charged God with being unfair in His judgments (see Revelation 12:10), but the investigative judgment shows that all of God's decisions are just. Paul suggested this concept in Romans 2:5, where he spoke of the "day of wrath and *revelation* of the righteous judgment of God" (emphasis added).

I wish I could tell you that every Seventh-day Adventist understands the judgment the way the church officially teaches it today. Unfortunately, I can't. Theological misunderstandings have a way of hanging on year after year. False theology that was embedded in our minds when we were young takes on an emotional component that is hard to change.

Every now and then I read of Adventists who left the church over the "false teaching" about the investigative judgment and who say that now they're rejoicing in the wonderful freedom they're experiencing in Jesus. I'm always glad that such people have found Jesus. But when I read their description of the investigative judgment, I feel sad because it isn't close to the view of the judgment that I hold or that the church teaches today. An Adventist friend once said to me, "I don't mind when people criticize us for what we *do* believe. What bothers me is when people criticize us for our 'beliefs' when we actually *don't* believe those things." Unfortunately, some of the critics who praise the Lord that they "escaped the Adventist Church," left us over what they *thought* we believed—no doubt over what they were *taught* that we believe—but their perception is not what we *in fact do believe today* about the investigative judgment.

What about Jesus' promise?

Some Christians object to the Adventist teaching about the investigative judgment because, they say, God's people won't be subject to a final judgment. And they cite Jesus' words in John 5:24 to prove their point: "Most assuredly, I say to you, he who hears My word and believes in Him who sent Me has everlasting life, and *shall not come into judgment,* but has passed from death into life" (emphasis added). The Greek word translated "judgment" in this verse is *krisis,* which can mean either "judgment" or "condemnation." And "condemnation" is how some versions of the Bible translate it, including the King James Version and the New International Version. It certainly is true that God's people will not come under *condemnation*—at least not by God. Satan is the "accuser of our brethren, who accused them before our God day and night" (Revelation 12:10). So God's true people will not be *condemned* in the judgment. To the contrary, God has already *acquitted* them. But their cases will be *considered* in the judgment with the result that the angels will agree that God's acquittal of them was justified.

Paul understood that God's people will appear in the final judgment. He made that very point twice in his epistles. Writing to the Christians in Corinth, he said, "We must all appear before the judgment seat of Christ, that each one may receive the things done in the body, according to what he has done, whether good or bad" (2 Corinthians 5:10). The "we" in this verse includes Paul and the Christians he was writing to. If Paul said that *he* of all people will have to appear before God's judgment, then certainly you and I won't escape!

Paul said the same thing in Romans 14:10–12:

> We shall all stand before the judgment seat of Christ. For it is written:
>
> "As I live, says the LORD,
> Every knee shall bow to Me,
> And every tongue shall confess to God."
>
> So then each of us shall give account of himself to God.

Obviously, the idea that God's people will appear in the judgment is biblical. And we can conclude that the major features of today's Adventist teaching about the investigative judgment are clearly biblical too:

• It will be investigative in nature.
• It will include an examination of the lives of God's own people.
• It will be for the benefit of the angels, not God, who passed His judgment on the lives of human beings at the time they lived.
• It doesn't threaten the assurance of God's acceptance that His people can have throughout their Christian walk.

These are the reasons why I insist that, when understood correctly, the concept of an *investigative judgment* in heaven prior to Christ's second coming is thoroughly biblical.

Where do we go from here? The relationship of the judgment to the gospel of righteousness by faith and the conflict between good and evil—the great controversy —is so crucial that I want to make sure these issues are absolutely clear before we get into the rest of this book. That's what the next two chapters are about.

---

1. Goldstein, *False Balances,* 18, 19.
2. Ibid., 19.
3. *Handbook,* 405.
4. *Seventh-day Adventist Church Manual,* 17th ed., 18; emphasis added.

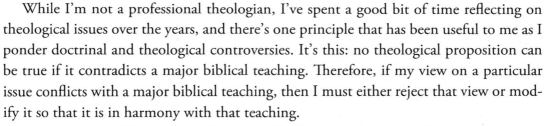

Chapter 3

The Investigative Judgment and Righteousness by Faith

While I'm not a professional theologian, I've spent a good bit of time reflecting on theological issues over the years, and there's one principle that has been useful to me as I ponder doctrinal and theological controversies. It's this: no theological proposition can be true if it contradicts a major biblical teaching. Therefore, if my view on a particular issue conflicts with a major biblical teaching, then I must either reject that view or modify it so that it is in harmony with that teaching.

An example of this is the popular view of hell as eternal torment. My primary objection to this doctrine is that it's in absolute conflict with the biblical teaching about a God of love, mercy, and justice. My friend George Knight wrote an article on hell for *Signs of the Times®* a number of years ago titled "The Infinite Hitler." That's precisely what God would be if He were to allow sinners to suffer in hell throughout the ceaseless ages of eternity. Hitler at least allowed his victims eventually to find peace in death. But the god of eternal torment never lets up. He won't even let his victims die! If we condemn Hitler as a brutal tyrant, then we must pass the same judgment on a god who would keep his victims alive throughout the ceaseless ages of eternity simply so he could keep on burning them. That simply isn't the just, merciful, and loving God described in the Bible. This is the primary reason why I reject the doctrine of eternal torment.

I applied this same principle as I pondered the objection to the Adventist teaching about the investigative judgment that was posed by my Church of Christ friend whom I mentioned in chapter 2. The righteousness by faith that provides Christians with assurance of acceptance by Christ *now* is one of those foundational teachings of Scripture against which every other teaching must be judged. Any doctrine that contradicts the gospel has to be a false doctrine. We must either revise our understanding of that doctrine so that it comes into harmony with the gospel, or we must reject it as error. I pointed out in the previous chapter why I believe the Adventist doctrine of the investigative judgment is scriptural, and I touched on its relationship to the gospel. In this chapter I will explain the gospel of righteousness by faith in greater detail, and I will hold the doctrine of the investigative judgment up to that standard.

What is righteousness by faith?

God has a problem—a *huge* problem: He can allow into heaven only people who are absolutely perfect. If there's one flaw in our lives, *we're out*! The problem is that while God loves us and *wants* us in His kingdom, every one of us is imperfect, which disqualifies us for entrance there. Fortunately, God has a solution to this problem. We read about it in Romans 3:20–24, which I've quoted below from the New International Version:

Therefore no one will be declared righteous in his sight by observing the law; rather, through the law we become conscious of sin. But now a righteousness from God, apart from law, has been made known, to which the Law

and the Prophets testify. This righteousness from God comes through faith in Jesus Christ to all who believe. There is no difference, for all have sinned and fall short of the glory of God, and are justified freely by his grace through the redemption that came by Christ Jesus.

Verse 20 says that you and I cannot be justified (the New International Version says "declared righteous") by our efforts at keeping God's law. Fortunately, verse 21 provides the solution to the problem: "But now a righteousness from God . . . has been made known" (NIV). Paul stated in verse 20 that no amount of law-keeping on our part will qualify us for acceptance by God. Since we have no righteousness of our own to offer God, He provides us with His own righteousness. That's what the words "a righteousness from God" mean. It's a righteousness *from* Him *to* us. (See also Philippians 3:8, 9.) God, of course, is perfect. His righteousness is perfect as well. So when He gives us His righteousness, we, too, are perfect—not within ourselves, but because His righteousness is now counted as our own.

God asks only one thing of us in exchange for His righteousness: faith in Jesus. Verse 22 says, "This righteousness from God comes through faith in Jesus Christ to all who believe" (NIV). Once you and I place our faith in Jesus as our Savior, God's righteousness is ours. That moment we stand justified—perfect in His sight. We are still very flawed, but God *counts* us as perfectly righteous because of the righteousness that He has given to us. Ellen White stated it clearly:

> He lived a sinless life. He died for us, and now He offers to take our sins and give us His righteousness. If you give yourself to Him, and accept Him as your Saviour, then, sinful as your life may have been, for His sake you are accounted righteous. Christ's character stands in place of your character, and you are accepted before God just as if you had not sinned.[1]

Notice the concepts Ellen White expressed:

- Christ takes our sins and gives us His righteousness.
- He accounts us righteous.
- Christ's character stands in place of our character.
- God accepts us just as if we had not sinned.

To be accepted by God *just as if we had not sinned* is to be accepted by Him as perfect. At that point we imperfect sinners have the qualification of absolute perfec-tion that we need for entrance into His kingdom. This perfection isn't ours in the sense that we achieved it ourselves. It's ours as a gift from God. And since every gift truly belongs to the person who receives it, when God gives us His righteousness, it truly is ours.

Verse 23 and the first three words of verse 24 express a profound truth about righteousness by faith. Here's what they say: "All have sinned and fall short of the glory of God, and are justified . . ." (NIV). Paul made two statements in verse 23. They're parallel to each other, but each has a different tense:

"All have sinned"	Past tense
"[All] fall short of the glory of God"	Present tense

The present tense in the Greek is a "continuous present." It expresses action that is ongoing. In order to translate the present tense line in English to reflect this quality of the continuous present, we'd have to say that we all "*keep on* falling short of the glory of God."

Notice what comes next: "and are justified" (NIV). It's important to understand that justification goes with each of the statements in verse 23:

"All have sinned" in the past	"and are justified"

"All keep on sinning" "and are justified"
   in the present

Thus, God's justification covers both our sins of the past and those we commit in the ongoing present.

Some people have a hard time with the idea that God justifies us despite the sins we commit in the present. However, this gives us an excellent insight into the nature of righteousness by faith. The experience of righteousness by faith puts us into a permanent relationship with Jesus that's similar to the legal states of marriage and adoption. While husbands and wives can break the marriage relationship, their marriage license isn't voided every time one of them does something that displeases the other. Nor do children who've been legally adopted become legally "unadopted" every time they disobey their parents. Similarly, while we can break our relationship with Jesus, this doesn't happen every time we sin. Even in our ongoing sins we're still married to Christ, still adopted as children in His family. We'll confess our sins and seek forgiveness—that's a given. But even in the meantime, we're still His bride, His children.

The gospel means that Jesus takes our hand and walks beside us in our Christian journey, and He doesn't let go of our hand every time we slip and fall. To the contrary, He stoops down, lifts us back up, and keeps walking beside us, helping us to overcome that temptation the next time it comes.

This was Ellen White's understanding of the gospel. She said, "When it is in the heart to obey God, when efforts are put forth to this end, Jesus accepts this disposition and effort as man's best service, and He makes up for the deficiency with His own divine merit."[2] Putting it in the fewest possible words, she also said, "When we do our best, He becomes our righteousness."[3]

These statements tell us that God asks us to be loyal—to *commit* to obey Him and to *try* to obey Him. Loyalty doesn't mean perfect obedience. It means we *want* to obey, and we're *trying our best* to obey. And when we fail to obey, we realize our mistake, are sorry for it, and determine to do better next time. Ellen White spoke in one place of those who "honestly desire to do right."[4] When we have that kind of loyalty yet fail to obey, Jesus makes up for that failure with His righteousness. And He does it instantly.

This is not the same thing as "once saved, always saved"—the idea that once we accept Christ we can't turn back. We *could* rebel. We *could* abandon our relationship with Christ. And, unfortunately, some people do. But as long as we maintain our loyalty and commitment to Him—as long as we honestly desire to do right—Jesus stays beside us, even when we slip and fall.

In Romans 5:1, Paul said, "Having been justified by faith, we have peace with God through our Lord Jesus Christ." I've found these words to be very true. There's tremendous peace of mind in knowing that God accepts me right where I am and doesn't demand that I be something I'm not. There's tremendous peace of mind in knowing that I don't have to be afraid of God when I make a mistake. I can get up, tell Him I'm sorry, and rest in the knowledge that He's still beside me to help me grow spiritually. Jesus doesn't abandon me when I slip and fall. He's absolutely committed to my spiritual growth. He walks beside me all day every day, and when I sin, He helps me overcome next time. There's also peace of mind in knowing that, if I should die tonight, my place in God's eternal kingdom is secure.

This is the gospel.

And it has everything to do with the judgment.

Righteousness by faith and the judgment

I mentioned in the previous chapter the fear that many Adventists have had over the years about their standing with God in the investigative judgment. Since their name could come up in the judgment at any time, they have to be sure they're living right at every moment. This has kept many Adventists in a continual state of anxiety. However, this view is a total denial of righteousness by faith, which assures us that throughout our lifetime God gives us the righteousness that makes us acceptable to Him. When it's our sincere desire to obey God, when we are committed to obeying Him, we can rest in the assurance that His righteousness covers us even when we fail, and we don't have to worry about whether these failures will affect our eternal destiny.

A bit of reflection will reveal that a fear-based view of the judgment is actually a righteousness-by-works theology because it suggests that a Christian's standing before God depends on whether or not he or she is "living right at every moment." This is not to minimize the importance of living right. *God is very interested in our living right!* But living right isn't the basis of His acceptance of us. The basis of His acceptance of us is Christ's righteousness, not ours. And that's as true when our name comes up in the judgment as it is at any other time in our life.

Adventists in more recent years have come to realize this, and the result has been a very grace-oriented understanding of the judgment. This is evident in our fundamental belief on the judgment:

The investigative judgment reveals to heavenly intelligences who among the dead are *asleep in Christ* and therefore, *in Him, are deemed worthy to have part in the first resurrection.* It also makes manifest *who among the living are abiding in Christ,* keeping the commandments of God and the faith of Jesus, and in Him, therefore, are ready for translation into His everlasting kingdom. This judgment vindicates the justice of God in saving *those who believe in Jesus.*[5]

According to this statement, our standing with God in the judgment depends on whether we're *asleep in Jesus* (if we've died before the judgment) or *abiding in Christ* (if we're still living). It depends on whether we *believe in Jesus,* not on how well we've lived—that is, on our good behavior.

The *Handbook of Seventh-day Adventist Theology* takes a similar view of the investigative judgment:

As believers, we may face each aspect of the judgment with *confidence.* With Paul we affirm, "It is God who justifies; who is to condemn?" (Rom. 8:33, 34). Our security of salvation and faith rests in the God who is both Saviour and Judge. . . .

The faithful are saved in the Lord, who graciously forgives their sins (1 John 1:9), our heavenly Mediator (1 Tim. 2:5; Heb. 9:15; 12:24), who stands good for our debt (Heb. 10:12–

14), and in whose merits we can face the judgment with *confidence.* Through our Lord Jesus Christ we can "with *confidence* draw near to the throne of grace" (Heb. 4:16), because He is our "advocate with the Father" (1 John 2:1). Our relationship with our Mediator, Advocate, and High Priest makes us *confident* in the day of judgment.[6]

Notice that the word *confidence* or one of its derivatives appears four times in these paragraphs. We can "face each aspect of the judgment with *confidence.*" Through the merits of Christ we can "face the judgment with *confidence.*" "We can 'with *confidence* draw near to the throne of grace,' " and finally, "our relationship with our Mediator, Advocate, and High Priest makes us *confident* in the day of judgment."

God wants us to view the judgment with confidence in the merits of Jesus that He has applied to our case so that we stand before God "just as if [we] had not sinned."[7]

What about our works in the judgment?

Does this mean that our works count for nothing in the judgment? Of course not! Solomon said, "God will bring every work into judgment, including every secret thing, whether good or evil" (Ecclesiastes 12:14). Jesus said, "For every idle word men may speak, they will give account of it in the day of judgment" (Matthew 12:36). And Paul said, "We must all appear before the judgment seat of Christ, that each one may receive the things done in the body, according to what he has done, whether good or bad" (2 Corinthians 5:10). Thus, the idea that our works will be considered in the judgment is entirely biblical.

Ellen White made some rather stern statements about our accountability in the judgment. In her book *The Great Controversy,* she said,

> All who would have their names retained in the book of life should now, in the few remaining days of their probation, afflict their souls before God by sorrow for sin and true repentance. There must be deep, faithful searching of heart. The light, frivolous spirit indulged by so many professed Christians must be put away. There is earnest warfare before all who would subdue the evil tendencies that strive for the mastery. The work of preparation is an individual work. We are not saved in groups. The purity and devotion of one will not offset the want of these qualities in another. Though all nations are to pass in judgment before God, yet He will examine the case of each individual with as close and searching scrutiny as if there were not

another being upon the earth. Everyone must be tested and found without spot or wrinkle or any such thing.[8]

Statements such as these can easily sound frightening, especially to immature Christians. I will point out, however, that they are no more frightening than some rather severe statements in the Bible. I mentioned a moment ago the words of Solomon, Jesus, and Paul. The author of Hebrews has also written, "If we sin willfully after we have received the knowledge of the truth, there no longer remains a sacrifice for sins, but a certain fearful expectation of judgment, and fiery indignation which will devour the adversaries. . . . It is a fearful thing to fall into the hands of the living God" (Hebrews 10:26, 27, 31).

It is essential, in evaluating statements such as these in both Scripture and Ellen White's writings, that we understand the statements in the light of the gospel of righteousness by faith. In the judgment, the standing of those who are saved will always be based upon their being covered with Christ's righteousness, never upon their own success in obeying God's laws. In the statement by Ellen White that I quoted above, she said, "Everyone must be tested and found without spot or wrinkle or any such thing."[9] The only way we can stand in the judgment "without spot or wrinkle" is through receiving the gift of

Christ's righteousness. This is why Ellen White said, "Christ's character stands in place of your character, and you are accepted before God just as if you had not sinned," and "when we do our best, He becomes our righteousness."

Christ our Mediator in the judgment

In recent years, some Seventh-day Adventists have emphasized that in the investigative judgment, Christ serves as our Mediator. I believe this is a very appropriate emphasis. In her chapter on the investigative judgment in the book *The Great Controversy,* Ellen White paints a vivid word picture of Satan standing before God in the judgment and accusing God's people of being unworthy of His favor:

> While Jesus is pleading for the subjects of His grace, Satan accuses them before God as transgressors. The great deceiver has sought to lead them into skepticism, to cause them to lose confidence in God, to separate themselves from His love, and to break His law. Now he points to the record of their lives, to the defects of character, the unlikeness to Christ, which has dishonored their Redeemer, to all the sins that he has tempted them to commit, and because of these he claims them as his subjects.[10]

Notice Jesus' response to these accusations:

> Jesus does not excuse their sins, but shows their penitence and faith, and, claiming for them forgiveness, He lifts His wounded hands before the Father and the holy angels, saying: I know them by name. I have graven them on the palms of My hands. . . . Christ will clothe His faithful ones with His own righteousness, that He may present them to His Father "a glorious church, not having spot, or wrinkle, or any such thing."[11]

Please notice that in the judgment, Jesus responds to Satan's accusations against God's people by asserting that they are righteous because of their faith.

Is it biblical?

I'm going to say something that may surprise you: I'm not aware of a text in the Bible that says that Jesus is our Mediator in the judgment. The New Testament identifies Him as a Mediator. First Timothy 2:5 says, "There is one God and one Mediator between God and men, the Man Christ Jesus." And other texts describe His mediatorial ministry even though they don't use the word *mediator.* For example, 1 John 2:1 says, "My little children, these things I write to you, so that you may not sin. And if anyone sins, we have an Advocate with the Father, Jesus Christ the righteous." And Hebrews gives an extensive description of Christ as our high-priestly Mediator in the heavenly sanctuary (e.g., Hebrews 8:1–6). Hebrews 9:24 says, "Christ has not entered the holy places made with hands, which are copies of the true, but into heaven itself, now to appear in the presence of God for us." But where do we get the idea that Christ is our Mediator in the heavenly sanctuary *during the investigative judgment?*

While the Bible doesn't directly say that He functions in this way, it's a logical conclusion based on what it *does* say about Christ as our Mediator. If He stands in the heavenly sanctuary as our Mediator in every other respect, then He will also be our Mediator during the judgment.

But why would a Mediator even be necessary during the judgment? For the answer to that question, we need to understand the investigative judgment in light of the conflict between good and evil that has been raging in the universe ever since Satan rebelled against God in heaven. We need to understand the investigative judgment in light of what Adventists have historically called "the great controversy."

---

1. White, *Steps to Christ,* 62.
2. White, *Selected Messages,* 1:382.
3. Ibid., 368.
4. White, *The Acts of the Apostles,* 232.
5. *Seventh-day Adventist Church Manual,* 17th ed., 18; emphasis added.
6. *Handbook,* 845; emphasis added.
7. White, *Steps to Christ,* 62.
8. White, *The Great Controversy,* 490.
9. Ibid.
10. Ibid., 484.
11. Ibid.

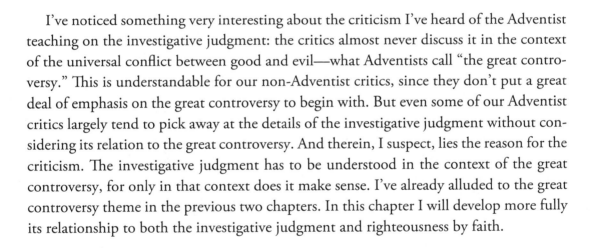

Chapter 4

The Investigative Judgment and the Great Controversy Theme

I've noticed something very interesting about the criticism I've heard of the Adventist teaching on the investigative judgment: the critics almost never discuss it in the context of the universal conflict between good and evil—what Adventists call "the great controversy." This is understandable for our non-Adventist critics, since they don't put a great deal of emphasis on the great controversy to begin with. But even some of our Adventist critics largely tend to pick away at the details of the investigative judgment without considering its relation to the great controversy. And therein, I suspect, lies the reason for the criticism. The investigative judgment has to be understood in the context of the great controversy, for only in that context does it make sense. I've already alluded to the great controversy theme in the previous two chapters. In this chapter I will develop more fully its relationship to both the investigative judgment and righteousness by faith.

What is the great controversy?

I suspect most Christians would agree that there's a conflict between good and evil in the world. Just watching a segment or two of the evening news makes apparent the reality of this conflict. The Adventist concept of the great controversy is an enlargement on that theme. It explains the origin and final resolution of the problem of evil.

Three propositions underlie the great controversy theme: (1) God has created intelligent beings in addition to humans; (2) God has created all intelligent beings with the ability to make rational, independent choices, including the choice to rebel against Him. Some of the nonhuman intelligent inhabitants of the universe (angels) have chosen to rebel against God. Humans as an entire race have made that same choice; and (3) God wants to resolve this rebellion in a way that will secure the universe against future rebellions. I will elaborate on each of these propositions on the next few pages.

There are intelligent beings other than humans. Genesis 3 says that a serpent spoke to Eve when she approached the tree of the knowledge of good and evil (verses 1–5). The assumption among most conservative scholars is that Satan was the intelligent agent who spoke to Eve (see Revelation 12:9) and that he simply used the serpent as a medium. If this is correct—and Adventists believe it is—then this is the first reference in the Bible to an intelligent created being who isn't a human.

Throughout Scripture there are references to intelligent beings—angels—appearing to and speaking to people. Genesis 16:7, for instance, says that an angel of the Lord appeared to Hagar and spoke to her after she fled from Sarah. Genesis 22:11, 12 says that an angel of the Lord spoke to Abraham to prevent him from sacrificing his son Isaac. And the story of Job tells of "a day when the sons of God came to present themselves before the LORD" (Job 1:6). It goes on to describe a conversation Satan had with God about whether Job deserved God's favor. Since only intelligent beings can speak, the reasonable assumption is

that these angelic beings are highly intelligent. This concept is crucial to the Adventist understanding of the great controversy theme.

Some angels have rebelled. The second proposition that we can draw from the Bible is that both angels and humans have the freedom to make choices contrary to God's will—that He won't force either us or the angels to obey Him. The Bible presents clear evidence that some of God's angels have used this freedom to rebel against Him. We read about this rebellion in Revelation 12:7–9,

> War broke out in heaven: Michael and his angels fought with the dragon; and the dragon and his angels fought, but they did not prevail, nor was a place found for them in heaven any longer. So the great dragon was cast out, that serpent of old, called the Devil and Satan, who deceives the whole world; he was cast to the earth, and his angels were cast out with him.

War is an act of aggression against a government. So, obviously, some of God's own angels—beings that He created—chose to rebel against Him. Revelation suggests that as many as a third of the angels in heaven joined Satan in his rebellion (see Revelation 12:1–4), and they were cast down to the earth (see verse 9). This explains Satan's presence in the Garden of Eden, where he tempted Eve.

We gain further insight into Satan's rebellion against God from Ezekiel and Isaiah. Ezekiel tells us that prior to Satan's fall, he stood in God's very presence as a "covering cherub" (Ezekiel 28:16). Isaiah suggests that Lucifer aspired to take over God's throne:

You said in your heart,
　"I will ascend to heaven;
I will raise my throne
　　above the stars of God;
I will sit enthroned on the mount of
　　assembly,
　　　on the utmost heights of the sacred
　　　　mountain.
I will ascend above the tops of the
　　clouds;
　　I will make myself like the Most
　　　High" (Isaiah 14:13, 14, NIV).

This text is somewhat symbolic. Thrones are a symbol of government, and governments have laws by which society is ordered. And stars are a symbol of God's loyal followers—angels or humans (see Daniel 12:3). Thus, Isaiah is telling us that in aspiring to establish his throne above the stars of God, Lucifer intended to usurp God's position as Head of the universe. That's why Isaiah says Lucifer intended to make himself "like the Most High." So,

the most exalted angel in heaven rebelled against God and His laws, and this set the stage for the great controversy between good and evil that has raged in our world ever since.

When a person rebels against the authority of someone who holds a higher position, the subordinate person obviously disagrees with certain policies or laws of the superior. Without such disagreement there would be no rebellion. We can say, then, that in rebelling against God, Lucifer had profound disagreements with God. He questioned some of God's decisions, His policies, and His laws. Lucifer believed that God was wrong and that he was right.

God intends to resolve the problem of evil. The third proposition of the great controversy theme is that God wants to resolve the problem of evil in a way that will ensure that it never rises again. The rest of this chapter deals with this issue.

Lucifer's rebellion

It isn't very likely that the angels who joined Lucifer in his rebellion against God did so because Lucifer forced them to follow him. Like all the other intelligent created beings, they were free to disobey God if they chose to, and a third of the angels made that choice. Why? Did all of them suddenly and simultaneously decide that they were going to rebel against God?

Probably not. The idea of rebelling against God probably never occurred to most of them until Lucifer introduced it to them. It's also reasonable to assume that this rebellion against God developed over a period of time. Here's how Ellen White described it in her book *Patriarchs and Prophets:*

> Leaving his place in the immediate presence of the Father, Lucifer went forth to diffuse the spirit of discontent among the angels. He worked with mysterious secrecy, and for a time concealed his real purpose under an appearance of reverence for God. He began to insinuate doubts concerning the laws that governed heavenly beings, intimating that though laws might be necessary for the inhabitants of the worlds, angels, being more exalted, needed no such restraint, for their own wisdom was a sufficient guide. They were not beings that could bring dishonor to God; all their thoughts were holy; it was no more possible for them than for God Himself to err. . . . Such were the subtle deceptions that through the wiles of Lucifer were fast obtaining in the heavenly courts.[1]

Lucifer must have been extremely persuasive to get a full third of the angels to buy into his line of reasoning and join him in his rebellion against God!

Why God allowed evil to exist

The existence of evil poses one of the most crucial theological problems of all time. To explain it, people have proposed a variety of theories:

- There is no God. We humans are the makers of our own trouble.
- Good and evil are coequal forces, and the struggle between them is eternal. While good will always exist, so will evil and suffering.
- God created the world and life, but beyond that He isn't interested in what happens to the planet or its inhabitants. We're on our own.
- The universe and life on our planet are the result of the random forces of nature operating through the laws of evolution, one of which is the reign of tooth and claw. Evil and suffering are inherent in the progress toward good.
- A loving God created our world, and we humans chose to rebel against Him. He will eventually bring the reign of sin and suffering to a close.

I'm sure you recognized the last explanation of the problem of evil as the typical Christian answer. It's certainly biblical, and Seventh-day Adventists agree with it. However, people then say, If God is truly a God of love, why has He allowed evil and suffering to plague our planet these thousands of years when He had the power to put a stop to the problem at its source? If Satan is the cause of our world's woes, why didn't God just destroy him and his rebellious companions immediately upon their sinning?

Reflecting on the question of why God didn't destroy Lucifer and his rebellious companions to begin with, Adventists point out what would almost certainly have been the result had He done so. If Lucifer was so persuasive that a third of the angels joined him in his rebellion, then surely those angels who maintained their loyalty must also have had serious questions about God. Had He destroyed Lucifer and his angels at the beginning of their rebellion, those questions would have remained unanswered. The loyal angels would have feared God, afraid that He would destroy them, too, because of their questions. They would have come to view God as a tyrant and would have served Him out of fear rather than from love and respect. But God's government is based on love, and He can accept only a loyalty that's based on love. A government in which the citizens feared the Ruler would have perpetuated the very evil God would have been trying to prevent by destroying Satan and his angels.

Of course, God could have responded to the questions in the minds of the loyal angels by explaining to them the ultimate consequences of Lucifer's rebellion. In fact, I'm sure He did exactly that, and I'm sure His explanation helped many of the angels who were wavering to return to loyalty. But verbal explanations can only go so far. In order for the loyal angels to be fully persuaded of the evil of Lucifer's rebellion, God had to let them *see* that rebellion in action. He had to give the universe a show-and-tell, if you please. Once the loyal universe saw the ultimate result of Satan's rebellion, they would understand that God truly was right, and they would fully and forever reject Satan and his plan for the universe.

However, I'm sure that by now the loyal universe has been fully persuaded that Satan is wrong and God is right. So why hasn't God brought the history of sin to a close? What need is there of an investigative judgment to show the angels that Satan's plan for ruling the universe is a tragic mistake? It isn't likely that an investigative judgment would make the case any better than history has.

Nevertheless, as we saw in chapter 2, the Bible makes it crystal clear that *there will be a judgment at the end of time.* Daniel shows us that judgment in progress, with the thousands of angels who surround God's throne examining the record books (see Daniel 7:9, 10). And Paul said that God's people must appear in that judgment to "give an account of [themselves] to God" and to "receive what is due [them] for the things done while in the body, whether good or bad" (Romans 14:12, NIV; 2 Corinthians 5:10, NIV). That there will be a judgment at the end of time prior to Christ's return is certain. That God's people will appear in that judgment (though obviously not in person) to give an account of their lives is also certain.

But why?

The answer is very simple. It has to do with God's plan to resolve the sin problem. And this is where the investigative judgment intersects with the great controversy theme.

The great controversy and the end of evil

The great controversy theme accomplishes a number of important functions. I'll point out two. The first, which I've already mentioned, is that it explains where evil came from. Heaven's highest created being rebelled against his Maker, and he succeeded in persuading a third of the angels and the entire human race to join with him in his rebellion. Evil didn't originate with God; it originated with Satan. God didn't introduce sin into our world—Satan did.

However, this explains only the *origin* of evil. The second function of the great controversy theme is to explain God's *solution* to the problem of evil. As I have pointed out, one aspect of God's solution has been to allow evil to run its course. That way, rather than God simply *telling* the loyal beings in the universe that evil is bad, they'll *see for themselves* the awful results it produces and reject it on their own initiative. Seventh-day Adventists believe that it is God's plan to eventually expel all evil from the entire universe* so that His law of love is the basis for all the thoughts, feelings, and actions of every living being.

Life is valuable. We all love life and resist death. Thus, the destruction of even one intelligent created being, whether angel or human, is a serious matter. That's why God instituted a plan to save as many human beings from eternal death as possible. So, let's consider God's plan of salvation, especially as it relates to the great controversy and the resolution of the problem of evil.

Something drastic happened in the minds of Adam and Eve when they sinned. Prior to their sin, they were happy in their Garden home. They were at peace with

---

*One of the major reasons why Adventists reject the doctrine of eternal torment is that it keeps evil present in the universe throughout eternity. While that doctrine no doubt suggests that the evil beings who are suffering eternal torture would be isolated in a remote corner of the universe, they would still be a part of the universe nonetheless, and in that small slice of the universe, evil would continue to exist. This would be contrary to God's purpose, which is to cleanse the universe of every bit of evil. Sin exists in the minds of intelligent beings, so God's purpose can be fulfilled only when all rebellious, sinful beings, both angels and humans, have been annihilated.

God and with each other. But one of the immediate psychological results of sin was the introduction of both fear and shame into their minds. When God came to meet them in the Garden, they fled from Him, and when God asked Adam why he had fled, Adam said, "I was afraid" (Genesis 3:10). Their fear also involved shame, which is evident in the fact that Adam and Eve made clothing for themselves out of fig leaves (see verse 7). Adam admitted his shame. He said, "I was afraid because I was naked; and I hid myself" (verse 10).

Fear and shame are two of the foundational characteristics of sin. The fact that Adam and Eve experienced these emotions as soon as they rebelled against God confirms that they had become infected with sin. Unfortunately, they passed that infection on to each of their descendants.

Will evil be reintroduced?

If human beings have been infected with sin, what's to say they won't reintroduce it into God's heaven if He allows them back in? We lock up criminals to protect society from their predatory deeds. Every now and then, a prison parole board will release a prisoner who the board members believed was ready to live in normal society, only to discover a day or a year later that the criminal has injured or killed another innocent victim. Then everyone asks why the parole board allowed him or her back into society.

I can assure you that if we have these concerns while living in a sinful society here on earth, the angels in heaven are even more concerned about who will be allowed into their perfect society. The loyal angels, under the leadership of Michael (Christ), cast Lucifer and his angels out of heaven several thousand years ago because they rebelled against God. They've spent several thousand years observing firsthand the horrible results of sin, and *they don't want to allow it back into their society*! They don't want to allow anyone back into heaven who would start the deadly cycle all over again. They want to be sure that every person who enters heaven is "safe to save."

Thus, the supreme issue in the great controversy for both God and the angels is to resolve the sin problem once and for all. God isn't going to force the angels to accept anyone into heaven whom any of the angels have doubts about. And frankly, you and I wouldn't want to live in a heaven where there was any question about whether we were welcome there. So, in order to ensure that we are welcomed into heaven by every single angel, God lets them review the life of every single human that He has decided to bring into His kingdom.

That's what the investigative judgment is all about!

The purpose of the investigative judgment is *not* for God to decide who is worthy to be saved. He made His decision about each saint's worthiness at the time he or she lived and died. Nor does this judgment give the angels veto power over God's decisions. Instead, the purpose of this judgment is to let the angels* see the grounds for God's decision regarding each of His people. God wants them to be convinced not only of His justice but also that neither you, nor I, nor any other saved person will reintroduce sin and rebellion into this universe. Love—the prime value of His kingdom—requires trust, and trust is based on evidence. That's why, at the time that "the judgment was set, and the books were opened" (Daniel 7:10, KJV), Daniel saw thousands upon thousands of angels ministering before God and ten thousand times ten thousand standing before Him.

Without this unique view that Daniel gives us of the angels' participation in the judgment, no statement about the final judgment anywhere in the Bible would make any sense. God knows every detail of the life of every single saint who has ever lived. He doesn't need a final judgment to determine our worthiness for salvation. The benefit that God derives from the final judgment is the affirmation by the angels of His decisions regarding our salvation. If even one angel had any question about the worthiness of even one saint whom God

brought to heaven, the law of love on which the universe operates would be compromised. God cannot afford to take that risk—that's why He has to be absolutely certain before He brings us into heaven that every single angel will welcome every single saint with open arms.

This is precisely the understanding of the investigative judgment that is reflected in the Seventh-day Adventist statement of belief about the judgment:

> The investigative judgment *reveals to heavenly intelligences* who among the dead are asleep in Christ and therefore, in Him, are deemed worthy to have part in the first resurrection. It also *makes manifest [to those same heavenly intelligences]* who among the living are abiding in Christ, keeping the commandments of God and the faith of Jesus, and in Him, therefore, are ready for translation into His everlasting kingdom. *This judgment vindicates the justice of God in saving those who believe in Jesus.*[2]

Satan's role in the judgment

Revelation 12:10 contains a statement that gives us a profound insight into the investigative judgment. It says that Satan is "the accuser of our brethren, who accused

---

*I make the argument for the purpose of the judgment primarily in terms of angels, but there may well be other unfallen intelligent beings who have the same questions as do the unfallen angels.

them before our God day and night." I can assure you that Satan is doing everything he can to ensure that you and I are *not* acquitted in the investigative judgment. In the previous chapter, I quoted a statement by Ellen White that highlights Satan's role as a prosecuting attorney in the investigative judgment. Here it is again:

> While Jesus is pleading for the subjects of His grace, Satan accuses them before God as transgressors. The great deceiver has sought to lead them into skepticism, to cause them to lose confidence in God, to separate themselves from His love, and to break His law. Now he points to the record of their lives, to the defects of character, the unlikeness to Christ, which has dishonored their Redeemer, to all the sins that he has tempted them to commit, and because of these he claims them as his subjects.[3]

This is simply another way of saying that Lucifer, now Satan, has profound disagreements with God—not simply about His policies and laws, but also about His decisions with respect to human beings. It should go without saying that Satan is happy with God's decisions regarding those who are lost. It's God's decision about those whom God deems worthy of salvation that Satan disputes. Thus, the investigative judgment is not simply about hu-

man beings. In this judgment God is as much on trial as we are because it is God's decisions about the eternal destiny of the righteous that Satan is challenging.

God doesn't ask the angels to accept Him blindly. He invites them, as He has us, to reason with Him (see Isaiah 1:18). This means that He wants to explain Himself to the angels so they can understand His decisions and decide for themselves what they think of them. Paul suggested as much in Romans 3:26, where he said that God wants "to *demonstrate* at the present time His righteousness, that He might be just and the justifier of the one who has faith in Jesus" (emphasis added). God wants to vindicate His name by letting the judgment demonstrate His fairness, His righteousness. Thus, the judgment is as much about God and His decisions as it is about us and our salvation.

The Satan who, thousands of years ago, was so persuasive that he convinced one-third of heaven's angels to join him in his rebellion against God, is still capable of bringing up to the angels very persuasive arguments against you and me. That's why we need a Mediator in the heavenly sanctuary during the investigative judgment, One who can counter all of Satan's deceptive arguments about us with the truth. And that's exactly how Ellen White describes Christ's mediatorial ministry in the judgment:

Jesus does not excuse [the sins of His people], but shows their penitence and faith, and, claiming for them forgiveness, He lifts His wounded hands before the Father *and the holy angels,* saying: I know them by name. . . . Christ will clothe His faithful ones with His own righteousness, that He may present them to His Father "a glorious church, not having spot, or wrinkle, or any such thing."[4]

The reason why those who have accepted Jesus as their Savior need have no fear of the judgment is that Jesus, their Mediator, is responding to every one of Satan's accusations against them. When the judgment is over, every angel in heaven will have had an opportunity to listen both to Satan's accusations and to Christ's responses. Sadly, in some cases, Christ will have had to admit that Satan is right: some of the professed people of God don't deserve a place in His kingdom; and the angels will agree. But Jesus will explain why every saint who has truly placed his or her trust in Jesus *does* deserve a place in His kingdom, and again, the angels will agree.

With Jesus on our side, you and I need have no fear of the investigative judgment!

Where to from here?

In this chapter, and the two that precede it, I have given what to me is the biblical jus-

tification for the Adventist teaching about a pre-Advent investigative judgment. If this doctrine didn't have this biblical foundation, there'd be no reason for Seventh-day Adventists as a Christian denomination to hold to it. Because it does have this biblical foundation, I have full confidence in it.

Having said this, however, it's important to recognize that there are a number of other critical pieces to the story. We need to examine the origin of the doctrine in the Millerite movement and the years that followed. We also need to examine carefully the prophecies on which we base our teaching of the investigative judgment, especially Daniel 7, 8, and 9. Closely related is the Day of Atonement in Leviticus 16. And finally, there is the New Testament book of Hebrews, which critics allege contradicts our teaching of the heavenly Day of Atonement as an investigative judgment. In the remainder of this book, I will examine each of these issues in detail, point out the biblical data that apply, and explain why, in spite of the many criticisms that have been raised about our Adventist teaching, this doctrine really does make sense.

---

1. White, *Patriarchs and Prophets,* 37.
2. *Seventh-day Adventist Church Manual,* 17th ed., 18; emphasis added.
3. White, *The Great Controversy,* 484.
4. Ibid.; emphasis added.

History of the Investigative Judgment

Chapter 5

Millerite Roots of the Investigative Judgment Doctrine

The Seventh-day Adventist teaching about the investigative judgment has as much to do with history as it does with theology. By that I mean that this doctrine arose out of a particular history: the Millerite movement. Had the events in the life of William Miller and his followers never occurred, it's doubtful that anyone would ever have conceived of the doctrine of the investigative judgment in just the form that Adventists now understand it.

Some people will use this observation as a reason to question the validity of our teaching about an investigative judgment. They'll agree that it developed as a consequence of the Millerite movement; but to them that's precisely the reason to doubt it. They consider it to be nothing more than a "colossal, psychological, theological face-saving phenomenon" that is *"stale, flat, and unprofitable."*[1] I will argue that God led in the Millerite movement and in the Seventh-day Adventist understanding of an investigative judgment that arose out of that movement.

Of course, it's impossible to demonstrate conclusively in the scientific way of proving things that God was behind the events in the latter part of Miller's life. The idea that God led in the Millerite movement and the establishment of the Seventh-day Adventist Church is a matter of faith. That history, along with the story of Sabbatarian Adventists in the years immediately following 1844, tells us how we came to an understanding of the investigative judgment. Many Seventh-day Adventists will be quite familiar with this story. I am reviewing it here for the benefit of those who may not be familiar with it.

The story of William Miller

William Miller lived much of his life in Low Hampton, New York, just across the state line from Vermont. During his early adult years, he was a Deist, believing that God created the world and then left it to operate on the laws He had established apart from any other intervention or even interest on His part.

Then, in 1816, Miller became a Christian. His skeptical Deist friends challenged his new beliefs, so he began a detailed study of the Bible. He was especially fascinated by the prophecies of Daniel. When interpreted by the historical method, they outline history from the time of the Babylonian Empire to the end of the world.

The vision of Daniel recorded in chapter 8 concludes with the words, "Unto two thousand and three hundred days; then shall the sanctuary be cleansed" (verse 14, KJV). Miller understood the sanctuary to be the earth and its cleansing to be the destruction of the world by fire at Christ's second coming. He concluded, then, that the prophecy foretold the approximate time when Christ would return. Considering the "two thousand and three hundred days" to be symbolic language representing 2,300 literal years and believing 457 B.C. to be the beginning point for this time period, he concluded that Jesus would return sometime in 1843. Miller reached this conclusion in 1818, and he was stunned, for this meant, in his own words, that "in about twenty-five years . . . all the affairs of our present state would be wound up."[2]

The conviction then settled upon Miller that he must tell the world what God had revealed to him. However, he fought the idea of preaching about his views because he felt inadequate as a public speaker. But the conviction kept growing in his mind that he must share his discoveries. Finally, on a Saturday morning in August 1831, the impression became so strong that he promised God he would preach if God opened the way. Half an hour later, he received an invitation to preach the very next day at a Baptist church in Dresden, New York, some sixteen miles from his home in Low Hampton. Convinced now that God had indeed called him to preach, he accepted the invitation.

The congregation was so impressed with Miller's presentation that they urged him to continue his explication of the prophecies during the week, which he did. People from nearby villages heard about his preaching and came to hear him. A revival took place, and several people were converted. Upon his return home, Miller found a letter inviting him to preach at a nearby church in Poultney, Vermont. The result there was the same as in Dresden. Thus began the Millerite movement.

The Millerite movement

For the next eight years, Miller preached mostly in small communities. However, in 1839, Joshua V. Himes, the pastor of the Chardon Street Chapel in Boston, invited him to speak at his church. This was the beginning of Miller's transformation from a small-town preacher to a major public evangelist. Himes caught Miller's vision for the nearness of Christ's return and his passion for souls, and he put Miller on the map, becoming an indefatigable promoter of his teachings. He published newspapers, helped to organize fifteen "general conferences" of Adventist leaders, and convened more than 130 camp meetings in the New England states. Crowds flocked to hear Miller speak. Scores of ministers accepted his views and began preaching them. Opposition set in, but it seemed only to add fuel to the fire. The Millerite movement rolled on.*

By January 1843, Miller had refined his prophetic interpretation to the point that he predicted Christ would return between March 21, 1843, and March 21, 1844. That increased the enthusiasm. However, March 21, 1844, came and went, and there was no Jesus. Miller and his followers were confused and disappointed, but they continued to believe that His coming was just around the corner.

Then came electrifying news in late August 1844. Samuel S. Snow, heretofore a relatively unknown Millerite preacher, spent several days at a camp meeting in Exeter, New Hampshire, explaining the relationship between the "cleansing of the sanctuary" in Daniel 8:14 and the Hebrew Day of Atonement, which also involved a "cleansing of the sanctuary" (see Leviticus 16). He said that Daniel 8:14 predicted the time when the antitype of the Jewish Day of Atonement would be fulfilled, which would be the second coming of Christ.

Snow argued further that Jesus' death fulfilled the Jewish Passover because Jesus died *on the very day* of that feast in the Jewish religious year. The outpouring of the Holy Spirit on the Day of Pentecost (see Acts 2) also occurred *on the very day* of that feast in the Jewish religious year. Snow concluded that in the same way, the Day of Atonement in the New Testament era, with its "cleansing of the sanctuary,"

---

*Estimates of the number of people who had accepted William Miller's teachings by October 22, 1844, vary from fifty thousand to five hundred thousand. One hundred thousand is probably a conservative number. That's one half of 1 percent of the estimated twenty million United States inhabitants in 1844, which at first glance seems to be a relatively small proportion. However, this half of 1 percent was generated in about five years. To put this figure in perspective, a similar movement in today's United States would have to generate 1.5 million adherents in just five years. I can assure you that a religious movement of that magnitude would generate a lot of attention! Miller's movement did.

should be fulfilled *on the very day* of the Day of Atonement in the Jewish religious calendar. And in 1844, the Jewish Day of Atonement was to occur on October 22. So, Snow predicted, *"Jesus will come on October 22!"*

At first, the major Millerite leaders opposed Snow's views, but the movement he had started spread like the turbulent waters rushing from a broken dam. A tremendous revival broke out. Confessions were made. Criminals gave themselves up for trial. People sold their property and donated the proceeds to "the cause." Joshua Himes accepted the October 22 date and canceled a European trip in order to print extras of his publications as fast as the steam presses could turn them out. On October 6, Miller himself accepted the October 22 date. Millerite meetings were held continuously throughout the last two weeks prior to October 22, and anticipation rose to a fever pitch. During the final week, shopkeepers closed their stores and farmers left their crops unharvested. And on October 22, believers met in groups all around New England. This was the day of Jesus' return! Soon they would be with their Lord!

But October 22 passed and Jesus didn't come!

The disappointment was as bitter as the anticipation had been sweet. "Our fondest hopes and expectations were blasted," wrote Hiram Edson, "and such a spirit of weeping came over us as I never experienced before. It seemed that the loss of all earthly friends could have been no comparison. We wept, and wept, till the day dawn."[3]

Aftermath of the Millerite movement

There was massive confusion in Millerite ranks on October 23, 1844. The skeptics had a heyday mocking the devastated believers. The vast majority of Miller's followers concluded that his prophetic interpretation was a tragic mistake, and they abandoned the whole movement as a pious but unfortunate fiasco. Some of his followers maintained their confidence in Miller's basic teaching but concluded that he had the date wrong. For a number of years, these Millerites continued setting more dates for the Second Coming until it became obvious that no one could calculate the time of Jesus' return to planet Earth on the basis of Daniel 8:14. Most of the leaders of the original Millerite movement were in this group.

However, another group emerged from the 1844 disappointment, one that eventually developed into the Seventh-day Adventist Church. This group concluded that Miller's date was correct—*the error was in the event that occurred on that date.* For the next several years, they studied and prayed until they finally reached the conclusion that October 22, 1844, marked the beginning of the investigative judgment. The story of how they reached that conclusion and what has developed since is the topic of the next chapter.

1. Donald G. Barnhouse, "Are Seventh-day Adventists Christians?" *Eternity,* September 1956; quoted by Ford, "Daniel 8:14," 98; emphasis in Ford's original.

2. *Seventh-day Adventist Encyclopedia,* s.v. "Miller, William."

3. Hiram Edson, fragment of a manuscript on his "Life and Experience," quoted in ibid., s.v. "Edson, Hiram."

Chapter 6

The Development of the Investigative Judgment Doctrine

I'm not aware of a single doctrine of the Christian faith that has arrived full-blown from the moment of its first conception. Some Christian teachings have arisen out of a crisis of faith on the part of either an individual or a group. One of the best examples is Christ's death, which overwhelmed His disciples at the time it occurred. Within a few weeks, Peter understood enough about Christ's death that he could preach a sermon on the Day of Pentecost that won three thousand souls. However, the believers' understanding of the meaning of Christ's death continued to increase throughout the apostolic period. Similarly, Luther came to understand the truth about justification by faith through a crisis in his personal life, and throughout his life he and other Protestant thought leaders continued to develop it. We today continue to grow in our understanding of righteousness by faith.

Similarly, it would be a mistake to suppose that the Adventist teaching about a pre-Advent investigative judgment arose out of thin air the day after the Great Disappointment. I pointed out in the previous chapter that this doctrine had its origin in William Miller's interpretation of Daniel 8:14, "Unto two thousand and three hundred days; then shall the sanctuary be cleansed" (KJV). However, it took some thirteen years—from 1844 to 1857—for the basic concept of an investigative judgment to develop among Adventists, and our understanding of this important doctrine continues to grow. I will summarize that development in this chapter.

When Jesus failed to appear on October 22, 1844, an obvious question faced those devastated Adventists who remained convinced of the accuracy of Miller's chronological calculations: since the 2,300 days didn't culminate in Christ's return in the clouds of heaven, what *did* happen on that date? Several theological concepts merged over the next thirteen years, and the Sabbath-keeping Adventists developed these concepts into the doctrine of the investigative judgment. Questions and objections have been raised about each of these theological ideas; I'll address them later in this book. For now, I'll simply share with you four basic theological concepts that were held by the Millerites before 1844 and/or by the Sabbath-keeping Adventists shortly after 1844. These four key ideas came together within a few years to form the Adventist teaching about a pre-Advent investigative judgment in heaven.

Basic theological concept 1: The sanctuary is in heaven

When Jesus failed to appear on October 22, 1844, it became painfully obvious that Miller and his followers were wrong. They had clearly misunderstood something about the words of Daniel 8:14. But what? Where was their mistake?

On October 23, 1844, Hiram Edson—the man who "wept, and wept, till the day dawn"—set out with a companion to visit some of the other believers who lived nearby. Wanting to avoid the scoffers they were sure to meet on a public road, they walked through Edson's cornfield. "Suddenly Ed-

son stopped. As he stood there an overwhelming conviction came over him—that instead of our High Priest *coming out* of the Most Holy of the heavenly sanctuary to come to this earth on the tenth day of the seventh month, at the end of the 2300 days, he for the first time *entered* on that day the second apartment of that sanctuary and that he had a work to perform in the Most Holy before coming to this earth."[1]

It would be difficult to overemphasize the significance of Edson's insight. Miller and his followers had been so convinced that the sanctuary represented the earth that Edson's insight almost certainly wouldn't have made sense to them prior to October 22, 1844. However, when Jesus failed to return on that date, their minds were open to a new understanding of the sanctuary of Daniel 8:14. And Edson's new understanding, that the sanctuary referred to in that verse is in heaven, was the first theological concept that would lead the Sabbath-keeping Adventists to their teaching about an investigative judgment in heaven beginning in 1844.

Basic theological concept 2: A two-apartment ministry

Once the early Adventists understood that the sanctuary referred to in Daniel 8:14 is in heaven, they naturally sought a greater understanding of that sanctuary. And since Hebrews clearly teaches that the

Old Testament sanctuary and its services were a type of Christ's death on the cross and His ministry as High Priest in the heavenly sanctuary (see Hebrews 8:1–6 and Hebrews 9), they turned to the Old Testament to see what the earthly sanctuary might teach them about the one in heaven.

One of the things these early Adventists recognized immediately was that the Old Testament sanctuary services were of two kinds. First, there were those services that the priests carried out every day of the year in the courtyard and in the First Apartment—the Holy Place—of the sanctuary. These included both the morning and evening sacrifices performed on behalf of the entire congregation and the sacrifices for specific sins, which individual Israelites could bring to the sanctuary at any time. Adventists have typically referred to these kinds of rituals as the "daily services" and the "First-Apartment ministry" in the earthly sanctuary.

The second kind of service consisted of several feast days that occurred once a year. The most important of these was the Day of Atonement, which required the high priest to sprinkle blood on various items throughout the sanctuary to cleanse them and the sanctuary as a whole. Most significant, he was to enter the Second Apartment and sprinkle blood on the ark of the covenant. The Day of Atonement was the only time in the year when the high priest carried out ministry in the Second Apartment—the Most Holy Place. Adventists have typically referred to this ritual as a "yearly service" and the "Second-Apartment ministry" of the earthly sanctuary.

As these early Adventists understood it, Christ began carrying out His daily, First-Apartment ministry in A.D. 31, when He ascended to heaven; at first, they believed that He concluded this ministry on October 22, 1844. They also believed that Christ began His yearly, Second-Apartment ministry on October 22, and that this was the heavenly antitype of the earthly Day of Atonement. They still didn't associate this with an investigative judgment, but the concept of a two-apartment ministry in the heavenly sanctuary was one of the building blocks that would eventually become a part of that teaching.

Basic theological concept 3: The blotting out of sins

Soon after the Great Disappointment, Sabbatarian Adventists began teaching that one of Christ's functions during the heavenly Day of Atonement was to blot out the confessed sins of the righteous. In early 1846, a young man by the name of O. R. L. Crosier wrote in a publication called the *Day-Star* that "the atonement which the priest[s] made for the people in connection with their daily ministration was different from that made on the tenth day of the 7th month. . . . The former was made for the *forgiveness of sins,* the latter for *blotting them out.*"[2] Notice also that Crosier clearly understood the distinction between the daily and the yearly services.

This concept of the blotting out of sins during the heavenly Day of Atonement has continued in Adventism to the present time. For example, writing in the *Handbook of Seventh-day Adventist Theology,* Gerhard Hasel said, "The earthly Day of Atonement cleansing meant the blotting out of sin. . . . The heavenly cleansing (Heb. 9:23, 24) involves a blotting out of sin from the heavenly records."[3]

The concept of the blotting out of sins in connection with the investigative judgment is another of the ideas that contributed to the development of the Adventist doctrine of the investigative judgment.

Basic theological concept 4: The judgment

James White appears to have been the first person to use the term *investigative judgment.** However, he was far from being the first person among Adventists to speak of a final judgment in connection with Daniel 8:14. Following the Great Disappointment, William Miller apparently began to rethink the meaning of

Daniel 8:14 because, in a letter he wrote to a friend in March 1845, he suggested that God's final judgment marked the end of the 2,300 days:

That the prophetic numbers did close in 1844, I can have but little doubt. What then was there worthy of note that could be said to answer to the ending of the periods under these numbers so emphatically describing the end? I answer. The first thing I will notice is, "The hour of his Judgment is come." I ask, is there any thing in the scriptures to show that the hour has not come, or in our present position to show, that God is not now in his last Judicial character deciding the cases of all the righteous, so that Christ (speaking after the manner of men) will know whom to collect at his coming, or the angels may know whom to gather, when they are sent to gather together the elect, whom God has in this hour of his Judgment justified?[5]

It's significant that Miller specifically related the end of the 2,300 days to the judgment, for he concluded that "the prophetic numbers [the 2,300 days] did close in 1844," and "the first thing I will notice is, 'The hour of his Judgment is come.' "

---

*He wrote, "The investigative judgment of the house, or church, of God will take place before the first resurrection."[4]

However, the early, Sabbath-keeping Adventists apparently didn't pick up on Miller's significant insight. The *Seventh-day Adventist Encyclopedia* notes, "Judging by their writings, Adventists who later formed the SDA Church did not notice William Miller's suggestion relating the judgment of Rev 14:6, 7 to the cleansing of the sanctuary mentioned in Dan 8:14."[6] It would be another nine years before J. N. Loughborough would connect the cleansing of the heavenly sanctuary in Daniel 8:14 with the judgment in Revelation 14:7. In early 1854, he said, "What was that work of cleansing? Is the work of cleansing the Sanctuary fitly heralded by the first angel's message? in other words, Is it a work of judgment? . . . It certainly looks as though [the high priest in the earthly sanctuary on the Day of Atonement] was going to do a judgment work."[7]

Note, however, the tentativeness with which Loughborough spoke. He asked whether the cleansing of the sanctuary in Daniel 8:14 *might* be related to the judgment, and he suggested that "it certainly looks" that way.

The first one to positively identify the Day of Atonement in the heavenly sanctuary with the judgment was Uriah Smith. Writing in the *Advent Review and Sabbath Herald* of October 2, 1855, he made the positive statement that "the work of cleansing the earthly sanctuary was a work of judgment."[8] Note how Smith spoke of the judgment in heaven as the antitype of the earthly Day of Atonement. After referring to Leviticus 16:33, which says that on the Day of Atonement the high priest made atonement for the sanctuary and the people, he said, "This prefigured a solemn fact; namely, that in the great plan of salvation, a time of decision was coming for the human race; a work of atonement, which being accomplished, God's people, the true Israel, should stand acquitted, and cleansed from all sin. . . . We read in Dan. vii, 10, that the *judgment* was set, and the *books* were opened."[9]

This correlation of the Day of Atonement in the heavenly sanctuary with the judgment was the last piece in the puzzle—the last of the four theological concepts held by Millerites before and/or after the Great Disappointment that came together to create a new doctrine: the investigative judgment. Thus, by 1857, Sabbath-keeping Adventists had developed their basic teaching about a pre-Advent investigative judgment out of these four theological concepts.

---

1. *Seventh-day Adventist Encyclopedia,* s.v. "Edson, Hiram"; emphasis in the original.

2. O. R. L. Crosier, "The Law of Moses," *Day-Star Extra,* February 7, 1846, 40; emphasis in the original. Quoted in Damsteegt, *Foundations,* 127; emphasis in the original.

3. Gerhard Hasel, "Divine Judgment," *Handbook,* 845.

4. James White, *Advent Review and Sabbath Herald,* January 29, 1857, quoted in *Seventh-day Adventist Encyclopedia,* s.v. "Investigative Judgment."

5. William Miller, letter, *Day-Star,* April 8, 1845; quoted in *Seventh-day Adventist Encyclopedia,* s.v. "Investigative Judgment."

6. *Seventh-day Adventist Encyclopedia,* s.v. "Investigative Judgment."

7. J. N. Loughborough, *Advent Review and Sabbath Herald,* February 3, 1853; quoted in *Seventh-day Adventist Encyclopedia,* s.v. "Investigative Judgment."

8. Uriah Smith, *Advent Review and Sabbath Herald,* October 2, 1855; quoted in *Seventh-day Adventist Encyclopedia,* s.v. "Investigative Judgment."

9. Ibid.; emphasis in the original.

Chapter 7

Critics of the Investigative Judgment Doctrine

Most of us don't like criticism of our beliefs, but we need to remember that responding to critics is one of the ways we grow in our understanding. And objections to the Adventist doctrine of the investigative judgment have been raised since 1857. It's important to understand that our critics haven't always been wrong. In some cases, they have pointed out aspects of our doctrine of the investigative judgment that needed correction. This is especially true with respect to the relationship of the judgment to righteousness by faith.

Adventist critics

The critics that I mention on the next few pages were all at one time Seventh-day Adventists. Some of them left the Adventist Church, some of them did not. For the most part, those who didn't leave us maintained their confidence that the Adventist movement was led by God, even while they disagreed with what we taught about the investigative judgment.

Dudley Canright was an Adventist evangelist and writer, and, for two years, he was a member of the General Conference Committee. Several times he became upset with the church and left the ministry, only to return. However, in February 1887, he totally severed his connection with the Adventist Church, was ordained as a Baptist minister, and became a " 'champion' of theological opposition to SDA teachings."[1]

In 1889, Canright published a book, *Seventh-Day Adventism Renounced,* which is still the classic work against Seventh-day Adventism. At least half of this 416-page book is devoted to arguments against the Sabbath. In his chapter on "The Sanctuary," Canright doesn't deal with the investigative judgment at all. Instead, his objection focuses solely on the Adventist concept that since 1844, Christ has been carrying on a unique ministry in the Most Holy Place of the heavenly sanctuary. His reasoning is that, according to Hebrews, "eighteen hundred years ago, [Christ] went directly to the right hand of God and sat down on his throne.* Heb. 8:1. Hence, he must have entered the most Holy then, instead of 1844."[2]

Ellet J. Waggoner is best known in Adventism for bringing our attention to the biblical truth about righteousness by faith. He and A. T. Jones were the main speakers at a ministerial institute that preceded the 1888 General Conference Session, and Waggoner's theme was the law in Galatians, which he used as the basis for an extended presentation on righteousness by faith. Ellen White gave strong support to Waggoner's understanding of righteousness by faith at that time. Unfortunately, during the 1890s, Waggoner veered off into an extreme form of perfectionism, claiming that the absolute perfection of the final generation of saints would vindicate God.[3]

Waggoner took strong exception to at least two aspects of the Adventist teaching about the investigative judgment. One disagreement was with the idea of a sinner's sin being transferred to the heavenly sanctuary. Arguing that "sin is not an entity but a condition that can exist only in a person," he concluded that "it is impossible that there could be any such thing as the transferring of sins to the sanctuary in heaven, thus defiling that place."[†] Waggoner went on to say that "there could, consequently, be no such thing, either in 1844 A.D. or at any other time, as the 'cleansing of the heavenly sanctuary.'" From this, Waggoner concluded that 1844 "had no foundation [in the Bible] whatever," and he "simply dropped it."[4]

Another aspect of the doctrine of the investigative judgment with which Waggoner took strong exception was our interpretation of the 2,300 days in Daniel 8:14 as 2,300 years.[‡] He reasoned that the words in Hebrew were 2,300 *evenings-mornings,* not 2,300 *days.* He said, "There is a Hebrew word that is everywhere rendered 'day,' and it is the only word for 'day' in the Hebrew Scripture. Has it never occurred to you to wonder why an exception should be made here?"[5]

---

*I will comment on the question of when Jesus entered the Most Holy Place of the heavenly sanctuary in chapter 28.

†I will comment on the transfer of sin to the sanctuary in chapter 19.

‡I will deal with the year-day principle in chapter 27.

By 1891, Waggoner had abandoned his belief in the basic aspects of the doctrine of the investigative judgment,[6] even though he continued working for the church for at least another ten years.

Albion F. Ballenger was a Seventh-day Adventist minister in the late 1800s and early 1900s. For a time in the 1890s, he served as the secretary of the National Religious Liberty Association, the forerunner of today's Public Affairs and Religious Liberty Department of the General Conference. About the year 1900, he was called to serve the church in the British Isles, becoming for a time the superintendent of the Ireland Mission.

It was during this time that Ballenger developed some ideas about the sanctuary that were unacceptable to the church.[7] One of his chief arguments was that Christ ministered in the First Apartment of the heavenly sanctuary for several thousand years prior to A.D. 31. Ballenger also agreed with Canright that, according to Hebrews, Christ entered the Second Apartment of the heavenly sanctuary at His ascension, not in 1844. However, Ballenger still believed in a judgment that began in 1844. He just didn't think it had anything to do with the saints.*

Ballenger published a book titled *Cast Out for the Cross of Christ,* and in about 1914, he began publication of a magazine called *The Gathering Call* as a way to bring his ideas to the attention of the church. The church published a response to Ballenger in 1911—the book *A More Excellent Ministry* by church administrator Elmer E. Andross.

W. W. Fletcher was an Australian who served the church in Australia and southern Asia as a colporteur, evangelist, administrator, and college Bible teacher for nearly thirty years. He left the church in 1930 because of disagreements with our doctrine of the sanctuary and the investigative judgment.[8]

While Fletcher didn't adopt Ballenger's extreme views of the sanctuary, he agreed with him fully that Hebrews placed Christ in the Most Holy Place of the heavenly sanctuary in A.D. 31. This, he said, negated the Adventist understanding of an investigative judgment that began in heaven in 1844 as the antitype of the earthly Day of Atonement. He also understood the sprinkling of sacrificial blood on the altar and before the veil in the Old Testament sanctuary to represent the expiation of sin, not its transfer to the sanctuary.

Unfortunately, when Fletcher left the church, many ministers and church members in Australia left with him.

Louis R. Conradi was a German and a leader of the Adventist Church in Europe during the latter part of the nineteenth

---

*I will respond on the topic of the judgment and the sins of the saints in chapter 11.

century and the first quarter of the twentieth century. He was troubled by the Adventist interpretation of Daniel 8:9–14.[9] Verses 10–12 describe the little horn's attack on God's people and the sanctuary. In verse 13, one "holy one" asks another "holy one" how long this situation will continue, and verse 14 gives the answer: "For two thousand three hundred days; then the sanctuary shall be cleansed." According to the Adventist interpretation, the cleansing of the sanctuary represents God's dealing with the sins of the saints, but verses 10–12 indicate that it's the sins of the little horn that defile the sanctuary.* Conradi also objected to the Adventist view that Christ entered the Most Holy Place of the heavenly sanctuary in 1844, when according to Hebrews, He entered that apartment at His ascension. Primarily because of his objections to the Adventist doctrine of the sanctuary and the investigative judgment, Conradi left the Adventist Church in 1932 and joined the Seventh Day Baptists.

Two recent Adventist critics

The critics of our doctrine of the investigative judgment that I mentioned in the previous pages all lived during the latter part of the nineteenth century and the first half of the twentieth century. Raymond F. Cottrell and Desmond Ford were two of the most prominent critics of the doctrine during the second half of the twentieth century.

Raymond F. Cottrell. Following several years of teaching in the religion department of Pacific Union College, Raymond Cottrell was invited to be an associate editor of the seven-volume *Seventh-day Adventist Bible Commentary.* He also became an associate editor of the *Review and Herald,* now called the *Adventist Review.*

Cottrell's interpretation of Daniel's prophecies differed widely from the church's official understanding. Cottrell had no use for the Adventist historicist method of prophetic interpretation.† He interpreted these prophecies according to what he called the "historical method," which is much different than the historicist method in spite of the similarity between the two terms. The following quote sums up Cottrell's historical method: "In order to understand chapters 8 and 9 [of Daniel] as heaven intended them to be understood, we must imagine ourselves in Daniel's historical circumstances and view them from his perspective of salvation history."[10] The first principle of Cottrell's historical interpretation is to "imagine ourselves in Daniel's historical circumstances." Obviously, the more we can know about the times in which a biblical author lived and the im-

---

*I will comment on the sins of the little horn and the sins of the saints in chapters 13–17.

†I explain the historicist method of prophetic interpretation in the next chapter.

mediate situation he was addressing, the better we can understand what both he and God meant by what he (the biblical author) wrote. However, Cottrell meant more than that, as we shall see.

The second principle of Cottrell's historical method is that we should try to view what Daniel said "from his perspective of salvation history." Daniel and his contemporaries understood that at some point in the future God would restore humanity to its Edenic perfection. However, it would never have occurred to them that twenty-five hundred years would pass before this would take place. Therefore, we must interpret Daniel's prophecies as Daniel would have understood them, in the light of his understanding of the Messiah's coming and the establishment of God's eternal kingdom. Cottrell believed that Daniel's visions don't provide us with any information about world history beyond the time of Christ and the New Testament, so it's a serious mistake for us to attempt to interpret those prophecies in the light of the history of the past two thousand years. He said,

> When given, Daniel's preview of the future applied specifically to the Jewish captives in Babylon anticipating [their] return to their homeland, and to [God's] plans for them culminating in the establishment of His eternal reign of righteousness in the long

ago. . . . The presupposition that Daniel 8:14, when given, anticipated events of our time was the basic cause of the 1844 error and the resulting disappointment. Continued disappointment will be inevitable until this error is recognized and corrected, *and the historicist principle on which it is based, is abandoned.*[11]

Cottrell granted that Christ didn't establish His eternal kingdom when He was on earth two thousand years ago. However, this didn't concern him because he believed Daniel's prophecies were conditional upon the positive response of the Jewish people. Thus, when the Jews rejected Christ, Daniel's prophecies lost their significance as predictors of human history.

Nevertheless, Cottrell claimed to have full confidence in the Adventist understanding of the sanctuary and the investigative judgment. He based this on the theory that God has given a special revelation to His people in each of three eras: (1) from Abraham to Christ, (2) from Christ to 1844, and (3) from 1844 to the Second Coming. Each era's revelation is built on the *principles* stated in the language of the revelations of the previous eras. The prophets in each era, Cottrell said, quoted from the Scriptures of previous eras, but they often interpreted the previous era's prophets in ways that were quite inconsistent with what the original prophets actually meant in the context of their historical situation.* Cottrell then reasoned that Ellen White was God's prophet for the Adventist era, and even though Daniel 8:14 had absolutely nothing to do with the antitype of the Day of Atonement or 1844, these were valid interpretations for the Adventist era *simply because Ellen White said so.*

Cottrell never did leave the Adventist Church, but for most of the second half of the twentieth century he was a critic of the church's views. However, during most of this time, he shared his opinions only in small circles of denominational theologians. He didn't discuss them publicly until after his retirement. Cottrell passed away in 2006.

Desmond Ford was a professor in the religion department of Avondale College in Australia during much of the second half of the twentieth century. He wrote numerous articles on Daniel, the investigative judgment, and related issues—all supportive of the church's position. And his book *Daniel,* published in 1978, was also largely supportive. In the late 1970s, Ford came to

Pacific Union College (PUC) in California as an exchange professor. In 1979, while still at PUC, he gave a presentation for the Adventist Forum in which he took strong exception to the Adventist interpretation of the 2,300 days and related issues. As a result, he was asked to step down from his position at the college, and the General Conference gave him several months to prepare a document defending his views. Ford presented this document at a convocation of Adventist theologians and administrators at the Rocky Mountain Conference's Glacier View summer camp in August 1980. At the conclusion of the convocation, the delegates rejected Ford's views, and the church revoked his ministerial credentials.

Ford stayed in North America for several years following Glacier View, presenting his views in small gatherings of Adventists and former Adventists around the United States. However, he eventually returned to Australia, where he taught for a time at a Baptist seminary. He was still living in Australia at the time I wrote this book.

Ford is without a doubt the most thorough critic of the Adventist view of the

---

*The New Testament writers sometimes interpreted Old Testament texts in ways that seem unrelated to the context in the Old Testament passage. For example, in Matthew 2:18, the Gospel writer applied the prophecy of Jeremiah 31:15, about Rachel weeping for her children, to Herod's slaughter of the baby boys in Bethlehem. Obviously, Jeremiah was unaware of that tragic event. However, the larger context of both Matthew 2:18 and Jeremiah 31:15 does justify Matthew's interpretation—see Richard Davidson's article "New Testament Use of the Old Testament," http://www.andrews.edu/~davidson/Publications/ Hermeneutics,%20Biblical/NT_use_of_the_OT.pdf; *Seventh-day Adventist Bible Commentary,* 5:292.

sanctuary, the investigative judgment, and related issues. The main body of the document he presented at Glacier View consists of nearly seven hundred pages, and his appendixes take up another three hundred, for a total of nearly one thousand pages.* Ford especially questions our interpretation of Daniel 8:14, the sanctuary in Hebrews, and the year-day principle.

In chapter 2—nearly 120 pages long—of his Glacier View manuscript, Ford discusses the sanctuary in Hebrews. He understands the antitypical Day of Atonement to be the basic theme of the book, and he considers it to have begun in A.D. 31, not 1844. Chapter 3 says Adventists have problems in Daniel, especially with our interpretation of the little horns in chapters 7 and 8 and with our interpretation of the cleansing of the sanctuary in Daniel 8:14. He considers Antiochus IV Epiphanes to be the primary fulfillment of the horns. Ford also takes strong exception to the year-day method of interpreting the time prophecies of Daniel and Revelation. Instead, he proposes what he calls the "apotelesmatic principle," which states that the prophecies of Daniel and Revelation have had numerous fulfillments throughout history.

Walter R. Martin

I will mention one non-Adventist critic of our sanctuary doctrine: Walter R. Martin, who, together with Donald G. Barnhouse, the editor of *Eternity* magazine, contacted Adventist leaders at the General Conference in the mid-1950s. Martin was a Protestant student of what were considered to be the American cults—Mormonism, Christian Science, Jehovah's Witnesses, and Seventh-day Adventists. At the request of Zondervan Publishing House, Martin was writing a book about each one. He approached the leaders of each group, requesting that they discuss all aspects of their doctrines with him and respond to his questions. Seventh-day Adventist leaders were the only ones who accepted—they welcomed the opportunity. The meetings occurred over a period of nearly two years.[12]

At the time Martin approached the Adventist leadership, he was of the opinion that Adventists should be included as a non-Christian cult along with Mormons, Christian Scientists, and Jehovah's Witnesses. However, after a careful examination of our literature and in-depth discussions with Adventist leaders, he became convinced that Adventists were in harmony with the major teachings of orthodox Christianity: the doctrines of God, the atonement, righteousness by faith, and so on. Martin affirmed this in a book, *The*

---

*In preparing to write this book, I read the main body of his document through once and some parts of it several times.

Truth About Seventh-day Adventism, which was published by Zondervan in 1960. His colleague Donald G. Barnhouse said the same thing in an article in *Eternity* magazine, which resulted in the magazine losing a significant portion of its subscriptions. Barnhouse declared in the foreword to Martin's book that "Seventh-day Adventists are a truly Christian group, rather than an antichristian cult," and Adventist members who adhere to church doctrine as presented by the denomination's leadership *"are to be considered true members of the body of Christ."*[13]

Since that time, Seventh-day Adventists have increasingly been viewed with respect by other Protestants. Some Adventists have questioned the appropriateness of that respect, presumably on the grounds that it somehow signifies a watering down of our doctrines. However, the fact is that on the basics of the Christian faith—the nature of God and of Christ, the atonement, and righteousness by faith—Seventh-day Adventists are fully orthodox and don't deserve to be placed in the same category as some of these other religious organizations.

Adventist responses to the critics

During the second half of the twentieth century, the General Conference appointed three committees to study Adventist teachings in greater detail, including the prophecies of Daniel and Revelation, the investigative judgment, the Day of Atonement, problems in Hebrews, the year-day principle, and so forth. The first committee, which consisted of eight or ten Adventist scholars, met in the early 1950s, but it produced no written document. The second committee met during the latter part of the 1950s, and its major accomplishment was the production of the book *Questions on Doctrine,* which responded to the issues raised by Walter Martin. The third committee met during the 1980s in response to the Desmond Ford controversy and the Glacier View conference in August 1980. Out of the work of this committee came a seven-volume set of books called The Daniel and Revelation Committee Series, published between 1986 and 1992 by the Biblical Research Institute of the General Conference.[14]

Several books on the investigative judgment and related issues have been published by individual Adventists during the 1990s and the first decade of the twenty-first century. One of the most prolific Adventist writers has been Clifford Goldstein, who wrote at least three books on the topic: *1844 Made Simple, False Balances,* and *Graffiti in the Holy of Holies.*[15] And, of course, there's the book you're holding in your hand.

With this introduction, it's time that we got into the biblical teaching about the investigative judgment.

1. *Seventh-day Adventist Encyclopedia,* s.v. "Canright, Dudley Marvin."

2. Canright, *Seventh Day Adventism Renounced,* 122.

3. See Whidden, *E. J. Waggoner,* 298–304. For my comments on the final generation, see my book *How to Think About the End Time,* 183–190.

4. Quoted in Whidden, *E. J. Waggoner,* 347.

5. Quoted in Desmond Ford, "Daniel 8:14," 60.

6. See Whidden, *E. J. Waggoner,* 347.

7. See Ford, "Daniel 8:14," 61–74. Ford describes at length Ballenger's objections to the sanctuary.

8. See Ford, "Daniel 8:14," 75–78. Ford comments at length on Fletcher's objections.

9. Ford, "Daniel 8:14," 78–81. Ford comments on Conradi's objections to the sanctuary.

10. Cottrell, "The 'Sanctuary Doctrine'—Asset or Liability?" This article is number 8 in a series by Cottrell responding to the 2006 *Adult Sabbath School Bible Study Guide* (Quarterly) titled "The Gospel, 1844, and Judgment."

11. Cottrell, " 'The Sanctuary Doctrine,' " article 9, August 23, 2006; emphasis added.

12. See *Questions on Doctrine,* 7, 8.

13. Martin, *The Truth About Seventh-day Adventism,* 7; emphasis in the original.

14. For a list of these books, see the footnote on page 11.

15. All three of Goldstein's books were published by Pacific Press®: *1844 Made Simple,* 1988; *False Balances,* 1992; *Graffiti in the Holy of Holies,* 2003.

Issues in Daniel 7

Chapter 8

Principles for Interpreting Daniel's Prophecies

What we know that the investigative judgment is largely based on Daniel. But the prophecies of Daniel and Revelation are without a doubt among the most challenging parts of the Bible to understand. So, before we get into the book of Daniel, we need to consider three issues that will significantly affect how we interpret that book.

1. Methods of interpreting apocalyptic prophecy

The first issue we need to consider is the interpretation of apocalyptic prophecy. The word *apocalypse* comes from the Greek word *apokalupsis,* which means "a disclosure of truth," "a revelation."* Daniel is the primary apocalyptic book of prophecy in the Old Testament.

Apocalyptic prophecy has several major characteristics. I will mention two.

- Apocalyptic prophecy focuses on the cosmic scope of history with an emphasis on the conflict between good and evil and its resolution at the end of world history when God establishes His eternal kingdom.
- Apocalyptic prophecy relies heavily on symbols such as beasts, stars, and horns, which quite obviously represent things other than literal beasts, stars, and horns.

Students of prophecy have developed three primary methods of interpreting the Bible's

---

Apokalupsis is the Greek name for the book of Revelation.

apocalyptic prophecies. They are the historicist method, the preterist method, and the futurist method. The historicist method is crucial to the Adventist understanding of the investigative judgment. I'll discuss that method in some detail and briefly explain the other two.

The historicist method. Historicist interpreters believe that Daniel's prophecies cover the sweep of history from Daniel's time down to the establishment of God's eternal kingdom. This pattern is particularly evident in Daniel 2, where the succession of nations is represented by four metallic segments of an image or statue. Daniel explained that these four metallic segments—comprised of gold, silver, bronze, and iron—represented four world kingdoms. He explicitly told King Nebuchadnezzar, the one who had dreamed of the statue, "You are this head of gold" (Daniel 2:38).

The fact that the head of gold represents Nebuchadnezzar and his kingdom, Babylon, clearly anchors the beginning point of this dream in Daniel's own time. The three other metallic segments represent Media-Persia, Greece, and Rome. The image's feet, a mixture of iron and clay, represent the breakup of the powerful iron kingdom, making what followed it "partly strong and partly fragile" (verse 42). This was fulfilled very accurately when barbarian tribes from northern Europe invaded the Roman Em-pire during the third, fourth, and fifth centuries A.D. These tribes settled in various parts of the empire, eventually evolving into the nations of Europe that we know today.

Next, Nebuchadnezzar had watched as a huge stone came flying out of the sky, struck the image on the feet, and ground it to powder that the wind blew away. The stone then became a great mountain that filled the whole earth. This, Daniel said, represented the fact that God will one day destroy all human kingdoms on planet Earth and establish His own eternal kingdom that will stand forever (see verse 44). So the end point of the vision is the second coming of Christ.

Daniel 7, with its four beasts and ten horns on the fourth beast, also covers history from the era of Babylon to the time when the kingdoms of this world are given over to the Son of man and the people, the saints of the Most High (see Daniel 7:13, 14, 27). Daniel 8 begins with Media-Persia instead of Babylon, and it extends to the time of the end rather than to the second coming of Christ (see Daniel 8:17, 19).

From this brief review you can see why this method of interpreting apocalyptic prophecy is called the *historicist* method: it interprets the segments of Daniel's (and Revelation's) prophetic visions as successive periods of history that begin with the prophet's time and continue to the end of the world. I've explained this method in some detail because, as I noted above, *the Seventh-day Adventist understanding of the investigative judgment is based on the historicist method.* Without this method, the doctrine of the investigative judgment as we understand it couldn't exist.

The preterist method. Historicists aren't the only people who interpret the details of Daniel's visions as having a fulfillment in history. Preterist interpreters of prophecy also understand the Bible's apocalyptic prophecies to have a historical fulfillment—but they limit that history to the prophet's own time. Thus, John Goldingay, in his commentary on Daniel, said, "The four *melechoth* [a Hebrew word for "king" or "kingdom"] have usually been interpreted as four empires, but Nebuchadnezzar personally is the head, so it is more natural to refer them to the regions of four kings over a single empire, destroyed at a blow by the rock."[1]

Goldingay interprets the image in Nebuchadnezzar's dream to represent the kings of Babylon from Nebuchadnezzar to the fall of that empire. A major problem with this interpretation is the obvious fact that God didn't establish His eternal kingdom when the Babylonian Empire was overthrown. On the other hand, history that stretches from Nebuchadnezzar's day to ours fulfills his dream exactly; though, of course, the final events are yet to happen. Beginning with Babylon, four major empires ruled the Middle East, Europe, and North Africa. Only Rome covered this entire area. And Rome wasn't succeeded by a fifth empire. As I pointed out a few paragraphs back, a series of barbarian invasions from northern Europe in the third, fourth, and fifth centuries A.D. broke up the Roman Empire, and the nations of Europe as we know them today evolved from the resultant conglomeration. This is an exact fulfillment of Nebuchadnezzar's dream. In contrast, Goldingay's interpretation that the dream represents only the four kings of Babylon doesn't fit with the feet of iron and clay.

The fact that the establishment of God's eternal kingdom is still in the future and the fact that the details of Nebuchadnezzar's dream so clearly match world history since his day are strong evidence that the historicist method of interpreting Daniel's prophecies is to be preferred over the preterist. And it would be impossible to arrive at the Adventist understanding of the investigative judgment by the preterist method of interpreting prophecy.

The futurist method. Futurists also understand Daniel's prophecies to have a literal historical fulfillment, and most would probably agree with the historicist interpretation of Daniel 2 that I have given here. The difference is in their interpretation of Daniel 7 and 8. Futurists apply the persecuting powers of those two chapters—the two "little horns"—to an end-time antichrist during the Tribulation (what Adventists refer to as "the time of trouble") rather than to the papacy of the Middle Ages. Thus, there is a huge period during the Middle Ages that, in their view, Daniel's prophecies skip.* I will discuss Daniel 7 and 8 in detail later in this book, and, consequently, won't comment on those chapters further here except to say that the futurist method also rules out the Adventist understanding of the investigative judgment.

2. Daniel: Who was he and when did he write his prophecies?

The second major issue that we need to discuss in this chapter is the dating of Daniel's prophecy. For nearly two thousand years, the majority of Christian and Jewish scholars understood the book of Daniel to have been written by Daniel himself at the time the book claims, during the Babylonian exile of the Jews in the sixth century B.C. However, modern critical scholarship dates the book to the time of the persecution of the Jews by a Seleucid king named Antiochus IV Epiphanes between 168 and 164 B.C. They view Antiochus as the fulfillment of the little horns of Daniel 7 and 8. And since they believe that the book of Daniel was written shortly after Anti-

ochus's attack on the Jews and their temple in Jerusalem, they believe that an unknown author adopted the name Daniel and wrote as though he were living in the sixth century B.C.

Conservative scholars, including Seventh-day Adventists, continue to defend the earlier authorship. One reason is that the book is set in the sixth century B.C., during the Babylonian and early Persian periods. Also, much of the book is written in the first person. The expression "I, Daniel" or something similar appears repeatedly throughout the last six chapters (e.g., Daniel 7:15; 8:1; 9:2; 10:2; 12:5). Of course, assumed authorship was a common practice in the mid-second century B.C., so the conclusion that Daniel was written at that time is reasonable. However, there are other factors to consider in dating the book.

What about inaccuracies in Daniel? For more than one hundred years, critical scholars have pointed to a number of supposed historical inaccuracies in Daniel as evidence that the author didn't know the true history of the Babylonian and early Persian empires. However, archaeological discoveries have shown that in many instances Daniel was right and the critics were wrong. For example, critics claimed that Daniel's chronology of the Babylonian captivity disagrees with Jeremiah's. Scholars have now harmonized the two

---

*That's why this method is sometimes called "the gap theory."

perfectly. Critical scholars also claimed that Nebuchadnezzar was not the great builder of Babylon that he claimed to be (see Daniel 4:28–30). Cuneiform records have shown that he *was* a great builder and that it was he who expanded and renewed the city of Babylon.

One of the primary reasons for accepting a sixth-century date for the authorship of Daniel is the fact that the book describes the Babylonian and early Persian cultures very accurately, and these details would have been known only to someone who lived at that time, not to someone living in the second century B.C. One scholar commented that "of all non-Babylonian records dealing with the situation at the close of the Neo-Babylonian empire the fifth chapter of Daniel ranks next to cuneiform literature in accuracy."[2]

To put the matter in perspective, suppose that a novelist today were to write a story about Jamestown, the first permanent English settlement in the United States. Jamestown was founded in 1607, which is about four hundred years ago as I write these words; that's about how much time elapsed between the sixth century B.C. and 165 B.C. Archaeologists have dug up and analyzed a significant amount of information about Jamestown, so some careful research should make it possible for an author to be fairly accurate in portraying life in seventeenth-century Jamestown. But to-

day's careful archaeological research was unknown in 165 B.C. There is simply no way that a second-century writer could have known about conditions in Babylon three to four hundred years earlier. Daniel's accurate portrayal of that earlier period is strong evidence in support of a sixth-century B.C. date for the writing of the book.

For many years, scholars rejected a sixth-century dating for Daniel because none of the historical records available at the time mentioned Belshazzar, who, according to Daniel 5, was king of Babylon at the time the Persian emperor, Cyrus, conquered the city. However, cuneiform tablets discovered in the past one hundred or so years make it very clear that Belshazzar was coregent with his father, Nabonidus. One scholar of the higher critical school commented, "We shall presumably never know how our author [Daniel] learned . . . that Belshazzar, mentioned only in Babylonian records, in Daniel, and in Bar. 1:11, which is based on Daniel, was functioning as king when Cyrus took Babylon."[3] The simple explanation, of course, is that Daniel knew because he was there! The biblical book of Daniel is accurate because Daniel himself wrote it at the time the events described were happening.

The reverse is also true. One would expect that if Daniel were written in the second century B.C., it would contain a great deal of information relative to that period. The apocryphal books of 1 and 2 Maccabees describe quite accurately the events surrounding Antiochus's desecration of the temple and its restoration three years later. But the Adventist scholar Arthur Ferch points out that "given the premise that chapter 11 (and so much else in the book of Daniel) was possibly written only a few months after the episodes took place, it is incredible that so little in [Daniel] reflects the events recorded in 1 and 2 Maccabees."[4] In other words, the author of Daniel knew a great deal about the life and times of sixth-century Babylon and very little about second-century Judea. Again, this is strong evidence in support of a sixth-century B.C. date for the writing of the book.

The real issue. Let's get to the heart of the difference between traditionalist scholars and contemporary critical scholars in the matter of the date for the composition of Daniel. It can be summed up in two words with an abbreviation between them: supernaturalism vs. naturalism. Traditional scholars believe that God intervenes in human history in miraculous—supernatural—ways. Thus, they understand the stories in Daniel about the deliverance of the three Hebrews from the fiery furnace and of Daniel from the lions' den to have really happened. They also believe that Daniel's account of the rise and fall of empires—Babylon, Media-Persia, Greece, and Rome—truly was a matter of divine prediction.

Daniel's accurate account of succeeding empires forces critical scholars, who deny the possibility of the supernatural and thus of divine foreknowledge, to conclude that the book was written in the mid-160s B.C. By that time, Babylon and Media-Persia had come and gone, Greece was on the decline, and the Roman Empire was in ascendancy. Thus, in their view, there was nothing supernatural that was required for Daniel to predict the rise of four great empires. He knew them from history (Babylon and Media-Persia) and from his own experience at the time he lived (Greece and Rome).

However, the supernatural view is not that easily explained away. Why wouldn't a second-century B.C. author have predicted that a fifth empire would replace Rome? But no, Daniel predicted that the fourth empire would be broken into many disunited parts (see especially Daniel 2:41–43). This prediction was fulfilled very accurately in the third, fourth, and fifth centuries A.D. by—as we have noted already—the various barbarian tribes from northern Europe that crushed the western Roman Empire and eventually established their own nations. In chapter 7, Daniel predicted that following the breakup of the Roman Empire, a religio-political power would dominate European politics. This prediction was accurately ful-filled in the history of the medieval papacy. There is simply no way that a second-century B.C. author could have foretold these major developments apart from the guidance of a God who knows the future as well as He knows the past. And a God who can predict the breakup of the Roman Empire by barbarian tribes could just as easily have predicted the rise and fall of Greece and Rome. (Daniel lived during the Babylonian and early Medo-Persian empires, so he didn't need divine guidance to tell their story.)

Thus, the conservative Christian conclusion that Daniel was written during the sixth century B.C. is well supported by history and archaeology.

3. The year-day principle

The third item that is important to understand as we seek to interpret Daniel's prophecies is known as the "year-day principle." According to this principle, in Bible prophecy, one symbolic day represents a year of literal time. Daniel 7, 8, and 9 each have a symbolic time period that Adventists interpret according to this principle.

- Daniel 7:25—Time, times, and half a time *equal* 1,260 symbolic days, which

equal 1,260 literal years
- Daniel 8:14—2,300 evenings-mornings (NIV) *equal* 2,300 symbolic days, which *equal* 2,300 literal years
- Daniel 9:24—70 weeks *equal* 490 symbolic days, which *equal* 490 literal years

I believe there is a solid biblical basis for the year-day principle. However, it will be easier for me to comment on that after we have examined the details of Daniel 7, 8, and 9. In the meantime, I will interpret these time periods according to the year-day principle without attempting to substantiate that principle from the Bible. Those who wish to see what I have to say about the year-day principle before reading my explanation of Daniel 7–9 can turn to chapter 27 of this book now.

---

1. Goldingay, *Daniel*, Word Biblical Commentary, vol. 30, 49.

2. Raymond P. Dougherty, *Nabonidus and Belshazzar*, 199, quoted in *Seventh-day Adventist Bible Commentary*, 4:808.

3. R. H. Pfeiffer, *Introduction to the Old Testament* (New York: Harper & Bros., 1941), 758, 759, quoted in *Seventh-day Adventist Bible Commentary*, 4:807.

4. Ferch, "Authorship, Theology, and Purpose of Daniel," *Symposium on Daniel*, 2:16, 17.

Chapter 9

Antiochus Epiphanes

Scholars have interpreted the prophecies of Daniel in a number of ways, most of which are not our concern in this book. However, we do need to pay attention to one interpretation that is widely accepted by today's scholars, namely, that the little horn in Daniel 8:9–12 represents a Seleucid king by the name of Antiochus IV Epiphanes. This view was adopted by both Desmond Ford and Raymond Cottrell.* Conservative Adventist expositors, however, have historically interpreted the little horns in both Daniel 7 and Daniel 8 as representing the papacy. In this chapter I will explain the Antiochus interpretation of these horns and why I reject it.

An overview of Daniel 8:1–14

Daniel 8 opens with the prophet by the river Ulai in the city of Shushan (or Susa), where he receives a vision from God. The vision begins with a ram that has two horns. The ram charges north, south, and west, and "no animal could withstand him," Daniel said, so "he did according to his will and became great" (verse 4). Daniel's angel interpreter told him that this ram represented the kingdom of Media-Persia (see verse 20).

However, the ram had a contender, for the prophet saw a goat rush toward the ram from the west. The goat had "a notable horn between his eyes" (verse 5), presumably like the horn on a unicorn, and the goat was moving so swiftly that its feet didn't even touch the ground. It overpowered the ram, shattered its two horns, and trampled it to the ground. The goat, Daniel said, "grew very great" (verse 8). However, at the height of its

*See chapter 7 of this book.

power the large horn broke off, and four other horns grew up in its place. Daniel said these four horns "grew up toward the four winds of heaven" (verse 8, NIV), meaning, no doubt, that they grew in all the directions of the compass. The identity of the goat is also certain because Daniel's angel interpreter told him that "the male goat is the kingdom of Greece," and "the large horn that is between its eyes is the first king [of Greece]" (verse 21). To my knowledge, all interpreters of Daniel agree that this king was Alexander the Great.

Alexander was an unusual man. Elevated to general in his early twenties, he conquered the Medo-Persian Empire and parts of India in just thirteen years—a fact that is represented in Daniel's vision by the goat's rushing toward the ram so fast that its feet didn't even touch the ground (verse 5). Unfortunately, Alexander died in his early thirties without clearly stating whom he wished to succeed him. As a result, four of his generals parceled out his empire among themselves. This division of the Greek Empire into four parts is appropriately represented in Daniel's vision by the four horns on the goat that grew up in place of the great horn that was broken. (The four heads on the leopard in Daniel 7 also represent the division of Alexander's empire, and its four wings suggest the speed with which he conquered Media-Persia.)

The "little horn"

Next Daniel saw something very strange: "Out of one of them," he said, "came a little horn which grew exceedingly great toward the south, toward the east, and toward the Glorious Land" (verse 9). Notice that Daniel said this horn "came" "out of one of them." What is "them"? Most interpreters understand this term to refer to the four horns—which would mean, of course, that, the "little horn" came out of one of the goat's four horns. We'll return to this key issue in chapter 12 of this book.

The "little horn" didn't stay little for long, though. Daniel said that it grew to be "exceedingly great." And having achieved this greatness, it went on a rampage. Daniel said the horn "grew up to the host of heaven; and it cast down some of the host and some of the stars to the ground, and trampled them. He even exalted himself as high as the Prince of the host; and by him the daily sacrifices were taken away, and the place of His sanctuary was cast down" (verses 10, 11).

Notice the objects of the horn's attack:

- The host and the stars
- The Prince of the host
- The sanctuary
- The sanctuary's rituals

I think I'm safe in saying that most interpreters understand the stars and the host to refer to God's people, and the horn's trampling on them means that the horn persecuted them. The horn also attacked "the Prince of the host." Several recent Bible translations capitalize the word *Prince,* suggesting that He is a divine Being. (See, for example, the NIV, NASB,* and NKJV.)

The last two objects of the horn's attack are the sanctuary and its rituals. This is a very important point because it means the horn attacked the center of the worship of God. And the tragedy is that the horn was very successful in its attack—verse 12 says he "prospered."

These attacks on God's saints, His Prince, His sanctuary, and the sacrificial system naturally raised the question of when this terrible state of affairs would end. And, indeed, that's what verse 13 asks, "Then I heard a holy one speaking; and another holy one said to that certain one who was speaking, 'How long will the vision be, concerning the daily sacrifices and the transgression of desolation, the giving of both the sanctuary and the host to be trampled under foot?' " And the answer is given, "For two thousand three hundred days; then the sanctuary shall be cleansed" (verse 14).

The question is, what does this horn represent? Because the majority of today's interpreters understand it to represent the Seleucid king Antiochus IV Epiphanes, I will give you a bit of background on Antiochus.

Who was Antiochus IV Epiphanes?

Antiochus ruled over what is known as the Seleucid Empire, which was one of the four sections into which the Greek Empire was divided following Alexander the Great's death. Antiochus reigned for about eleven years—from 175 B.C. until his death in 164. His empire consisted largely of Syria and Judea.

One of Antiochus's ambitions was to force the Jews to adopt the secular Greek culture—to be "Hellenized" (from the Greek word *Hellas,* the Greek name for their empire). Some Jews favored Hellenization, but conservative Jews opposed it bitterly. Antiochus appointed a man by the name of Menelaus, who was strongly pro-Hellenization, as high priest over the temple in Jerusalem. Conservative Jews resisted Menelaus mightily, and while Antiochus was on a military campaign in Egypt, they rioted, forcing Menelaus to flee Jerusalem. On his return from Egypt, Antiochus executed the leaders of the riot, set up an image of the Greek god Zeus in the temple in Jerusalem, and sacrificed a pig on the altar

---

*The New American Standard Bible uses the word *Commander* instead of *Prince,* but the word is capitalized.

of sacrifice there. He also forbade the Jews to offer their own sacrifices, banned their Sabbaths and feast days, and outlawed the rite of circumcision. The image of the god Zeus stood in the temple courtyard for the next three years.

Horrified at the banning of their religion and the desecration of their temple, the Jews rallied behind a man named Judas Maccabeus, who raised an army to fight against Antiochus and the Seleucids. The apocryphal books of 1 and 2 Maccabees, which are named after Judas and his family, tell the story of their war against the Seleucids. The Maccabees defeated Antiochus, and three years to the day after Antiochus set up the image to Zeus in the courtyard of the temple, they drove him out of Jerusalem, ritually cleansed their temple, and reestablished the conservative Jewish religion. With the defeat of Antiochus, the Jews enjoyed about a hundred years of independence: their only period of independence from the time of their Babylonian captivity until they were conquered by Rome in 63 B.C.

The majority of today's Bible scholars, both liberal and conservative, understand the little horn of Daniel 8:9–12 to represent Antiochus IV Epiphanes. And the similarities are striking. The little horn appears to spring from one of the four horns that replaced the great horn between the goat's eyes, and Antiochus was a king of the Seleucid Empire, which was one of the four divisions of Alexander's empire. Daniel's vision also matches Antiochus's attack on the Jewish people (the "stars" and the "host" in Daniel's vision) and their sanctuary and his banning of—taking away of—their sacrifices. This is by far the most widely accepted interpretation of the little horn in Daniel's vision in chapter 8. Any reasonable observer can understand why this interpretation makes sense to so many people. However, it also has significant problems, as we shall now see.

Problems with the Antiochus theory

While Antiochus does match some of the specifications of the horn in Daniel's vision, I will point out six that he does not match.

1. The horn's greatness. Daniel 8:4 says that the Medo-Persian ram "did according to his will and became *great.*" Verse 8 says that the goat "grew *very great,*" and verse 9 says that the little horn "grew *exceedingly great*" (all emphasis added). Notice the progression—from "great" to "very great" to "exceedingly great." Media-Persia, represented by the ram, was a great empire. Greece, the goat, was an even greater empire, if for no other reason than that it conquered Media-Persia. But the greatest of them all was the little horn.

Antiochus simply does not fit this description. His kingdom wasn't greater than

Media-Persia and Greece. Antiochus was a minor king of one of the four divisions of Alexander's Greek Empire.

2. The horn's growth. When Antiochus began his reign, the Seleucid Empire included Syria and Judea. Daniel 8:9 says the horn "grew exceedingly great toward the *south,* toward the *east,* and toward the *Glorious Land*" (emphasis added). Most interpreters understand the words *Glorious Land* to refer to the land of the Jews—that is, Judea. But if Antiochus already ruled over Judea at the time he began his reign, then it would be incorrect to say that he *grew* in that direction. In fact, the Maccabees reconquered Judea and threw Antiochus out. Thus, far from *growing* in that direction, by the time of Antiochus's death, he had *lost* Judea!

Daniel also said that the little horn grew toward the south and the east. Antiochus did carry on a military campaign against Egypt, which is south of Syria, but it was short lived. He returned to Judea with his tail between his legs, defeated by the Romans without so much as even a battle! And as for the east, the Seleucid Empire had extended as far as India, but Antiochus's predecessors lost control over that territory. Antiochus tried to regain it but was only partially successful. Thus, Antiochus didn't grow in the directions that Daniel said the horn grew.

3. The horn's attack on the sanctuary. Daniel 8:11 says, "By him [the horn] the daily sacrifices were taken away, and the place of His sanctuary was cast down." Antiochus did put a stop to the sacrifices and other services at the temple in Jerusalem. However, he didn't cast down "the place of His [God's] sanctuary." The word *place* is from the Hebrew word *makown,* which means "foundation." In order to fulfill this part of Daniel's prediction, Antiochus would have had to destroy the sanctuary itself—the structure, the building. But Antiochus didn't do that. As far as the historical record is concerned, Antiochus left the Jewish temple intact.

4. The 2,300 days. Daniel 8:14 gives a specific time period of 2,300 evenings and mornings, after which the sanctuary would be restored. Interpreted as 2,300 literal *days,* this represents a period of about 6.3 years. However, Antiochus's defamation of the sanctuary in Jerusalem lasted three years to the day, which is only 1,095 days, not 2,300.

In an effort to make the number 2,300 fit the facts of history, most interpreters today assume that the words *evenings* and *mornings* refer to the evening and morning sacrifices, and they count each sacrifice separately. Twenty-three hundred evenings and mornings amount to 1,150 days, which is closer to the length of time that the temple in Jerusalem remained desecrated, but it is still fifty-five days longer than

1,095 days. Thus, this part of Daniel's prophecy doesn't line up with the historical facts of Antiochus's attack on the temple in Jerusalem. This is especially significant in view of the fact that preterist interpreters of Daniel claim that the book was written in the mid-second century B.C. But an author writing at that time would surely have known the exact length of time the sanctuary was desolate, and he would have stated the time more precisely.

5. The horn and the end time. When the angel Gabriel interpreted the vision of chapter 8, one of the first things he told Daniel was that "the vision refers to the time of the end" (verse 17). Verse 19 says, "At the appointed time the end shall be." Thus, Gabriel told Daniel twice that his vision in chapter 8 was to stretch to the end time. But the three years of Antiochus's defamation of the temple in Jerusalem hardly extended to the time of the end!

6. The big picture. One of my most significant objections to the Antiochus Epiphanes interpretation is that the visions of both Daniel 7 and Daniel 8 describe the universal conflict between good and evil and its resolution—what Adventists have traditionally called "the great controversy." This is evident from the fact that Daniel 7 shows God passing judgment on the dragon* and its little horn, destroying them, and establishing His own eternal kingdom in their place. This describes the process by which God will bring the history of sin to a close. Obviously, then, Daniel 7 and 8 don't refer to the activities of Antiochus IV Epiphanes, who was, after all, just a minor actor in that drama.

The six problems with the Antiochus interpretation that I have shared with you in this chapter are among the reasons why Seventh-day Adventists reject the Antiochus interpretation of the little horn in Daniel 8.

---

*Deciding what term or name to use for this fourth beast of Daniel 7—and the quite-closely corresponding first beast of Revelation 13—is difficult. Calling it "the fourth beast" makes for some awkward sentences. So, because of its resemblance to Revelation's great red dragon, and for the sake of convenience, I have chosen to call it a dragon.

Chapter 10

The Time of the Judgment in Daniel 7

The Adventist understanding of the investigative judgment is based primarily on Daniel 7. Chapters 8 and 9 add important information, but they rely on chapter 7 for the basic concept of the judgment. In this and the next chapters of this book, I will discuss several questions that Seventh-day Adventists have raised about the judgment in Daniel 7.

The first issue is the time when this judgment is to occur in relation to the second coming of Christ. Adventists believe that it is to begin some time *before* the Second Coming, and Daniel 7 is one of our primary sources of evidence for this conclusion. I think I'm safe in saying, however, that most Christians believe God's final judgment will take place *at* Christ's second coming, and they object to our concept of a judgment in heaven that begins some time *prior* to the Second Coming. In recent years, Desmond Ford in particular has challenged our view of a pre-Advent investigative judgment in heaven.

Near the end of this chapter, I will also comment briefly on a second issue—the objection that 160-plus years is much too long a time for God's final judgment—He doesn't need that much time to do what He wants to do. However, before we get into these issues, let's take a quick look at Daniel's vision in chapter 7.

An overview of Daniel 7

In the vision that Daniel recorded in chapter 7 of his book, he saw four great beasts arise from the sea: a lion, a bear, a leopard, and a dragon. According to the historicist method of prophetic interpretation, these beasts represented the empires of Babylon,

Media-Persia, Greece, and Rome. The dragon had ten horns on its head, which we have always understood to represent the breakup of the Roman Empire by barbarian tribes between about A.D. 250 and 500. A little horn arose among the ten and spoke great words against God, persecuted His saints, and attempted to change His laws. This little horn was given power over the saints "for a time and times and half a time" (verse 25). Obviously, this power is in rebellion against God and His people. Adventists believe it represents the medieval papacy.

Immediately following the depiction of the little horn, Daniel's vision turns from events on earth to a judgment scene in heaven. This judgment condemned the little horn and vindicated the saints (see verses 21, 22, 26). Then a Being "like the Son of Man" approached God's throne (verse 13). Many interpreters of Daniel understand this Son of man to be Jesus, and Adventists agree. The Son of man is then given dominion over the kingdoms of this world (see verse 14). That, in a nutshell, is Daniel's chapter 7 vision.

We can outline that vision like this:

Symbol	Fulfillment
Lion	Babylon
Bear	Media-Persia
Leopard	Greece
Dragon	Rome
Ten horns	European nations
Little horn	Papacy
	Judgment
	Son of man
	World's kingdoms given to the Son of man

Notice that the last three items on the list aren't represented by a symbol. Daniel described them literally.

The judgment in Daniel 7

Our focus is on the judgment and the giving of the kingdoms of the world to the Son of man in verses 9–14, so we need to spend some time examining that part of the vision. Verses 9 and 10 provide us with a vivid word picture of the judgment:

> I watched till thrones were put in place,
> And the Ancient of Days was seated;
> His garment was white as snow,
> And the hair of His head was like pure wool.
> His throne was a fiery flame,
> Its wheels a burning fire;
> A fiery stream issued
> And came forth from before Him.
> A thousand thousands ministered to Him;
> Ten thousand times ten thousand stood before Him.

The court was seated,
And the books were opened.

Verse 9 begins with Daniel seeing "thrones," plural, being set in place. What are these thrones, and what purpose do they serve?

From verse 10 we learn that this is a court scene, so what we apparently are seeing in the first part of verse 9 is the preparation of the courtroom for the judicial process that is to follow. Daniel says that once the courtroom is prepared, "the Ancient of Days was seated." His throne is described as having "wheels [of] burning fire." In his book *Selected Studies on Prophetic Interpretation,* William Shea says, "This description underlines the idea of motion onto the scene of action. . . . The implication is that it was through some kind of locomotion related to these wheels that, riding upon His throne, God came into the audience chamber where He met with His angelic host."[1] This suggests a formal opening of the court session.

It's also possible that, as in today's courts, the angelic host stood when the Ancient of Days entered because verse 10 says that the millions of angels in God's presence "stood before Him." Shea comments that "the emphasis may not be so much on the hosts continuing to stand before God as upon their rising to demon-strate honor and respect for Him as He arrives on His chariot throne."[2]

Verse 10 goes on to say that "the court was seated." In other words, once the Judge was seated at His place in the courtroom, everyone else sat down. This also explains the reason for the plural "thrones" that were set in place. It was on these thrones that the millions of angels surrounding the Ancient of Days sat.

Now the real purpose of this court session becomes apparent: the books were opened. It seems rather obvious that the decisions of the court will be based on the information contained in these books. I will have more to say about the books later in this chapter. Our first question about this judgment is when it will occur in relation to Christ's second coming.

When will this judgment occur?

I mentioned at the beginning of this chapter that most Bible interpreters understand that God's final judgment will take place *at* Christ's second coming. Indeed, Christians sometimes refer to the Second Coming as "the great Judgment Day." Adventists, on the other hand, have believed that the judgment described in Daniel 7:9, 10, began in 1844, *long before* Christ's second coming. We even refer to this judgment as the "pre-Advent judgment." However, some Adventists today question that conclusion.

Ford does have a concept of a pre-Advent judgment, but it is quite different from the Adventist understanding. He says,

> It is just as certain that while the great judgment has its public revelation at the coming of Christ, destinies are judged and sealed while Christ is still high priest above. This is the truth of the pre-advent judgment. At every point of His intercession Christ knows whether professed believers are truly abiding in Him. While they trust Him as Saviour, a trust manifested by loyalty and obedience, He represents them before the Father and their destiny is never in doubt.
>
> We must ever keep in mind 1 Cor. 4:4 which speaks of a pre-advent judgment of us all by our Lord.[3]

In the quotation above, Ford says a couple of things that clarify his concept of a pre-Advent judgment. For him, "the truth of the pre-advent judgment" is that "destinies are judged and sealed while Christ is still high priest above." According to Ford, the pre-Advent judgment happens whenever Christ makes a decision regarding someone's destiny as a part of His high priestly ministry because "at every point of His intercession Christ knows whether professed believers are truly abiding in Him." He also refers to 1 Corinthians 4:4,

which says, "I know of nothing against myself, yet I am not justified by this; but He who judges me is the Lord." Ford then says that this "speaks of a pre-advent judgment of us all by our Lord." Thus, for Ford, the pre-Advent judgment is God's judgment of all human beings during their life.

Like many other Christians, Ford also speaks of a judgment that will take place *at* Christ's second coming. He says, "True it is that the judgment spoken of in Scripture vindicates God's righteousness to the universe in the sense of making public His righteous decisions. *But this transpires in the split second division of the living at the advent and the subsequent resurrections.*"[4]

I don't disagree with Ford's idea that God judges people during their lives. Of course He does! The investigative judgment is not meant to be a time when God decides anything. By the time of that judgment, He's already made His decisions. Nor do I disagree with the idea that there will be a "great Judgment Day" at Christ's second coming in the sense that at that time people will go to their rewards. The problem is that Ford's version of the pre-Advent judgment is a relatively private affair. In a sense, it takes place entirely in God's head, where no one else has the opportunity of examining His verdicts and questioning them before He carries them out.

The pre-Advent investigative judgment

as Adventists understand it is a formal, public event that opens to the angels the judgments about the saints that God has been making all along. Its purpose is to reveal the carefulness and love with which God has considered every case and the justice of His decisions. It's to give the angels the opportunity of asking any questions that they may have so God can answer them before He gives people unending life or sorrowfully sentences them to eternal death.

So, the question is whether Adventists are correct in their conclusion that there is to be an open, public judgment in heaven *prior* to Christ's second coming or whether the closed form of judgment *at* His coming envisioned by Ford and most other Christians is correct. From a careful examination of the evidence, I have concluded that Scripture very much supports the Adventist position. I find this scriptural evidence in both Daniel and Revelation. I will begin with Daniel.

Judgment in Daniel 7

Verses 13 and 14. A careful examination of Daniel's description of the judgment in chapter 7 makes it very clear that it will begin *prior* to the Second Coming, not *at* Christ's return. Daniel said that following the judgment mentioned in verses 9 and 10, "One like the Son of Man" approached God's throne. Notice that the Son of man came "with the clouds of heaven" (verse 13). At first glance, we are reminded of the descriptions in the New Testament of Jesus returning to earth on clouds at His second coming. (See, for example, Matthew 24:30; Revelation 1:7.) However, the coming Daniel viewed clearly *is not* Christ's second coming because Daniel sees the Son of man come to the Ancient of Days in heaven, not to this earth.

The New International Version says that the Son of man "approached the Ancient of Days and was *led* into his presence" (emphasis added), and the New King James Version says, "He came to the Ancient of Days, and *they* brought Him near before Him" (emphasis added). Who are the "they" that "led" the Son of man into God's presence? Apparently, Daniel was given a glimpse of a formal ceremony in which Jesus was escorted into God's presence, presumably by a retinue of angels from among the millions standing before God's throne. The purpose of this grand entrance of the Son of man into the courtroom and His presentation before the Ancient of Days follows.

> Then to Him was given dominion and
> glory and a kingdom,
> That all peoples, nations, and languages
> should serve Him.
> His dominion is an everlasting dominion,
> Which shall not pass away,

And His kingdom the one
Which shall not be destroyed (verse
14).

During my years as a pastor, I gave many Bible studies on Daniel 7, and I always told those I was studying with that verse 14 was a prediction of Christ's second coming. However, a careful reading of the text makes it clear that this is not quite the case. Verse 14 has Christ's second coming in view, but what it describes *precedes* His return. The Son of man is given the authority to destroy earth's kingdoms and establish His own eternal kingdom, but this takes place *before* His second coming.

Let's review the order of events up to this point:

1. The judgment takes place in heaven (verses 9, 10).
2. Following the judgment, the Son of man is led into God's presence (verse 13).
3. The Son of man is given authority to rule the world (verse 14).

The point is that the judgment in heaven *precedes* Christ's second coming. This is also evident from the fact that the verdicts of the judgment are rendered prior to Christ's second coming. These verdicts include condemnation of the dragon and the little horn (see verses 11, 25, 26), vindication of the saints (see verses 21, 22), and the conferring on the Son of man and the saints the authority to possess the world (see verses 13, 14, 21, 22). If these verdicts are rendered prior to Christ's second coming, then obviously the judgment that renders them also has to occur prior to His return. It would be difficult to make this point any more clearly than Daniel makes it in chapter 7.

Verses 26 and 27. We find this same order of events outlined in verses 26 and 27:

But the court shall be seated,
And they shall take away his [the little
horn's] dominion,
To consume and destroy it forever.
Then the kingdom and dominion,
And the greatness of the kingdoms un-
der the whole heaven,
Shall be given to the people, the saints
of the Most High.

Please pay careful attention to the order of events in these verses. Verse 26 begins with the court being seated, and its verdict is to remove dominion over the world from the little horn and give it to the saints. Again, Christ's second coming is in view, but it has not yet occurred. Thus, this passage also has the judgment in Daniel 7 *preceding* Christ's second coming rather than taking place *at* His return.

Verse 22. Another, earlier statement in Daniel 7 helps us to understand when the judgment will occur in relation to Christ's second coming. Verse 22 says, "Judgment was made in favor of the saints of the Most High, and the time came for the saints to possess the kingdom." Notice that here the saints actually *possess* the kingdom (see also verse 18). This, of course, will happen at Christ's second coming. Thus, verse 22 is helpful in determining the relationship between the judgment and Christ's return because it mentions both events, with the judgment occurring first. And the words "*the time came* for the saints to possess the kingdom" suggest the passing of a certain amount of time between the judgment and the saints' possession of the kingdom (emphasis added).

Again, the point is that the judgment does not occur *at* Christ's second coming; rather, it *precedes* His return.

Books in Daniel 7. One other factor in Daniel 7 contributes to our understanding of the chronological relationship of the judgment to the Second Coming. According to verse 10, angels and books are both involved in this judgment. If this were the only place in Scripture that mentioned books in heaven, we might be mystified as to their content. However, other parts of the Bible mention the existence of books in heaven and give us an indication of what they contain; specifically, a record of the lives of God's professed people—a record of their thoughts, words, and actions (see Psalm 56:8; Malachi 3:16; Philippians 4:3; Revelation 20:12–15; 21:27). I propose that these books also contain a record of the history of the world and of God's involvement in that history. Daniel informs us that these books will be used in God's judgment, and they will be opened *while millions of angels surround God's throne.*

Books are simply a method of keeping records for future reference.* But since God is omniscient, He hardly needs records in order to remember anything. Thus, we can safely say that the books in Daniel's judgment scene are for the benefit of the angels who surround God's throne.

Ford says, "Does not God do this work of investigative judgment for the sake of the angels? . . . No, the angels themselves are familiar with the thoughts and intents of our hearts."[5] I beg to disagree. Angels are not omniscient and therefore they cannot possibly be as familiar with the thoughts and intents of human hearts as God is. They need accurate records to preserve this information for them. This is why we see books in Daniel's judgment scene. Daniel specifically says that "the books were opened" (verse 10). In other words, the angels are being given an opportunity to examine the record of God's dealings with

_____

*Surely, heaven's method of record keeping is vastly superior to literal bound volumes on library shelves.

the world and its people.

Now here's my point: *An examination of records by created beings suggests the need of time for examining them.* Thus, the judgment that Daniel describes in chapter 7 has to begin *some time before* Christ's second coming in order to give the angels an opportunity to review the books thoroughly. This cannot happen "in the split second division of the living" when Christ returns. It has to precede His return by quite some time in order for the angels to have the opportunity to review heaven's record books thoroughly.

Judgment in Revelation

Revelation's description of God's judgment also suggests that it will take place some time before Christ's second coming. Two passages are particularly relevant to the pre-Advent timing of the judgment.

Revelation 14:6, 7. This passage records what is commonly referred to in Adventist circles as "the first angel's message," and it contains a significant reference to the judgment: "Then I saw another angel flying in the midst of heaven, having the everlasting gospel to preach to those who dwell on the earth—to every nation, tribe, tongue, and people—saying with a loud voice, 'Fear God and give glory to Him, for the hour of His judgment has come; and worship Him who made heaven and earth, the sea and springs of water.' "

Two ideas in this text are especially im-

portant to our discussion. The first is that this angel has "the everlasting gospel to preach to those who dwell on the earth." Clearly, the gospel is still being preached at the time this angel proclaims his message. Souls are still being saved for God's kingdom. Thus, this angel's proclamation precedes Christ's second coming because Christ will not return until the preaching of the gospel has been finished (see Matthew 24:14).

The second significant point in Revelation 14:6, 7 is the angel's announcement that "the hour of [God's] judgment has come." Notice: it *has come,* not *will come.* Clearly, God's judgment in heaven is going on at the same time that the gospel is being preached. Thus, it has to begin *prior* to Christ's second coming, not *at* His coming.

Revelation 16:4–6. From Revelation 16 we learn that God's judgment will also *conclude* prior to Christ's second coming. Revelation 16 describes seven last plagues that will devastate the world immediately prior to Christ's return. Notice what verses 5 and 6 say.

> You are righteous, O Lord,
> The One who is and who was and who
> is to be,
> *Because You have judged these things.*
> For they have shed the blood of saints
> and prophets,
> And You have given them blood to
> drink.

For it is their just due (emphasis added).

These are the words of an angel following the outpouring of the third plague, and here the judgment is clearly an event in the past because the angel says that God has judged—past tense. And since the seven last plagues occur *before* the second coming of Christ, the judgment that precedes these plagues must both begin and end prior to His return (see also Revelation 19:1, 2). Adventists understand this to be the judgment that is described in Daniel 7:9, 10.

So, Revelation also leaves absolutely no doubt that a judgment will occur in heaven *prior to* Christ's second coming. I conclude, therefore, that the Adventist teaching about a *pre-Advent* investigative judgment is thoroughly biblical.

The date for the judgment

Daniel 7 doesn't provide us with an exact date for the beginning of the investigative judgment. However, the concluding sentence in verse 25 gives us a clue about the approximate time when the judgment should begin, and, again, it occurs *before* Christ's second coming, not *at* His coming. Speaking of the little horn, verse 25 says, "The saints shall be given into his hand for a time and times and half a time."

The Aramaic* word translated "time" in this verse is *'iddan*. This word also occurs in chapter 4, which tells the story of Nebuchadnezzar's dream of the great tree. Only a stump was left after the tree was cut down, and a heavenly watcher cried out that the king's heart would be changed to that of a beast, and "seven times" (*'iddan*) would "pass over him" (verse 16). Most interpreters understand *'iddan* in this passage to mean "years." In fact, the New King James Version and the New International Version add footnotes to the word *times* in verse 16 that give "years" as an alternate translation.† Based on this, Seventh-day Adventists have traditionally interpreted the word *time* in Daniel 7:25 to also mean a year. (The plural *times* in most English versions is actually a translation of a dual form of the word *'iddan*—that is, "two times.")‡ Here is how this time period works out mathematically:

Time ("year")	360 days
Times (two times)	720 days
Half a time	180 days
Total	1,260 days

You may wonder why these calculations

---

*Daniel 2:4b–7:28 is written in Aramaic.

†The word *times* (*'iddan*) also occurs in verses 23, 25, and 32.

‡ *The Seventh-day Adventist Bible Commentary* says, "Scholars generally agree that [the plural *times*] should have been pointed as a dual, thus denoting 'two times' " (4:833). The Revised Standard Version of Daniel 7:25 says "two times."

are based on years that are 360 days long rather than the usual 365 or 366 days. This is done based on a double presentation of this prophecy in Revelation 12. Verse 6 of Revelation 12 says that "the woman fled into the wilderness, where she has a place prepared by God, that they should feed her there *one thousand two hundred and sixty days*" (emphasis added). However, verse 14 uses the language of Daniel 7:25 to say the same thing: "The woman was given two wings of a great eagle, that she might fly into the wilderness to her place, where she is nourished for *a time and times and half a time,* from the presence of the serpent" (emphasis added). We can be certain, then, that the "time and times and half a time" of Daniel 7:25 should be interpreted as three and one-half years of 360 days each.

The next question is whether these three and one-half years should be interpreted as literal or symbolic time. Based on what is known as the year-day principle (which I will discuss in detail in chapter 27 of this book), Adventists have always interpreted Daniel's statement as symbolic, with one day representing a year of literal time. The full prophecy, then, comprises 1,260 years.

The key question, of course, is when these 1,260 years should begin and end. Adventists understand the period to have started in A.D. 538 and to have ended in 1798. I have given a fairly detailed explanation of the basis for these dates in my

book *Could It Really Happen?*[6] I will give a summary here.

Adventists have traditionally referred to the 1,260 days/years as the period of papal supremacy. This way of stating the prime characteristic of the period leads to the misconception that the papacy achieved its political supremacy in Europe in 538 and lost it in 1798. It is much more accurate to say that 538 opened the way for the papacy to becoming increasingly influential in European politics. It reached the zenith of its political power between 1100 and 1300, following which it went into a gradual decline. It lost the last of its political influence during the French Revolution, which was a violent secular revolt against all religion, especially Catholicism. In February 1798, the French general Berthier took Pope Pius VI prisoner, and this pope died in exile a year or so later. For approximately the next one hundred years, popes fretted and fumed over their political isolation, but there was precious little they could do about it. The Jesuit author Malachi Martin noted in 1990 that the Vatican had suffered "two hundred years of inactivity [that were] imposed on the papacy by the major secular powers of the world."[7] Note that 1990 is less then ten years short of two hundred years from 1798. From Adventism's historicist point of view, Martin was right on target.

With 1798 established as the end point

of the 1,260 years, a bit of math gives us 538 as the starting point of that period. What happened in 538? During the previous hundred or so years, Rome and Constantinople had kept up a tug-of-war for supremacy over the Christian churches in the Roman Empire. In 533, the emperor Justinian settled the debate with a letter to the pope establishing the pope as the " 'head of all the holy churches' and 'head of all the holy priests of God.' "[8] That, of course, is five years short of 538. Adventists and other historicists have explained that the Ostrogoths had laid a siege around Rome at the time of Justinian's letter, and thus, the pope was unable to exercise the power that the letter conferred on him. However, in 538, Justinian's army drove the Ostrogoths away from Rome, opening the way for the pope to begin to exercise the prerogatives the letter gave him.

Returning our attention to Daniel's prophecy, it's important to note that the 1,260 years is the period given to the little horn to exercise its power. This figure doesn't establish the date for the judgment. However, we can expect the judgment to have begun shortly after that period. And indeed, by Adventist calculations, it began in 1844, less than fifty years later. We'll see more on that in later chapters of this book. The point again is that the judgment described in Daniel 7:9, 10 will occur *prior* to Christ's second coming, not *at* His coming.

How long does the judgment have to continue?

Before concluding this chapter, we need to consider one final objection that I hear now and then regarding the timing of the investigative judgment. The basic idea is that if the judgment began in 1844, then it's been going on for more than 160 years, and surely neither God nor the angels need *that long* to review heaven's records and make up their minds about conferring the kingdom on the Son of man. Nor does it have to take *that long* for the angels to review the lives of the saints and Jesus' declaration that they are worthy of salvation. For example, Ford said, "Even neophytes in religion are hard to convince that the omniscient God takes so long ferreting out the evidence about His creatures, especially when Scripture so clearly affirms that He reads the thoughts and intents of each soul, and that every heart is open to Him with whom we have to do."[9] "Were we soundly based when we concluded that in 1844 Christ began a new form of ministry which had to be pursued to the bitter end for more than fourteen decades before His living saints could see His face?"[10]

I will respond to Ford's objection in four ways. First, God probably didn't intend for the investigative judgment to continue for 160 years either. Had the church fulfilled its mission in the years following 1844, Jesus would have returned already.

Second, the objection that 160-plus years is much too long for God's judgment has always struck me as a bit odd. God is in heaven; we're on the earth. Who are we to tell Him how long His judgment process should take? It often seems to us that God operates on a very slow timetable. He let four thousand years pass after the fall of Adam and Eve before He sent the Messiah. Most of the empires in Daniel's vision lasted hundreds of years. The Roman Empire lasted at least five hundred years. Why should we be surprised that the judgment phase of Daniel 7 takes more than 160 years?

My third response to Ford's comments cited above is that in the first quotation he assumes the judgment to be for God's benefit, to give Him an opportunity to ferret out the evidence about His creatures. Many Adventists in the past assumed this to be the case, but it isn't the church's present understanding. I pointed out in chapter 4 that Adventists today understand the judgment to be for the benefit of the angels, not God. The judgment reveals to the angels the reasons for God's decisions about each of His children.

Fourth, the objection that 160-plus years is too long a time for God's judgment assumes that the judgment in heaven is a continuous process. However, it's entirely possible that the judgment progresses in stages, with breaks between sessions that may last several years. We simply don't know enough about the judgment in heaven to express an opinion about how long it should take.

We're humans, and it's understandable that we would like to see the judgment wrapped up and Jesus come back to redeem us *tomorrow*! But God takes His time to let history work out His will.

In conclusion

The primary issue in this chapter has been whether God's final judgment, which is mentioned several times in Scripture, will take place *at* Christ's second coming or some time *prior* to His return. Most Christians, Desmond Ford included, understand it to occur *at* the Second Coming. However, the Adventist teaching of the investigative judgment requires that it occur in heaven some time *before* His return. And the evidence that I have provided in this chapter makes it clear that the Adventist position has strong biblical support.

_____

1. Shea, *Selected Studies in Prophetic Interpretation*, 119.
2. Ibid., 121.
3. Ford, "Daniel 8:14," 477.
4. Ibid., 476; emphasis added.
5. Ibid.
6. See Moore, *Could It Really Happen?* 43–52.
7. Martin, *The Keys of This Blood*, 22.
8. Quoted in the *Seventh-day Adventist Bible Commentary*, 4:827.
9. Ford, "Daniel 8:14," 277.
10. Ibid., 293.

Chapter 11

The Judgment and the Sins of the Saints

Adventists believe that one of the primary purposes of the investigative judgment is to provide the angels with an opportunity to review God's dealings with His professed people, so they can see the justice of His decisions about each one. Out of necessity, this will include the angels' review of the sins of the saints. However, Desmond Ford insists that the primary function of the judgment in Daniel 7 is to condemn the wicked little horn and that it has nothing whatsoever to do with the sins of the saints. He says,

> It is the little horn that is being investigated, not the suffering saints. The books enshrine the records of willful transgressions of Satan's followers, not the failures of the worshippers of Yahweh.[1]

> Never are the saints the focus of divine investigation. If they are in right covenant relationship with God, their status is not open to question at any time.[2]

> The "books" of Dan. 7:10 apparently contain the record of the evil deeds of the fourth beast and the little horn. There is nothing here whatever about the saints being scrutinized by the heavenly court. None of *their* sins are indicated, and there is nothing to indicate that these books contain a record of their lives.[3]

Note Ford's words: "It is the little horn that is being investigated, not the suffering saints," "never are the saints the focus of divine investigation," and "there is nothing here whatever about the saints being scrutinized by the heavenly court." Ford is essentially correct in that Daniel 7 doesn't *say* that the judgment in heaven prior to Christ's second coming will consider the sins of the saints. I will point out that neither does Daniel 7 directly state that the sins of the dragon and its little horn are being investigated. The sins of the little horn are listed in verse 25, and the reasonable conclusion is that the judgment will investigate those sins, but Daniel doesn't actually say so. The point of the vision is the conflict between the little horn and the saints, and the focus of the judgment is on the resolution of that conflict, not on the sins of either the little horn or the saints.

The sins of the saints aren't mentioned in Daniel 7 because it's the saints who are being attacked. Their sins aren't the issue in this particular prophecy, but that doesn't mean the judgment won't consider their sins, as we shall see in a moment. What the prophecy does say is that a verdict is rendered for both parties. The dragon and its little horn are condemned (verses 11, 26), and "a judgment was made in favor of the saints of the Most High" (verse 22). The saints are vindicated. The obvious implication is that the judgment examines both the little horn and the saints, for if a judgment is rendered in favor of the saints, then they had to have been investigated.

God's judgment elsewhere in the Bible

As with any other biblical topic, *it's important to include all the biblical evidence.* It's a mistake to consider the judgment in Daniel 7 in isolation from everything else the Bible says about the judgment. And the evidence elsewhere in the Bible makes it very clear that the sins of the saints *will be* a consideration in the final judgment. Notice the following:

Ecclesiastes 12:14—"God will bring every work into judgment, including every secret thing, *whether good or evil*" (emphasis added).

Matthew 12:37—"By your words you will be justified, and by your words you will be condemned."

Romans 14:10–12—"We shall all stand before the judgment seat of Christ. For it is written: 'As I live, says the LORD, every knee shall bow to Me, and every tongue shall confess to God.' So then each of us shall give account of himself to God."

2 Corinthians 5:10—"We must all appear before the judgment seat of Christ, that each one may receive the things done in the body, according to what he has done, *whether good or bad*" (emphasis added).

James 2:12—"So speak and so do as those who will be judged by the law of liberty."

Two conclusions are very obvious from these texts: (1) God's people will appear in God's final judgment, and (2) their deeds, both good and bad, will be a consideration in that judgment. Thus, while Daniel's description of the judgment in chapter 7 doesn't mention the sins of the saints, the judgment as it is described elsewhere in the Bible *does* include those sins. Daniel 12:1 says that at the resurrection when Christ returns, "Your people shall be delivered, every one who is found written in the book." The statement that God's people will be "*found* written in the book" is obviously a statement about judgment. And when will God's people have been "*found* written in the book"? Obviously, at the time of the judgment mentioned in Daniel 7:9, 10, which is the only other place in Daniel where books are mentioned in the context of judgment.

The only way to conclude that the judgment in Daniel 7 has nothing to do with the sins of the saints is to believe that God plans to conduct two final judgments: one that is described in Daniel 7 and another one that is mentioned elsewhere in the Bible. But that doesn't make much sense to me. It seems much more reasonable to assume that the judgment in Daniel 7 is the same as the one mentioned by other Bible writers and that putting them all together gives us our most complete picture of heaven's final judgment.

We can say, then, that even though Daniel doesn't state it directly, the judgment he speaks of in chapter 7 will involve a review of the lives of God's people, including both their good and bad deeds. Granted, there is a sense in which Scripture describes Christ's second coming as a day of judgment. However, I hardly think God is going to wait until Christ's second coming to bring up the sins of the saints for judgment! If they're to be brought up at all—and Scripture makes it very clear that they will—then it's much more reasonable to conclude that they will be investigated in the pre-Advent judgment rather than at whatever judgment takes place at Christ's second coming.

The investigative judgment and the great controversy

In chapter 4 of this book I pointed out that the Adventist teaching about the investigative judgment especially makes sense in the context of the great controversy. Revelation 12 provides one of the primary evidences for the great controversy, and it has a bearing on the investigative judgment.

Revelation 12 begins with a woman giving birth to a male Child, whom a dragon tries to destroy. However, God saves the Child by snatching it up to heaven (verses 1–6). This is an obvious reference to Christ's birth and ascension. When the dragon sees that he can't destroy the Child, he turns on the woman. Adventist interpreters understand a woman in apocalyptic prophecy to be a symbol of God's people, those professing to follow Him. Revelation 12:13 says that the dragon persecuted the woman, and verse 14 says that "the woman was given two wings of a great eagle, that she might fly into the wilderness to her place, where she is nourished for a time and times and half a time, from the presence of the serpent" (i.e., the dragon—see verse 9). Notice that Revelation brings in two concepts from Daniel 7:25: the persecution of the saints, and the length of that persecution, which is "a time and times and half a time," or 1,260 days.

Revelation contains a third allusion to Daniel 7 as well. According to Daniel 7:25, the little horn will "intend to change times and law." Adventists understand this to refer to the papal change of the Ten Commandments in two ways: (1) the worship of images, which the second commandment forbids, and (2) the substitution of the first day of the week for the seventh as the weekly day to be "kept," in violation of the fourth commandment. Revelation 12:17 also suggests an attack on God's law: "The dragon was enraged with the woman, and he went to make war with the rest of her offspring, *who keep the commandments of God* and have the testimony of Jesus Christ" (emphasis added). Here the dragon

attacks God's commandments in the person of His commandment-keeping saints. Thus, three of the specifications about the little horn in Daniel 7 reappear in Revelation 12:

- The attack on God's people
- The period of a time, times, and half a time
- The attack on God's law, His commandments

This leads to an extremely significant conclusion: the little horn of Daniel 7 and the dragon in Revelation 12 are related. The dragon, of course, is Satan, for Revelation 12:9 speaks of "the great dragon . . . called the Devil and Satan." I don't mean to suggest that the little horn of Daniel 7 *is* Satan, however. I agree with our Adventist historicist interpretation that the little horn represents the medieval papacy. But Satan rarely appears in person to human beings. He works through his human agents. Thus, I'm suggesting that a comparison of Daniel 7 with Revelation 12 makes it evident that the little horn in Daniel is simply an agent of Satan. Satan is the power behind the little horn.

Satan, our accuser. This conclusion about the little horn is extremely significant, for it adds another dimension to the attack on God's people in Daniel 7. We find that added dimension in Revelation

12:10, in which the revelator says, "I heard a loud voice saying in heaven, 'Now salvation, and strength, and the kingdom of our God, and the power of His Christ have come, *for the accuser of our brethren, who accused them before our God day and night, has been cast down*' " (emphasis added). Daniel 7:25 shows the little horn attacking God's people, and Revelation 12:10 shows the dragon—Satan, the power behind the little horn—also attacking God's people. And please notice the nature of Satan's attack: *he is the accuser of God's people.*

Accusing them of what?

Two other texts in the Bible show Satan accusing God's people. In the first chapter of Job, Satan joins other heavenly beings in appearing before God. Then God challenges Satan: "Have you considered My servant Job, that there is none like him on the earth, a blameless and upright man, one who fears God and shuns evil?" (Job 1:8). Satan answers, "Does Job fear God for nothing? Have You not made a hedge around him, around his household, and around all that he has on every side? You have blessed the work of his hands, and his possessions have increased in the land. But now, stretch out Your hand and touch all that he has, and he will surely curse You to Your face!" (verses 9–11). The issue is Job's character, and *Satan's specific accusation is that Job doesn't deserve God's favor.*

We see essentially the same thing in Zechariah 3. The prophet writes,

He showed me Joshua the high priest standing before the Angel of the LORD, and Satan standing at his right hand to oppose him. And the LORD said to Satan, "The LORD rebuke you, Satan! The LORD who has chosen Jerusalem rebuke you! Is this not a brand plucked from the fire?" Now Joshua was clothed with filthy garments, and was standing before the Angel. Then He answered and spoke to those who stood before Him, saying, "Take away the filthy garments from him." And to him He said, "See, I have removed your iniquity from you, and I will clothe you with rich robes" (verses 1–4).

While the text doesn't actually *say* that Satan accused Joshua of unworthiness, this is clearly implied. Notice that Satan opposes the Angel of the Lord. And what is the Angel's response? He rebukes Satan, saying that Joshua is a brand plucked from the fire. The Angel of the Lord then removes Joshua's filthy garments, puts rich robes on him, and says, "I have removed your iniquity from you." Zechariah's vision is a perfect description of righteousness by faith, by which God removes our sins from us and clothes us in the robe of Christ's righteousness. It's also a perfect description of Satan's effort to oppose this transaction. Satan obviously means that Joshua's sinfulness disqualifies him for God's favor.

Similarly, I propose that when Revelation 12:10 calls Satan "the accuser of our brethren," the accusations referred to are the same as those in Job and Zechariah—Satan is claiming that God's people are unworthy of His favor. What else would Satan accuse God's people of?

Now here's the point: In Revelation 12, Satan's accusations are a direct attack on the saints. And because of the close relationship between Revelation 12 and Daniel 7, that conclusion contributes profoundly to our understanding of the attack on the saints in Daniel 7. While the historical focus in Daniel 7 is on the medieval papacy's persecution of God's people through the Inquisition, Revelation 12 shows us that the power behind the little horn is Satan, and that his attack on the saints includes attacking them before God as unworthy of His favor. And *we have to take this attack into account in our evaluation of the judgment in Daniel 7.* Two other pieces of evidence in the Bible fully justify our taking this approach: (1) heaven's books include a record of the lives of God's people, and (2) their deeds, both good and bad, will come up for review in God's final judgment.

If what I've said here is correct—and I believe it is—then please notice *why* the sins of the saints come up in the judgment.

It isn't because God and Christ bring them up, for they have already forgiven those sins, nor is it because the angels bring them up. It's because *Satan brings them up!* He's the accuser of God's people. I will remind you of a paragraph in Ellen White's *The Great Controversy* that I quoted in an earlier chapter:

> While Jesus is pleading for the subjects of His grace, Satan accuses them before God as transgressors. The great deceiver has sought to lead them into skepticism, to cause them to lose confidence in God, to separate themselves from His love, and to break His law. Now he points to the record of their lives, to the defects of character, the unlikeness to Christ, which has dishonored their Redeemer, to all the sins that he has tempted them to commit, and because of these he claims them as his subjects.[4]

This brings us to another thought that Ford expressed in one of the quotes I shared with you earlier in this chapter. He said, "If [the saints] are in right covenant relationship with God, their status is not open to question at any time." This is certainly true as far as God and Christ are concerned. However, it definitely is not true as far as Satan is concerned. He *does* question the status of God's saints. *That's what his role as accuser is all about.* Let me repeat it, then: The reason the sins of the saints come in review during the final judgment is not because God and Christ bring them up or because the angels bring them up. It's because Satan brings them up! The books of record are God's response, and when the angels have completed their review of the lives of the saints, they will all be satisfied that God is right and Satan is wrong. All of Satan's charges against those who are truly God's saints will be proved groundless. The tragedy is that in some cases Satan's accusations are correct—some of those who have claimed to be on God's side have actually been on Satan's side (see Matthew 7:22, 23; 25:11, 12), although, of course, God has known their true spiritual condition all along.

Thus, while Ford is essentially correct that Daniel 7 doesn't state that the sins of the saints will be considered in the judgment of which it speaks, the description of that judgment elsewhere in the Bible makes it very clear that the deeds of God's people, both good and bad, *will* be reviewed in the judgment at the end of time. This is very biblical.

---

1. Ford, "Daniel 8:14," 353. This quotation is part of Ford's comment on Daniel 8:14, not his comment on the judgment in Daniel 7. However, his argument regarding the sins of the saints is the same regarding both chapters of Daniel.
2. Ibid., 355.
3. Ibid., 371; emphasis in the original.
4. White, *The Great Controversy*, 484.

Issues in Daniel 8

Chapter 12

Where Is Rome in Daniel 8?

Daniel 8 is one of the parts of the Bible most foundational to the Adventist doctrine of the investigative judgment. Our interpretation of this chapter has also been one of the focal points of the criticism we have received over the years. Thus, it's important that we take the time to examine this chapter carefully. I will begin with a comparison of Daniel's vision recorded in chapter 8 with the visions in chapters 2 and 7.

I've noted in the previous chapters of this book the parallel nature of chapters 2 and 7 of Daniel. The four metals in chapter 2 represent the same political powers as the four beasts in chapter 7: Babylon, Media-Persia, Greece, and Rome. And the feet of iron and clay in Daniel 2 represent the breakup of Rome by the barbarian tribes, as do the ten horns on the dragon's head in chapter 7. Finally, both chapter 2 and chapter 7 conclude with the establishment of God's eternal kingdom. The question we have to ask about Daniel 8 is whether it is parallel to chapters 2 and 7.

Three symbols and one statement by the angel Gabriel in Daniel 8 *are* clearly parallel to these other chapters:

1. *The ram.* The angel told Daniel that the ram in chapter 8 represents "the kings of Media and Persia" (verse 20). This symbol is parallel to the arms and chest of silver in Daniel 2 and the bear in chapter 7.
2. *The goat.* This symbol in chapter 8, which the angel said represents Greece (verse 21), is parallel to the belly and thighs of bronze in chapter 2 and the leopard with four heads and four wings in chapter 7.

3. *The little horn.* Most scholars agree that the little horn in chapter 8 is parallel to the little horn in chapter 7.

4. *The end time.* Daniel's angel interpreter told him that the vision in chapter 8 concerned the time of the end (verses 17, 19), and the establishment of God's eternal kingdom in Daniel 2 and 7 is also an end-time event.

However, the Roman Empire, which is so clearly represented by the legs of iron in chapter 2 and by the dragon in chapter 7, appears to be absent in chapter 8. Hence the question that titles this chapter: where is Rome in Daniel 8?

Many Adventist interpreters understand the little horn to represent Rome in both its pagan and its papal phases, and I agree. The rest of this chapter explains the basis for this interpretation. I will begin by quoting verses 8 and 9:

Therefore the male goat grew very great; but when he became strong, the large horn was broken, and in place of it four notable ones came up toward the four winds of heaven. And out of one of them came a little horn which grew exceedingly great toward the south, toward the east, and toward the Glorious Land.

I pointed out in chapter 9 of this book that most scholars understand the little horn to represent Antiochus IV Epiphanes. The most obvious reason for this conclusion is that Antiochus was a Greek king of one of the divisions of Alexander's empire, and, at first glance, it appears that the horn grows out of one of the goat's four horns. However, historicist students of prophecy (which includes Adventists) interpret the little horn in Daniel 8 as representing Rome in both its pagan and papal phases. One of the primary reasons they do so is that the problems with the Antiochus interpretation raise serious questions about its validity.

Problems with the Antiochus interpretation

I discussed several of the problems with the Antiochus interpretation in chapter 8. I'll begin here by summarizing them.

- Daniel 8 says the ram was "great," the goat was "very great," and the horn became "exceedingly great." But Antiochus wasn't greater than the Medo-Persian and Greek empires. He was a rather minor ruler of the Seleucid Empire.
- Antiochus's holdings didn't grow in the directions Daniel said the horn would grow.
- Antiochus didn't destroy the temple in Jerusalem as was prophesied of the little horn.

- Nor did he desecrate the sanctuary for 2,300 days or even for 1,150 days.
- The end time didn't follow Antiochus's rampage in Jerusalem.
- Antiochus doesn't fit the "big picture" in Daniel's prophecies.

An important reason, then, why historicists reject the Antiochus interpretation of the little horn in chapter 8 is that Antiochus doesn't fit several of the specifications Daniel gave for that symbol.

Comparison of the horns. The actions of the horns in Daniel 7 and 8 are quite similar. Both attack God, both attack His people, and both attack His truth. In chapter 7, the little horn attacks God's law, and in chapter 8, the little horn attacks His sanctuary. This has led many interpreters— probably a majority—to consider the little horns in chapters 7 and 8 to represent the same evil entity. This presents a problem, of course, for those who understand the little horn in chapter 8 to represent Antiochus because then they have to find a way to make the little horn in chapter 7 represent Antiochus as well. But in chapter 7, the little horn grows out of the dragon, which represents Rome. How could Antiochus be pictured as a power that grows out of the Roman Empire when he was part of the preceding Greek Empire? Scholars who want the little horn in Daniel 7 to represent Antiochus try to make it work by

splitting Media-Persia into two separate entities. Here is an outline of that interpretation of the vision of chapter 7:

Lion	Babylon
Bear	Media
Leopard	Persia
Dragon	Greece
Little horn	Antiochus

There are several problems with this interpretation of the beasts in chapter 7. First, it breaks the unity between chapters 2 and 7. The image in chapter 2 has four metals that represent Babylon, Media-Persia, Greece, and Rome. It seems most reasonable that the four beasts of chapter 7 should match whatever these four metals of chapter 2 represent. It's a historical fact that Babylon was succeeded by Media-Persia, Greece, and Rome. So we break the unity between chapters 2 and 7 if we split Media and Persia apart in chapter 7 just so we can make the little horn on the dragon's head represent Antiochus.

A second problem with breaking Media and Persia apart in chapter 7 is that in chapter 8:20, Daniel's angel interpreter told him that a single ram represented both Media and Persia. If Media and Persia are represented by a single beast in chapter 8, it seems reasonable that they should be represented by a single beast in chapter 7. There's also a significant similarity between the bear in Daniel 7 and the ram in chapter 8. The bear raised itself up on one side, and the ram had two horns, one of which became higher than the other. Thus, it seems very reasonable to understand the bear and the ram as representing the same power—the combined Media and Persia.

A third problem with separating Media and Persia in Daniel 7 is that the leopard has four heads, which are analogous to the four horns on the Greek goat in chapter 8. Also, the leopard's four wings suggest the speed with which Alexander the Great conquered the Medo-Persian Empire—and they parallel the point in chapter 8 that the goat rushed at the ram so fast that its feet didn't even touch the ground. Thus, the leopard most logically represents Greece, not Persia.

For these reasons, I conclude that the bear in chapter 7 represents both Media and Persia, and the leopard represents Greece, not Persia.

Antiochus and the ten horns. Yet another problem with the Antiochus interpretation has to do with the symbols in both Daniel 2 and 7 for the breakup of the Roman Empire in the third, fourth, and fifth centuries A.D. This breakup is represented in Daniel 2 by the feet and toes of iron and clay and in Daniel 7 by the ten horns. According to Daniel 7:24, the little horn arises *after* the ten horns. If the dragon represents Greece, then those ten horns have to fit into the

history of Greece prior to Antiochus so that Antiochus can arise out of them. But there is simply no way to make them do that. Those horns only make sense in light of the breakup of the Roman Empire several centuries after Antiochus passed from the scene of action. Therefore, the little horn in Daniel 7 cannot represent Antiochus.

In conclusion, the problems associated with identifying the little horn of Daniel 7 as Antiochus seem all but insurmountable to me.

Problems with the historicist interpretation

I would be less than candid, however, if I were to pretend that all of the problems with the interpretation of the little horn in Daniel 8 lie with the idea that it represents Antiochus. The historicist interpretation falls short of being perfect for at least two reasons.

Why not two symbols? One of the problems is that in chapter 7 the Roman Empire and the papacy are represented by separate symbols: the dragon represents Rome, and the little horn represents the papacy. However, Adventists generally understand the little horn in chapter 8 to represent both pagan and papal Rome. The question is, Why does chapter 8 have only one symbol to represent both Rome and the papacy when chapter 7 has two?

This actually is not as much of a problem as it might seem at first glance. The little horn in Daniel 7 is only *somewhat* of a separate symbol from the dragon, for it grows out of the dragon's head. Thus, during the entire time of the little horn's existence, it's a part of the dragon, and the dragon is in existence during the entire period represented by the horn. So if the horn in chapter 7 represents the papacy, then so does the dragon. There's a very good reason for this melding of symbols. Historians recognize that the papacy grew out of the Roman Empire and succeeded that empire, the pope simply replacing the emperor. Indeed, one of the titles of the ancient Roman emperors was Pontifex Maximus, which is one of the titles of popes to this day. Thus, it shouldn't surprise us to find Daniel's vision in chapter 8 providing us with a single symbol to represent both the pagan and the papal phases of Rome, for in a very real sense they *are* one entity.

Origin of the little horn. A second problem with the historicist interpretation of the little horn in Daniel 8 is that the horn appears to grow out of one of the goat's four horns—that is, out of one of the divisions of Alexander's empire. And, of course, Antiochus was an emperor of the Seleucid Empire, which was one of the divisions of Greece. Historicists need a very credible

response to the idea that the little horn grows out of one of the goat's four horns, both because the Antiochus interpretation seems so obvious and because that interpretation is so widely accepted in the scholarly world.

It is to that response that I will now turn.

Reasons that the little horn fits Rome

The first thing to notice is that the Hebrew in Daniel 8:9 doesn't say that the little horn *grew* out of one of the four horns on the goat's head. Most of our modern versions translate the Hebrew accurately to say that "out of one of *them came* a little horn" (emphasis added). The two significant words are *them* and *came*. I'll begin by commenting on the pronoun *them*.

The antecedent to them. The question is, What is the antecedent* of the *them* from which the little horn came? Verse 8 provides two possibilities. I will quote that verse again and italicize each possibility. "Therefore the male goat grew very great; but when he became strong, the large horn was broken, and in place of it four notable *ones* came up toward the four *winds* of heaven." Then Daniel said, "Out of one of *them* came a little horn . . ."

So, did the little horn come out of one of the four horns or out of one of the four

---

*The antecedent of a pronoun is the noun it represents. For example, verse 8 says that "the male goat grew very great; but when he became strong . . ." The antecedent of the pronoun *he* is the goat.

winds? The most obvious reason for concluding that the little horn came out of one of the four horns is that the four horns and the little horn are all *horns*. In real life, horns don't grow out of winds. It seems reasonable, then, that the little horn should grow out of another horn. However, the symbols in apocalyptic prophecy quite often defy reality. Lions and leopards don't have wings, and goats don't have horns between their eyes, nor do they run without touching the ground. In real life, horns don't have eyes and mouths, they don't speak, they don't try to change God's laws, and they don't attack His sanctuary. Thus, while the idea of a horn growing out of one of the four winds seems bizarre to our understanding of the normal world, it's no more bizarre than some of the other symbols in Daniel's prophecies.

A second consideration in determining the antecedent of the word *them* is that usually the antecedent of a pronoun is the noun that precedes it most closely. For example, suppose that I say, "John tossed the ball in the air and threw his glove on the ground. Then he picked *it* up." Is the antecedent of *it* the ball that went in the air and fell back on the ground, or is it the glove that John threw on the ground? The most natural assumption is that the antecedent of *it* is the glove because the word *glove* is the noun that precedes the pronoun *it* most closely. Similarly, the four winds are closer to the pronoun *them* than are the four horns, making the winds the more logical antecedent.

The Hebrew word meaning "came." According to the Antiochus interpretation, the little horn *grew* out of one of the four horns on the goat's head. Several Hebrew words are translated "grow" in our English Bibles, depending on the particular shade of meaning the author intended. However, Daniel didn't use any of the words for "grow" to describe the origin of the little horn. The word he used was *yatsa*. This word occurs more than a thousand times in the Hebrew Old Testament.[1] It is occasionally translated "grow." (See, for example, Job 31:40.) However, that isn't its basic meaning. By far the most common translation is "to come out from" or "to go out from." For example, Genesis 2:10 says "a river *went out of* [*yatsa*] Eden to water the garden," and in Genesis 15:4, God told Abraham that a son "who will *come from* [*yatsa*] your own body shall be your heir." In his dissertation on Daniel 8:9–14, Martin Proebstle says, "In the Hebrew Bible *yatsa* is never used for the developing of horns, and the verb used for [the developing of horns] in the vision of Dan 8 is *alah* (Dan 8:3, 8). Semantically, it is then difficult to support the idea that in vs. 9a the horn *grows* 'from one of them,' rather it *comes forth*."[2]

One of the more frequent uses of *yatsa*

in the Old Testament is in the sense of an army "going out" to battle. For example, in his prayer dedicating the temple, Solomon said, "When Your people *go out* [*yatsa*] to battle against their enemy, . . . then hear in heaven their prayer" (1 Kings 8:44, 45; emphasis added). Numbers 1:20 speaks of "the children of Reuben, . . . every male individually, from twenty years old and above, all who were able *to go* [*yatsa*] to war" (emphasis added). Through the next twenty-one verses the same thing is repeated for each tribe. This military use of the word *yatsa* fits Antiochus's attempts to conquer Egypt and subdue the Jews, but it's especially appropriate to describe the military conquests of the Romans as they conquered Greece and took control of the Mediterranean region.

Coming back now to Daniel 8:9, the little horn *came out from* something, and the two options are (1) that it came out from one of the four horns, or (2) that it came out from one of the four winds. The view that the little horn *came out from* one of the four horns on the goat's head is certainly reasonable. The significance of *yatsa* is that it makes the "winds" option more plausible than a Hebrew word for growth would have. It's easier to think of a horn *coming out* from one of the four winds than to think of it *growing* from one of the four winds.

Jacques Doukhan, who grew up as a Jew speaking Hebrew and who now teaches in the Old Testament Department at the Andrews University Theological Seminary, made the following comment about the origin of the little horn:

Unlike the little horn of chapter 7, which emerged from one of the four beasts, the little horn of chapter 8 arises from one of the four winds of heaven (Dan. 8:8). This expression brings us back to the origins of the four beasts in chapter 7: the sea churned up by the four winds of heaven (Dan. 7:2). The little horn would, then, have emerged from one of those winds and not from one of the horns, as some translations seem to imply. . . .

Grammatically speaking, the Hebrew expression translated as "out of one of them" (Dan. 8:9) we should actually read as "out of one [feminine] of them [masculine]," suggesting a link with the preceding expression: "the four winds [feminine] of heaven [masculine]."[3]

Growth of the little horn. So what does it mean that the little horn came out from one of the four winds? I think most interpreters understand the four winds to mean the four directions of the compass. Daniel said that the little horn "grew exceedingly great toward the south, toward the east, and toward the Glorious Land." This is a prediction of the directions of the compass in which the little horn would grow.

I pointed out in chapter 9 that Antiochus did *not* grow exceedingly greater than what he was when he began his reign. If anything, his defeat by the Maccabees made him weaker than he had been. So, of course, Antiochus didn't grow east and south as the prophecy specifies. Neither did he *grow* toward the "Glorious Land" (Judea) because he already controlled that area at the beginning of his reign, and, by the end of his reign, he had lost it. On the other hand, from the perspective of the Bible writers, the Roman Empire *did* come from the West; it expanded east and south; and it subjugated Judea, the Glorious Land. And it is absolutely true that Rome became exceedingly great in comparison to Media-Persia (the ram) and Greece (the goat). Thus, Rome did fulfill Daniel's spec-ifications about the origin of the little horn. This is yet another reason favoring the view that the little horn represents Rome rather than Antiochus.*

In conclusion, neither the Antiochus nor the Rome interpretations of the little horn in Daniel 8 are straightforward. Both have problems that require explanations. However, in my opinion, the problems associated with the Antiochus interpretation are significantly greater and more difficult to resolve. The evidence that I have presented in this chapter persuades me that interpreting the little horn as Rome makes more sense than interpreting it as Antiochus.

---

1. See Holbrook, *Symposium on Daniel,* 395.
2. Proebstle, "Truth and Terror," 101.
3. Doukhan, *Secrets of Daniel,* 124, 125; brackets in original.

---

*Some Adventist commentators see the grammar of verses 8 and 9—and particularly the tenses of the verbs—being decisive for determining that the little horn originates from one of the four winds. (See, for example, Gerhard Hasel, "The 'Little Horn,' " in *Symposium on Daniel,* 388, 389.) Others find this argument to be inconclusive (see Proebstle, "Truth and Terror," 125, 126).

Chapter 13

Which Sanctuary in Daniel 8?—Part 1

When Jesus didn't arrive on October 22, 1844, the immediate question that pressed upon Adventist minds was, *Where were we wrong?* I pointed out in chapter 6 that part of the answer came the very next day. As Hiram Edson was walking across a cornfield to visit other disappointed Millerites on the morning of October 23, the strong impression came upon him that the sanctuary mentioned in Daniel 8:14 was not this earth—it was the sanctuary in heaven. From that day to this, Adventists have held firmly to the belief that the sanctuary mentioned in Daniel 8:14 is the heavenly sanctuary, not the earthly sanctuary.

However, this belief has been challenged both from without and from within our church. Raymond Cottrell was one of those within the church who disagreed with this conclusion. He wrote, "In the Book of Daniel, as throughout the Old Testament, the 'sanctuary' is always, without exception, the Temple in Jerusalem. In order for the analogy between Daniel 8:14 and the Book of Hebrews to be valid it would be essential to demonstrate from the context that Daniel, here, intentionally refers to the sanctuary in heaven rather than to the Temple in Jerusalem, as he consistently does elsewhere."[1]

Analyzing Cottrell

Cottrell raised two issues that I will comment on. The first is whether the Hebrews conceived of a sanctuary in heaven. It would probably be correct to say that no one in Old Testament times had a full-blown concept of a heavenly sanctuary in which ministry was carried out that was an antitype of the ministry carried on in their own earthly sanctuary.

However, God's people in Old Testament times did have a good concept of a sanctuary in heaven. A number of years ago, Elias Brasil de Souza made a study of the sanctuary/temple references in the Old Testament. His doctoral dissertation concluded that the Hebrew people in Old Testament times *did* understand that God dwelt in a sanctuary in heaven, from which He provided forgiveness and salvation.[2] Isaiah, for example, spoke of seeing God "sitting on a throne, high and lifted up, and the train of His robe filled the temple" (Isaiah 6:1). Indeed, some fifty passages in the Old Testament speak of a sanctuary in heaven (see, for example, Psalms 11:4; 102:19, 20).

The second issue Cottrell raised is the question of which sanctuary Daniel had in mind. In the statement Cottrell made that I quoted above, he said that for the Adventist interpretation of Daniel 8 to be correct, it would be "essential to demonstrate from the context that Daniel, here, intentionally refers to the sanctuary in heaven rather than to the Temple in Jerusalem." I don't think it can be demonstrated from the context or in any other way that Daniel himself intentionally referred to the sanctuary in heaven because I don't think Daniel had any such thought in his head. Indeed, it's quite obvious from chapter 9 that Daniel understood the sanctuary that was desolate to be the one in Jerusalem. (See Daniel 9:4–19, especially verse 17.)

On the other hand, I believe it *can* be demonstrated that the sanctuary in Daniel 8:14 refers to the heavenly sanctuary even though Daniel himself didn't understand it that way. For one thing, Daniel 7 locates the little horn at a very specific point in history: it appears following the rise of the barbarian tribes that overthrew the western Roman Empire. If the little horn in chapter 8 represents the same evil power as does the little horn in chapter 7, which most scholars believe to be the case, then the depiction of the horn's activities in chapter 8 must be fulfilled in the same time frame—namely, beginning in the sixth century A.D. This was long after Titus had destroyed the temple in Jerusalem—the only alternative to the sanctuary in heaven. That's why Adventists have historically identified the sanctuary in Daniel 8:14 with the heavenly sanctuary. *It was the only one in existence when the prophecy was fulfilled.*

However, because the sanctuary that is cleansed in Daniel 8:14 is the one that was attacked in verses 10–12, we also need to demonstrate that verses 10–12—the context that Cottrell referred to—also speak of God's sanctuary in heaven. I'll introduce my discussion of this issue with a question: Did God give His Old Testament prophets a preview of important aspects of the plan of salvation hundreds of years in advance? The obvious answer to that question is Yes. God devised the plan of salvation even before the creation of our world (see Revelation 13:8), and He began giving glimpses of that plan as far back as Eden (see Genesis 3:15). Over the next several millennia, He gave continuing insights into His plans regarding salvation, with Isaiah 53 pointing forward quite specifically to a suffering Messiah.

Christ's death is not the only important part of the plan of salvation. His mediatorial ministry in the heavenly sanctuary is also an essential part of that plan. This ministry is clearly revealed in the New Testament, especially in Hebrews and Revelation. The question we're asking here is this: if God gave His prophets information about Christ's sacrificial death centuries and even millennia before that event actually occurred, is it possible that He might also have given advance glimpses of Christ's high-priestly ministry in the heavenly sanctuary? I propose that the answer is Yes. I believe God gave Daniel glimpses of Christ's priestly ministry several centuries before that ministry began. In the remainder of this chapter and all of the next one, I will point out evidence from Daniel 8:10–12 that the sanctuary in these verses is the heavenly sanctuary.[3]

DANIEL 8:10

Verse 10 says, "It [the little horn] grew up to the host of heaven; and it cast down some of the host and some of the stars to the ground, and trampled them." You'll recall that verse 9 says the little horn "grew exceedingly great toward the south, toward the east, and toward the Glorious Land." That's horizontal movement, along the surface of the earth. That's a good description of the growth of the Roman Empire, which grew "horizontally" across Europe, the Middle East, and North Africa. Verse 10, on the other hand, shows the little horn growing "up to the host of heaven." This is vertical movement—that is, it's *up* rather than *across*. What does this vertical movement represent? A careful examination of verses 10–12 suggests that it represents movement *up* to heaven.

Who or what is "the host of heaven"?

In the Old Testament, the term "host of heaven" most often refers to the literal sun, moon, and stars in the context of false worship of these heavenly bodies. (See, for example, in Deuteronomy 4:19; 2 Kings 17:16; Jeremiah 19:13.) But Daniel went on to say that the little horn would "cast down some of the host and some of the stars to the ground." It's rather difficult to think of the little horn, which is a human organization, trying to attack the literal sun, moon, and stars. It seems more reasonable to think of the host and the stars as symbols of God's people on earth, especially since sometimes that's what they *do* represent in the Bible. (See Genesis 15:5; Daniel 12:2, 3.) Understood this way, the horn's casting down the host and the stars to the ground represents the persecution of God's people on earth. (Compare the description of the little horn's activities in chapter 7, where Daniel said it would "wear out the saints of the most High" [Daniel 7:25, KJV].) Adventists understand this wearing out of the saints to have been fulfilled by the papal persecution of dissenters during the medieval period, and the horn's attack on "some of the host and some of the stars" in chapter 8:10 can almost certainly be understood to mean the same thing.

I suggest, however, that it's also possible to understand the host of heaven and the stars in Daniel 8:10 as symbolizing *both* God's earthly people *and* His angels in heaven. Heavenly beings are clearly the meaning of "the host of heaven" in 1 Kings 22:19, where the prophet Micaiah said that he saw "the LORD sitting on His throne, and all the *host of heaven* standing by, on His right hand and on His left" (emphasis added; see also 2 Chronicles 18:18). Micaiah's vision is similar to Daniel's vision in Daniel 7:9, 10, in which he saw thousands of angels surrounding God's throne. The question is how the little horn in Daniel 8:10, which we have always identified as a human entity, could cast heavenly beings down to the ground and trample on them. Obviously, it couldn't. But these "stars" may have another meaning.

In chapter 11 of this book, I pointed out that while the little horn in Daniel 7 represents the papacy during the Middle Ages, there is an even more evil entity behind the little horn. This becomes very clear in Revelation 12, which repeats several of the symbols from Daniel 7:25 and applies them to Satan, the dragon. Revelation 12 pictures the dragon as persecuting the woman, which symbolizes the church (see verses 6, 13, 15, 17), and as attacking God's law through attacking His people (see verse 17). And most significantly for our purpose here, verses 6 and 14 of Revelation 12 apply Daniel's 1,260 days to the period during which the dragon would persecute God's people. Verse 14 even uses Daniel's actual terminology: "time and times and half a time." There can be no doubt that Revelation is expanding our understanding of Daniel's little horn by relating it to Satan and the broader great controversy between Christ and Satan. This is not to say that the little horn and Satan are the same entity. They are distinct, but Satan is the power behind the horn.

Revelation 12 also takes some of the symbols related to the little horn in Daniel 8 and applies them to Satan. In verses 3 and 4, John says he saw the dragon, Satan, draw "a third of the stars of heaven and [throw] them to the earth." This terminology is nearly identical to Daniel 8:10, where the little horn "cast down . . . some of the stars to the ground." Verses 7–9 expand on this idea, portraying Satan and his angels as engaging Michael and his angels in a battle that results in Satan being "cast to the earth, and his angels . . . with him" (verse 9). Thus, it seems very reasonable to apply the little horn's casting down "some of the host and some of the stars to the ground" first of all to the medieval papacy's persecution of God's people, but in a secondary sense to Satan, who fought a war against Michael and His angels. And Revelation 12:4 says that the dragon, Satan, cast a third of the stars to the earth.

In his dissertation on Daniel 8:9–14, Martin Proebstle devotes twenty pages to a detailed examination of the grammar and syntax of the words "the host of heaven" in verse 10. He concludes that "as a human power the horn apparently fights against other human powers. Thus, the 'host of heaven' should be understood as referring to God's people. Still, on a larger scale, the horn . . . typifies the role of a transcendent, anti-divine demon who wages war against the good angels and against God himself. In a similar way, the expression the 'host of heaven' refers to the host of saints which is God's army on earth, but at the same time

hints at the heavenly army that is also involved in this cosmic battle."[4]

Thus, the most significant lesson to be drawn from the attack of Daniel's little horn against the host of heaven and the stars is that it depicts the universal conflict between good and evil—what Adventists have historically called "the great controversy." Antiochus played a minor role in that conflict, but Daniel's description reaches all the way to heaven!

Let's return now to the question posed in the title of this chapter: "Which Sanctuary in Daniel 8?" Is it strictly the sanctuary on earth, or does the little horn extend its reach to the sanctuary in heaven? I've suggested that the evidence indicates that the phrase "the host of heaven" includes not only God's people on earth (its primary meaning), but also the angels in heaven, whom the little horn, which represents Satan himself as well as his earthly agent, also attacks. In what way could Satan do that? He certainly couldn't attack the angels in any kind of physical persecution. He couldn't have done that in heaven even before he was cast out. I suggest that his attack on them is in the sense of taunting them for their loyalty to God and His people. (See, for example the last part of chapter 19 of this book.)

The suggestion that "the host of heaven" in verse 10 includes more than God's people on earth—that it can be understood in some sense to refer to the angels in heaven—gets us started toward answering the question of whether the sanctuary in verses 10 and 11 is in heaven. Verse 11 provides the final answer.

DANIEL 8:11

Three clauses in this verse need our attention:

1. He [the little horn] even exalted himself as high as the Prince of the host;
2. and by him the daily sacrifices were taken away,
3. and the place of His sanctuary was cast down.

I will discuss these three clauses separately.

Exalting itself up to the Prince of the host

In Hebrew, the language in which Daniel wrote chapter 8, the phrase *Prince of the host* reads *sar ha-tsaba*. The word *sar* means "prince," "commander," "chief," and so on; *ha* means "the"; and *tsaba* means "host" or "army."

A Divine Being. Some of those who interpret the little horn to be Antiochus see the expression "the Prince of the host" as

representing Onias III, who was high priest at the time that Antiochus rose to power. If Onias is this "Prince of the host," then it would be appropriate to say that Antiochus "exalted himself as high as the Prince of the host" because Antiochus deposed Onias from the position of high priest. But can Onias reasonably be understood to be the "Prince of the host" in Daniel 8:11? Notice that the New King James Version capitalizes the word *Prince.* A number of other modern versions of the Bible do likewise,* indicating that the translators consider this Prince to be a Divine Being—a designation that hardly fits Onias! According to Proebstle, "The majority of exegetes agree that the 'prince of the host' designates Yhwh [Jehovah]."[5]

On what basis do these translators and exegetes interpret this Prince of the host to be a Divine Being? The evidence is actually very strong. Several times in Daniel the word *prince* (*sar*) seems to clearly refer to a Divine Being. In Daniel 8:25, which is part of the angel Gabriel's interpretation of the vision of that chapter, Gabriel speaks of the "Prince of the host" as the "Prince of princes" (*sar sarim*). And Daniel 12:1 speaks of "Michael . . . , the great prince [*sar*] who stands watch over the sons of your people." (See also Daniel 10:13.) It's especially clear in this verse that this Per-

---

*Including the New International Version. The New American Standard Bible says "the Commander of the host," also indicating a Divine Being.

son is much more than a human prince, and it seems reasonable to conclude that the same is true of the Prince in 8:11.

The Commander of the Lord's army. The Old Testament clearly uses the word *sar* to refer to a Divine Being in two other places. One is Isaiah 9:6, which speaks of the Messiah as "Mighty God, Everlasting Father, Prince [*sar*] of peace." The other place, Joshua 5:14, 15, is particularly significant to our discussion.

Joshua had just led the Israelites across the Jordan River, and he was apparently away from the camp alone, meditating on the upcoming battle for Jericho. Suddenly, the "Commander of the army of the LORD" appeared before him. The Hebrew words are *sar tsava Yahweh.* You will recognize the words *sar* and *tsava,* and *Yahweh* is what some Bible versions translate as "Jehovah." So the One who appeared to Joshua was the Commander (*sar*) of Jehovah's army (*tsava*). Joshua clearly recognized this Person as a Divine Being because he "fell on his face to the earth and worshiped" (verse 14). Then this "Commander of the army of the LORD" ordered Joshua to "take your sandal off your foot, for the place where you stand is holy" (verse 15). The only other place in the Bible where such a command was given is in Exodus 3:5, where the Angel of the LORD—again, Jehovah (see verse 14)—told Moses at the burning bush to remove

his shoes "for the place where you stand is holy ground." There can be no doubt, then, that Joshua was in the presence of a Divine Being.

This story in Joshua is significant for our understanding of Daniel 8:11 because in the original language the words translated "Prince of the host" (in Daniel) and "Commander of the army" (in Joshua) are the same. Both are *sar tsava.* The fact that the Commander of the host who appeared to Joshua was a Divine Being supports the conclusion that the "Prince of the host" in Daniel 8:11 should also be understood as a Divine Being. Thus we can understand the "Prince of the host" in Daniel 8:11 to be the Commander of heaven's armies, a fact that reminds us again of Revelation 12:7–9, where Michael, who is Christ, leads the army of heaven.

The little horn's self-exaltation. Daniel said that the little horn "exalted himself as high as the Prince of the host" (Daniel 8:11). The word *exalted* comes from the Hebrew word *gadal,* which means "to grow" and can also mean "to become great [or important]." The idea behind *gadal* in Daniel 8:11 seems to be not so much that the little horn *attacked* the Prince of the host as that it claimed to be *as great as* the Prince of the host. God didn't exalt the little horn. It exalted itself. And notice its goal: it exalted itself as high as the Prince of the host. This reminds us of Isaiah's description of Lucifer, who said, "I will ascend into heaven, I will exalt my throne above the stars of God; . . . I will be like the Most High" (Isaiah 14:13, 14). Satan's rebellion in heaven occurred several millennia prior to Daniel's time; but his attitude toward Christ has been the same throughout history. Thus, again, the little horn in Daniel 8 can be understood as representing a demon as well as a human being. What we're seeing here is the great controversy. The focal point of the horn's attack is the Prince of the host, whom we identify as Christ. *And Christ is in heaven.* This is another step on our way toward identifying the sanctuary in Daniel 8:10–12 as Christ's sanctuary in heaven.

Taking away the daily sacrifice

The New King James Version says that "by him [the little horn] the daily sacrifices were taken away." At this point Daniel 8 introduces us to sanctuary language. The third clause in verse 11, which we will examine in a moment, actually uses the word *sanctuary.* And again, there is evidence that this sanctuary is in heaven.

What are "the daily sacrifices"? In the clause "by him the daily sacrifices were taken away," the English words *daily sacrifices* are a translation of the Hebrew word *tamid.* The simplest meaning of *tamid* is activities that are carried out on a regular basis, at fixed times. For example, the Bab-

ylonians gave the exiled King Jehoiachin "a regular [*tamid*] ration . . . a portion for each day, all the days of his life" (2 Kings 25:30).

Often in the Old Testament, though by no means always, *tamid* refers to activities *in the sanctuary* that were carried out on a regular basis. For example, Exodus 29:42 speaks of a "continual [*tamid*] burnt offering," and Numbers 4:16 speaks of a "daily [*tamid*] grain offering."

So far as I know, all interpreters understand *tamid* in Daniel 8:11 to refer to sanctuary activities. This is evident from the fact that many Bible versions translate *tamid* as "daily *sacrifice*" (NIV, KJV, NKJV; emphasis added in this and the following quotations), or "regular *sacrifice*" (NASB), or "continual *burnt offering*" (RSV). An important question is whether *tamid* in verse 11 refers to continual sanctuary activities in general or whether it refers specifically to the daily sacrifices. Please note that the words *sacrifice* and *burnt offering* have been added by the translators. The Hebrew simply says, *tamid,* which means "regular." The morning and evening sacrifices were certainly carried out on a regular basis, but so were a number of other sanctuary activities. Had Daniel meant exclusively the daily or regular *sacrifices,* he would have had to include the word *olah,* which means "burnt sacrifice."

Another indication that *tamid* in Daniel 8:11 refers to sanctuary activities as a whole is that the Hebrew says *ha-tamid,* which means "**the** *tamid.*" Proebstle points out that whenever *tamid* is used with the article—"**the** *tamid*"—it links the term to its occurrences in the Pentateuch, and thus to a sanctuary context.[6] This would include the daily sacrifices, but it does not limit *tamid* to them.

Having determined that *tamid* refers to sanctuary activities, the next question is whether those activities take place in the earthly or the heavenly sanctuary. Here is where the translation of a Hebrew preposition is critical. The King James Version says, "*By him* [that is, the little horn], the daily sacrifice was taken away" (emphasis added), and the New King James Version says essentially the same thing. However, from a grammatical point of view, the preposition could just as well be translated, "*From him* [that is, from the Prince of the host] the daily sacrifices were taken away." In fact, most of today's scholars prefer "from him," as is evidenced by the fact that the New International Version, the Revised Standard Version, and the New American Standard Bible all say it that way.

Now, if the *tamid* is taken away *from* the Prince of the host, who is a Divine Being, then the little horn's attack is on the Prince's sanctuary. This means that the

Prince of the host is also a Priest. Proebstle concludes that "*ha-tamid* in Dan 8:11–13 designates (1) the cultic* activities of the *sar ha-tsava* as high priest, and/or (2) the continual cultic worship directed toward the *sar ha-tsava* as divine being."[7] In taking the *tamid* from the Prince of the host, the little horn is attempting to take over His priestly activities. The Old Testament contains no record of any Divine Being ever ministering as a priest in the earthly sanctuary. On the other hand, the book of Hebrews in the New Testament speaks in detail about Christ's high-priestly ministry in the heavenly sanctuary. This brings us closer to the idea that the sanctuary in Daniel 8 is in heaven.

But how could an earthly, human little horn reach up to heaven and take away Christ's high-priestly ministry? I will deal with that question in the next several chapters. For now, it's enough to say that the horn attacks Christ's plan of salvation—something Satan does both personally and through his human agents.

Casting down His sanctuary

Verse 11 concludes by saying that "the place of His [the Prince of the host's] sanctuary was cast down." Note first of all that Daniel directly states here that the Prince of the host has a sanctuary. The fact that

*In today's popular usage, the word *cult* means a false religious system. However, as it is used by scholars, *cult* means any kind of religious worship or ritual, true as well as false.

this Prince who has a sanctuary is a Divine Being supports the conclusion that sanctuary He has is in heaven.

The Hebrew word translated "place" is *machon* (pronounced *mah-kone*), which means "a fixed or established place," "a foundation." Proebstle points out that the word "*machon* in the singular (found 16 times in the OT) exclusively designates the place of the sanctuary and/or the presence or dwelling of YHWH."[8] Even on this earth, it would obviously be impossible to cast down, take away, or destroy the foundation of a building without at the same time destroying the building itself. And the idea of a human organization, or even Satan himself, destroying any part of Christ's sanctuary in heaven is ridiculous in the extreme. So in what sense does the little horn attempt to cast down or destroy the foundation, the place, of the sanctuary? Proebstle offers a helpful suggestion.

Scholars who take the foundation of the sanctuary as referring to the literal temple explain that the verbal notion is not one of overthrowing or destroying but rather of rejecting or desecrating. On the other hand, vs. 11c could refer to the throwing down of the concept or principles upon which the sanctuary is based. This activity does not necessarily affect the architecture of the sanctuary but attacks the *raison d'etre* [reason for the existence] of the sanctuary and thus of the whole sanctuary system.

The semantic features of vs. 11c as well as contextual considerations appear to provide enough reasons to argue for a metaphorical understanding of *machon*, . . . [since] it does not seem possible to throw down the site of the sanctuary, and it is rather unlikely to throw down the foundations of a building/structure.[9]

Proebstle concludes his discussion of the third clause in Daniel 11 with these words: "The clause describes an action by which the metaphorical foundations of the sanctuary of the prince of the host, consisting of the principles upon which the sanctuary and its cultic system are based, are thrown down by the little horn."[10] This moves us toward an understanding of how the little horn could attack God's sanctuary in heaven. Verse 12 will lead us to our conclusion.

DANIEL 8:12

Daniel 8:12 says, "Because of transgression, an army was given over to the horn to oppose the daily sacrifices; and he cast truth down to the ground. He did all this and prospered."

Two possible translations

The first half of Daniel 8:12—the part that says, "Because of transgression, an army [*tsava,* "host," KJV, NIV] was given over to the horn to oppose the daily sacrifices"—can be translated in two ways. One way is to understand the host (the *tsava*) to be the same host that was under attack in verse 10 and whose Prince was under attack in verse 11—in other words, God's people. The other way is to understand the host in verse 12 to be some other group than the one in verse 10. At first glance, this second view doesn't seem to make sense. However, there are good reasons to support this second view.

Verse 12 says that the host is "*given over to* the horn" (emphasis added) so that it can oppose the continual services (the *tamid*) in the sanctuary. In verse 10, the little horn initiates its attack on God's people and His sanctuary. The Hebrew word in verse 12 is in the passive voice: "was given over." It's one thing for the horn to initiate its own attack on God's people. It's quite another for someone to hand God's people over to the horn to be attacked.

Who would give God's host over to the little horn? The list of options is fairly limited. Indeed, there's really only one option: God. No one else would have the authority to hand God's people over to

the rebellious little horn. But it seems rather unlikely that God would hand His own people over to the horn. So, what's going on here?

Martin Proebstle offers a very helpful solution to this problem. His grammatical analysis of the first half of verse 12 is fairly complex (sixty-five pages in his dissertation!), so all I can give you here are his most essential arguments. I'll share two grammatical details that he points out. First, the word *host* (KJV; *tsava* in the original Hebrew) in verse 12 has no article. It's "*a* host," not "*the* host." If Daniel had said "*the* host," then there would be no question that he had in mind the same host that he had described in verses 10 and 11. The fact that he said "*a* host" rather than "*the* host" suggests that he had a different host in mind.

Second, the Hebrew word *natan,* "to give," can also mean "to set." In verse 12, the word is in the passive voice, so it's translated "was given" or "was set." Proebstle's solution to the problem of the identity of the host is to suggest that Daniel had a different host in mind in verse 12 than in verses 10 and 11—an evil host that the horn itself set up against the sanctuary and its continual services, the *tamid.* Here is how Proebstle translates the first half of verse 12: "And a host will be set against the *tamid* in rebellion."[11] Thus, the horn is continuing its attack on the sanctuary, but in verse 12 it has engaged the services of its own host to assist it.*

Rebellion against God

The New International Version translates the first three words of verse 12 "Because of rebellion." The Hebrew word for "rebellion" is *pesha'*, which is used elsewhere in the Old Testament to describe deliberate rebellion against God. The point is that the little horn's attack on the sanctuary, including everything Daniel describes in verses 10 and 11, is a supreme act of rebellion against the God of heaven.†

The problem gets worse. Verse 12 goes on to say that the little horn "cast truth down to the ground." In writing about Daniel 8:12, Jacques Doukhan made the following comment:

> The [Hebrew] word *emeth* rendered here by "truth" is synonymous with "law" (see Ps. 43:3; 119:43, etc.). In Hebrew, truth is a concrete action of obedience to God and has nothing to do with our abstract conception of truth. It is anything in accordance with the law. . . . Jewish commentators (Ibn Ezra, Rashi) interpreted the verse

[Daniel 8:12] to mean that "the little horn shall annul the Law [Torah] and the observance of the commandments.[12] [Compare the warning in Daniel 7:25 that the little horn seeks to change God's law.]

Daniel 8:12 concludes by saying that the little horn "prospered"—meaning that its rebellion actually succeeds! So, Daniel 8:10–12 doesn't describe a short-term problem. *This situation will continue for some time.*

If the analysis of these verses that I've given in this chapter is correct, then the problem described in Daniel 8:10–12 extends far beyond Antiochus and, in fact, beyond all human rebellion on planet Earth. It reaches up to God's sanctuary in heaven. This conclusion is critical to the Adventist understanding of Daniel 8:14 because ever since the mid-1800s we have insisted that the sanctuary in that verse is the heavenly sanctuary, where God, Christ, and the angels are engaged in an investigative judgment. If the sanctuary that is "cleansed" in verse 14 is the heavenly sanctuary, then the sanctuary that is attacked in verses 10–12 must also be the heavenly sanctuary.

---

*Proebstle's conclusion that the host in verse 12 refers to an evil host rather than to the host of God's people in verses 10 and 11, is not shared by all Adventist scholars. The arguments on both sides are quite technical and go beyond the scope of this book.

†In the Hebrew of Daniel 8:12, the word *pesha'* doesn't begin the verse; it comes at the end, after the word *tamid*. That is why Proebstle translates the verse the way he does, "And a host will be set against the **tamid in rebellion**."

I will continue the discussion of this important question in the next chapter.

1. Cottrell, "A Hermeneutic for Daniel 8:14," 8.

2. De Souza, *The Heavenly Sanctuary/Temple Motif in the Hebrew Bible*.

3. One of the primary sources that I have used in my analysis of Daniel 8:9–14 (in chapters 12–17 and 21 of this book) is the 871-page dissertation on these verses by Martin Proebstle, "Truth and Terror." At the time I wrote this book, Proebstle was a professor at the Bogenhofen Adventist Seminary in Austria.

4. Ibid., 153.

5. Ibid., 167.

6. Ibid., 212.

7. Ibid., 231.

8. Ibid., 235.

9. Ibid., 242.

10. Ibid., 243.

11. Ibid., 290.

12. Doukhan, *Secrets of Daniel*, 124.

Chapter 14

Which Sanctuary in Daniel 8?—Part 2

From the discussion in the previous chapter, you can see that I understand the sanctuary of the Prince to be particularly Christ's sanctuary in heaven, from which He has been carrying out His plan to save human beings from sin. If that's true—if the sanctuary in Daniel 8:10–12 does indeed refer in some way to God's sanctuary in heaven—what does that mean, or what will it mean, regarding the little horn's activities?

We'll start to answer that question by considering the relationship of the little horn to the sanctuary in heaven. Whether one believes that the little horn represents Antiochus Epiphanes or the papacy of the Middle Ages, all interpreters identify it as a human organization, and, as I pointed out in the previous chapter, it would be ludicrous in the extreme to suggest that anything human could attack God's sanctuary, which is probably thousands and perhaps millions of light-years from planet Earth. Even Satan and his angels couldn't do that. However, I will remind you of a suggestion by Martin Proebstle, which I quoted in the previous chapter: "The clause [Daniel 8:11c] describes an action by which the metaphorical foundations of the sanctuary of the prince of the host, consisting of the principles upon which the sanctuary and its cultic [sanctuary] system are based, are thrown down by the little horn."[1]

We must keep in mind that the whole purpose of the heavenly sanctuary is to save human beings. Thus, while human beings can't literally reach up to heaven and destroy its sanctuary, they *can* distort the principles of salvation on which that sanctuary operates. The plan of salvation is based on the assumption that human beings will understand it and accept it. But people can develop such false teachings about Christ's ministry in the heavenly sanctuary that they make void His ministry in the minds of those who believe those false teachings.

The papacy

For the past 150-plus years, Seventh-day Adventists have maintained (as did the Reformation Protestants before them) that this distortion of the truth about salvation is indeed exactly what has happened through the teachings of the papacy. Following are some ways that Catholic teachings contradict this biblical truth.

- Catholicism leads people to pray to Mary and the saints instead of directing their prayers to Jesus Christ.
- The pope claims to be the vicar of Christ, that is, Christ's representative on earth during the time of His absence, whereas Jesus said that He would send the Holy Spirit to be His Representative on earth after He returned to heaven (see John 14:16, 17).
- Catholic priests supposedly re-enact Christ's sacrifice for human sin thousands of times each day on church altars all over the world, whereas the Bible clearly teaches that Christ made one sacrifice for all time.
- Human priests listen to confessions of sin and offer absolution, when it is God to whom we should confess our sins.

- Mary is presented as a co-mediator and co-redeemer with Christ, and Catholics are continually urged to seek her mediation rather than Christ's.

These false teachings and practices began developing in the Christian church shortly after the close of the New Testament era (about A.D. 100), and by the Middle Ages they had become well enshrined in Catholicism. For more than 150 years, Adventists have identified the little horn of Daniel 8 as the medieval papacy and have explained the horn's desecration of the heavenly sanctuary as being fulfilled in the papal distortions of Christ's heavenly mediation, causing that ministry to be irrelevant and ineffective in the minds of Catholics. I agree with this interpretation. But is that all that the little horn's attack on the sanctuary represents?

Satan's attack on the sanctuary

I propose that the little horn also attacks the heavenly sanctuary. I will begin my explanation of this phase of the horn's attack by once again calling your attention to the very close relationship between, on the one hand, Daniel 7 and 8 in the Old Testament and, on the other, Revelation 12 and 13 in the New Testament. The following chart shows that relationship.

Daniel	Revelation
7:25; 8:10 The little horn persecutes the saints.	12:13; 13:7 The dragon persecutes the saints.
7:25; 8:12 The little horn tries to change God's law; it casts down the truth (the law) to the ground.	12:17 The dragon persecutes those who keep the commandments.
7:25 Time, times, and half a time.	12:6, 14; 13:5 1,260 days; time, times, and half a time; forty-two months.
7:25 The little horn speaks great words against God.	13:6 The sea beast blasphemes God.
8:10 The little horn casts down some of the stars to the ground.	12:4 The dragon threw a third of the stars of heaven to the earth.
7:1–7 Four beasts—a lion, a bear, a leopard, and a dragon—arise from the sea.	13:2 The sea beast looks like a leopard, has the mouth of a lion, the feet of a bear, and the the dragon gives him his seat and authority.
8:11 The little horn attacks God's sanctuary.	13:6 The sea beast blasphemes God's tabernacle, His sanctuary.

So, there are at least seven similarities between Daniel's visions in Daniel 7 and 8 and John's visions in Revelation 12 and 13. Thus, Revelation gives us an expanded view of the same conflict between good and evil that Daniel describes in chapters 7 and 8. It's also evident that Satan, in Revelation 12, and the beast from the sea, in Revelation 13, parallel the little horns of Daniel 7 and 8. The little horns in Daniel and the beast power in Revelation 13 are simply Satan's surrogates, whom he works through to accomplish his purposes on the earth. Proebstle notes that "behind the reality symbolized by the horn stands nothing else than the archfiend, the satanic figure."[2]

Satan's attack on the sanctuary in Revelation 13. Let's look more closely at Revelation 13:6, which says that the beast from the sea "opened his mouth in blasphemy against God, to blaspheme His name, *His tabernacle,* and those who dwell in heaven" (emphasis added). There are a couple of reasons to consider the beast's attack on God's "tabernacle" to be an attack on the heavenly sanctuary. First, the Greek word for "tabernacle" in Revelation 13:6 is *skēnē.* And Hebrews 8:1, 2 says, "We have such a High Priest, who is seated at the right hand of the throne of the Majesty in the heavens, a Minister of the sanctuary and of the true tabernacle [*skēnē*] which the Lord erected, and not man." Here, *skēnē* clearly refers to God's heavenly sanctuary, so the New Testament does use the word in that way.

Second, conservative Bible scholars generally agree that John wrote Revelation sometime in the last decade of the first century. This would have been twenty to thirty years after the destruction of Jerusalem and its temple, and it was some sixty to seventy years after Jesus' death on the cross, which brought the services in the earthly sanctuary to a close.* Thus, if at that time John saw the beast from the sea blaspheming God's sanctuary, it would have to have been the sanctuary in heaven. The temple/sanctuary on earth and its services no longer existed.

I propose, then, that the entity that Daniel 8:11 and Revelation 13:6 portray as attacking the heavenly sanctuary is a more than human power. Revelation helps us to understand that the real power behind the little horns in Daniel 7 and 8 is Satan himself. Revelation's beast from the sea also receives its power and authority from Satan, the dragon (Revelation 13:2). Thus, Satan is not just the moving power behind the papacy's attacks on the heavenly sanctuary. He is not just the instigator. I propose that Satan himself attacks the heavenly sanctuary. And his attack has much more potential for damaging the heavenly sanctuary than does that of any human power.

How Satan attacks the sanctuary

How does Satan attack the sanctuary? Keep in mind that the heavenly sanctuary is all about God's plan of salvation. Jesus is interceding for His people *in the heavenly sanctuary.* He forgives their sins *in the heavenly sanctuary.* He covers them with His

---

*The Jews continued to offer their sacrifices until the destruction of Jerusalem in A.D. 70, but those sacrifices no longer had any spiritual or theological significance.

righteousness *from the heavenly sanctuary.* All of this and much more is a part of His mediatorial ministry *in the heavenly sanctuary.* So when Daniel and Revelation suggest that Satan is attacking the heavenly sanctuary, what they really mean is that he is attacking the plan of salvation. And how does he do that? *In his role as the accuser of God's people.* Revelation 12:10 specifically calls him "the accuser of our brethren, who accused them before our God day and night." In chapter 4 of this book, I pointed out two other biblical texts that show Satan accusing God's people. A brief review is in order here.

Satan's accusation against Job. Job 1:7 records the beginning of a conversation between God and Satan that was apparently prompted by Satan's charge that God had no faithful followers on the earth. God says to Satan, "Have you considered My servant Job, that there is none like him on the earth, a blameless and upright man, one who fears God and shuns evil?" (verse 8). And Satan replies, "Does Job fear God for nothing? Have You not made a hedge around him, around his household, and around all that he has on every side?" (verses 9, 10).

In essence, Satan is claiming that Job had ulterior motives for serving God, so he wasn't nearly as faithful to God as God claimed. As the story continues, of course, God allows Satan to test Job to the limit,

and Job maintains his loyalty to God. My point, however, is not Job's loyalty. It's Satan's haughty accusation that Job was unworthy of God's favor.

Satan's accusation against Joshua. We see a similar situation in Zechariah 3, where Joshua the high priest is "standing before the Angel of the LORD, and Satan [is] standing at his right hand to oppose him"—that is, to oppose the Angel of the Lord (verse 1). While the text doesn't explicitly *say* that Satan was accusing Joshua of being unworthy of God's favor, this seems clearly to be the point of the story. And what does the Angel of the Lord do? He removes Joshua's filthy garments and places a clean, rich garment on him. This is a symbol of the righteousness of Christ that covers His people. *And Satan doesn't like that because he was accusing Joshua of being unworthy of God's favor!*

So, Satan appears as an accuser of God's people in two places in the Bible besides the book of Daniel. And in those two places, Satan's basic charge is that God's people are unworthy of God's favor. This is crucial for our understanding of the little horn's attack on the sanctuary in Daniel 8:10–12. Since it is from the heavenly sanctuary that Jesus administers His plan of salvation, any attack on the plan of salvation is also an attack on the heavenly sanctuary.

On the human, earthly level, the little horn's attack on the heavenly sanctuary is fulfilled by the papacy's distortion of the truth about God's plan of salvation. If people misunderstand that plan, then it is of no benefit to them. And that is Satan's whole purpose—to prevent people from understanding God's plan of salvation so they won't benefit from it.

But Satan himself also attacks God's sanctuary and His plan of salvation. He does so through his accusations that God's people are unworthy of divine favor, unworthy of God's forgiveness, unworthy of the eternal life that Jesus died to give them—when Jesus says that through His grace *they are worthy*!

To whom does Satan make his accusation?

We need to consider one further aspect of Satan's accusations: to whom is he making those accusations? Revelation doesn't address that question, but a bit of reflection should point us in the direction of the answer.

Surely Satan doesn't hope to persuade God that His people are unworthy of salvation. Surely he doesn't hope to persuade the Savior. Jesus knows His sheep (see John 10:14). He knows those who are His and those who are not. I propose that the ones whom Satan hopes to influence by his accusations are the angels. They aren't omniscient, and doubts *can* be raised in their minds.

The idea that Satan aims his accusations at the angels adds to the case that the sanctuary under attack in Daniel 8:10–12 isn't just the earthly sanctuary. It isn't just the sanctuary that Antiochus defiled. It is God's sanctuary in heaven, where Christ is ministering as our High Priest. And the power behind the little horn is the accuser of God's people, Satan himself, who insists that Jesus is wrong when He grants His people forgiveness and the guarantee of eternal life. I'm sure he presses his accusations against every single saint, one saint at a time. And as God's holy angels travel back and forth between heaven and earth, they have to listen to those malicious charges. None of us can escape their hateful indictments. Fortunately, we have a Mediator who is extremely qualified to respond to every charge—One who covers each of His saints with His robe of righteousness.

While I intend this study to be primarily a careful analysis of Scripture, I will repeat here a couple of paragraphs written by Ellen White that I quoted in chapter 3.

While Jesus is pleading for the subjects of His grace, Satan accuses them before God as transgressors. The great deceiver has sought to lead them into skepticism, to cause them to lose confidence in God, to separate themselves from His love, and to break His law. Now he points to the record of their lives, to the defects of character, the unlikeness to Christ, which has dishonored their Redeemer, to all the sins that he has tempted them to commit, and because of these he claims them as his subjects.[3]

Notice Jesus' response to these accusations:

Jesus does not excuse their sins, but shows their penitence and faith, and, claiming for them forgiveness, He lifts His wounded hands before the Father and the holy angels, saying: I know them by name. I have graven them on the palms of My hands. "The sacrifices of God are a broken spirit: a broken and a contrite heart, O God, Thou wilt not despise." Psalm 51:17. And to the accuser of His people He declares: "The Lord rebuke thee, O Satan; even the Lord that hath chosen Jerusalem rebuke thee: is not this a brand plucked out of the fire?" Zechariah 3:2. Christ will clothe His faithful ones with His own righteousness, that He may present them to His Father "a glorious church, not having spot, or wrinkle, or any such thing."[4]

Satan, the power behind the little horn, attacks Christ's sanctuary in heaven by accusing God's people before the angels of being unworthy of the salvation Christ provides.

The bold rebellion

In Daniel 8:12, the prophet wrote that "a *host* will be set [by the horn] against the *tamid* in rebellion."[5] In other words, the little horn will set up a host of his own followers against Christ's mediatorial ministry. How are we to understand this?

Keep in mind that Satan is not the only fallen angel on this earth. Revelation 12:3, 4 tells us that when he was cast out of heaven, he drew a third of the angels with him. I can't imagine that he alone is accusing God's people of being unworthy of salvation. Satan's companion angels work tirelessly with him, day and night, to tempt and annoy God's people, to get them to yield to temptation, and then to accuse them of being unworthy of God's grace. Unfortunately, in some cases they are right. Some professed Christians are actually covered with their own righteousness, trusting in their own good deeds to save them instead of relying on the righteousness of Christ. But Satan and his angels don't bring their charges against only these faltering people. They accuse every single saint of being unworthy of God's grace.

Daniel said that the little horn would "cast truth down to the ground." Satan and his angels don't limit their efforts to deceiving humans with their falsehoods.

To be sure, they do aim at them. But all the evil angels are making every possible effort to distort the truth about God's saints before the angels in heaven as well. They make a blasphemous attack against Christ's ministry in the heavenly sanctuary. It is high-handed, deliberate rebellion against God.

Daniel 8:10–12 is about much more than an ancient Seleucid king (Antiochus) attacking the Jews in Jerusalem and Judea and desecrating their sanctuary. That was one minor act in the drama as well. However, this passage in Daniel's book is about the conflict between good and evil that's been unfolding on our planet—and indeed throughout the entire universe—for at least the past six thousand years. And God has allowed it to happen. Daniel was very correct when he said that the little horn "practised, and prospered" (Daniel 8:12, KJV). God has given Satan time to work out his plan for running our world as a demonstration of what he would do throughout the universe if he were given a chance.

The chronology of Daniel 8:10–12

We need to deal with one more issue before concluding this chapter. The question is very simple: when was Daniel's prediction about the little horn and its attack on God's people, on their Prince, and on His sanctuary to be fulfilled?

Adventists have always maintained that these verses predict the medieval papacy, its persecution of God's people, and its distortion of the truth of the gospel. As you know, I agree with that interpretation, for the little horn in Daniel 7 arises after the barbarian tribes defeated the western Roman Empire, and, therefore, so does the horn in chapter 8. I've shown you that the medieval papacy fits the chronology of Daniel 2, 7, and 8 the way a hand fits a glove. Through its various false teachings, the papacy also fits the description of the little horn's attack on the sanctuary.

However, I have also shown that the power behind the little horn is Satan himself. So are we to suppose that Satan's attack on Christ's mediatorial ministry—his accusation that God's people are unworthy of Christ's grace—is limited to the medieval period? Of course not! He has been attacking God's saints ever since Adam and Eve sinned in Eden, and he will continue doing so until Christ returns. How, then, do we fit Satan's accusations against God's people into the chronology of the four metals and the feet of iron and clay in Daniel 2? How do we fit them into the chronology of the four beasts and the dragon's ten horns in Daniel 7?

I propose that we don't.

Allow me to take you back to Daniel 7 for a moment. Immediately following the judgment scene in verses 9 and 10, Daniel said, "I watched then because of the sound of the pompous words which the horn was speaking; I watched till the beast was slain, and its body destroyed and given to the burning flame" (verse 11). The point is that the judgment condemned the horn and the dragon and turned them over for destruction. So, does this mean that the judgment in verses 9 and 10 deals only with the medieval papacy? In chapter 2 of this book I pointed out that the judgment scene in the vision of chapter 7 pictures the same judgment as the one prophesied by Solomon (Ecclesiastes 12:14), Jesus (Matthew 12:36, 37), and Paul (Romans 14:10–12; 2 Corinthians 5:10). It's the same judgment that John prophesied in Revelation (chapter 14:6, 7; 15:3, 4; 16:5; 19:2).

Thus, I propose that the little horns in Daniel 7 and 8 *do* represent the medieval papacy. However, as I've said before, Satan is the power behind these little horns. While the final judgment will condemn the medieval papacy, its broader purpose is to settle the entire conflict between good and evil that has been raging in the universe ever since Satan rebelled against Christ in heaven. The little horn's attack on the saints, their Prince, and His sanctuary as portrayed in Daniel 8 is simply an important segment of the great controversy that began in heaven before our world was created and will conclude at the end of the millennium.

In conclusion, the primary purpose of this chapter and the previous one has been to determine whether the sanctuary mentioned in Daniel 8:10–12 is the earthly sanctuary or the heavenly sanctuary. I have concluded, on the basis of a careful analysis of the verses themselves, that it is the sanctuary in heaven. Therefore, from the biblical evidence I have shared with you, it seems reasonable to understand the sanctuary that is cleansed or restored in verse 14 also to be the heavenly sanctuary.

---

1. Proebstle, "Truth and Terror," 243.
2. Ibid., 521, 522.
3. White, *The Great Controversy*, 484.
4. Ibid.
5. Proebstle, "Truth and Terror," 290.

C h a p t e r   1 5

How Long, O Lord?

An obvious question comes to mind after one reads the three verses that describe the little horn's attack on God's people, His Prince, and His sanctuary. It's the anguished cry, "God, where are You?" that comes from the lips of millions of sufferers around the world. When life takes a difficult turn, we pray, "God, how long must I endure this pain? When are You going to bring this horrible state of affairs to an end?" This is the cry of the souls under the altar in Revelation 6:10, "How long, O Lord, holy and true, until You judge and avenge our blood on those who dwell on the earth?"

We find this same question following the little horn's devastating attack on God's people, His Prince, and His sanctuary: "Then I heard a holy one speaking; and another holy one said to that certain one who was speaking, 'How long will the vision be, concerning the daily sacrifices and the transgression of desolation, the giving of both the sanctuary and the host to be trampled underfoot?' " (Daniel 8:13).

The holy ones

Apparently, the question, "How long?" was asked by an angel. Daniel said, "Then I heard *a holy one* speaking; and another *holy one* said to that certain one who was speaking" (emphasis added). Daniel doesn't tell us who these holy ones are. He gives us no names. However, he does leave us a couple of clues. First, in Daniel 7:9, 10, he gave us a snapshot of millions of angels surrounding God's throne, and it seems most likely that it was one of these angels who asked the question in Daniel 8:13. We find another clue in Daniel 8:15, 16, where someone commands the angel Gabriel to explain the vision to

Daniel. It seems reasonable to conclude that Gabriel was one of the angels in verse 13—probably the one who answered the question, "How long?" In other words, it's likely that it was Gabriel who gave the answer that we read in verse 14. However, before we get into the answer, we need to examine the question in a bit more detail, for if we misunderstand the question, we may get the wrong answer, or at least we may misunderstand the answer we get.

Given our understanding of the little horn's horrible attack in verses 10–12, we would naturally expect the angel to ask, "When will the little horn's attack end?" But that's not what he said. Instead, he asked, "How long will the vision be?" These two questions are quite different. In order to ensure that you understand the difference between them, I have repeated them below:

"When will the little horn's attack end?"
(The question we might expect.)

"How long will the vision be?"
(The question the angel actually asked.)

Analyzing the question

Two differences between these questions are particularly relevant to our discussion: (1) When, versus How long? and (2) the little horn's attack versus the vision.

When? versus How long? A simple illustration will clarify the first difference between these two questions. Suppose that I'm scheduled to leave on March 7 for a week-long business trip. If my wife asked, "When will you return?" my answer would be, "On March 14." But if she asked, "How long will you be gone?" my answer would be, "One week." The answer appropriate to the second question would require my wife to do a bit of mathematical calculation in order to know when I will return. A glance at the calendar would tell her that if I leave on March 7, my weeklong trip would end on March 14.

Returning to the angel's question, notice that it was "How long?" not "When?" Because the question was asked this way, we have to know both the starting point of the period and the length of the period to calculate the ending point. Verse 14 gives us the length of the period: 2,300 days, which I will discuss in the next chapter of this book. Several chapters after that we will determine the beginning point of the period involved, which will then enable us to calculate its ending point.

The little horn's attack versus the vision. The question the angel might have asked, "When will the little horn's attack end?" inquires only about the end point of the little horn's destructive activities. The question the angel actually asked, "How long will the vision be?" inquires about the length of time covered by the entire vision, which began with the Medo-Persian ram.

The last part of the angel's question mentions four things that are included in the vision: "How long will the vision be, concerning [1] the daily sacrifices and [2] the transgression of desolation, the giving of both [3] the sanctuary and [4] the host to be trampled underfoot?" You will notice that each of these has to do with the little horn and its vicious attack. From this, some interpreters have concluded that the angel's question about time is restricted to the period of the little horn. However, I will point out again that the angel's question was, "How long will the *vision* be."

The Hebrew word translated "vision" is *hazon*. It occurs three times in the first two verses of chapter 8. Daniel says, "[1] In the third year of the reign of King Belshazzar a vision [*hazon*] appeared to me. . . . [2] And I saw in the vision [*hazon*], . . . and I saw in the vision [*hazon*] . . ." In these verses that introduce the vision of chapter 8, the word *hazon* clearly refers to the entire vision. In verse 17, a voice commands the angel Gabriel to "make this man understand the vision [*hazon*]." Gabriel then began his explanation with the Medo-Persian ram, the first animal in the vision (verse 20). Thus, again, the word *hazon* clearly refers to the entire vision. Therefore, we should also understand the question in verse 13, "How long will the vision [*hazon*] be?" to refer to

the entire vision and not just to the period of the horn's attack. The significance of this detail will become evident in a later chapter.

The short list

In asking his "How long?" question in verse 13, the angel brought up at least two of the things that the previous three verses had pictured the little horn attacking, and a possible third item. The angel definitely had in mind the *tamid* (what most Bible versions call the "daily sacrifice") and the host and possibly the sanctuary. I say "possibly" because the Hebrew word translated "sanctuary" is *qodesh,* the basic meaning of which is "holy." The Hebrew word for "sanctuary" is *miqdash,* which is related to but not the same as *qodesh. Miqdash* is used only in verse 11, which says, "The place of His sanctuary [*miqdash*] was cast down." In verse 13, the angel literally asked, "How long will the vision be, concerning the . . . giving of . . . the [holy] [*qodesh*] . . . to be trampled underfoot?" He didn't ask about the sanctuary (*miqdash*) being trampled underfoot. This is a significant point that I will discuss in further detail in the next chapter.

Verses 10–12 picture the little horn attacking a number of items and people. As I noted above, verse 13 picks up several of these objects of the little horn's attack. But it leaves out the stars (verse 10), the Prince of the host (verse 11), and the truth (verse 12). However, the angel did mention "the transgression."

The Hebrew word for "transgression" in this verse is *pesha'*, which first appeared in verse 12: "Because of transgression [*pesha'*] . . ." I pointed out in the previous chapter that the word *pesha'* means "rebellion," in the sense of a shameless, deliberate choice to disobey God. And the horn's attack on God's people, His Prince, and His sanctuary certainly qualifies as a shameless, deliberate attack on God! It's an abominable rebellion! In the question in verse 13, the angel called the horn's attack a "transgression of *desolation*" (emphasis added). The Hebrew word *shamem* means "to be desolate," or "to be appalled." The latter word may be more what Daniel had in mind—an *appalling* rebellion. This un-derscores the awfulness—the sense of horror—that we should have at the little horn's rebellion.

An important issue is whether the list of items from verses 10–12 in the angel's question is deliberately short. That is, was the angel asking only about these specific items? The reasonable answer seems to be No. The four items he brought up from the previous three verses are sort of a summary. He really seems to be asking, When will *all* of the terrible problems associated with the little horn's attack be corrected?

So one angel has asked another, "How long will the vision's ram, goat, and rebellious little horn carry on? When will the events seen in this horrible vision wind up?" The answer comes in verse 14, which we will consider in the next chapter.

Chapter 16

The Cleansing of the Sanctuary

We finally come to Daniel 8:14, the key text of this whole book, and the verse that prompted William Miller to predict that Jesus would return in 1844. You are very familiar with this verse, I'm sure, but for the record, here's what it says, "And he said to me, 'For two thousand three hundred days; then the sanctuary shall be cleansed.'"

As I noted in chapter 5, throughout most of Miller's public preaching career, he didn't set a specific date for Christ's second coming. He accepted the October 22, 1844, date only about two weeks prior to the Great Disappointment. In any case, the October 22 date is based on an extrapolation from the Jewish Day of Atonement, not on Daniel 8:14.

For the purpose of this discussion, we can divide Daniel 8:14 into three parts:

- 14a: And he said to me,
- 14b: "For two thousand three hundred days;
- 14c: then the sanctuary shall be cleansed."

The first part, "And he said to me," hardly needs comment. Briefly, in verse 13, two holy ones engaged in a short conversation about how long the events revealed in the vision of verses 3–14 would last, and one of them gave the answer that comprises verse 14. Interestingly, the angel who answered the question addressed Daniel directly. Daniel reported, "He said to *me*" (emphasis added), not, "He said to *the other 'holy one.'*" However, I'm not aware that this detail has any effect on our interpretation of the rest of verse

14. Our exclusive concern in the remainder of this chapter will be on the cleansing of the sanctuary and the 2,300 days.

THE CLEANSING OF THE SANCTUARY

Two words in verse 14c are especially critical to a correct understanding of the text: "For two thousand three hundred days; then the *sanctuary* shall be *cleansed.*"

Sanctuary

I pointed out in the previous chapter that the Hebrew word for "sanctuary" is *miqdash,* which is the word Daniel used when he said, "The place of His sanctuary [*miqdash*] was cast down" (Daniel 8:11). However, the Hebrew word translated "sanctuary" in both verses 13 and 14 is *qodesh,* the basic meaning of which is "holy." So, what is the difference between *qodesh* and *miqdash*?

The Hebrew word *qodesh* is used to designate holy persons, places, and things. It occurs three times in the preceding verse, Daniel 8:13. The first two times are when a "*holy* one" spoke to another "*holy* one" (emphasis added). The third time it is translated "sanctuary," as it is in verse 14. The question is whether the clause in verse 14 should perhaps be translated "then the *holy* shall be cleansed."

I don't mean to imply that the word *sanctuary* in our English Bibles is a mistranslation. The sanctuary is an important theme in verses 10–12. In the Old Testament, the word *qodesh* occurs primarily in the books of Exodus, Leviticus, Numbers, and Ezekiel. This suggests that the word is used especially in connection with the sanctuary, since that is a major theme of those books. And the majority of commentators agree that *qodesh* in Daniel 8:14 means "sanctuary," and almost all versions translate it that way.

However, perhaps it's significant that the angel used the word *holy* (*qodesh*) rather than *sanctuary* (*miqdash*) in both verses 13 and 14. Keep in mind that verse 14 is the answer to the angel's question about how long the vision—in other words, the little horn's attack in verses 10–12—would be allowed to continue, and remember, too, that the sanctuary is not the only thing the little horn attacked. It also attacked God's people (the host and the stars), His Prince, the services (*tamid*) in God's sanctuary, and His truth, all of which are holy. Had Daniel used the actual Hebrew word for "sanctuary" (*miqdash*), it might appear that the solution in verse 14 was intended for just the sanctuary that was cast down in verse 11. Instead, the word *holy* (*qodesh*) suggests that there must be a solution for all of the holy things that were attacked in verses 10–12—people, Prince, sanctuary, services, and truth. Proebstle concludes,

The results of the semantic study of *qodesh*—it refers to the sanctuary but also has associations to the holy ones—corroborate the conclusion that . . . Dan 8:14c encompasses the solution to all the different elements stated in the question in vs. 13c. Thus, the particular use of . . . *qodesh* in 8:14c strongly suggests that the restoration of the holy to its right includes both the vindication of the sanctuary as well as of the host.[1]

Cleansed

The Hebrew word translated "cleansed" in Daniel 8:14 (in both the KJV and the NKJV) is *nitsdaq*. It's the passive form of the active verb *tsadaq*. A great deal has been written about both *tsadaq* and *nitsdaq,* so all we can do here is summarize the points that are especially relevant to our study.

Tsadaq *and "cleansed."* The early Adventists, who used the King James Version, associated the word *cleansed* in Daniel 8:14 with the cleansing of the sanctuary on the Day of Atonement in Leviticus 16. Many critics—Adventist as well as non-Adventist—have challenged this association because the Hebrew word for "cleansed" in Leviticus 16 is *taher,* not *tsadaq*—the basic meaning of which is "to be just," "to be righteous," and "to be in the right." Therefore, the critics say, a direct correlation between Daniel 8:14 and Leviticus 16 isn't justified.

However, we must keep a couple of other considerations in mind. First, the ancient versions of the Old Testament in languages other than Hebrew are nearly unanimous in translating *nitsdaq* as "cleansed."[2] This is especially significant with respect to the Septuagint because it was a translation of the Old Testament into Greek by Jews, who understood their own Hebrew language very well.*

Second is the conclusion of Dr. Richard Davidson, the chair of the Old Testament Department at the Seventh-day Adventist Theological Seminary, in an article he wrote that appeared several years ago in the *Journal of the Adventist Theological Society.* Davidson compared the Hebrew word *tsadaq* with other Hebrew words that stand parallel to it in Old Testament poetry.† He concluded that the words used in parallel with *tsadaq* suggest three meanings for the word.

- The basic meaning is "to be right."
- In some contexts, it means "to be clean/pure" or "to cleanse/purify."

---

*Proebstle doesn't give the ancient versions much credit. In a personal comment to the author, he said, "It is quite possible that the translators, especially of the Septuagint, thought Daniel 8:14 found its fulfillment in the cleansing of the temple in Maccabean times."

†Often, biblical poetry expresses the same thought twice in slightly different form. This is called "parallelism." (See for example Psalms 5:1; 6:1; 15:1.)

- In the context of judgment, it means "to be vindicated."[3]

With respect to the second item above, Davidson points out that in Job 4:17 and 17:9, *tsadaq* is used in parallel form with *taher,* the word translated "cleansed" in Leviticus 16. *Tsadaq* is also used in parallel with the Hebrew word *zakah,* which means "to be pure" (see Job 15:14; 25:4; Psalm 18:20). Thus, while "cleansed" may not be the most basic meaning of *tsadaq,* it can have that meaning.

Judicial use of tsadaq. Also significant for our discussion is the fact that the Old Testament often uses *tsadaq* in a judicial context. Richard Davidson states that "according to one count, of the 117 occurrences of *tsedeq* [a variant form of *tsadaq*] in the OT, 67 (or 57%) are found in a legal context." He concludes that "in these legal settings it is clear that *tsedeq* takes on an extended meaning with the connotation of 'vindication.' "[4] Following are three examples.

- Moses instructed the people, "If there is a dispute between men, . . . they [should] come to court, that the judges may judge them, and they justify [*tsadaq*] the righteous and condemn the wicked" (Deuteronomy 25:1).
- In his effort to undermine his father's rule and establish himself as king in Israel, Absalom said to the people,

"Oh, that I were made judge in the land, and everyone who has any suit or cause would come to me; then I would give him justice [*tsadaq*]" (2 Samuel 15:4).
- Solomon said, "He who justifies [*tsadaq*] the wicked, and he who condemns the just, both of them alike are an abomination to the LORD" (Proverbs 17:15).

These texts make it clear that in the Old Testament, *tsadaq* is often used in the sense of judgment in a court of law, when judges are called to vindicate the innocent and condemn the wicked.

Proebstle points out that in certain Hebrew verb forms, *tsadaq* "designates an activity by which someone is declared in the right, justified, or vindicated," and this is often true of "a person who by means of the context is already characterized as righteous."[5] Certainly, the context in Daniel 8:10–12 characterizes God's people, His Prince, and His sanctuary as already righteous. In a court of law, when a defendant is found to be innocent, the jury in essence declares that he was in the right all along. He is vindicated. Thus, an appropriate translation of Daniel 8:14 would be "then shall the holy be *vindicated*," and this would apply to all of the holy things that the little horn attacked in verses 10 to 12, not just the sanctuary.

The judicial use of *tsadaq* provides a significant contextual relationship between Daniel 8:14 and the judgment theme in chapter 7. In both chapters, a little horn attacks God, His saints, and His truth, and in both chapters, the issue is resolved with vindication. Chapter 7:22 says, "Judgment was made in favor of the saints of the Most High"—which means that they are vindicated. And chapter 8:14 says that the *holy*—that is, all of the holy things that were under attack in verses 10–12—are *nitsdaq*, that is, vindicated. This is important evidence for understanding the cleansing or vindication of the holy things in verse 14 to refer to a work of judgment.

Passive voice. The passive voice of *tsadaq* is *nitsdaq*. That's the form of the verb used in Daniel 8:14. Here's a brief explanation about the difference between active and passive voice, which will help to clarify the significance of the use of the passive in verse 14. The active voice requires that the subject of the sentence name the doer of the action and that a direct object name the recipient of the action. Thus the sentence "John hit the ball" is active because it contains the subject, *John;* the verb, *hit;* and, in this case, the direct object of the action of the verb, *the ball.* In English, a passive sentence reverses the subject and the direct-object relationship. It puts the direct object in the place the subject holds in an active sentence, and it may or may not tell who did the action. Thus, "The ball was hit"—a passive sentence—is a complete sentence even though it doesn't tell us who hit the ball. In order to know who hit the ball, we would have to say, "The ball was hit *by John.*"

In Hebrew, the form of the verb indicates whether a sentence is active or passive. The verb *nitsdaq* in Daniel 8:14 is the passive form of the verb *tsadaq,* which is the active form. It tells us *what* will be cleansed (the sanctuary), but it doesn't tell us *who* will do the cleansing. In order for us to know that, the sentence would have had to have said something like "the sanctuary was cleansed *by* _____ (whoever did the cleansing)."

Of course, the obvious One to have cleansed the sanctuary is God. But perhaps the word *tsadaq* is in the passive in Daniel 8:14 because God isn't the only One who will be involved in that cleansing, that vindication. We'll explore this issue further in the next chapter.

THE 2,300 DAYS

We noted in the previous chapter that in Daniel 8:13, one "holy one" asked another, "*How long* will the vision be, concerning the daily sacrifices . . ." (emphasis added). And verse 14 gives the answer: "For two thousand three hundred days." (The Hebrew terms translated "days" in the King James and New King James versions literally mean "evenings-mornings." Thus many recent versions read something like the New International Version's "2,300 evenings and mornings.")

This is a clear indication that the 2,300 days constitute a time prophecy. And, indeed, nearly all interpreters of Daniel understand the 2,300 days to be a period in history. The issue regarding Daniel 8:14 is not whether it's a time prophecy, and Seventh-day Adventists are not wrong to understand it to be a time prophecy. The real issue is *how much time* the verse indicates. Are we to understand 2,300 days as being literal or as being symbolic?

Those who adopt the literal interpretation apply it to actual days during the reign of terror imposed on the Jews by Antiochus. Two hundred years ago, many prophetic interpreters understood the 2,300 days as representing years, and a large number of them ended the period in 1843, 1844, or 1847.[6] However, so far as I know, today, Seventh-day Adventists are the only ones who adopt the view that the 2,300 days symbolically represent 2,300 literal years that began in the Medo-Persian period and extend to the mid-1800s. I will summarize for you the basic issues involved in each interpretation.

The literal interpretation

I pointed out in chapter 9 that Antio-

chus Epiphanes' desecration of the sanctuary in Jerusalem lasted three years to the day. But three years amounts to only 1,095 days. On the other hand, 2,300 days equals six years and four months. Most people who adopt the Antiochus interpretation want to make the number 2,300 more nearly approximate the facts of history. So they assume that the words *evenings* and *mornings* refer to the evening and morning sacrifices in the Jewish sacrificial system, and then, by interpreting half the 2,300 units to represent evening sacrifices and half of them the morning sacrifices, they arrive at the total of 1,150 days—half of the 2,300 days. This is closer to the length of time that the temple in Jerusalem remained desecrated, but it's still fifty-five days more than Antiochus's 1,095 days. For most scholars, this is close enough— it's the best they can do to make the facts fit their interpretation.

This literal interpretation, shaky as it is, is obviously demanded if the little horn in Daniel 8 represents Antiochus. So the basic question is whether that's the case. I presented evidence in chapters 9 and 12 that it isn't; thus, I won't comment further on that issue here.

The symbolic interpretation

The Adventist interpretation of the 2,300 days as 2,300 years is based on the year-day principle, in which a day in symbolic prophecy stands for a year of literal time. However, since I will discuss that principle in detail in chapter 27, I will limit my discussion here to two other issues: (1) how the context of Daniel 8:14 impacts the interpretation of the 2,300 days, and (2) the meaning of the words *evening* and *morning* in the Hebrew language.

The context. Daniel's vision ended with verse 14. As soon as the vision ended, the angel Gabriel appeared to Daniel (see verse 16), and Gabriel said, "Understand, son of man, that *the vision refers to the time of the end*" (verse 17; emphasis added). Two verses later, Gabriel said, "I am making known to you what shall happen in the latter time of the indignation; for *at the appointed time the end shall be*" (verse 19; emphasis added). So, the 2,300-day period is supposed to extend to the time of the end.

I pointed out in the previous chapter that the angel asked, "How long will the *vision* be?" not, "When will the *little horn's attack* end?" (emphasis added). The issue is the length of time the entire *vision* covers. Daniel's vision began with the Medo-Persian ram. This means that the 2,300 days must begin during the Medo-Persian period, and from there it must extend to the time of the end—which Adventists, along with many other Christians, believe is our own time. Six years and four months would obviously be a very short bit of time

during the reign of the Medo-Persian Empire. This leaves us with no choice but to interpret the 2,300 evenings and mornings symbolically.

Do the "evenings and mornings" refer to the daily sacrifices? I mentioned a few paragraphs back that most interpreters understand the "evenings and mornings" in verse 14 to refer to the Levitical evening and morning sacrifices. But is this correct? I will begin by giving you the words in the original language that are translated "evening" and "morning."

The Hebrew word for "evening" is *erev,* and the word for "morning" is *boqer.* Both words are singular in the Hebrew, and there is no conjunction between them. Also, the words translated "two thousand three hundred" come after *erev boqer.* Thus, a literal English reading would be "evening-morning two thousand three hundred," not "two thousand three hundred evenings and mornings."

The word order *evening-morning* is significant. Adventists argue against the idea that in Daniel 8, these words are sanctuary language. One of the evidences favoring our position is that the when the daily sacrifices are spoken of in the Old Testament, the word order is always *morning-evening,* never *evening-morning.** Daniel's word order, *evening-morning,* is most evident in the Creation story, which says, "The evening

---

*See Numbers 28:4; 2 Kings 16:15; 1 Chronicles 16:40; 2 Chronicles 2:4; 13:11; 31:3; Ezra 3:3.

and the morning were the first day," and uses the same terms for the second day through the sixth day (Genesis 1:5). (See also verses 8, 13, 19, 23, 31.) Understood this way, the obvious interpretation of "evening-morning two thousand three hundred" is full days, not half days.

The Creation theme is significant for another reason. The little horn's attack on the host, the Prince of the host, the *tamid*, the sanctuary, and the truth, was very destructive. Thus, the restoration would be a work of *creation*, or, perhaps more correctly, *re-creation*. Proebstle says, "After the question [in verse 13] until which point in time the destructive situation will continue, the first thought triggered by the answer is regarding creation. Thus, the idea is that creation counters destruction."[7] "The notion of creation fits as counterpart to the destruction carried out by the horn and its host. Thus, the singular 'evening-morning' raises the expectation of a creative act. However, this creative act will come only after a period of '2300 evening-morning.' "[8]

Adventists have historically identified the cleansing of the sanctuary in Daniel 8:14 as a reference to the antitype of the Day of Atonement in Leviticus 16. Since I will devote chapters 20 and 21 to a discussion of the Day of Atonement, I will make only one comment about it here. In the vision of Daniel 8, Media-Persia was represented by a ram and Greece by a goat. Sig-

nificantly, in the Israelite sanctuary services, rams and goats were common sacrifices, and both were sacrificed on the Day of Atonement (see Leviticus 16:15, 3, 24). Here, then, is another reason to understand verse 14 in Day of Atonement terms. Proebstle makes the following significant comment: "If the cultic [sanctuary] terminology in the vision of Dan 8 leads to the belief that the phrase 'evening-morning' should denote a day from evening to evening and have cultic significance, one would have to opt for a reference to the Day of Atonement which explicitly runs from evening to evening."[9]

Proebstle's point is easily verified. A major Adventist "proof text" that Sabbath should begin and end at sunset is Leviticus 23:32, which says, "From evening to evening, you shall celebrate your sabbath." What most people don't realize is that this text is in the context of the Day of Atonement. As part of a passage that gives instruction on the observance of the Day of Atonement, the entire verse reads, "It [the Day of Atonement] shall be to you a sabbath of solemn rest, and you shall afflict your souls; on the ninth day of the month at evening, from evening to evening, you shall celebrate your sabbath." The point is that the Day of Atonement—as every other day by Hebrew reckoning—began in the evening (at sunset), continued through the morning, and ended in the evening (sunset). While morning is not mentioned in the instruction for observing the Day of Atonement, the succession of time periods is clearly the "evening-morning-(evening)" that we find in Daniel 8:14.

In conclusion, interpreters of Daniel 8:14 have given a variety of explanations for the "cleansing" of the "sanctuary" following "evenings-mornings two thousand three hundred." The Adventist explanation differs from these others in several significant ways. We understand the sanctuary to be in heaven and its cleansing to mean a judicial vindication of all the holy things that the little horn attacked in verses 10–12. And we understand the 2,300 evenings-mornings to be *days,* which are to be interpreted according to the year-day principle as *years.* We also understand verse 14 to refer to a work of judgment that is an anti-type of the Day of Atonement in the earthly sanctuary. And, it seems to me, there is a reasonable basis in Scripture for each of these conclusions.

All of this is getting us started on an understanding of Daniel 8:14, but there's more to consider.

---

1. Proebstle, "Truth and Terror," 425.

2. See Holbrook, ed., *Symposium on Daniel,* 2:451. (This is in the chapter by Gerhard F. Hasel titled "The 'Little Horn,' the Heavenly Sanctuary and the Time of the End: A Study of Daniel 8:9–14.")

3. Davidson, "The Meaning of *Nitsdaq* in Daniel 8:14," 107–119.

4. Ibid.

5. Proebstle, "Truth and Terror," 400, 402.

6. See Edwin Froom, *The Prophetic Faith of Our Fathers,* 4:404.

7. Proebstle, "Truth and Terror," 374, 375

8. Ibid., 394.

9. Ibid., 390.

Chapter 17

The Cleansing of the Sanctuary and the Sins of the Saints

For more than 150 years, ever since 1857, Seventh-day Adventists have said that the cleansing (restoration, vindication) of the sanctuary in Daniel 8:14 points to an investigative judgment that began in heaven in 1844. The purpose of this investigative judgment is to review the lives of the saints for the purpose of blotting out their sins from heaven's record books, or, in the case of those who are not found worthy, to retain the record of their sins. We've said that the cleansing of the sanctuary that Daniel speaks of is the heavenly antitype of the Levitical Day of Atonement, which points forward to this blotting out of the sins of the saints. I'll deal with the Levitical sanctuary service, including the Day of Atonement, in the next four chapters. This chapter focuses on the cleansing of the sanctuary and the sins of the saints in Daniel 8:14.

For at least one hundred years, the critics of the traditional Adventist understanding have pointed to a major contextual problem with our interpretation of Daniel 8:14. In verses 10–12, the wicked little horn attacks God's people, His truth, His Prince, and the sanctuary that belongs to His Prince. Verse 12 concludes by saying that the little horn *succeeded* in its attack. And in verse 13, an angel asks how long the horrible devastation of God's people and His sanctuary conveyed in this vision will continue.

The answer comes in verse 14: "For two thousand three hundred days; then the sanctuary shall be cleansed." But if context has anything to do with the interpretation of this text, this cleansing of the sanctuary doesn't appear to be at all about removing the sins of the *saints* from the sanctuary. It's about reversing the nefarious deeds of the *little horn*. If the sanctuary needs to be cleansed of any sins, it's the sins of the wicked little horn that should be removed, not the sins of the saints. Desmond Ford stated the issue succinctly in his Glacier View manuscript:

> After describing the successes of the wicked little horn against the sanctuary and its worshippers, the inquiry was made by an angel as to how long such ravages would be permitted to continue. When would heaven intervene to punish the wicked aggressor? Verse 14 was the answer to that inquiry, but the traditional exposition by Seventh-day Adventists never relates the two. Instead, we switch from the theme of the verses about the evil deeds of anti-God powers and concentrate instead on the sins of the saints defiling the sanctuary. *Let it not be missed—the context says nothing about believers doing despite to the sanctuary, but unbelievers.*[1]

I remember learning about this problem back in the early 1960s. At the time, I was aware of the traditional Adventist interpretation that the little horn represented the papacy and that its attack on the sanctuary represented certain false papal teachings. Therefore, I concluded that the cleansing of the sanctuary must represent the restoration of the truths that the papacy had distorted. God began this restora-

tion with the Reformation in the 1500s, and He brought it to its final fulfillment with the establishment of the Seventh-day Adventist Church in 1844.* For the next forty-five or so years, that's the best I could do with Daniel 8:14.

I still believe that my explanation back then is one appropriate way to understand this verse. However, I've also been aware all along that this explanation didn't solve the basic contextual problem. If Daniel 8:10–13 deals exclusively with the sins of the wicked little horn, how can Adventists say that verse 14 points to an investigative judgment in which *the sins of the saints* will be reviewed and blotted out? This is obviously a critical problem. I've resolved it to my satisfaction. The interpretation of Daniel 7 and 8 that I shared with you in chapters 10–16 of this book provides the background for my explanation, which I will now share with you. Two issues are especially critical: (1) which sanctuary does Daniel 8:14 refer to, and (2) what does its cleansing mean?

Which sanctuary?

The first question we have to settle is whether the sanctuary mentioned in Daniel 8:14 is in heaven or on this earth. The majority of contemporary interpreters apply the sanctuary in Daniel 8 to the temple

---

*The Seventh-day Adventist Church was formally organized in 1863, but its roots go back to the Millerite movement and the Great Disappointment on October 22, 1844.

in Jerusalem that Antiochus Epiphanes attacked in 168 B.C., which of course was an earthly sanctuary. William Miller thought the sanctuary represented the entire earth, our globe, and none of those who were looking for Jesus' coming on October 22, 1844, questioned that interpretation until Jesus failed to appear. The very next day—the morning of October 23—Hiram Edson gained the insight that the sanctuary to be cleansed is the one in heaven. Adventists have maintained that view ever since. I agree with it for three reasons.

1. The 2,300 days/years. The first reason is based on the interpretation of the 2,300 days as a period of years that began in 457 B.C. and ended in 1844. (I will discuss the historical basis for the year 457 B.C. in chapters 23 and 25.) These 2,300 years obviously extend far beyond the time of Christ's ascension to heaven, when He began His ministry in the heavenly sanctuary. The services in the earthly sanctuary ended with Christ's death, and the temple in Jerusalem was destroyed in A.D. 70 and has never been rebuilt. Thus, the

Daniel 7	Daniel 8	Interpretation
Lion	Not represented	Babylon
Bear	Ram	Media-Persia
Leopard	Goat	Greece
Dragon	Little horn (verse 9)	Rome
Ten horns	Not represented	Divided Europe
Little horn	Little horn (verses 10–12)	Papacy
Judgment in heaven	**Cleansing of the sanctuary**	
Kingdom given to the Son of man	Time of the end	Christ's second coming is imminent

only sanctuary that Daniel 8:10–14 could possibly have referred to as functioning in the years following A.D. 70 is Christ's sanctuary in heaven. I find this to be a very reasonable argument and a strong support for the conclusion that the sanctuary in verse 14 is in heaven.

2. Comparison of Daniel 7 and 8. My second reason for concluding that the sanctuary in Daniel 8:14 is the one in heaven is based on a comparison of Daniel 7 and 8. As I've already said several times, the majority of the interpreters of Daniel understand the horns in both chapters to represent the same evil power. The two most common interpretations are that these horns represent Antiochus Epiphanes and that they represent the papacy. I laid out the difficulties with the Antiochus explanation of the little horns in chapter 9; we won't review those details here. Instead, in this chapter, we need to examine the traditional Adventist interpretation of the two horns. The chart on page 159 summarizes that interpretation. Please pay special attention to the last two rows, especially the one that is in bold-faced type.

Notice that in chapter 7, *the judgment in heaven* resolves the crisis brought on by the little horn, and in chapter 8, *the cleansing of the sanctuary* resolves the crisis brought on by the little horn. Also note that the judgment scene in chapter 7 comes at the very same point on the chart as the cleansing of the sanctuary in chapter 8, which suggests that they're different aspects or views of the same process. And in Daniel 7, the judgment clearly takes place in heaven because it includes millions of angels surrounding God's throne. All this lends strong support to the conclusion that the sanctuary that is cleansed in chapter 8 is Christ's sanctuary in heaven and that its cleansing includes a judgment process.

Desmond Ford agrees with this comparison of Daniel 7 and 8. In his Glacier View manuscript, he said, "Adventists have not always capitalized as they should have done on the fact that in the corresponding sequences of the visions in chapters 7 and 8 of Daniel, while the former chapter culminates its portrayal by the scene of the judgment and the coming of the Son of Man, the following chapter at its climax promises that 'the sanctuary shall be cleansed.' Thus we have the following parallel which shows that the sanctuary's cleansing is identical with the judgment."[2] Ford then goes on to give essentially the same chart that I've shared with you on the previous page.

3. The sanctuary in Daniel 8:10–12. My third reason for concluding that the sanctuary mentioned in Daniel 8:14 is Christ's heavenly sanctuary, is found in the previous several verses. I discussed this in some detail in chapters 13 and 14, but a brief review is in order here.

You will recall that in Daniel 8:10–12, the little horn attacks the Prince of the host. This Prince of the host is clearly a Divine Being, and several of the modern versions of the Bible recognize this because they capitalize the word *Prince* (*Commander* in the New American Standard Bible). The Prince of the host obviously has a sanctuary because the little horn is said to throw it down and to remove from Him the *tamid*—that is, the regular services in His sanctuary. Thus, the Prince is also a priest. It seems most likely that this Prince is Christ because the New Testament informs us that Christ is a Priest, and He officiates in the heavenly sanctuary (see Hebrews 8:1, 2). This is my third reason for concluding that the sanctuary that is cleansed in Daniel 8:14 is Christ's sanctuary in heaven.

The question is, How does the little horn "cast down" the sanctuary in heaven? The answer, of course, is that it doesn't in any literal sense. Rather, the historic Adventist interpretation is that the papacy "cast down" Christ's ministry in the heavenly sanctuary by attacking the principles God established on which that sanctuary operates and thus distorting the plan of salvation that Christ is administering there. In chapter 14, I pointed out that the pa-

pacy does this by leading people to seek salvation through a human priesthood and by substituting the so-called mediation of Mary and other saints in place of Christ's mediatorial ministry. With these and other false teachings, the papacy has as effectively nullified Christ's mediation in the heavenly sanctuary as if it had reached up to heaven and forced Christ to step down as our High Priest.*

This is one way to understand the cleansing of the sanctuary in verse 14. However, we still have not resolved the contextual problem—namely, that the cleansing of the sanctuary in verse 14 has to do with the sins of the saints when the previous verses seem to deal exclusively with the sins of the wicked little horn. As Ford pointed out in his Glacier View manuscript, "Let it not be missed—the context says nothing about believers doing despite to the sanctuary."

How is the heavenly sanctuary "cleansed"?

In order to find something in Daniel 8:14 that indicates it's about the sins of the saints, we have to understand that verse in light of the universal conflict between good and evil—what Adventists have historically called "the great controversy."

---

*Fortunately, the Reformation began to correct these false doctrines, and Adventists believe that God raised up our movement to complete the restoration of truth that the teachings of the little horn had so distorted.

The Adventist understanding of the investigative judgment doesn't make sense apart from that theme.

How does the great controversy theme bring the sins of the saints into Daniel 8:14? Revelation 12 is one of the key chapters in the Bible from which we gain an understanding of the great controversy, and Revelation 12 and 13 repeat several of the key symbols from Daniel 7 and 8, including the persecution of the saints, the attack on God's law, the casting of the stars to the ground, the blaspheming of God, and the attack upon His sanctuary (see chapter 14 of this book).

These similarities between Daniel and Revelation make it apparent that both of Daniel's little horns have a very clear demonic component. I'm aware that throughout our history we have understood the primary fulfillment of Daniel's two little horns to be the papacy, and I have no argument with that conclusion. However, Revelation helps us to understand that Satan is the power behind these two horns, and he has a significant role to play in the fulfillment of the prophecies by the power that the horns represent.

Satan's attack on the sanctuary. Daniel 8:11 says, "By him [the little horn] the daily sacrifices [the *tamid*] were taken away, and the place of His sanctuary was cast down." We find a similar situation in Revelation, where the beast power in chap-ter 13 attacks God's sanctuary (verse 6). This beast, of course, is a surrogate of Satan because Revelation says that the dragon—Satan—gave this beast "his power, his throne, and great authority" (verse 2). Thus, it is Satan who inspires the little horn's attack on God's people, His commandments, and His sanctuary.

In fact, Satan himself is also involved in this attack because of his role as "the accuser of our brethren, who accused them before our God day and night" (Revelation 12:10). He accuses God's people before the angels as being unworthy of God's favor—undeserving of the salvation that Jesus died to provide them. I pointed out in chapter 11 that the judgment in Daniel 7 is the same as the judgments mentioned by Jesus and Paul in which the deeds of God's people, both good and bad, will be examined. Jesus said, "By your words you will be justified, and by your words you will be condemned" (Matthew 12:37), and Paul said, "We must all appear before the judgment seat of Christ, that each one may receive the things done in the body, according to what he has done, *whether good or bad*" (2 Corinthians 5:10; emphasis added). Thus, there is no question that the sins of the saints will be brought up in the final judgment. But I will emphasize again that God is not the One who brings them up. It is Satan who brings them up, and he does so through his accusations. Of course, Satan's accusations don't take God by surprise. He expects them. The judgment is His way of responding to them.

Satan's accusations against God's people are also a direct and powerful attack on the heavenly sanctuary, because in challenging the worthiness of God's people for salvation, Satan has challenged the plan of salvation that Jesus is mediating from His heavenly sanctuary. Satan's accusation that God's people don't deserve salvation raises serious questions in the minds of the angels—questions that demand answers. It is the purpose of the investigative judgment to provide those answers.

How the sins of the saints cause the sanctuary to need "cleansing." We must understand that the sanctuary in heaven doesn't need cleansing from the sins of the saints because the saints committed those sins, nor is heaven's sanctuary cleansed of those sins in the final judgment in the sense of God saving His people from them at that time. That was taken care of when the sins were confessed. The sanctuary in heaven needs cleansing from the sins of the saints only in the sense that Satan has thrown those sins up before God and the angels as evidence for his claim that the saints don't deserve to be granted eternal life.

I'm sure God responds to those charges the moment Satan brings them up; I wouldn't expect less of Jesus our Mediator. But for the purpose of settling the great controversy between Christ and Satan, God's final response is to open heaven's record books for every angel in heaven to examine in whatever detail he wishes. Satan's attacks against God's people—and especially his challenge that they are unworthy of salvation—are dealt with once and for all at that time. *This is why an investigative judgment is needed.*

Vindicating the saints and the sanctuary. In the King James Version and the New King James Version of Daniel 8:14, this judgment is represented as the *cleansing* of the sanctuary. The Revised Standard Version translates it as *restoring* the sanctuary to its rightful state. I believe the best word is *vindicating.* This is entirely justified because the Hebrew word translated "cleansed" in the King James and New King James versions of Daniel 8:14 is *nitsdaq,* the passive form of *tsadaq,* which in the Old Testament is very commonly used in a judicial context.

Under Jesus' skilled guidance, the angels in heaven will vindicate every one of God's true people of guilt in regard to every one of Satan's false accusations. This vindication of Jesus' ministry is also a vindication of the sanctuary. This understanding of the vindication, or cleansing, of the sanctuary is especially evident in the judgment in Daniel 7. Verse 22 says that in response to the little horn's attack upon the saints, "judgment was made in favor of the saints of the Most

High." In other words, through that judgment, they are vindicated.

Please note that the ones who make decisions at that time are the angels,* not God. He made His decision about the worthiness of each human being for salvation at the time that person lived and died. The investigative judgment is when the books are opened for the angels to examine. That's what the judgment scene in Daniel 7:9, 10 is all about. When that judgment is concluded, every angel in heaven will declare that every one of God's decisions about the salvation of His people is fair and just. God will be confirmed in His decisions, both about those who are saved and those who are lost.

Adventists have maintained for 150 years that the forgiven sins of the saints are maintained in heaven's record books until the time of the judgment. It's extremely important to understand that the records are kept there only for the purpose of responding to Satan's attacks against the saints in the judgment. When the angels see "forgiven" written across the record of those sins, and as they read the motives that prompted God's people to seek forgiveness, they will justify God in every single decision He has ever made.

Then the record of the sins of the saints will be forever erased from heaven's books. Because of the sins recorded there, Satan had accused the saints of being unworthy of God's forgiveness. This was a direct attack on the plan of salvation and on the heavenly sanctuary, where that salvation had originated. Daniel 8:10, 11 represents this symbolically as an attack by the little horn on God's people (the stars), their Prince (Jesus), His sanctuary, and its services (the *tamid*). The resolution comes in verse 14, which speaks of the vindication of the saints and the removal of their sins from the record books in heaven. This "cleanses" the heavenly sanctuary of those sins, the sins of the saints, and repels the attack by Satan, the little horn.

Frankly, I'm *glad* that the record of my sins remains on the books of heaven till the judgment because I also know that "forgiven" is written beside each one. Thus, I can be assured that when I enter heaven, a huge welcoming committee will be on hand to throw their arms around me and tell me how glad they are to see me!

If you and I are maintaining an ongoing relationship with Jesus, then we need not spend one single minute in fear of the judgment. Nor should we have a moment's apprehension about the record of our sins that has been kept in heaven's books. Rather, we

---

*The angels don't make decisions in the sense of having a vote against God's judgments of His saints. Rather, they make decisions in the sense of examining for themselves the charges Satan brings against God's people, noting Christ's response, and recognizing that God's decisions are just.

should praise God that an accurate record has been kept of everything, including our repentance and God's forgiveness. We should praise God that Jesus, our Mediator, will make a fair and accurate presentation of our situation when our name comes up in the judgment, and that when it's all over, He'll be vindicated in every one of His decisions. And if He is vindicated, then so are we.

Satan, be gone! I can't wait to meet my welcoming committee!

---

1. Ford, "Daniel 8:14," 346; emphasis added.
2. Ibid., 283.

The Investigative Judgment and the Sanctuary

Chapter 18

The Daily Services in the Earthly Sanctuary

A small band of Adventists came out of William Miller's failed movement with their confidence in Miller's basic mathematical calculations intact. They believed that God had done something important on October 22, 1844, after all. And Hiram Edson's insight that the sanctuary involved in that "something important" is in heaven got them thinking in a new direction.

Edson, together with a Dr. Franklin B. Hahn and a young man by the name of Owen R. L. Crosier, entered upon a serious study of the biblical teaching about the sanctuary. Crosier wrote out their conclusions in the *Day-Star Extra,* a lengthy supplement to a Millerite publication. There, Crosier laid out many of the conclusions that Adventists have accepted ever since. One of those conclusions was that the services in the earthly sanctuary were divided into two parts: those that were conducted every day of the year, and those on the Day of Atonement that were conducted just once a year. Ever since that time, Adventists have referred to these as the "daily services" and the "yearly services."*

This division of services in the Israelite religious calendar is clearly supported in the New Testament book of Hebrews. Chapter 9:6, 7 says that when the construction of the Old Testament sanctuary had been completed, "the priests always went into the first part of the tabernacle, performing the services. But into the second part the high priest went alone once a year." From Crosier's time to the present, Adventists have maintained that this division in the Israelite sanctuary rituals represents two great divisions of Christ's

---

*There were six annual feast days in the Israelite calendar (see Leviticus 23; Numbers 28; 29), but when Adventists speak of the "yearly service," they generally have in mind only the Day of Atonement.

ministry in the heavenly sanctuary. The daily services of the earthly sanctuary represent Christ's work in the heavenly sanctuary for nearly 2,000 years, from His ascension in A.D. 31 until the close of probation. The Day of Atonement in the earthly sanctuary—the yearly service—began in 1844 and continues to the close of probation. The early Adventists believed that the part of Christ's heavenly ministry that was typified by the daily services ended in 1844, when the yearly Day of Atonement began. However, I believe I am correct in saying that all Adventist theologians today understand the "daily service" in the heavenly sanctuary to continue alongside the Day of Atonement all the way to the close of probation.

In this chapter and the next, we will examine the daily services in the earthly sanctuary. A number of books have been written on the Levitical sanctuary rituals, including three by Dr. Roy Gane,[1] a professor of Old Testament at the Andrews University Theological Seminary in Berrien Springs, Michigan. My comments and conclusions in this chapter and the next three are largely based on Gane's work. I will begin by explaining the sacrifices.

The sacrifices

God had a problem. He created us human beings, and He loves us. He wants to have a relationship with us. He wants to dwell among us (see Exodus 25:8). Unfortunately, we are imperfect. We fall into various kinds of sins, and these sins make it impossible for Him to have the kind of relationship with us that He would like. In order to have that relationship, He had to figure out a way to deal with our imperfections while maintaining the integrity of His laws. That's what the Israelite sacrificial system was all about. They made it possible for God to have a loving relationship with His people who were loyal to His laws and at the same time maintain His justice when they violated those laws.

What did this sacrificial system consist of?

Each morning and each evening the priests slew a lamb and offered its body on the altar of sacrifice. This was called the "morning and evening" sacrifice (see 1 Chronicles 16:40; 2 Chronicles 2:4; 13:11; 31:3). However, that isn't the aspect of the Israelite sacrificial system that we will focus on in this chapter. Our concern here is with the sacrifices of individual Israelites.

Whenever an Israelite committed a sin, he or she was required to bring an animal sacrifice to the sanctuary. By this act, the Israelite acknowledged violating God's law. The sacrifice also showed that the sinner had repented, though Leviticus doesn't say anything about repentance. Depending on whether the sinner was a priest, a ruler, or a common person, the sacrifice required was a bull, a goat, or a lamb. People who couldn't afford to bring one of these could bring two doves or pigeons, or, in cases of extreme poverty, an offering of fine flour.* In the case of the bull, goat, or lamb, the sinner placed one hand on the animal's head and then killed it by slitting its throat and cutting the jugular vein. The priest then collected the animal's blood in a bowl. If the sinner was a commoner or a ruler, the priest daubed some of the blood on the horns of the altar of sacrifice in the courtyard (see Leviticus 4:25, 30). When a priest had sinned, or in the case of a sin by the entire congregation, the priest carried some of the blood into the Holy Place, the first room in the sanctuary, sprinkled it seven times before the veil, and then daubed it on the horns of the altar of incense (see Leviticus 4:6, 7, 17, 18). The priest then skinned the animal and burned certain parts of it on the altar of sacrifice (see Leviticus 4:10, 19, 20, etc.).

This ritual sounds very strange to our ears. As Roy Gane points out in his book *Cult and Character:*

> Slaughtering an animal, putting its blood on various parts of a dwelling and its furniture, and then burning the suet and carcass (Lev 16:11–28) do not accomplish any kind of cleansing in physical terms. To the contrary, these activities create a mess and are impractical and wasteful, transforming a live, valuable animal into bloodstains, smoke, and ashes, none of which are put to practical use. Nevertheless, the text informs us that the goal of another transformation is achieved at a higher level: nonphysical pollution, consisting of ritual impurities and moral faults, is purged from the sanctuary of supramundane YHWH on behalf of the Israelites (vv. 18, 19, 33). While the activities themselves do not produce this goal through physical cause and effect, as they would be expected to in ordinary life, they serve as a vehicle for transformation that takes place on the level of symbolic meaning.[2]

The meaning of the sacrifices

Gane means that, strange as the rituals of the Levitical sacrifices seem to us, they had an important purpose. The sinners had violated God's law when they sinned, putting themselves out of favor with God. In order to continue their relationship with God, they needed God's forgiveness. And that's what the sacrificial ritual accomplished. Speaking of a sinner who had brought his animal sacrifice, Leviticus 4:26 says, "The priest shall make an atonement for him concerning his sin, and *it shall be forgiven him*" (emphasis added; see also

*One of our primary sources of information about these sacrificial offerings is Leviticus 4 and 5.

verses 20, 31, 35; 5:10, 13, 16, 18). The animal died in the sinner's place. It took the sinner's sin upon itself and gave its life in place of the sinner's life. By means of this ritual, the sinner's transgression was purged from himself or herself, and he or she was forgiven. Thus, God could continue His loving relationship with the sinner.

The New Testament helps us to understand the extended meaning of these sacrifices. John the Baptist, pointing to Jesus, exclaimed, "Behold! The Lamb of God who takes away the sin of the world!" (John 1:29). In 1 Corinthians 5:7, Paul said, "Christ, our Passover, was sacrificed for us." And the author of Hebrews wrote, "If the blood of bulls and goats and the ashes of a heifer, sprinkling the unclean, sanctifies for the purifying of the flesh, how much more shall the blood of Christ, who through the eternal Spirit offered Himself without spot to God, cleanse your conscience from dead works to serve the living God?" (Hebrews 9:13, 14). Finally, Revelation 5:6 depicts Christ as "a Lamb as though it had been slain" standing in the midst of God's throne.

From this it is very evident that the animal sacrifices in the earthly sanctuary were a type of Christ's death on the cross by which He took our sins upon Himself, paid the death penalty we should have paid, and obtained our salvation from those sins. Thus, Christ achieved in reality what the sacrifices in the Jewish sanctuary ritual could only illustrate.

A crucial aspect of this whole ritual was the transfer of sin from the sinner to the sanctuary, which we will examine in the next chapter.

---

1. *Altar Call*; *Cult and Character: Purification Offerings, Day of Atonement, and Theodicy;* and *Leviticus and Numbers.*

2. Gane, *Cult and Character,* 17.

Chapter 19

The Transfer of Sin to the Sanctuary

From the very early days of Adventist history, the transfer of sin has been a major part of our understanding of the sanctuary and the investigative judgment. However, there have also been significant questions about that idea. Ellet J. Waggoner, of 1888 fame, questioned the whole idea of the transfer of sin. He said, "Sin is not an entity but a condition that can exist only in a person," and, therefore, "it is impossible that there could be any such thing as the transferring of sins to the sanctuary in heaven, thus defiling that place."[1]

However, that sin can be transferred from one individual to another is obvious from the fact that Christ bore our sins on the cross (see Isaiah 53:4–6, 11; 1 Peter 2:24). Thus, the idea of the transfer of sin to the sanctuary shouldn't be all that surprising. Gane points out that "in ritual a nonmaterial entity (e.g., sin) can be treated as if it belongs to the material domain, so that it can be subject to physical interaction and manipulation."[2] Thus, the issue is not so much *whether* sin can be transferred but what that transfer *means*.

I will discuss the meaning of the transfer of sin later in this chapter. For now, it's enough to note that it seems rather obvious that the sins of the Israelites got *into* the sanctuary because on the Day of Atonement they had to be cleansed *out* of the sanctuary. If they had to be removed, then somehow they must have gotten in. But how? When? And under what circumstances?

The traditional Adventist explanation is that an Israelite's sin was transferred to the sanctuary at the time he or she brought the sacrifice and went through the ritual I described in the previous chapter. However, some scholars understand the transfer of sin from the sinner to the sanctuary quite differently. The Israelites' sins didn't wait till they brought their sacrifices to be transferred to the sanctuary, they say. *The sins went to the sanctuary at the time the people committed them.*

So which way is it? Did sins get transferred to the sanctuary the moment they were committed or only after the sinner had brought his or her sacrifice? Let's examine both the traditional Adventist view and the different view of some scholars.

The traditional Adventist view. According to this view, the transfer of sin into the sanctuary was actually a two-step process. Assuming that the sinner had repented of his sin by the time he arrived at the sanctuary with his sacrifice, the first step was the transfer of sin from the sinner to his offering, usually an animal. Gane says, "The offering material as a whole, whether it consists of an animal or grain item, absorbs evil from the offerer, thereby purifying him/her."[3] In the case of an animal sacrifice, the animal took upon itself the death penalty that the sinner should have paid. This, of course, is a type of Christ's great sacrifice by which He took our sins upon Himself and paid the death penalty for them.

The second step in the Adventist understanding was the transfer of sin from the animal to the sanctuary. When the animal had been slain, the priest collected some of its blood in a bowl and daubed it on the horns of either the altar of sacrifice in the courtyard or the altar of incense in the Holy Place. Adventists have always said that by this process the sin was transferred

to the sanctuary. Gane said, "Through . . . purification offerings performed at the sanctuary, imperfection removed from [the] offerers is transferred to YHWH's sanctuary. Now the imperfection, in a contained/controlled form, is in his 'ballpark,' that is, it is his problem."[4]

This is the traditional Adventist view of how sins got *into* the sanctuary. But how did they get *out?* The answer to that question is very simple: on the Day of Atonement, the high priest sprinkled the blood of the Lord's goat on the ark of the covenant in the Most Holy Place, on the furniture in the Holy Place, and on the altar of sacrifice in the courtyard (see Leviticus 16:15–18). These rituals purged the sins of the Israelites from the sanctuary. The high priest then confessed these sins over the scapegoat, placing them on the goat, which was banished far enough into the wilderness that it couldn't return to the camp. Thus, the sins of the Israelites were forever removed from both the people and the sanctuary.

The view of some scholars. An alternative view is that the sins of the Israelites were transferred to the sanctuary at the moment they were committed.[5] Desmond Ford agrees with that position. In his Glacier View manuscript, he said, "Even on earth the sanctuary was defiled by the *act* of sin, not its confession."[6] In other words, the sins went to the sanctuary at the time they were committed, not through the sacrificial ritual.

Scholars who adopt this view support it with three texts, one from Leviticus and two from Numbers. I have quoted these texts below with the relevant words italicized.

- **Leviticus 20:2, 3**—"Say to the Israelites: 'Any Israelite or any alien living in Israel who gives any of his children to Molech must be put to death. The people of the community are to stone him. I will set my face against that man and I will cut him off from his people; for by giving his children to Molech, *he has defiled my sanctuary* and profaned my holy name' " (NIV).
- **Numbers 19:13**—"Whoever touches the body of anyone who has died, and does not purify himself, *defiles the tabernacle of the LORD.*"
- **Numbers 19:20**—"The man who is unclean and does not purify himself, that person shall be cut off from among the assembly, because *he has defiled the sanctuary of the LORD.*"

The italicized words in these texts make it very clear that sin defiled the sanctuary—it was transferred to the sanctuary—*at the moment it was committed.* This is why Ford said that "the sanctuary was defiled by the *act* of sin, not its confession." In support of

that statement, he referred to the texts I quoted above.[7]

So if sin was transferred into the sanctuary at the time it was committed, how and when did it get out? As scholars who adopt this view understand it, when the priest applied the blood of an individual's sacrifice to the horns of the altar, it was the altar that was purged of the sin. After all, if the sinner's sin was transferred to the sanctuary when it was committed, then at the time the sinner brought his* sacrifice to the sanctuary it was the sanctuary—not the sinner—that needed purging from the sin. Jacob Milgrom, a leading expert on the Israelite sanctuary rituals, said, "By daubing the altar with the . . . blood or by bringing it inside the sanctuary, . . . the priest *purges the most sacred objects and areas of the sanctuary* on behalf of the person who caused their contamination by his physical impurity or inadvertent offense."[8] This is how some scholars, including Ford, interpret the transfer of sin into and out of the sanctuary.

It's important to note that according to this theory, the Levitical system didn't purge sin from the Israelite who brought the sacrifice. It only removed the sin from the sanctuary—that is, from God. This has profound implications for Christian theology. Does Christ's death on the cross, the antitype of all Levitical sacrifices, remove our sins from

---

*Through the rest of this chapter and the next I use masculine singular pronouns to refer to the sinner for the sake of convenience and to avoid awkward sentences.

us, or does it only remove sin from the heavenly sanctuary—that is, from God? Let's analyze the evidence in a bit more detail.

Analyzing the evidence

I will begin our more detailed examination of the evidence by summarizing the two views:

The Adventist view
- When the sinner came to the sanctuary, his sin was still upon him.
- The animal symbolically absorbed the sinner's sin.
- Applying the animal's blood to the altar transferred the sin to the sanctuary.

The view of some scholars
- The sin defiled (was transferred to) the sanctuary at the time it was committed.
- By the time the sinner came to the sanctuary, his sin had already been transferred.
- Thus, the blood applied to the altar purged the sanctuary, not the sinner, of the sin.

So, was sin transferred to the sanctuary the moment it was committed or was it transferred when the sinner brought his sacrifice? The answer is *either,* depending on the kind of sin. The Hebrew language has several words for sin, just as we do in English. In addition to the word *sin,* we also sometimes speak of *iniquity, evil,* and *rebellion.* The three most common Hebrew words for sin are *hatta't, awon,* and *pesha'.* We met the word *pesha'* in earlier chapters. A word from the same root means "to rebel." *Pesha'* is most often translated "transgression," and it means "rebellion." The Hebrew word *hatta't* is usually translated "sin." Gane considers it to be "a broad term denoting a deed that violates an existing relationship/partnership."[9] *Awon* means "to be guilty," "to be culpable for a wrong." It is most often translated "iniquity."

We know that all three kinds of sin were transferred *to* the sanctuary because all three were removed *from* the sanctuary on the Day of Atonement. Leviticus 16:21 says that when the high priest laid his hands on the live goat, he was to "confess over it all the iniquities [*awon*] of the children of Israel, and all their transgressions [*pesha'*], concerning* all their sins [plural of *hatta't*], putting them on the head of the goat."

How did these sins get *into* the sanctuary? None of them is ever mentioned by

---

*Roy Gane prefers the translation "as well as" rather than "concerning" here. This is important because "concerning" makes it appear that the *awon* and *pesha'* sins are summarized under *hatta't* sins. Following a careful and very technical analysis (see *Cult and Character,* 285–291), Gane concludes that "the live goat carries away three distinct kinds of moral faults (*awon, pesha',* and *hatta't*)." *Cult and Character,* 290.

name as being transferred from the sinner into the sanctuary, but the evidence suggests that *pesha'* sins reached the sanctuary in one way, and *hatta't* and *awon* sins reached the sanctuary in another way. We need to examine these two ways in more detail.

1. Pesha' sins. A page or so back I shared with you three texts which state that certain sins defiled the sanctuary at the time they were committed. The Bible doesn't use any of the three Hebrew words for sin in these texts, but a careful examination makes it quite clear that all of them were *pesha'* sins of deliberate rebellion against God.[10] Leviticus 20:2, 3 condemns the worship of the pagan god Molech, to which the Canaanites sacrificed their children. Such sacrifices would be obvious acts of rebellion against the God of heaven. Offering them would be the same as you and I today giving up our Christian faith, going to India, and bowing down to one of the many Hindu gods. We call this apostasy, which is an obvious act of rebellion. That's what an Israelite did when he worshiped the pagan god Molech.

This act of apostasy defiled the sanctuary—and thus was transferred to the sanctuary—at the time it was committed. God often forgave sinners their *pesha'* sins when they repented (e.g., Exodus 34:7; Psalm 32:1; Isaiah 43:25), but the forgiveness came directly from Him. The sacrificial system provided forgiveness only for *hatta't* and *awon* sins.[11]

The other kind of sin that defiled the sanctuary at the time it was committed was the deliberate refusal to perform the ritual required for purification from ceremonial impurity. Numbers 19:20, which I quoted earlier, says, "The man who is unclean and does not purify himself, that person shall be cut off from among the assembly, because *he has defiled the sanctuary of the LORD*" (emphasis added; see also verse 13). The man's refusal to participate in a required purification ritual indicated a rebellious spirit on his part and an unwillingness to repent. It was a refusal to comply with God's condition for cleansing. This was an obvious *pesha'* sin of rebellion against God's laws that was so serious that the individual was to be "cut off from among the assembly." In today's language, we would say that the individual was to be disfellowshiped; his membership removed from the church books.* There was no sacrifice for *pesha'* sins of rebellion, which is why they defiled the sanctuary—were transferred to the sanctuary—at the moment they were committed. Gane says,

---

*However, for the Israelite, "cutting off" was more than banishment from the community. It was a terminal divine penalty that could result in execution, cutting off the person's line of descendants, and denying him or her an afterlife.

"Automatic defilement of the sanctuary when the sin is committed is attested only in certain kinds of serious cultic sins for which no sacrificial expiation is available: Molech worship (Lev 20:3) and wanton neglect to be purified from corpse impurity (Num 19:13, 20)."[12]

2. Hatta't *and* awon *sins.* The sacrificial service dealt only with *hatta't* and *awon* sins. Indeed, the sacrifice itself was called a *hatta't* sacrifice, which is why some English translations call it a "sin offering." Gane points out that these sacrifices were also commanded for cleansing from ritual impurities, which didn't involve the committing of wrong actions (although they could be regarded as having to do with the state of sinfulness that results from sinful action). Thus, *sin offerings* is an inadequate term. Gane calls them "purification offerings"[13] because they purified both from sinful actions and from physical ritual impurities. *Hatta't* sacrifices are described in detail in Leviticus 4, where, depending on the Bible version, they are called unintentional sins (NIV), unwitting sins (RSV), or sins of ignorance (KJV) (see verses 2, 13, 22, 27). The idea seems to be that although the sinner could be aware of his actions, he didn't realize that it was sinful at the time he committed it. In other words, these sins weren't acts of rebellion against God. Gane

calls them "nondefiant sins."[14] *Hatta't* and *awon* sins that weren't deliberate acts of rebellion are the sins that were transferred to the sanctuary at the time the sinner brought his animal and went through the sacrificial process.

However, Leviticus doesn't actually *say* that these sins were transferred to the sanctuary. We know it from a careful analysis of what was purged of sin when the sinner brought his sacrifice to the altar. The details are quite technical, so pay careful attention to what follows.*

Purging sin

The second half of Leviticus 4:26 states the purpose of the sacrificial ritual: "The priest shall make atonement for him [the sinner] concerning his sin, and it shall be forgiven him." The word *atonement* is from the Hebrew word *kippur,* from which we get the name of the well-known Jewish feast day, *Yom Kippur* (*yom* means "day," hence "Day of Atonement"). However, a better translation of *kippur* is "purge." Using this word, Leviticus 4:26 would read, "The priest shall make [purgation *from* his sin], and it shall be forgiven him." For the rest of our study I will use the word *purge* instead of *atone* or *atonement.*

Gane highlights the key issue with the following question: "When the priest car-

---

*For a complete discussion, see Roy Gane, "Purification Offering: Purgation of Sanctuary or Offerer?" in *Cult and Character,* 106–143.

ries out the goal of a purification offering by effecting purgation (*kippur*) on the offerer's behalf, what does he purge? Does he remove evil from the altar to which he applies the blood or from the offerer who has sinned?"[15]

If the answer to this question is that the sacrificial ritual purged the sin from the altar (that is, from the sanctuary), then the sin would have already been transferred to the sanctuary at the time it was committed, and it would have ceased to reside on the sinner. On the other hand, if the sacrificial ritual removed the sin from the sinner, then it would not have been transferred to the sanctuary at the time it was committed. Which was the case?

The answer is found in the second half of Leviticus 4:26, which I will quote again with the relevant words italicized. "The priest shall make atonement *for him* [the sinner] concerning his sin, and it shall be forgiven him." The word *for* in this verse is a translation of the Hebrew preposition *min,* and many Bible versions adopt the translation *for* (for example, see the NIV, NASB, NKJV, KJV). However, *min* can also be translated *from.* Please notice the difference in meaning between these two possible translations:

- The priest shall purge his sin *for* him.
- The priest shall purge his sin *from* him.

The first translation provides no suggestion about where the sin resided at the time the sinner brought his sacrifice to the sanctuary. It could have been on the sinner or on the sanctuary. Either way, the priest purged the sin *for* the sinner, that is, on his behalf. However, the second translation leaves no doubt about where the sin resided at the time the sinner brought his sacrifice—the priest purged the sin *from* him, that is, *from* the sinner. Obviously, it had to reside *on* or *in* the sinner in order to be purged *from* him. Clearly, if it still resided on or in the sinner at the time he brought his sacrifice to the sanctuary, then it hadn't been transferred from him to the sanctuary at the time he committed the sin. Instead, it was transferred to the sanctuary through the sinner's participation in the sacrificial ritual.

Gane analyzed the Hebrew preposition *min* in great detail in his book *Cult and Character.* He prepared a two-page chart that showed every occurrence of *min* in connection with the purification sacrifices.[16] At the conclusion of his analysis, he made the following statement: "Controlled syntactic analysis of the [*kippur*] formulas that state the goals/functions/meanings of the various kinds of purification offerings has forced me to the inescapable conclusion that all . . . purification offerings [performed on behalf of sinners] . . . remove evil from their offerer(s), rather than from the sanctuary."[17]

If Gane is correct—and I believe he is—then the sin remained on the sinner until he brought his sacrifice, and it was transferred to the sanctuary by means of the sacrificial ritual. Thus, the account of the sacrificial system in Leviticus supports the traditional Adventist view that the sacrifices of sinful Israelites removed the sin from the sinner not the sanctuary, and the sin was transferred to the sanctuary at that time, not when the sin was committed.

What I have just shared with you may seem like a technical discussion that's important to scholars but has little relevance to the likes of you and me. However, the issue of the transfer of sin is very relevant to the Adventist understanding of the sanctuary and the investigative judgment, as we shall now see.

What does the "transfer of sin" mean?

A key question that we must address is the meaning of the transfer of sin to the sanctuary. A statement by Gane that I quoted earlier provides a suggestion: "Through . . . offerings performed at the sanctuary, imperfection removed from [the] offerers is transferred to YHWH's sanctuary. Now the imperfection, in a contained/controlled form, is in his 'ball park,' that is, it is his problem."[18]

Gane's comment helps us to understand the meaning of the transfer of sin from the perspective of the earthly sanctuary. By accepting the sin into His sanctuary, God took the sinner's moral imperfection upon Himself. The sinner was forgiven, and he was thus no longer accountable for his wrong action. God had assumed the responsibility for the sin, and that responsibility remained upon Him until the Day of Atonement, when it was removed even from Him.

An even more important question that we must now address is the meaning of the transfer of sin from the sinner to the *heavenly* sanctuary. Earlier in this chapter I pointed out that the transfer of sin to the earthly sanctuary was a two-step process. The first was the transfer of sin from the sinner to the sacrificial victim, which then "paid" for the sin with its life. This, of course, represents the transfer of our sins to Christ, who bore them on the cross and truly did pay for them by His death. The New Testament is very clear about this. Peter said that Christ "bore our sins in His own body on the tree [the cross]" (1 Peter 2:24; see also Isaiah 53:4–6, 11).

However, sins were transferred from the sacrificial victim to the sanctuary in the earthly sanctuary as well. What did that mean in God's plan of salvation?

While the New Testament clearly indicates that our sins are transferred to Christ, nowhere does the New Testament state the antitypical meaning of the transfer of sin from the sacrificial victim to the sanctuary—that is, from Christ to the heavenly sanctuary. However, the book of Hebrews makes it very clear that in the New Testament era, the Israelite sanctuary rituals had their antitypical fulfillment in the various aspects of Christ's death and mediatorial ministry. Therefore, the transfer of our sins from the sacrificial victim to the sanctuary must have some meaning in the antitype. That is, in some way, our sins must be transferred from Christ, the sacrificial Victim, to the sanctuary in heaven. But what does this mean? How does it happen?

Adventists have always said that the transfer of sins to the sanctuary in the antitype refers to the fact that, throughout world history, the sins of God's professed people have been written in heaven's record books so that they will be available for consideration at the time of the investigative judgment.

I agree, and I will suggest a reason why this is necessary. Revelation 12:10 tells us that Satan is the accuser of God's people, and we have narrative examples of this in both Job 1 and Zechariah 3. And in both cases, the evidence suggests that angels were present to hear the accusations. The Bible tells us that Satan accused Job at a time when "the sons of God" (Job 1:6, KJV, NASB, NKJV), "the angels" (NIV), had come together for a conference.

This is also evident in the story about Joshua and the angel in Zechariah 3. Verse 4 says, "The angel said *to those who were standing before him*, 'Take off his [Joshua's] filthy clothes' " (NIV; emphasis added). We can reasonably assume that "those who were standing before" were God's angels. We can also reasonably assume that Satan is still accusing all of God's people before the loyal angels of being unworthy of God's favor. Satan has been doing this throughout the centuries and millennia of earth's history.

Let's consider an imaginary exchange between Satan and a heavenly angel whom I will call Raphael. This "conversation" took place some three thousand years ago.

Satan approaches Raphael as he is about to make his way back to heaven, and Satan says, "Can I have a word with you, please?"

Raphael stops and looks at Satan, and there's an uncomfortable pause. Finally, Raphael responds, "Well?"

Satan steps closer, a gleam in his eye and a sneer in his voice. "I understand your Master has accepted King David. Surely you're aware of his adultery."

"I've heard about it."

"And your Master plans to keep this miserable wretch of a sinner as one of His own?"

"He says David has repented."

"Ha! *Repentance!* And then he marries the woman and sleeps with her the rest of her life. David's repentance was as flimsy as a piece of papyrus! I have people on my side who haven't been a fraction as evil as David is, but because David is your Master's favorite, he's forgiven! How fair is that?"

"I'll convey your objection to my Master," Raphael says, and he turns and wings his way toward heaven.

Reaching the Holy City, Raphael hurries to find Michael, the Archangel, whom we know as Jesus. He finds Him at the entrance to the heavenly throne room, and he bows low. Then he speaks. "Michael," he says, "I just came from planet Earth, and Satan approached me, complaining about Your forgiveness of King David. Satan challenged my statement that David had repented."

Michael smiles and puts a hand on Raphael's shoulder. "Thank you for letting Me know about Satan's objection," He says. "I'm not prepared to respond at the moment. But a day is coming—it will be many earth years from now—when I will open the record books of heaven for you and all of your angel friends to examine. At that time, I will give Satan all the time he needs to make his most convincing arguments in the presence of all the angels in My kingdom, and I will give you and your friends all the time you need to examine the records for yourselves. When you're through reviewing the evidence, I believe you will agree that I am right in the decisions I've made about David, and Satan is wrong."

Michael pauses to let Raphael think about what He's said. Then He continues. "Between now and the judgment, I'm taking personal responsibility for the sins of all My people." He puts a hand on Raphael's shoulder, looks into his eyes, and smiles. "Until then," He says, *"trust Me."*

Gane pointed out that the transfer of sin to the sanctuary means that "now the imperfection, in a contained/controlled form, is in his 'ball park,' that is, it is his problem." Gane is speaking of the earthly sanctuary, and his point is that the transfer of the sinner's sin to the sanctuary meant that God assumed the responsibility for the sin until the Day of Atonement, when it would be removed from the sanctuary and transferred to the scapegoat.

I believe the same principle applies to the heavenly sanctuary. In the face of Satan's accusations against us, which raise serious questions in the minds of the angels, Jesus assumes the responsibility for our confessed and forgiven sins *until the judgment.*

As I understand it, the transfer of our sins to the heavenly sanctuary means that they are written in heaven's record books, awaiting the judgment. But, as the chronology of Daniel 7:9, 10 indicates, those record books weren't available for the angels to examine throughout most of world history. Therefore, an additional meaning of the transfer of sins to the heavenly sanctuary is that, until the judgment (which we understand is now in progress), Christ took upon Himself the responsibility for our forgiveness. His response to all of Satan's accusations and to any questions these accusations might raise in the minds of the angels was simply, "Trust Me until the judgment."

It's important to note that only sins that had been transferred to the sanctuary through the sacrificial animal could be forgiven. As we have seen, sins of rebellion were also transferred to the sanctuary, and these *pesha'* sins had to be removed from the sanctuary on the Day of Atonement,* but without the benefit of forgiveness for the sinner. All the sins of God's professed people are recorded in heaven's record books, and all will be considered in the judgment.†

Unforgiven sins of rebellion will stand as evidence against those who committed them, and those people will be condemned. On the other hand, those whose sins have been forgiven will be acquitted because their repentance and confession and Christ's forgiveness are recorded beside their sins. Christ, our Mediator and great Defense Attorney, will represent us against all of Satan's accusations. That's why we need have no fear of the judgment!

This has been a rather lengthy and somewhat technical discussion, but I trust that you can recognize its relevance to our study of the investigative judgment. Again, I have demonstrated that the Adventist interpretation of the Old Testament sacrificial ritual with its transfer of sin from the sinner to the sanctuary has strong biblical support.

---

1. Whidden, *E. J. Waggoner,* 347.
2. Gane, *Cult and Character,* 8.
3. Ibid., 176.
4. Ibid., 177.
5. Jacob Milgrom, an expert on Leviticus, adopts this view; see Gane, *Cult and Character,* 268–270.
6. Ford, "Daniel 8:14," 348; emphasis in the original. See also pages 5 and 290 for similar statements.
7. Ibid., 348; emphasis in the original.

---

*See Leviticus 16:16, where the English word *transgressions* is a translation of *pesha'*.

†The only people whose names are considered in the investigative judgment are those who have made a profession of faith in Christ, just as the Day of Atonement dealt only with the sins of Israelites—not those of pagan foreigners. The judgment of the wicked happens at the end of the millennium (see Ellen G. White, *The Great Controversy,* 480).

8. Jacob Milgrom, *Studies in Cultic Theology and Terminology* (Leiden: Brill, 1983), 75, quoted in Gane, *Cult and Character,* 107, 108; emphasis added.

9. Gane, *Cult and Character,* 292.

10. Ibid., 296.

11. Ibid., 297, 298.

12. Ibid., 274.

13. Ibid., 50.

14. Ibid., 233.

15. Ibid., 51.

16. Ibid., 110, 111.

17. Ibid., 142; see also page 273, item 2.

18. Ibid., 177; see also page 276.

Chapter 20

The Day of Atonement and the Problem of Evil

From the beginning of our movement in the mid-1840s, Seventh-day Adventists have seen the 1844 event as in some way an antitype of the Day of Atonement in the earthly sanctuary. Following the first disappointment in the spring of 1844, some Adventists came to believe that there was a relationship between Christ's second coming and the Day of Atonement. The *Seventh-day Adventist Encyclopedia* explains this Millerite understanding: just as "at the close of the Day of Atonement the high priest came out and blessed the waiting congregation," so they believed that "Christ would come out of the Holy of Holies at His second advent to bless His waiting people."[1] However, the Millerites also still believed that the earth was the sanctuary to be cleansed at Christ's second coming. The *Seventh-day Adventist Encyclopedia* points out that "no one explained how the Holy of Holies . . . could be heaven itself, and yet the sanctuary could be the earth, to be cleansed by fire at the Second Advent."[2]

The immediate significance of this focus on the Day of Atonement by the Millerites is that it led them to establish the specific date October 22, 1844. There is, of course, no direct biblical evidence for that specific date. This particular bit of time-setting arose out of the Millerites' reflection on the feast days in the Hebrew calendar and their fulfillment in the antitype. Samuel Snow explained this view (though he probably didn't originate it) at a camp meeting held in Exeter, New Hampshire, from August 12–17, 1844. Snow argued that Passover and Pentecost were both fulfilled in the antitype on the very day that these feast days occurred in the type. That is, Jesus, the true Passover, was crucified *on the very day of the Jewish Passover,* and the outpouring of the Holy Spirit at Pentecost occurred *on the very day of the Jewish Feast of Weeks*. In the same way, Snow reasoned, the Day of Atonement should be fulfilled *on the very day of that feast in the Jewish calendar*. The year 1844 had already been established on the basis of Daniel 8:14. All that was left was to determine *when* in that year the Day of Atonement would occur. And, according to the calendar of the Karaite Jews,* in 1844, the Day of Atonement was to occur on October 22. This is where our pioneers got the date October 22, 1844.

Up to this point, everyone had assumed that the cleansing of the sanctuary in Daniel 8:14 referred to the cleansing of the earth by fire at Christ's second coming. However, Jesus didn't come on October 22, 1844. This led to Hiram Edson's insight on October 23 that the sanctuary was in heaven and "that instead of our High Priest *coming out* of the Most Holy of the heavenly sanctuary [on that date] . . . he for the first time *entered* on that day the second apartment of that sanctuary."[3] The only time the high priest ministered in the Most Holy Place in the earthly sanctuary was on the Day of Atonement, so Edson's conclusion that Christ entered the Second Apartment of the sanctuary in heaven on October 22 meant that He entered upon His heavenly Day of Atonement ministry on that day.

Adventists still had a lot to learn about the heavenly sanctuary and the Day of Atonement, as well as a lot to unlearn. Nevertheless, from that primitive beginning, we eventually developed the idea that the antitype of the Day of Atonement is an investigative judgment that will take place in heaven prior to Christ's second coming. Thus, we need to examine more closely the Day of Atonement.

The Day of Atonement in the earthly sanctuary

The Day of Atonement was the high point in the Jewish religious year.[†] Five animals were used for the rituals performed on that day: a young bull, two rams, and two male goats. The day began with the high priest bathing himself. Then he dressed in a linen undergarment and a plain linen tunic, tied a linen sash around his waist, and placed a linen turban on his head.

Next, the high priest brought the two goats to the door of the tabernacle and cast lots over them, selecting one of them for the Lord and the other "for the scapegoat" (verse 8). He slaughtered the bull as a sin offering

---

*The Millerites chose this calendar because it preserved the original dating by continuous tradition from the second temple times, whereas rabbinic Judaism had changed the dating.

†Leviticus 16 is our primary source of information for the activities on the Day of Atonement. Unless otherwise noted, everything that follows is found in that chapter.

for himself. Then he took a lit censer into the Most Holy Place and put incense on it so that its smoke would shield him from God's presence, which was manifested above the ark of the covenant. Exiting the sanctuary, he picked up the container in which he had collected the bull's blood,* reentered the Most Holy Place, and sprinkled the blood once on the cover of the ark and seven times in front of the ark.

The high priest then exited the sanctuary again and slaughtered the Lord's goat. Collecting some of that blood in a container, he reentered the Most Holy Place and sprinkled the blood once on the ark and seven times in front of the ark. Then he exited the Most Holy Place, mixed the blood of the goat and the bull together, and sprinkled the combined blood on and before the altar of incense in the same way that he had the ark of the covenant. He also daubed some of the blood on the horns of the altar of incense (see Exodus 30:10).† When he was through with the blood manipulations in the Holy Place, the high priest exited to the courtyard, where he daubed blood on the horns of the altar of sacrifice and sprinkled blood on the altar seven times.

Next the high priest took the live goat, laid both of his hands on its head, and confessed over it all the sins that had just been purged from the sanctuary (see verse 21). The goat was then turned over to a man who had been appointed to take the animal far enough into the wilderness that it could never return to the Israelite camp.

With the ritual of the live goat completed, the high priest reentered the Holy Place, removed his linen garments, bathed again, and put on his regular high-priestly clothes. Then he exited the Holy Place, slaughtered the two rams, and sacrificed them on the altar in the courtyard as a burnt offering. This completed the high priest's activities on the Day of Atonement. The only remaining task was for a designated man to burn the carcasses of the sacrificial animals outside the camp.

Purpose of the Day of Atonement

Even more important than all the activity on the Day of Atonement is its purpose. Leviticus 16 mentions five things that were accomplished on that day:

- The sins of the people that had been accumulating in the sanctuary throughout the year were purged from the sanctuary (verse 16).
- The sanctuary was cleansed (verse 19).

---

*On page 225 of his book *Cult and Character*, Roy Gane lists eight activities that must have taken place on the Day of Atonement which Leviticus doesn't mention. One of these is the priest exiting the sanctuary to pick up the bull's blood.

†Leviticus 16 is vague about the ritual in the Holy Place. Roy Gane provides a detailed analysis in his book *Cult and Character*, pages 76, 77; see also page 225, number 8.

- The people were purged (verse 30).
- The people were cleansed (verse 30).
- The sins were sent away on the scape-goat (verse 21).

We'll examine each of these in a bit more detail.

1. The purging of the sanctuary. Leviticus says that on the Day of Atonement the high priest sprinkled the goat's blood on the ark of the covenant and the altar of incense. The purpose of this ritual was to "make atonement [*kippur*] for the Holy Place [what we call the Most Holy Place], because of the uncleanness of the children of Israel, and because of their transgressions, for all their sins; and so he shall do for the tabernacle of meeting [what we call the Holy Place] which remains among them in the midst of their uncleanness" (verse 16).

As noted in chapter 19, the Hebrew word for "atonement" is *kippur,* which means "to purge." Thus, the Day of Atonement was a day of purgation, when the high priest *purged* the sins of the Israelites from (or "out of") the sanctuary. Their sins, which had been *transferred into* the sanctuary throughout the previous year, were now *removed from* the sanctuary.

2. The cleansing of the sanctuary. A related idea is that the sanctuary was *cleansed* of the people's sins on the Day of Atonement. Verse 19 says, "Then he [the high priest] shall sprinkle some of the blood on it [the ark of the covenant] with his finger seven times, *cleanse it,* and consecrate it from the uncleanness of the children of Israel." The Hebrew word translated "cleanse" in this verse is *taher,* which means "to make clean," "to cleanse." Thus, we can say that the sanctuary was both purged (*kippur*) and cleansed (*taher*) from the sins of the Israelites on the Day of Atonement.

3. The purging of the people. One of the most important purposes of the Israelite sanctuary service was the purgation of sin not just from the sanctuary but also from the people themselves. However, the purgation of sin was a two-stage process. The first stage occurred throughout the year. As the people brought their animal sacrifices to the sanctuary, their sins were purged (*kippur*) from themselves and transferred to the sanctuary, that is, to God. As a result of this ritual, the people were forgiven. However, the responsibility for those sins didn't really belong to God, so the second stage of purgation occurred on the Day of Atonement, when the sanctuary was cleansed of the forgiven sins that had accumulated there throughout the year. As a result, the people themselves experienced an additional form of purgation. That's why Leviticus says that on the Day of Atonement "the priest shall make atonement [*kippur*] for *you*" (verse 30; emphasis added), that is, for the people.

However, there are at least two differences between the purging from sin that took place throughout the year and the purging that took place on the Day of Atonement. First, only the purgation in the daily services provided forgiveness. The word *forgive* doesn't appear even once in Leviticus 16, nor does it appear in any of the other passages that prescribe the rituals for the Day of Atonement (see Leviticus 23:26–32; Numbers 29:7–11). Second, the purgation on the Day of Atonement was corporate, not individual. All the sins of all the people were removed from the sanctuary at one time. Even the *pesha'* sins of rebellious Israelites were purged from the sanctuary on that day. However, this purgation didn't provide forgiveness to those who had committed these *pesha'* sins, for, as I mentioned, the word *forgive* doesn't appear in any of the descriptions of the Day of Atonement.

4. The cleansing of the people. Earlier we saw that the sanctuary was cleansed of sin on the Day of Atonement. Leviticus says that as a result of this ritual the people themselves were also *cleansed* of their sins: "On that day the priest shall make atonement for you, to *cleanse you,* that *you may be clean* from all your sins before the LORD" (verse 30; emphasis added). The Hebrew word for "cleanse" and "be clean" is *taher,* the same word that Leviticus uses to say that the sanctuary was cleansed of sin on the Day of Atonement. Now it's used to describe the cleansing of the people as well.

Throughout the year, the peoples' sins were purged (*kippur*) from them as individuals and they were forgiven. But they still were not cleansed of these sins. The word *taher,* "cleanse," doesn't occur in the daily service in connection with the purging of the peoples' moral faults, just as forgiveness of sin was not provided by the rituals of the Day of Atonement. And the cleansing (*taher*) on the Day of Atonement was corporate. The people could, of course, consider themselves cleansed of their sins as individuals, but the cleansing ritual was carried out for everyone all at the same time.

Thus, the purpose of the Day of Atonement was to accomplish a final, corporate purgation (*kippur*) of sin from the sanctuary, and the result of this purgation was the cleansing (*taher*) of both the sanctuary and the people.

5. The removal of the sins from the camp. The final purpose of the Day of Atonement was to permanently remove the sins of the Israelites not only from the sanctuary and the people, but also from the camp. It was the ritual with the scapegoat that accomplished this. Leviticus specifically says that after the high priest laid his hands on the live goat's head, he was to "confess over it all the iniquities [*awon*] of the children of

Israel, and all their transgressions [*pesha'*], concerning [or "as well as"] all their sins [*hatta't*], putting them on the head of the goat" (verse 21). Notice that all three Hebrew words for sin are mentioned in this text. Throughout the year, *hatta't* and *awon* sins had been transferred into the sanctuary through the peoples' purification sacrifices, and the *pesha'* sins of rebellious Israelites went to the sanctuary directly at the time they were committed (see chapter 19). All of these sins were purged (*kippur*) from the sanctuary on the Day of Atonement and placed on the scapegoat, which then carried this toxic load away from the camp. The transfer of sins *into* the sanctuary throughout the year may not be so clearly defined in Leviticus, but their transfer *out* of the sanctuary is stated very explicitly.

The scapegoat ritual

A crucial part of the Day of Atonement was the ritual with the scapegoat, by which the sins of the people were permanently removed from the camp of the Israelites. The word *scapegoat* in our English Bibles is a translation of the Hebrew word *azazel*. Some translators and commentators understand *azazel* to be a compound word because the Hebrew word *az* means "goat," and *azel* means "to go away," hence "escape goat," or "scapegoat."[4] However, that almost certainly isn't correct, as I will show

(though I will continue to use the word *scapegoat*).

The question of the meaning of the scapegoat in the antitype has been particularly controversial. Some commentators understand the scapegoat to represent Christ. Those who adopt this view give at least three reasons for their conclusion:

- Both goats are called a *sin offering* in most English translations. (See verse 5. "Purification ritual" is a better translation because the live goat wasn't an offering to God; see my comments below.)
- *Atonement* was made with both goats (see verses 15, 16 regarding the Lord's goat; see verse 10 regarding the scapegoat).
- The scapegoat was to "*bear* on itself" all the iniquities of the children of Israel "to an uninhabited land" (verse 22; emphasis added).

And, of course, serving as a sin offering and an atonement and bearing sin are all part of Christ's role in the plan of salvation. This is why some commentators have concluded that the scapegoat represents some aspect of Christ's work for our salvation.

However, other commentators have interpreted the scapegoat as Satan. You are perhaps aware that throughout our history,

Seventh-day Adventists have adopted this latter view. And we have endured severe condemnation for this interpretation from critics, who claim that it makes Satan our atonement for sin—our sin offering, our sin bearer. One of our most recent critics, Dale Ratzlaff, is a former Adventist minister and academy Bible teacher who now operates a ministry that is dedicated to opposing some teachings of the Adventist Church and getting as many people out of Adventism as he can. In his magazine *Proclamation!* Ratzlaff wrote, "Some teach that the scapegoat represents Satan. Personally, after thorough study, I feel this is the height of blasphemy."5

So, does the scapegoat represent Christ or Satan? The answer that makes the most sense to me is that it represents neither, though the interpretation that it represents Satan is closer to the truth. I will explain why.

A couple of paragraphs back I pointed out that our English word *scapegoat* is a translation of the Hebrew word *azazel,* which some interpreters consider to be a compound word. What seems more likely is that *azazel* is a single word that is the name of someone or something other than the goat. This seems evident from the fact that verse 8 says the high priest was to "cast lots for the two goats: one lot *for* the LORD and the other lot *for* the scapegoat" (em-

phasis added). The Hebrew literally says, "One lot for YHWH and the other lot for *azazel.*" One of the goats is *for* YHWH (Jehovah), that is, for His use. Since YHWH is clearly a personal Being, it seems most logical to understand *azazel* to also be a personal being (Azazel), and the goat is designated *for* him—in other words, for his (Azazel's) use. Thus, the goat itself is not Azazel. It is *for* Azazel.

So who or what is Azazel? Leviticus 16 is the only place in the entire Bible where the word appears, and Leviticus doesn't tell us who or what Azazel is. It simply uses the name.* However, Leviticus does provide us with clues.

Throughout the year, when an Israelite had sinned, he brought his sacrificial animal to the sanctuary, slaughtered it, and the priest performed the appropriate ritual. I pointed out in chapter 19 that this ritual transferred the person's sin from himself to the animal and from the animal to the sanctuary. The transfer of the sin to the sanctuary meant that God took upon Himself the responsibility for it. However, it was not in fact God's sin. He was simply assuming temporary responsibility for it.

On the Day of Atonement, then, all the sins that had accumulated in the sanctuary during the previous year were removed—not just from the sanctuary, but from God

*On page 251 of his book *Cult and Character,* Gane says, "The nature of Azazel's personality is not revealed in Leviticus, perhaps to avoid the danger that some might be tempted to worship him."

Himself. These sins were loaded onto the scapegoat, and the goat was banished far enough into the wilderness that it could never return. The fact that the scapegoat was designated *for* Azazel suggests that the goat was sent into the wilderness for the purpose of delivering the sins of the Israelites *to* Azazel. In other words, the *responsibility* for these sins was removed from God and His sanctuary and transported to Azazel.

So who is Azazel? Gane comments,

> The fact that YHWH is supernatural could be taken to imply that Azazel is also some kind of supernatural being. . . .
>
> . . . Because YHWH is the authority who commands the Israelites to perform the ritual (vv. 1–2), it appears that Azazel is his enemy. Therefore, it is likely that Azazel is some kind of demon and that his presence in an uninhabited region . . . represents "the extreme opposite of God's holy presence in the Holy of Holies."[6]

Although Azazel is a shadowy figure in Leviticus, his overall profile is clear and there is only one being in the universe who fits it: Satan.[7]

Thus, it seems most reasonable to conclude that Azazel is Satan, and the scapegoat was simply the vehicle that transport-ed the sins of the Israelites to him. Gane calls the scapegoat "a ritual 'garbage truck' carrying controlled toxic waste to Azazel."[8] He points out that "the Lord's goat belonged to the Lord and was offered to the Lord, but it also *represented* the Lord. . . . So the goat that belonged to Azazel and was sent to him *must also represent Azazel*."[9] When an attorney represents someone, he speaks in the place of that person, can sign documents for that person, and, in a sense, *is* that person. Similarly, the goat that carried the Israelite sins to Azazel represents Azazel and in that sense can be thought of as Azazel.

I pointed out earlier that Adventists have been severely criticized for identifying the scapegoat as Satan. In response, we have pointed out that the scapegoat was not slaughtered and offered as a sacrifice. Gane says that "the goat for Azazel is not a sacrifice."[10] The live goat "is not conceived, then, as an offering but as a vehicle for carrying off sin. What the community sends to Azazel is not so much the goat as the sin it bears."[11] The conclusion that Azazel is a demonic figure is also suggested by Leviticus 17:7, where God warned the Jews against worshiping demons. The word *demons* in this verse is from the Hebrew word *sa'iyr,* one meaning of which is "a he-goat, a buck."

Back in the mid-1950s, the evangelical author Walter R. Martin made a thorough investigation of Adventist teachings. While he disagreed with our doctrine of the investigative judgment, he made the following comment about our understanding of the scapegoat as Satan: "To be sure, the Seventh-day Adventists have a unique concept of the scapegoat, but in the light of their clearly worded explanation, no critic could any longer with honesty indict them for heresy where the atonement of our Lord is concerned. The Adventists have stated unequivocally that Jesus Christ is their sole propitiation for sin and that Satan has no part whatsoever in the expiation of sin."[12]

But what about the idea that the scapegoat helps to atone for the sins of the Israelites? Leviticus says clearly that the scapegoat was to be "presented alive before the LORD, to *make atonement* upon it" (Leviticus 16:10; emphasis added). In today's Christian theology, the word *atonement* refers to Christ's saving activity on behalf of sinful human beings. Thus, it seems like rank heresy to suggest that the scapegoat has a part in the atonement process. What we must keep in mind is that the Hebrew word translated "atonement" is *kippur*, which means "to purge," and the scapegoat *did* have a role to play in purging or removing sin from the sanctuary—but only in the sense that it was the vehicle that carried the peoples' sins away from the camp. This is clearly an aspect of purging or re-

moving sin, but it had nothing to do with *paying* for sin or *substituting* for sinners. Gane points out: "The customary rendering of [*kippur*] as 'atone,' coupled with the powerful association between 'atonement' and substitution in Christian theology, has obfuscated the meaning of the live-goat ritual for many Christians. But once we realize that [*kippur*] refers to removal of evil and does not specify substitution, which is only one kind of 'atonement,' the purification ritual of Azazel's goat makes good sense."[13]

My conclusion, then, is that the Adventist identification of the scapegoat as either Satan himself (our traditional view) or "*for* Satan" (a more recent understanding) is not "the height of blasphemy" that our critics have made it out to be. Rather, it represents an important part of the process for totally removing sin from God's people on the Day of Atonement in both the type and the antitype.

The Day of Atonement and the problem of evil

Roy Gane wrote his doctoral dissertation on Leviticus, and, since then, he's produced three books on the topic,[14] one of which is titled *Cult and Character: Purification Offerings, Day of Atonement, and Theodicy.* I've referred to and quoted from this book several times in this chapter and the two previous ones. I've repeated the title here to call attention to the last word: *theodicy.*

My guess is that the average person is unfamiliar with the word *theodicy.* Webster's dictionary defines it as "a system of natural theology aimed at seeking to vindicate divine justice in allowing evil to exist."[15] It seems to us that if we were God, we'd feed all the hungry people, heal all the sick people, provide for the needs of all the poor people, get rid of all the bad people, and as the ultimate benefactors of the human race, we'd help everyone else to live forever. So, if God is good and all powerful, why doesn't He carry out what seems to us such a logical solution to the problem of evil? Why does He allow it to continue to exist? Theodicy is the theological effort to explain this apparent conundrum.

Of course, when we speak of God as a God of *love,* it's important to understand that in order to be truly loving, He must love every human being, not just us and our friends. He must love even the evil people in the world. Furthermore, a God of love would want to do more than settle scores and relieve suffering. The ultimate objective of a truly loving God would be to completely rid the world of evil, because as long as evil exists, suffering will also continue to exist. The problem is that evil exists in us humans. Evil exists because *we* are evil. And it isn't just the so-called *bad* people who are evil. *All of us* are infected with

evil tendencies. Some of us manifest these tendencies more than others, but all of us have them. Thus, in order to get rid of evil in the *world,* God must get rid of evil in *human beings.*

And removing evil from humans is, in fact, what Leviticus is all about. I mentioned earlier that in Leviticus, God's method of removing evil from His sinful people was a two-stage process. The first stage was the daily service, in which sin was purged from the sinner and placed on a sacrificial animal, which had to die for that sin. This illustrated the fact that God took the sinner's sin upon Himself and paid the death penalty that the sinner should have borne, opening the way for the sinner to be forgiven. And when the death penalty was paid, the sin was transferred to the sanctuary, illustrating the fact in some sense God continued assuming responsibility for it. At this point, God still had not dealt fully with the problem of evil. All He had done was to take it upon Himself. But God didn't commit the sin, and, thus, He didn't deserve to be held responsible for it.

This brings us to the second stage in God's process of eliminating evil. Every year on the Day of Atonement, all the sins, for which God had assumed the responsibility during the previous twelve months, were purged out of the sanctuary and placed on a live goat, which toted them off into the wilderness to Azazel, who represented Satan. By this process, the sanctuary was "cleansed" of the people's sins, which means that God had removed them from Himself and placed them on the originator of sin. And, as I pointed out earlier, Leviticus also says that the people themselves were also fully cleansed of these sins on that day (see verse 30).

A page or so back I quoted Webster's definition of theodicy as "a system of natural theology aimed at seeking to vindicate divine justice in allowing evil to exist." However, the ultimate theodicy cannot merely vindicate God for allowing evil to *exist*. The ultimate theodicy has to include God's *solution* to the problem of evil so that it no longer exists. I hardly need to document the fact that according to Scripture, God's final resolution of the problem of evil will take place at the end of time with the establishment of His eternal kingdom of righteousness. Thus, the Day of Atonement, with its resolution of the problem of evil and its occurrence at the end of the Israelite religious year, has a strong eschatological sense to it. The Day of Atonement also reminds us of the great controversy theme as it is understood by Seventh-day Adventists. Indeed, we can say that theodicy—the great controversy theme—is the whole point of the Israelite sanctuary ritual.

In chapter 4, I pointed out that the investigative judgment doctrine makes sense only when it is viewed from the perspective of the great controversy theme, and, thus, the investigative judgment is also about theodicy. Therefore, it shouldn't surprise us to find that there is a relationship between the investigative judgment and the Levitical sanctuary ritual. But to see that, we must return to Daniel. In this chapter we've reviewed theodicy as it's illustrated in the Hebrew sanctuary rituals. In the next chapter, we'll examine theodicy as it's illustrated in the prophecies of Daniel, and we'll bring these two illustrations of theodicy together.

---

1. *Seventh-day Adventist Encyclopedia,* s.v. "Sanctuary."

2. Ibid.

3. *Seventh-day Adventist Encyclopedia,* s.v. "Edson, Hiram"; emphasis in the original.

4. See Gane, *Cult and Character,* 254.

5. Ratzlaff, "What Is the Meaning of the Cross?" 16.

6. Gane, *Cult and Character,* 250, 251.

7. Gane, *Altar Call,* 250.

8. Gane, *Cult and Character,* 247.

9. Gane, *Altar Call,* 250; emphasis in original.

10. Gane, *Cult and Character,* 251.

11. Y. Kaufman, *The Religion of Israel,* trans. and abridge. M. Greenberg (Chicago: University of Chicago Press, 1960), 114, quoted in Gane, *Cult and Character,* 247, note 11.

12. Martin, *The Truth About Seventh-day Adventism,* 188.

13. Gane, *Cult and Character,* 265.

14. See the bibliography at the end of this book.

15. *Webster's New World Dictionary of the American Language,* 2nd college ed., s.v. "Theodicy."

Chapter 21

The Day of Atonement in Daniel 7 and 8

In chapter 5 of this book, I pointed out that in the months leading up to the Great Disappointment on October 22, 1844, the Millerites interpreted the cleansing of the sanctuary in Daniel 8:14 as the antitype of the Levitical Day of Atonement. Seventh-day Adventists have maintained this view ever since. But is it correct? Can what Daniel 8:14 says about the sanctuary be reasonably interpreted from the Bible itself as the heavenly counterpart of the earthly Day of Atonement? That is the question I will address in this chapter.

The idea that the Day of Atonement in Leviticus was related to Daniel 8:14 would probably never have occurred to the early Adventists had it not been for the particular way that verse was translated in the King James Version: "And he said unto me, Unto two thousand and three hundred days; then shall the sanctuary be *cleansed*" (emphasis added). With minds already focused on the Day of Atonement, those Adventists looked at the word *cleansed* in Daniel 8:14 and they read the same word in Leviticus 16:19 (KJV): "And he shall sprinkle [some] of the blood on it [the altar of sacrifice] with his finger seven times, and *cleanse* it, and hallow it from the uncleanness of the children of Israel." Putting together the words *cleansed* in Daniel 8:14 and *cleanse* in Leviticus 16:19, they concluded that the two must refer to the same thing. Thus, Daniel 8:14 was about the cleansing of the heavenly sanctuary! It was about the heavenly Day of Atonement! How could they have missed seeing it!

Of course, with no background in the biblical languages, they were unaware that the Hebrew word translated "cleansed" in Daniel 8:14 is the passive of *tsadaq,* while the

Hebrew word translated "cleanse" in Leviticus 16:19 is *taher*. *Tsadaq* means "to be just," "to be righteous," while *taher* means "to be clean," "to be pure." The two ideas are similar, but they aren't the same. Thus, the fact that both words speak of cleansing in the King James Version is not necessarily the strongest basis on which to make a connection between Daniel 8:14 and the Levitical Day of Atonement.

Critics of the early Adventist interpretation have been quick to point out this problem. Ford, for example, said that *tsadaq* "has no vital connection with the *taher* of ritual cleansing in Lev. 16. Thus *taher* is not found in Dan. 8, and *sadaq* [Ford's spelling of the word] is not found in Lev. 16."[1]

Does this mean that Daniel 8:14 has nothing to do with the Day of Atonement in the heavenly sanctuary? Not at all. But the link between the two is more subtle than the appearance of the words *cleansed* and *cleanse* in Daniel and Leviticus. I will begin to present the case for that link by sharing with you what I consider to be the strongest evidence that Daniel 8:14 speaks to the Day of Atonement in the heavenly sanctuary.

Leviticus, Daniel, and theodicy

In the preceding chapter, I noted that the dictionary defines *theodicy* as "a system of natural theology aimed at seeking to vindicate divine justice in allowing evil to exist."[2] However, I went on to point out that we can't restrict theodicy to a mere explanation of how a good God can allow evil to *exist*. If God is truly good, if He is truly all powerful, and if He truly loves human beings, then His ultimate objective must be to *solve* the problem of evil—to end it. This is the great controversy theme, and for me, it's the very best evidence of the relationship between the Day of Atonement and Daniel 8:14.

Leviticus is a symbolic, minipicture of God's plan to eliminate evil from the lives of His people. Every day of the year the Israelites brought their animal sacrifices to the sanctuary, and each time they did, they were purged of their sins and forgiven. These sins were ritually transferred to the sanctuary, where God assumed temporary responsibility for them. However, on the Day of Atonement, all of the accumulated sins from the previous year were purged out of the sanctuary and were forever removed from the camp of Israel. This was a symbolic representation of God's plan to ultimately rid the universe of evil.

Daniel 7 shows a little horn attacking God, His law, and His people. Chapter 8 shows a little horn attacking God's people and His sanctuary, its services, and its High Priest (the Prince of the host). In both of these chapters, the power of evil is alive, well, and active in the world, and God allows it to be so for a time. However, in both chapters, the problem of evil is eventually resolved. In chapter 7, a judgment takes place in heaven and God's people are vindicated and granted eternal life, while the beast power and its little horn are condemned and destroyed by fire; the kingdom of God is then turned over to a Son of man and His saints. In chapter 8, the resolution to the problem of evil is the cleansing or "vindication" of the holy things that have been under attack: the sanctuary, its services, its High Priest, and its people.

Thus, both Leviticus and Daniel give symbolic representations of God's plan to eliminate evil from the universe. However, the approach in each is quite different. Leviticus uses religious ritual to tell us how God will deal with evil, whereas Daniel does so through apocalyptic prophecy. But the end result in both Leviticus and Daniel is the same: the problem of evil is resolved. And the point is that if both the Day of Atonement and Daniel 7 and 8 deal with God's plan for the elimination of evil, then we should expect that in some way they are related. We shouldn't be surprised to find the Day of Atonement reflected in Daniel.

Let's examine Daniel in detail for evidence of the Day of Atonement in chapters 7 and 8.

The Day of Atonement in Daniel 7

At first glance, it may seem like a stretch to view Daniel's vision of the Ancient of Days seated on His throne in chapter 7 as a sanctuary scene, let alone a Day of Atonement scene. However, please consider the following analysis.

To begin with, any scene of God seated on His throne is a sanctuary scene because, according to the Old Testament writers, God's throne was located in His temple, that is, in His sanctuary. Isaiah, for example, saw "the Lord [Jehovah] sitting on a *throne,* high and lifted up, and the train of His robe filled the *temple*" (Isaiah 6:1; emphasis added). And the psalmist said, "The LORD is in His holy *temple,* the LORD's *throne* is in heaven" (Psalm 11:4; emphasis added). Both of these texts make it clear that God's throne is located in the sanctuary—in His temple in heaven.

The book of Revelation makes the same point. In chapter 4, John writes of seeing God's throne room in heaven, and among other things, he says he saw "seven lamps of fire . . . burning before the throne, which are the seven Spirits of God" (verse 5). These seven lamps of fire are the heavenly counterpart of the menorah—the seven-branched lamp stand in the earthly sanctuary. And in Revelation, these seven lamps of fire are "before the throne." Thus, God's throne is in the heavenly sanctuary.

Revelation 8 also locates God's throne in the heavenly temple. In verse 3, an angel with a golden censer stands before an altar.

This is clearly the altar of incense because the angel is "given much incense, that he should offer it with the prayers of all the saints upon the golden altar which was before the throne." The presence of an altar of incense is clear evidence that the heavenly sanctuary is in view, and Revelation says that this altar of incense is "before the throne." Thus, there is no question that God's throne is located in the heavenly sanctuary.

Adventists have always maintained that the ark of the covenant in the earthly sanctuary is a type of God's throne in heaven because God's visible presence appeared over the mercy seat, between the cherubim. This view—that God's throne is located in His temple, the heavenly sanctuary—is supported by the evidence we have just examined. Thus, Daniel's vision of the Ancient of Days seated on His throne in chapter 7 takes us into the Most Holy Place of the heavenly sanctuary. And since the Day of Atonement is the only ritual in the entire Hebrew religious year that took place in the Most Holy Place, we should consider the possibility that Daniel's vision of God's throne in chapter 7 involves the heavenly counterpart of the earthly Day of Atonement.

Of course, we can't assume that every Old Testament mention of God's throne in the heavenly sanctuary is a reference to the Day of Atonement. For example, I don't know of anything to suggest that Isaiah's vision of God seated on His throne in His temple should be understood as a Day of Atonement scene. However, four factors about Daniel's vision of the Ancient of Days on His throne in Daniel 7 support the conclusion that this is indeed just such a scene.

1. When it occurs. First is the fact that the vision concerns what occurs at the end of world history, immediately prior to the establishment of God's eternal kingdom. I pointed out in the previous chapter that the Day of Atonement, with its resolution of the problem of evil at the end of the Israelite religious year, has a strong eschatological sense to it. And Daniel's vision of the Ancient of Days seated on His throne in the heavenly sanctuary at the end of world history just before the establishment of His eternal kingdom is clearly eschatological. Thus, it comes at the appropriate time in world history to be a heavenly Day of Atonement scene.

2. A heavenly judgment scene. Second, the Israelite Day of Atonement was a day of judgment. Roy Gane, in his book *Cult and Character,* has titled a section of one chapter "The Day of Atonement Is Israel's Judgment Day."[3] He begins his explanation by pointing out that "YHWH wants people who are loyal and remain loyal."[4] Throughout the year, the people demonstrated their loyalty by doing their best to obey God's moral laws and by carrying out the appropriate rituals when they failed to obey. On the Day of Atonement, they demonstrated their loyalty by denying themselves and by abstaining from all work. Gane concludes,

> By the end of this day [the Day of Atonement] there are only two classes of Israelites: (1) a remnant who are morally "pure," that is, having no impediments to their relationship with Yhwh (Lev 16:30), and (2) those who have no future with Yhwh and his people (23:29–30). So we find that, within the Israelite cultic year, the Day of Atonement completes the determination of destinies on the national level and in this sense can be regarded as Israel's judgment day.[5]

Daniel 7:9, 10 shows us a judgment transpiring in heaven in the presence of God, the Ancient of Days, who is seated on His throne. The result is that the powers of evil in the world are condemned and destroyed (verses 11, 26), while God's people are vindicated and given dominion over the world (verses 21, 22, 27). Thus, again, the world is divided into just two classes of people: those who are loyal to God and those who are not.

From this I conclude that Israel's judgment day on the Day of Atonement is a type of God's final judgment near the end of world history that we see pictured in Daniel 7:9, 10.

3. The angels. The two cherubim upon the ark of the covenant before which the high priest ministered on the Levitical Day of Atonement represent the millions of angels around God's throne in Daniel 7:9, 10. (See also Revelation 5:11.)

4. The "Son of Man." There is a fourth factor supporting the conclusion that the judgment scene in Daniel 7 is a heavenly Day of Atonement. At the conclusion of this judgment, "One like the Son of Man" approaches the Ancient of Days "with the clouds of heaven" (verse 13). Jesus repeatedly applied the term *Son of Man* to Himself (see, for example, Matthew 8:20; Luke 6:5). Thus, this "Son of Man" in Daniel 7 is none other than Jesus Himself. And His coming into God's presence "with the clouds of heaven" reminds us of the high priest entering the Most Holy Place on the Day of Atonement, shielded by a cloud of incense smoke. Martin Proebstle comments, "In a temple setting, the coming of the one like a son of man 'with the clouds of heaven' naturally brings to mind the entrance of the high priest with the clouds of incense on the Day of Atonement."[6]

For these reasons, I conclude that Daniel's vision of the Ancient of Days in Daniel 7:9, 10 is the heavenly counterpart of the Day of Atonement in the Levitical sanctuary. And, of course, these verses describe a heavenly judgment.

The Day of Atonement in Daniel 8

However, the text that Adventists have associated with the Day of Atonement from the very beginning is in chapter 8, not chapter 7. Thus, the key question is whether we can find the Day of Atonement in chapter 8.

The first thing to notice is that chapter 8 is filled with sanctuary imagery. The vision opens with two sanctuary animals in conflict with each other—a ram representing Media-Persia, and a goat representing Greece. And both of these animals figured prominently in the rituals of the Day of Atonement. Even more to the point, the little horn in Daniel 8 attacks God's sanctuary, its people, its rituals (the *tamid*), and its High Priest (the "Prince of the host"). And the sanctuary that is under attack, as we saw in chapters 13 and 14 of this book, is God's heavenly sanctuary.

Adventists have said that this attack was fulfilled by the medieval papacy through the distortion it effected in the minds of the people about God's plan of salvation. However, the power behind the little horns in both Daniel 7 and 8 is none other than Satan himself, who attacks God's people continually, day and night, through his accusations that they don't deserve salvation. This is a direct attack on the heavenly sanc-

tuary, from which God the Father and the Son are carrying out their plan of salvation. Then comes the anguished cry in verse 13 that asks when this terrible condition will end. And the answer comes in verse 14, with its assurance that after 2,300 days, the problem will be resolved; the sanctuary will be cleansed, restored, and vindicated.

Is this resolution a reference to the Day of Atonement in the heavenly sanctuary? I will mention six reasons why I believe that it is.

1. The relationship of Daniel 7 and 8. I have provided significant evidence that the heavenly court scene in Daniel 7:9, 10 is actually a heavenly Day of Atonement. If that is correct, then the fact that Daniel 8:14 comes at the same point of time in the outline of world history requires us to view this verse as portraying a Day of Atonement scene as well.

2. Theodicy. Daniel 7 and 8 are about God's great plan to bring an end to sin and cleanse it from the universe. This is particularly evident in chapter 7, where the world's evil powers are destroyed and their kingdoms are turned over to the Son of man and His saints (Daniel 7:13, 14, 26). Daniel 8 shows the same evil powers attacking God's people (the stars), Jesus Christ (the Prince of the host), His sanctuary, and its services (the *tamid*). This is an attack on Christ's heavenly sanctuary ministry! And verse 14 shows that the sanctuary will be vindicated *during the end time* (see verses 17, 19). Clearly, it's picturing the solution to the attack of both the little horn and its sponsor, Satan, on Christ's mediatorial ministry. Both Daniel 7 and Daniel 8 are snapshots of the conflict between good and evil stated as prophecy. This is the Seventh-day Adventist great controversy theme, which is the ultimate theodicy.

The Levitical sanctuary system that purged sin in a symbolic way both from individuals throughout the year and from God and His sanctuary on the Day of Atonement is also a symbolic representation of God's solution to the problem of evil—this time stated as ritual. So, these rituals were also about the ultimate theodicy. This, to me, is a powerful link between Daniel 7 and 8 and the Day of Atonement.

3. The horn's attack and its resolution. I've pointed out that the little horn in Daniel 8 attacks God's people, His sanctuary, its rituals, and its High Priest. This creates a huge problem that needs an answer, which verse 14 provides. As translated by most versions of the Bible, this verse mentions only the restoration or vindication of the *sanctuary.* However, in its context, the verse seems to have in view all of the problems caused by the little horn. This is particularly evident from the fact that the text literally says, "Then shall the *holy*

[Hebrew *qodesh*] be vindicated," not "then shall the *sanctuary* [*miqdosh*] be vindicated." The word *holy* suggests that everything the little horn attacked was to be restored or vindicated, not just the sanctuary. Proebstle points out that

> there is only one cultic [sanctuary] ritual by which all these entities come rightfully into their own again: the Day of Atonement. In other words, the objects of purification on the Day of Atonement—the sanctuary and the people of God—and the vindication of God himself correspond conceptually to both the target of the horn's assault in Dan 8 and the intended goal of what is restored to its right place in 8:14c, that is, the sanctuary, the host, and God himself.[7]

4. Resolving the horn's "transgression of desolation." I've pointed out in previous chapters that the Hebrew word *pesha'* means a sin of deliberate rebellion against God. It is typically translated as "transgression" in English. I've also pointed out that no provision was made throughout the Levitical year for *pesha'* sins to be purged and forgiven. The daily sacrificial system dealt only with *hatta't* and *awon* sins.

In the entire book of Leviticus, the word *pesha'* occurs only two times—both of them in connection with the Day of Atonement

(Leviticus 16:16, 21). You will recall that *pesha'* sins were transferred into the sanctuary immediately at the time they were committed, and all sins, *pesha'* included, were cleansed *out of* the sanctuary on the Day of Atonement. The significance of this detail is that in Daniel 8:13, the horn's attack is called a *pesha'* sin—the "transgression of desolation." The horn's activities were clearly an utter rebellion against the God of heaven, His people, His sanctuary, and His High Priest, so the word *pesha'* is entirely appropriate.

Now notice this: Daniel 8:14 says that all this *pesha'* was to be resolved after 2,300 evenings and mornings. And, of course, in the earthly sanctuary, it was the Day of Atonement ritual that removed *pesha'* sins, along with *hatta't* and *awon* sins, from the camp of Israel. This suggests that the cleansing/restoration/vindication of the sanctuary in Daniel 8:14 refers to a Day of Atonement process. Proebstle says, "The sanctuary can only be purified from *pesha* on the Day of Atonement. Thus, if *pesha* in Dan 8 is dealt with in a cultic [sanctuary] way, and the context does suggest it, [then] *pesha* has to be set right by a Day of Atonement activity, the only cultic ritual that deals with *pesha*."[8]

5. Qodesh in Daniel 8:14. I pointed out in chapter 16 that the word *sanctuary* in verse 14 is a translation of the Hebrew word *qodesh,* which means "holy." This word occurs several times in Leviticus 16, including seven occurrences where it clearly refers to the Most Holy Place (verses 2, 16, 17, 20, 23, 27, 33). In addition, variants of the word *qodesh* appear several times in Leviticus 16, such as in verses 4 and 32, where it is an adjective describing Aaron's clothing as "*holy* garments." Thus, the use of *qodesh* in Daniel 8:13, 14 provides what Proebstle calls a "terminological link"[9] between these verses and the Day of Atonement in Leviticus 16.

6. The Greek translation. While the words translated "cleanse" and "cleansed" in Leviticus 16:19 and Daniel 8:14 are different in the original Hebrew, the Septuagint version, which is the original Greek translation of the Old Testament, uses the same word, *katharizo,* in both Leviticus and Daniel. This is no doubt one of the factors that influenced the King James Version translators to use the same word in their English translation of Daniel 8:14. The assumption is that the Jewish scholars who translated the Old Testament into Greek would have been quite aware of the differing words in Leviticus and Daniel, and the fact that they used the same word in Greek suggests that they saw the same meaning in both Leviticus and Daniel.

I have provided six suggestions for understanding that Daniel 8:14 refers to a Day of Atonement process in the heavenly sanctuary. To summarize them:

1. The judgment scene in Daniel 7:9, 10, which comes at the end of world history, is the heavenly counterpart of the earthly Day of Atonement. The cleansing of the sanctuary in Daniel 8:14 comes at precisely the same point in the outline of earth's history and thus can be considered another aspect of heaven's Day of Atonement.

2. Leviticus 16 and Daniel 7 and 8 give us varying snapshots of God's plan to rid the universe of evil, which is *theodicy*. Therefore, Daniel 8:14 is also about theodicy—heaven's Day of Atonement.

3. Daniel 8:14 resolves all of the issues involved in the little horn's attack in verses 10–12, and the Day of Atonement in the earthly sanctuary is "[the] only . . . cultic ritual by which all these entities come rightfully into their own again."[10]

4. In the system of Levitical rituals, the Day of Atonement was the only one that dealt with *pesha'* sins—not by forgiving them, but by removing them forever from the Israelite people.

5. The use of the word *qodesh*, "holy," in Daniel 8:14 provides a link between that verse and Leviticus 16, where *qodesh* is used multiple times in reference to the sanctuary and especially the Most Holy Place.

6. The Septuagint uses the same Greek word for "cleanse" and "cleansed" in Leviticus 16:19 and Daniel 8:14.

These are my reasons for concluding that Daniel 7 and 8, and especially 8:14, are about a heavenly Day of Atonement.

Desmond Ford on Daniel 7 and 8 and the Day of Atonement

While Desmond Ford takes exception to significant aspects of the Adventist interpretation of Daniel 7 and 8, the investigative judgment, and the Day of Atonement, he agrees that Daniel 8:14 is about a heavenly Day of Atonement. In his book *Daniel,* which was published by the Southern Publishing Association, Ford said,

If the sanctuary is the microcosm of the kingdom of God, then its cleansing, vindication, restoration, must point to the reestablishment of that kingdom over the kingdom of men.

Furthermore we would expect to find something in the typical services of the sanctuary that comprehends all the concepts so far specified—something which would point to a finishing of sin, an atonement, a reconciliation, and a new beginning, with joy for the righteous and sorrow for those who have refused the sanctuary's provisions. [Note Ford's emphasis on theodicy.]

Was there any familiar sanctuary

ritual that spoke of all these things to the Jew? Indeed there was! The Day of Atonement, the crucial service of the seventh month, to the Jew was a summation of God's salvation. Coming at the end of the religious year, it pointed to the end of time. It belonged to the second complex of feasts, each member of which had eschatological significance. . . .

Here then was the cleansing, vindicating, restoring, of the sanctuary in type. . . .

. . . Lev 16 is indeed the final clue for the exposition of [Daniel] 8:14. Pointing forward to the great atonement made on Calvary for us by Christ, the antitypical Lord's goat, it also prefigures the last work for us by Christ, our High Priest. It pictures the placing of the responsibility for evil upon its true instigator, the true little horn—Satan himself. Thus God's character, so long trampled in the dust by the scandal of sin, will be vindicated.[11]

Ford's book *Daniel* was published in 1978, just two years prior to the time he presented his manuscript at the Glacier View summer camp in Colorado. At Glacier View, he maintained his view that Daniel 8:14 points to a heavenly Day of Atonement:

While in the days of Adventism's original position on Dan. 8:14 most contemporary scholars rejected any eschatological meaning for that verse, the last half century has seen a significant reversal of that trend. Today many non-Adventist scholars recognize Dan. 8:14 as eschatological, applying to the establishment of the Kingdom of God, and being equivalent in significance to the judgment picture of Dan 7:9–13.

In summary, Dan 8:14 points to the same judgment as Dan. 7:9–13—a judgment upon wicked powers resulting in the establishment of the kingdom of God, and the vindication of the saints. This event is the antitypical Day of Atonement which, while fulfilled at the cross, is consummated by the judgment of the end.[12]

Dan. 8:14 does indeed point to the final purification of the universe from sin and sinners which was prefigured in the ancient Day of Atonement, that passion-play of old which also came as a climax in Israel's worship, and which once every 49 years ushered in the great jubilee of liberty and joy.[13]

The one qualification to these statements, especially to what Ford said at Glacier View in 1980, is that he understands the heavenly Day of Atonement to have begun with the Cross, whereas Seventh-day Adventists see it commencing in 1844. Ford bases his conclusion about the Day of Atonement beginning at the Cross on Hebrews. We'll look at Hebrews in chapters 28 to 31 of this book.

In conclusion

The October 22, 1844, Great Disappointment provided an immediate and necessary correction to William Miller's view that the sanctuary in Daniel 8:14 represented the earth that was to be cleansed by fire at Christ's second coming. Within twenty-four hours, Hiram Edson gained the insight that the sanctuary was in heaven and that "instead of our High Priest *coming out* of the Most Holy of the heavenly sanctuary to come to this earth on the tenth day of the seventh month, at the end of the 2300 days, he for the first time *entered* on that day the second apartment of that sanctuary."[14] The early Adventists put the word *cleansed* in Daniel 8:14 together with the word *cleanse* in Leviticus 16:19 and concluded that Daniel 8:14 pointed forward to an antitypical Day of Atonement. From that time to this, Adventists have continued to insist that Daniel 8:14 does indeed point to the Day of Atonement in the heavenly sanctuary.

As I mentioned near the beginning of this chapter, students of Hebrew have challenged this interpretation, pointing to the differing words for "cleanse" and "cleansed" in Leviticus and Daniel. However, it seems to me that there was something providential about the Millerite and early Adventist interpretation. I believe God wanted our Adventist pioneers to make the association between the Day of Atonement in Leviticus and the judgment and the restoration of the sanctuary in Daniel. But they almost certainly wouldn't have made this connection at that time had the King James Version not used the word *cleansed* in Daniel 8:14. The more extended evidence I have presented in this chapter would almost certainly never have occurred to them in the decade or so following October 22, 1844. Thus, it was to their advantage that they didn't understand that the English words *cleanse* and *cleansed* in Daniel and Leviticus came from two different Hebrew words. This distinction has been pointed out repeatedly in the years since 1844, but *it does not invalidate the original conclusion.* The comparison of Leviticus 16 with Daniel 7 and 8 that I have made in this chapter bears out the validity of the original Adventist conclusion.

However, today we don't have to rely exclusively on the terms in Daniel and Leviticus to make the connection between the Old Testament Day of Atonement in Leviticus 16 and God's great heavenly Day of Atonement in Daniel 7 and 8. Furthermore, this broader understanding of the

Levitical Day of Atonement and Daniel's prophecies coincides perfectly with the great controversy theme on which Adventist theology is based. Daniel 7 and 8 share the theodicy of Leviticus 16—God's plan to solve the problem of evil and restore His people to the perfection that Adam and Eve knew at the moment they came from God's creative hand.

My conclusion, then, is that there is strong biblical support for the historic Adventist conclusion that Daniel 8:14 points to an eschatological Day of Atonement.

1. Ford, "Daniel 8:14," 349.

2. *Webster's New World Dictionary of the American Language,* 2nd college ed., s.v. "Theodicy."

3. Gane, *Cult and Character,* 305–309.

4. Ibid., 306.

5. Ibid., 306, 307.

6. Proebstle, "Truth and Terror," 659.

7. Ibid., 491.

8. Ibid., 492, 493.

9. Ibid., 493.

10. Ibid., 491.

11. Ford, *Daniel,* 175.

12. Ford, "Daniel 8:14," 645.

13. Ibid., 397.

14. *Seventh-day Adventist Encyclopedia,* s.v. "Edson, Hiram"; emphasis in the original.

Chapter 22

The Blotting Out of Sins

Soon after the Great Disappointment, Sabbatarian Adventists began teaching that one of Christ's functions during the heavenly Day of Atonement is to blot out the confessed and forgiven sins of the righteous. This is one of the basic theological concepts that they developed to explain what happened on October 22, 1844. (See chapter 6.)

Adventists still hold to the idea that the sins of God's people will be blotted out at the conclusion of the investigative judgment. A couple of examples will suffice. The first is from the *Handbook of Seventh-day Adventist Theology:*

> The heavenly cleansing [of the sanctuary] . . . involves a blotting out of sin from the heavenly records. Subjectively, the sinner receives personal forgiveness upon daily repentance and confession of sins, being saved in the Lord; objectively, the recorded and forgiven sins in heaven are blotted out once the case of each professed follower has been presented in the pre-Advent judgment.[1]

Ellen White wrote one hundred and more years ago; however, because her views are normative for Seventh-day Adventists, what she said about the blotting out of sins continues to have relevance for our consideration. Writing in the chapter on the investigative judgment in *The Great Controversy,* she said, "All who have truly repented of sin, and by faith claimed the blood of Christ as their atoning sacrifice, have had pardon entered against their names in the books of heaven; as they have become partakers of the righteousness of Christ, and their characters are found to be in harmony with the law of God, their sins will be blotted out, and they themselves will be accounted worthy of eternal life."[2] She also said, "Sins that have not been repented of and forsaken will not be pardoned and blotted out of the books of record, but will stand to witness against the sinner in the day of God."[3]

What are we to make of the idea that the sins of God's people won't be blotted out until the conclusion of the investigative judgment? Does this mean that for the past thousands of years the sins of God's people have stood recorded against them, awaiting a decision by the investigative judgment? Doesn't the Bible teach that our sins are blotted out at the time God forgives them? What kind of assurance of salvation can God's people have if their sins are still recorded in heaven's record books after they have confessed them and received God's forgiveness? I pointed out in chapter 3 that any teaching is false if it compromises the gospel of righteousness by faith and leads to unnecessary anxiety on the part of God's people. Therefore, we must understand this issue of the blotting out of sins in the light of the gospel.

What the Bible says

The Bible speaks of both names and sins being blotted from God's record in heaven. For example, when Israel worshiped a golden calf at the foot of Mount Sinai, God said, "Let Me alone, that I may destroy them and *blot out their name* from under heaven" (Deuteronomy 9:14; emphasis added). Moses interceded with God, "If You will forgive their sin—but if not, I pray, *blot me* out of Your book which You have written" (Exodus 32:32; emphasis added).*

The Bible also speaks of the blotting out of *sins*. For example, in confessing his adulterous relationship with Bathsheba, David prayed, "According to the multitude of Your tender mercies, *blot out my transgressions.* . . . Hide Your face from my sins, *and blot out all my iniquities*" (Psalm 51:1, 9; emphasis added).†

When does God blot out the sins of His people? In Isaiah 43:25, God said, "I, even I, am He who blots out your transgressions for My own sake; and I will not remember your sins." This text suggests that the sins of God's people are blotted out at the time they are confessed and forgiven. Peter suggested the same thing. In one of his sermons to the people of Jerusalem, he said, "Repent therefore and be converted, that your sins may be blotted out, so that times of refreshing may come from the presence of the Lord" (Acts 3:19). The implication is that as soon as the people repented and were converted, their sins would be blotted out.

---

*Regarding the blotting out of names, see also 2 Kings 14:27; Psalms 9:5; 69:28; 109:13; Revelation 3:5.
†Regarding the blotting out of sins, see also Nehemiah 4:5; Psalm 109:14; Isaiah 43:25; Jeremiah 18:23.

Commenting on Peter's statement, the *Seventh-day Adventist Bible Commentary* says, "The immediate result to those who accepted Peter's call to repentance was the forgiveness of their sins. In this sense the blotting out of their sins may be regarded as having occurred immediately. In the ultimate sense, however, the final blotting out of sin takes place just before the second advent of Christ in connection with the close of Christ's work as High Priest."[4] This, of course, is standard Adventist theology about the blotting out of sins.

The judgment and the sins of the saints. I'm not aware of any explicit statement in the Bible that says the sins of the saints will be retained in heaven's record books until the judgment. However, it is a reasonable conclusion from what we do know about the judgment and what we know about the Day of Atonement. The key question is this, Will the forgiven sins of the saints come up for review in the judgment? If the sins of the saints won't be reviewed in the judgment, then it's reasonable to conclude that they were blotted out of heaven's record books at the time those who committed them confessed and were forgiven. On the other hand, if the sins of the saints will be reviewed in the judgment, it's reasonable to conclude that those sins are retained in heaven's record books until the judgment.

I presented evidence in chapter 11 that the sins of all those who have professed to be followers of God—God's people—*will be* reviewed in the judgment, as the following texts clearly state.

Ecclesiastes 12:14—"God will bring every work into judgment, including every secret thing, *whether good or evil*" (emphasis added).

Matthew 12:37—"By your words you will be justified, and by your words you will be condemned."

2 Corinthians 5:10—"We must all appear before the judgment seat of Christ, that each one may receive the things done in the body, according to what he has done, *whether good or bad*" (emphasis added).

So, the Bible makes it clear that the judgment will consider *all* sins, including the sins of the saints. For that to happen, of course, those sins must be retained in heaven's record books until the judgment, and they will be blotted out as a consequence of the judgment. The Bible doesn't say whether each individual's sins will be blotted out at the time his or her name is considered or whether the sins of all the saints will be blotted out together at the conclusion of the judgment. However, the Day of Atonement ritual suggests that the blotting out will be corporate—done all at one time.

The Day of Atonement. In the Levitical rituals, the complete removal of sin from the people was a three-step process. The first two steps occurred each day throughout the year. In the first step, sin was transferred from the sinner to an animal, which was then slain. The second step, which followed immediately, was the transfer of sin from the sacrificial victim to the sanctuary. The third step was the corporate removal of the sins of all God's people from the sanctuary that had been accumulating there throughout the year. It occurred once a year on the Day of Atonement. The high priest loaded these sins onto the scapegoat, which carried them to Azazel.

The Bible clearly states the meaning of the first step in the antitype. The transfer of sin from the sinner to the sacrificial victim represented Christ bearing our sins on the cross and paying the death penalty for them (see 1 Peter 2:24; Isaiah 53:12). However, the Bible doesn't discuss the antitypical meaning of the transfer of the sin to the sanctuary in the daily service, nor does it discuss the antitypical meaning of the transfer of sin from the sanctuary to Azazel once a year on the Day of Atonement. Yet both of these were important parts of the Levitical ritual that should have some counterpart in the plan of salvation.

As a first step in attempting an explanation, it's important to note that the transfer of sin from the sacrificial victim to the sanctuary occurred *after* the death of the animal. Only forgiven sins were transferred into the sanctuary through the sacrificial process. Therefore, in whatever way this transfer of sin from the sacrificial victim to the sanctuary is fulfilled in the heavenly sanctuary, it happens *because of* Christ's death, and the only sins that are transferred are those that have been forgiven.

In chapter 19, I shared with you a statement by Roy Gane that is relevant here: "Through . . . purification offerings performed at the sanctuary, imperfection removed from [the] offerers is transferred to YHWH's sanctuary. Now the imperfection, in a contained/controlled form, is in his 'ballpark,' that is, it is his problem."[5] Commenting on Gane's statement, I said, "By accepting the sin into His sanctuary, God took the sinner's moral imperfection upon Himself. The sinner was forgiven, and he was thus no longer accountable for his wrong action. God had assumed the responsibility for the sin, and that responsibility remained upon Him until the Day of Atonement, when it was removed even from Him." The question, again, is, What is the meaning of all this in the antitype, the heavenly sanctuary? What does it mean for God to accept the responsibility for our sins? And what does the removal of those sins from the heavenly sanctuary during heaven's Day of Atonement mean?

From the beginning of our history,

Seventh-day Adventists have said that the transfer of our forgiven sins *into* the heavenly sanctuary means that they are recorded in heaven's record books, and the transfer of sin *out of* the sanctuary on the Day of Atonement represents the blotting out of those sins from those books at the time of heaven's Day of Atonement—the investigative judgment. This is an interpretation since neither the Old Testament nor the New Testament actually says this. However, it seems to me to be a reasonable interpretation, *provided it can be harmonized with the gospel.*

The blotting out of sins and the gospel

The idea that the sins of God's people won't be blotted out until the judgment raises a very significant question about the gospel of righteousness by faith: how can God's people be assured of salvation throughout their lives if their sins won't be blotted out until their case has been finalized in the judgment?

Note this statement that Isaiah attributes to God: "I have blotted out, like a thick cloud, your transgressions, and like a cloud, your sins. Return to Me, for I have redeemed you" (Isaiah 44:22). Please notice the last sentence in that verse: "Return to Me, for *I have redeemed you.*" God sometimes spoke of redeeming His people in the sense of delivering them from Egyp-

tian bondage or Babylonian captivity. However, in the context of the blotting out of sins in the first part of the verse, it's evident that when God said, "I have redeemed you," He had in mind the redemption of His people from their sins. But had God actually redeemed Israel from their sins at the time Isaiah wrote these words? No. Christ's redeeming act on the cross was still several hundred years in the future. How, then, could Isaiah speak of redemption from sin as an accomplished fact?

I will suggest a couple of reasons. First, as Paul points out in Romans 4:17, God "calls those things which do not exist as though they did." God spoke of Israel's redemption as an accomplished fact because He can speak of that which is future as though it were present.

This fact leads to the second reason: God always assures His people that they *have received* all the benefits of His salvation, even if the legal transaction that will secure one or more of those benefits is still future. Imagine God saying to the Old Testament Israelites, "Your redemption hasn't happened yet, but I *will* redeem you someday in the future." That would have been technically correct since Christ hadn't died yet. But what kind of assurance would that have given to God's Old Testament saints? So, instead, God proclaimed boldly through Isaiah, "I *have* redeemed you," even though the legal transaction that would secure the Israelites' redemption was still several hundred years in the future.

In the very same sense, I propose that God proclaimed through Isaiah that Israel's sins *had already been blotted out* even though in this case the legal transaction by which those sins would actually be blotted out was still several thousand years in the future.

But why must the sins of God's people be preserved in heaven's record once they have been forgiven? Again, I propose that the reason is not because God *wishes* to bring them up again, but because Satan *will* bring them up in the presence of the angels in the pre-Advent investigative judgment, and God must respond. However, this needn't threaten the assurance that God's people have of His acceptance. Please note again Ellen White's statement that I quoted a few pages back: "All who have truly repented of sin, and by faith claimed the blood of Christ as their atoning sacrifice, have had pardon entered against their names in the books of heaven; as they have become partakers of the righteousness of Christ, and their characters are found to be in harmony with the law of God, their sins will be blotted out, and they themselves will be accounted worthy of eternal life."

The important point is that the sins that are blotted out in the final judgment are those that have already been truly repented of, that have been forgiven by the blood of Christ, and that, consequently, have been recorded in heaven's books as pardoned. The sins that are blotted out in the judgment are the sins of those who "have become partakers of the righteousness of Christ," whose "characters are found to be in harmony with the law of God."* In the judgment, when Satan claims God's people as his subjects because of "all the sins that he has tempted them to commit,"[6] heaven's infallible records will show that those sins have been repented of and confessed. The word *pardoned* has been entered in the record alongside them, and Satan's claims will be proven groundless. Because God's people have a Mediator in the heavenly sanctuary, they can be absolutely certain that Satan's misrepresentations will be fully exposed as false, and the angels will pronounce them completely innocent.

---

*Lest there be any misunderstanding, please note how Ellen White defines a character that is in harmony with God's law: "Christ's character stands in place of your character, and you are accepted before God just as if you had not sinned" (*Steps to Christ*, 62). Those who have a character that is in harmony with God's law are those who have Christ's character standing in place of their character. This isn't to deny the importance of God's people putting forth efforts to develop a Christlike character. But it *is* to say that our standing in the judgment will depend on whether Christ's character stands in place of our character and not on the level of character development we have achieved or failed to achieve.

The blotting out of sins and theodicy

In considering the issue of the blotting out of sins, it's important to keep in mind that God's broad purpose in conducting an investigative judgment is theodicy—He wants to solve the problem of evil. Ultimately, God doesn't want merely to blot out the sins of His people—He wants to eliminate sin from the universe altogether. Ellen White understood this very clearly. In the book *The Great Controversy* she wrote, "When Christ, by virtue of His own blood, removes the sins of His people from the heavenly sanctuary at the close of His ministration, He will place them upon Satan, who, in the execution of the judgment, must bear the final penalty. The scapegoat was sent away into a land not inhabited, never to come again into the congregation of Israel. So will Satan be forever banished from the presence of God and His people, and *he will be blotted from existence* in the final destruction of sin and sinners."[7] So, the ultimate blotting out of sin will occur when, in the lake of fire, Satan himself is blotted from existence.

You are no doubt aware that Adventists divide God's final judgment process into three phases: an investigative phase before Christ's second coming, in which the angels are given the opportunity to review heaven's records (see Daniel 7:9, 10); a second phase during the millennium, when God's people are given the opportunity to review those records (see Revelation 20:4); and a third, postmillennial phase, when God will cause the history of sin on earth to pass in panoramic review before the eyes of the wicked.[8] This will be followed by the lake of fire, when sin and sinners will all be destroyed (see Revelation 20), making the earth clean again. This will be the ultimate blotting out of sin.

Edward Heppenstall, a professor at the Andrews University Seventh-day Adventist Theological Seminary in the 1950s and 1960s, wrote,

> The blotting out of sin involves more than forgiveness. It involves also the banishment of sin and Satan. The gracious purpose of our Lord is not only to forgive sin but to triumph over it and eradicate it. The ministry of Christ will bring the universe back into complete harmony with God. . . . Sin and sinners will finally be isolated, banished, and destroyed. . . . [Christ's] ministry will not stop short until all sin is blotted from the universe. If there is any place in the Levitical sanctuary and its services where this truth is taught and symbolized, it is on the Day of Atonement.[9]

The issue of the sins of God's people in the judgment is crucial because any misunderstanding can compromise the assurance of salvation that God wants all of us to experience. Some Adventists in the past *have* held serious misunderstandings about this topic, and the result has been anxiety about their acceptance by God. This is most unfortunate. However, it is no different from other misunderstandings about biblical teachings that God's people have held through the centuries—and in some cases still hold—which have also led to unnecessary spiritual anxiety. Satan is constantly trying to distort our understanding of the Word, and all too often he has succeeded. The challenge for all Christians is to arrive at a correct understanding of God's Word so that they can experience the peace that passes all understanding. Sometimes it

takes a while for that understanding to mature, both in our individual minds and in our corporate teachings. This has been true of the Adventist teaching about the investigative judgment and related topics such as the blotting out of sins. But I insist that these teachings are biblically sound when properly understood.

---

1. *Handbook,* 845.
2. White, *The Great Controversy,* 483.
3. Ibid., 486.
4. *Seventh-day Adventist Bible Commentary,* 6:158.
5. Gane, *Cult and Character,* 177.
6. White, *The Great Controversy,* 484.
7. Ibid., 422; emphasis added.
8. See ibid., 666–669.
9. Heppenstall, *Our High Priest,* 81.

Issues in Daniel 9

Chapter 23

The Beginning of the 2,300 Days

Seventh-day Adventists believe that the 2,300 days/years of Daniel 8:14 began in 457 B.C. and ended in A.D. 1844. From this, we have concluded that heaven's investigative judgment began in 1844. We got that date from one interpretation of Daniel 8:14 and 9:24–27. Gerhard Hasel, a former professor at the Andrews University Seventh-day Adventist Theological Seminary in Berrien Springs, Michigan, said that Daniel 9:24–27 is "one of the most controversial [passages] in the entire OT [Old Testament]."[1] He cited one interpreter who called the history of the interpretation of these verses "the Dismal Swamp of OT criticism."[2]

Thus, it is with some fear and trepidation that I enter the "swamp." Nevertheless, Daniel 9:24–27 plays an important role in the Adventist interpretation of Daniel 8 and 9, and we must deal with them. What I share with you in this chapter and the three that follow is pretty much the way Adventists have understood Daniel 9 throughout our history. The discussion is somewhat technical, so you'll have to put on your thinking cap.

I'll begin by pointing out that Daniel 8 gives us a very general idea of when the 2,300 days began. In verse 13, one "holy one"—almost certainly an angel—said to another "holy one," "How long will the vision [of Daniel 8] be?" We know that this vision began with the Medo-Persian period, which was represented by the ram. The Persian Empire was the primary force that lasted in the Middle East from 539–331 B.C., so the 2,300 years should begin sometime between those two dates. When we add 2,300 years to each one, we find that the 2,300 years should end sometime between A.D. 1762 and 1970. That's a long stretch—208 years. When in those 208 years did the 2,300 days begin, and, thus, when did they end? Unfortunately, Daniel 8 doesn't tell us. Fortunately, Daniel 9 does.

Now, let's examine the relationship between Daniel 8 and Daniel 9.

The relationship of Daniel 8 and 9

In Gabriel's explanation of the vision in chapter 8, he made it clear to Daniel that "the vision refers to the time of the end," and "at the appointed time the end shall be" (Daniel 8:17, 19). Thus, Daniel's vision in chapter 8 should extend to our own time. Of course, Daniel had no idea that thousands of years would pass before that "appointed time of the end" arrived. In his day, the Jews were still captive in Babylon because of their rebellion against God. Therefore, Daniel almost certainly understood the desecration of the sanctuary described in chapter 8:10–12 to refer to the destruction of Solomon's temple earlier in his own lifetime. The pronouncement in verse 14 that the sanctuary would be restored must surely have seemed to him to be good news.

In verses 20–27 of chapter 8, Gabriel explained most of that chapter's vision to Daniel. He concluded by saying, "The vision of the evenings and mornings [that is, the 2,300 days] which was told is true; therefore seal up the vision, for it refers to many days" (verse 26). Unfortunately, at this point Daniel "fainted and was sick for days" (verse 27). Thus, Gabriel's explanation of the cleansing of the sanctuary and

the 2,300 days was interrupted.

Let's try for a moment to put ourselves in Daniel's place. He was born in Jerusalem and lived there through the early part of his youth. He had observed the apostasy of his Jewish contemporaries and had heard Jeremiah's severe rebukes against them. (See, for example, Jeremiah 2 and 3.) He was very aware of Jeremiah's prediction that the Babylonians would invade Judea and destroy Jerusalem. (See Jeremiah 4:5–31). It must have been frightening for Daniel to live through the fulfillment of this terrible prediction. Worst of all, the Babylonians captured him and several of his friends and hauled them off to Babylon, where they were trained for service in the court of King Nebuchadnezzar. By the time Daniel received the vision of chapter 8, he had served Nebuchadnezzar and two or three other kings of Babylon faithfully for many decades. Nevertheless, he was always the loyal Jew who mourned what had happened to his people.

Daniel was very aware of a prediction by Jeremiah that after seventy years of captivity, the Jews would be restored to their homeland (see Jeremiah 25:11, 12; 29:10). He was also aware that the time for that restoration was drawing near. And now Gabriel was saying that 2,300 evenings and mornings must pass before the sanctuary would be restored. Daniel's fainting spell suggests that something about that announcement shocked him. However, he didn't say what it was that shocked him. We know that Gabriel didn't return immediately after Daniel's illness. In fact, Daniel didn't hear from Gabriel again for about eleven years, by which time the seventy years had almost ended—and Daniel was getting quite worried. Was the rebellion of his people so terrible that God intended to postpone their return?

Daniel did two things in response to his concern. First, he studied the prophecies of Jeremiah about the seventy years (Daniel 9:2). And second, he prayed earnestly that God would forgive the sins of His people and return them to their homeland (verses 4–19). This is a good lesson for us. Any time we're concerned about an important issue in our lives, we need to do the two things Daniel did; we need to search the Bible for an answer, and we need to ask God for divine guidance. If we do so, we can be sure that He will guide us to the right answer—as He did Daniel. Let's see what He told Daniel.

Gabriel's explanation

In response to Daniel's prayer, God sent Gabriel to the prophet's side again. Gabriel said, "I have now come forth to give you skill to understand. . . . Therefore consider the matter, and *understand the vision*" (verses 22, 23; emphasis added). From what I have just shared with you, it should be quite apparent that the vision Gabriel came to explain to Daniel was the

vision of chapter 8. I pointed out a moment ago that Gabriel had explained most of that vision immediately after Daniel received it (see Daniel 8:17–26). The only part that remained unexplained was the crucial 2,300 days and the restoration of the sanctuary (Daniel 8:26). This was the part of the vision Daniel had found so shocking that he fainted and got sick. It was the part of the vision that eleven years later prompted him to search Jeremiah's prophecies and pray earnestly for the restoration of his people to their homeland. And Gabriel came to Daniel precisely to relieve his mind of the worry that God might have changed His mind about allowing the Jews to return to Judea. The point I'm making is this: a careful comparison of Daniel 8 and 9 makes it obvious that the primary purpose of the seventy-week prophecy in Daniel 9:24–27 was to answer Daniel's question about the 2,300-day prophecy in chapter 8:14.

There's even more specific evidence to support this conclusion. Two Hebrew words in chapters 8 and 9 are translated "vision" in our English Bibles: *hazon* and *mar'eh*. The English language doesn't have exact equivalents for these words; however, using the word *vision* for both of them works quite well for a casual reading of the text. But the specific meaning of each of these Hebrew words can assist us greatly in understanding Gabriel's precise meaning in chapter 9.

William Shea's* explanation of the meaning of these words is helpful. He says,

> [Mar'eh] comes from the root ra'â, which is the common verb used 1,140 times in the OT for the idea of seeing. Hāzôn comes from hāzâ, which appears much less frequently in the OT and which generally refers (although not exclusively) to the more specific act of seeing in prophetic vision. . . . [Mar'eh] is commonly used in contexts not connected with prophecy. [Mar'eh] refers to that which can be seen with the natural eye. . . . Generally, it should be noted in this connection that [mar'eh] refers to some aspect of the appearance of individuals, or personal beings.[3]

Notice that last sentence. Shea says that "[mar'eh] [generally] refers to some aspect of the appearance of individuals, or personal beings." So, in verse 16, where Gabriel is told to "make this man understand the [mar'eh]," he is especially being told to explain to Daniel the conversation between the two holy ones who show up in verses 13 and 14, and particularly the statement by one of them that the sanctuary would be cleansed after 2,300 evenings and mornings.

With this understanding of mar'eh in mind, let's look at how this word and also the word hazon are used in Daniel 8. In verses 1 and 2, Daniel said, "In the third year of the reign of King Belshazzar a vision [hazon] appeared to me. . . . I saw in the vision [hazon] that I was by the River Ulai" (emphasis added). Both of these occurrences of hazon obviously refer to the entire vision that Daniel received in chapter 8:3–14.[†]

The English word vision appears next in verse 13, where one holy being says to another, "How long will the vision [hazon] be?" Again, hazon means the entire vision.

Verses 15, 16, and 17 also contain the English word vision, but the Hebrew original alternates between hazon and mar'eh: "Then it happened, when I, Daniel, had seen the vision [hazon—the entire vision] and was seeking the meaning, that suddenly there stood before me one having the appearance of a man. And I heard a man's voice between the banks of the Ulai, who called, and said, 'Gabriel, make this man understand the vision [mar'eh—the interchange between the two holy ones about the 2,300 days and the sanctuary].' So he came near where I stood, and . . . said to me, 'Understand, son of man, that the vi-

---

*William Shea is a former professor at the Andrews University Adventist Theological Seminary in Berrien Springs, Michigan, and a former member of the General Conference Biblical Research Institute.

†The vision itself seems to have ended with verse 12. Verses 13 and 14 are audition, not vision; they are a part of the explanation of the vision Daniel received in verses 3–12. However, Daniel seems to still have been in a visionary state when he heard the two saints speaking in verses 13 and 14.

sion [*hazon*—the entire vision] refers to the time of the end' " (emphasis added). And Gabriel went on to explain the vision recorded in the first half of the chapter.

The English word *vision* occurs three times in the last two verses of the chapter, which contain the end of Gabriel's explanation of the entire vision and Daniel's reaction to it: "[Gabriel said,] 'The *vision* [*mar'eh*—the interchange about the 2,300 days and the sanctuary] of the evenings and mornings which was told is true; therefore seal up the *vision* [*hazon*—the entire vision], for it refers to many days in the future.' And I, Daniel, fainted and was sick for days; afterward I arose and went about the king's business. I was astonished by the *vision* [*mar'eh*—the interchange about the 2,300 days and the sanctuary], but no one understood it."

Notice that it was especially this *mar'eh* of the evenings and mornings—the 2,300 days and the sanctuary—that so shocked Daniel that he fainted and became ill. No wonder the next chapter pictures him trying to figure out how this information related to Jeremiah's seventy years!

Finally, let's look at the word *vision* in chapter 9:21, 23. Daniel said, "While I was speaking in prayer, the man Gabriel, whom I had seen in the vision [*hazon*—the entire vision] at the beginning, . . . [came to me and said,] . . . 'Consider the matter, and understand the vision [*mar'eh*—the interchange about the 2,300 days and the sanctuary]." So

Gabriel, who had explained almost the entire *hazon* to Daniel in chapter 8, came again to finish his explanation of the *mar'eh*—the cleansing of the sanctuary and the 2,300 evenings and mornings—which had ended prematurely when Daniel fainted.

The seventy weeks

Interestingly, however, in his explanation in chapter 9:24–27, Gabriel never mentioned either the 2,300 days or Jeremiah's seventy-year prophecy. Instead, he addressed Daniel's primary concern, the fate of the Jewish people. In his prayer, Daniel had pled with God to "open Your eyes and see our desolations, and the city which is called by Your name. . . . O Lord, hear! O Lord, forgive! O Lord, listen and act! Do not delay for Your own sake, my God, for *Your city* and *Your people* are called by Your name" (verses 18, 19; emphasis added).

Now notice the first words of Gabriel's explanation: "Seventy weeks are determined for *your people* and for *your holy city*" (verse 24; emphasis added). Gabriel began his explanation with the very issue that most concerned Daniel. He said that seventy weeks had been "determined," or set aside, for the Jews ("your people") and Jerusalem ("your holy city"). That was enough for Daniel. His people would return to their homeland, and their city would be rebuilt. My guess is that with this answer, he didn't spend any more nights worrying about the 2,300 evenings and mornings.

But the return of the Jews and the rebuilding of Jerusalem are ancient history to us. We want to know exactly when in the 208 years between 1762 and 1970 those 2,300 years are supposed to have ended. Did Gabriel's answer to Daniel provide us with *that* information?

The answer is Yes. It's in the Hebrew word *hatak*.* Gabriel said, "Seventy weeks are determined [*hatak*] for your people and for your holy city" (verse 24).

What does *hatak* mean? The King James Version and the New King James Version translate the word as "determined," while the Revised Standard Version, New American Standard Bible, and most other modern translations say "decreed." Seventh-day Adventists have quite consistently over the years said that *hatak* means "to cut." Is that what it means in Daniel 9:24?

The best way to learn the meaning of a word in the Bible is to look for its use elsewhere, especially in the Bible. However, the word *hatak* doesn't appear anywhere else in the Old Testament. Thus, we're left looking for its use in other ancient Hebrew sources, such as the Mishnah and the Talmud.† William Shea has made a detailed study of *hatak* in the ancient Hebrew literature. Because the definition of this word is crucial to the Adventist understanding of the 2,300 years, I'll quote Shea's conclusions somewhat at length:

Hatak is used more often in Mishnaic sources in the sense of "cut" than it is in the sense of "determine." *Hatak* is used as a verb in at least ten Mishnaic passages, where it refers to cutting off parts of the bodies of animals according to the dietary laws. It is also used in connection with circumcision, for cutting a lamp wick, and for a miner cutting out ore. On two other occasions it refers to the lips or mouth cutting off words and to [the] cutting into two parts a verse of Scripture being read.

As a verb with the less-frequent meaning of "decide or determine," *hatak* is used twice to refer to the action of a judge in deciding a case and once for deciding the affairs of state. *Hatak* occurs as a noun in Mishnaic sources at least 18 times with the meaning of "that which is cut off"; whereas it occurs only once with reference to the law as given in the form of decisions. Thus the more common verbal meaning and the very common nominal meaning of *hatak* in Mishnaic Hebrew have to do with the idea of cutting.[4]

---

*The word used in Daniel 9:24 is *nehtak,* which is the passive form of *hatak.*

†The Talmud is a commentary by ancient rabbis on Jewish law, customs, and history. The Mishnah is a part of the Talmud, though it is often referred to as if it were a separate body of writings.

Words change in meaning over time, as any English-speaking person knows who has ever tried to read Shakespeare's original works, so it's possible that in Daniel's time *hatak* meant something different than what it meant several hundred years later when the Mishnah was written. This, of course, is as much a problem for those who understand *hatak* to mean "decreed" as it is for those who understand it to mean "cut." On this point, Shea comments,

Working from the principle of Semitic philology, that the extended meanings of roots developed from concrete concepts in the direction of abstract concepts, we must posit "cut" as the original Proto-Semitic connotation of . . . *hatak*. Thus from the action of cutting came the idea of cutting a decision* and finally just deciding. . . .

We may summarize this discussion thus far by suggesting that *hatak* originally derived from the idea of "cut" and that idea still predominates in its use in Mishnaic Hebrew. . . . We may [also] suggest that the idea of "cut" probably predominated even more in Daniel's time than in the Mishnaic period. [5]

Shea isn't the only scholar to suggest

that "cut" is the original meaning of *hatak*. In his doctoral dissertation, *The Chronology of Daniel 9:24–27*, Brempong Owusu-Antwi noted several other scholars who affirmed the same thing.[6] And Desmond Ford said, "All lexicographers declare that [*hatak*] literally means 'cut off,' "[7] and, "*Chathak* [his transliteration of *hatak*] means 'cut' or 'decree.' "[8]

The seventy weeks and the 2,300 days

How then does the word *hatak* give us the starting point for the 2,300 days of Daniel 8:14? Notice how Daniel 9:24 reads when the word *cut* is used. "Seventy weeks are [*cut off*] for your people and for your holy city." From the time of William Miller to the present, Adventists have said that the 490 days/years were *cut off* from the longer 2,300 days/years.[†] The reasoning is simple.

- The only part of Daniel's vision in chapter 8 that Gabriel hadn't explained to Daniel was the cleansing of the sanctuary and the 2,300 days.
- The first nineteen verses of chapter 9 make it obvious that the cleansing of the sanctuary, the 2,300 days, and their relationship to Jeremiah's seventy years were of tremendous concern to Daniel.
- While chapter 9 doesn't quote Gabriel

---

*I'm reminded of the English expression "cutting a check."

†William Miller understood the seventy weeks to have been "cut off" from the longer 2,300 days; see P. Gerard Damsteegt, *Foundations of the Seventh-day Adventist Message and Mission*, 36, footnote 178.

as mentioning the 2,300 days when he came to Daniel, it says he told Daniel that he had come to explain the *mar'eh*—that is, the part of the vision in chapter 8 that dealt with the cleansing of the sanctuary and the 2,300 days.

- The seventy weeks were "cut," which means that they were *cut from* a larger whole—namely, the 2,300 days that Gabriel had come to explain.
- Therefore, the beginning point of the 2,300 days is the same as the beginning point of the seventy weeks.

That's the logic of the Adventist interpretation of Daniel 8 and 9, the 2,300 days, and the seventy weeks. Ford, in his Glacier View manuscript, said, "There is no way of proving that the cutting off of the 490 from [the] 2300 is intended."[9] This, of course, is true. Daniel didn't say in so many words that the 490 years were a part of the 2,300 years or that they were to be cut from that time period. However, scholars draw many conclusions from the Bible based on reasonable inferences from the evidence that the Bible provides, and it makes sense to me that this is one of those instances. I accept this explanation for a couple of reasons. First, Gabriel stated very specifically that he had come to Daniel for the purpose of explaining more about chapter 8:14—that is,

the 2,300 days and the cleansing of the sanctuary at the end of that period. And second, cutting the seventy weeks from the 2,300 days is the *only* way to arrive at a date for the beginning and ending of the 2,300-day prophecy. The alternative is a nebulous 208-year period for beginning and ending the 2,300 days.

This is the biblical basis for concluding that the 2,300 days/years of Daniel 8:14 began at the same time as the 490 years of Daniel 9:24, 25. However, what I have explained up to this point still doesn't give us the date 457 B.C. as the time when the seventy weeks began. For that, we must turn to Daniel 9:24, 25, which I will deal with in the next two chapters.

---

1. Gerhard Hasel, "Interpretations of the Chronology of the Seventy Weeks," in *70 Weeks, Leviticus, Nature of Prophecy*, 5.

2. J. A. Montgomery, *A Commentary on Daniel*, ICC (1927), 400, quoted in Gerhard Hasel, "Interpretations of the Chronology of the Seventy Weeks," in *70 Weeks, Leviticus, Nature of Prophecy*, 6.

3. William Shea, "The Relationship Between the Prophecies of Daniel 8 and Daniel 9," in *The Sanctuary and the Atonement*, 232.

4. Ibid., 242.

5. Ibid., 243.

6. Owusu-Antwi, *The Chronology of Daniel 9:24–27*, 228.

7. Ford, *Daniel*, 225.

8. Ford, "Daniel 8:14," 288.

9. Ibid.

Chapter 24

The Purpose of the Seventy Weeks

Have you ever had a truly inspiring moment? Maybe you've experienced one while looking at a painting of a gorgeous sunset or hearing a beautiful piece of music. Think of how the artist who painted the sunset or the composer who wrote the beautiful music must have felt at the time he or she was painting or composing! All of us have inspiring moments from time to time, and when the inspiration is related to something we're talented at doing, we feel a special joy in carrying out that activity.

Daniel must have felt that way when Gabriel came to him because he wrote out what Gabriel told him as a poem. This isn't surprising, given the good news that Daniel's people would return to their homeland and rebuild their city. In the previous chapter of this book, we examined the first two lines of the poem in Daniel 9:24, which were about the seventy weeks. In the remainder of verse 24, which I will discuss in this chapter, Gabriel explained the purpose of the seventy weeks. And because the passage is in a poetic format, it will be easiest to analyze it poetic line by poetic line. I've numbered the lines in order to facilitate the discussion.

William Shea points out that the last six lines of verse 24 are divided into three pairs, like this:[1]

First pair
1. "To finish the transgression,
2. To make an end of sins,"

Second pair

3. "To make reconciliation for iniquity,
4. To bring in everlasting righteousness,"

Third pair

5. "To seal up vision and prophecy,
6. And to anoint the Most Holy."

In the first two lines of verse 24, Gabriel had just told Daniel that seventy weeks were "set aside" for his people and their city, Jerusalem. Seventh-day Adventists understand that Gabriel meant God was extending the probation of the Jewish nation by seventy weeks, which equals 490 days, or 490 years on the year-day principle.* This probationary period began in 457 B.C., and it ended in A.D. 34. I'll explain the mathematics behind these dates in the next chapter; our primary concern in this chapter is what Gabriel said was to occur *during* those 490 years. That's what the last six lines of verse 24 tell us. In the discussion that follows I'll comment on each of the six lines.

The first pair

In the first pair of lines, Gabriel pointed out the righteous society that God wanted the Jews to establish during their 490 years of probationary time.

Line 1: "To finish the transgression." The Hebrew word for "transgression" in this clause is *pesha'*, which we saw in several previous chapters has the primary meaning of "rebellion." Prior to their captivity in 605–586 B.C., the Jews had rebelled against Nebuchadnezzar. However, their primary rebellion had been against God, and it was this that led to their exile in Babylon. Now Gabriel was telling Daniel that God was giving the Jews 490 years to end their rebellion and demonstrate their loyalty to Him. As William Shea put it, "The opening phrase of [Gabriel's explanation] delimits a period of probation during which God's people are called to manifest their loyalty and not their rebellion toward Him."[2]

Line 2: "To make an end of sins." The Hebrew word for "make an end of" is *hatam*, which means "to seal up," "to complete," or "to bring to an end."[3] Nearly all English translations of the Bible recognize Gabriel's meaning to be "to bring to an end."

The Hebrew word for "sins" in this line is *hatta't*, which, as we saw in previous chapters, means sin in general. Thus, this clause is complementary to the previous one. Together, they are an encouragement to the Jews "to bring an end to the sinful state of their society, . . . [and] to construct a righteous society."[4] Had they done this, they would still be the people through whom God especially communicates His love and salvation to the world. However,

*I'll discuss the year-day principle in detail in chapter 27.

the New Testament indicates that, unfortunately, they chose otherwise.

The second pair

The second pair of lines tells what Jesus would do near the end of the seventy weeks of Jewish probation.

Line 3: "To make reconciliation for iniquity." The Hebrew word for "iniquity" is *awon,* which means "to be guilty." Thus, Daniel 9:24 includes all three of the basic Hebrew words for sin: *pesha'* ("rebellion"), *hatta't* ("sin"), and *awon* ("iniquity"). The only other chapter in the Old Testament where these three words occur together is Leviticus 16, which describes the activities on the Day of Atonement. Thus, Daniel 9:24 has strong Day of Atonement overtones. And, of course, Jesus, by His death on the cross, fulfilled all the sacrifices of the Israelite tabernacle service, including those that were offered by the high priest on the Day of Atonement. The rest of heaven's Day of Atonement is being fulfilled by the investigative judgment that is going on right now in the heavenly sanctuary, and it will end with the final eradication of sin in the lake of fire at the close of the millennium.

The Hebrew word for "reconciliation" in Daniel 9:24 is *kippur.* In Leviticus, this word states the purpose of the sacrifices the Israelites brought to the sanctuary for their sins throughout the year. For example, Leviticus 4:26 says that as a result of the sinner's sacrifice, "the priest shall make atonement [*kippur*] for him concerning his sin, and it shall be forgiven him." Thus, Gabriel was telling Daniel that at some point during the 490 years of Jewish probation, Jesus would die for the sins of the world, and, in so doing, He would make "reconciliation for iniquity."

Line 4: "To bring in everlasting righteousness." We've already met this concept in Daniel, though not expressed in these particular words. Daniel 7:27 says that as a result of the investigative judgment, dominion over the world will be given to the Son of man and His saints, and "His kingdom [will be] an everlasting kingdom, and all dominions shall serve and obey Him." The whole world's service and obedience to the Son of man in God's eternal kingdom means the same thing as "everlasting righteousness."

Today, we still look forward to the establishment of God's eternal kingdom. What, then, did Gabriel mean in Daniel 9:24 when he said that everlasting righteousness would be established during the 490 years of Jewish probation?

Jesus often spoke of His "kingdom" as a reality in His day. For example, in the parable of the wheat and the weeds, He said, "The kingdom of heaven *is* like a man who sowed good seed in his field" (Matthew 13:24; emphasis added). Notice the present tense: "is." The parable doesn't show the establishment of Jesus' dominion over the world until His second coming (see verses 41–43). Nevertheless, the entire parable describes "the kingdom of heaven" as if it had already been established. The same is true of the parables of the ten virgins and the ten talents in Matthew 25. In both, Jesus began by stating what the kingdom of God "is" like, and then He stated the mission and condition of His people in the world prior to His second coming.

In this sense, the kingdom of God means the change that occurs in the minds and hearts of those who accept Jesus as their Savior. The Bible speaks of this change as "conversion" or "the new birth" (see Matthew 18:3; John 3:1–8). While people in Old Testament times experienced conversion, Jesus achieved the legal basis for this transformation by His death on the cross. It is in this sense that Gabriel said "everlasting righteousness" would be ushered in during the 490 years of Jewish probationary time. The everlasting righteousness that we will experience following Christ's second coming begins in our lives whenever we accept Jesus and experience His converting power.

The third pair

In the third pair of lines, Gabriel told Daniel two things that would happen at the end of the seventy weeks or 490 years.

Line 5: "To seal up vision and prophecy." In Hebrew, this clause consists of three words: *hatam,* which is translated "seal up"; *hazon,* which means "vision"; and *navi,* which means "prophet." Let's examine each of these words.

Hatam. Most English versions translate this clause "*to seal up* [*hatam*] vision and prophecy" (emphasis added). Translated this way, *hatam* can be understood to mean that the exact fulfillment of the seventy-week prophecy would "seal up," or confirm, the validity of the vision of chapter 8 and Gabriel's explanation of it in chapter 9. After all, only the God of heaven would have the kind of accurate and detailed knowledge about the future that we find in Daniel 9:24, 25. This has been a fairly common explanation among Adventists. However, it's also possible to translate this clause, "to *make an end* of vision and prophet." I'll explain the significance of this translation after examining the other two words in the clause.

Hazon. I pointed out in chapter 23 that *hazon* means "vision." There is no article with *hazon*—a detail that is reflected in the translation of most English versions: "to seal up vision and prophecy," not "to seal up *the* vision and prophecy." The significance of this will also become apparent in a moment.

Navi. This word means "prophet." Most English versions translate it as "prophecy," but the Revised Standard Version says "prophet," and this seems to be the more accurate rendition.

We are now ready to discuss the significance of this clause when it is translated "to make an end of vision and prophet." Seventh-day Adventists have always said that the martyrdom of Stephen marked the end of the seventy weeks, and I agree with that interpretation. (I'll explain the chronological basis for it in the additional note at the end of the next chapter.) Shea points out that Stephen's speech before the Sanhedrin, which led to his martyrdom, was "what is known in Hebrew as a *rib* or 'covenant lawsuit.' "[5] A "covenant lawsuit" is a prophet's condemnation of the nation of Israel for their violation of God's covenant with them. Beginning with Abraham, Stephen reviewed the history of Israel up to the time of Solomon. Then he rebuked the members of the Sanhedrin: "You stiff-necked and uncircumcised in heart and ears! You always resist the Holy Spirit; as your fathers did, so do you. Which of the prophets did your fathers not persecute? And they killed those who foretold the coming of the Just One, of whom you now have become the betrayers and murderers, who have received the law by the direction of angels and have not kept it" (Acts 7:51–53).

At this point, Stephen received a vision of God. He said, "Look! I see the heavens opened and the Son of Man standing at the right hand of God!" (verse 56). The members of the Sanhedrin understood perfectly well that by "Son of Man," Stephen meant Jesus. This so enraged them that they dragged Stephen out of Jerusalem and stoned him to death. By this act they closed their probation, bringing to an end the seventy weeks or 490 years of probationary time for their nation.

Shea points out that "when the Holy Spirit came upon Stephen, he was given a vision of heaven. By definition Stephen became a prophet at this time. [For] it is to prophets that God gives visions of Himself like this."[6] So Stephen brought the covenant lawsuit against the Sanhedrin in his God-given role as a prophet. And when the Sanhedrin—the official representatives of the Jewish nation—rejected God's message to them through His new prophet, they closed their probation as a nation. Of course, individual Jews could still receive salvation through faith in Jesus, but as a nation they were no longer His chosen instrument to carry the message of salvation to the world. From then on, God worked through the Christian church. This is the background we need to understand Gabriel's words to Daniel that part of the purpose of the seventy weeks was "to make an end of vision and prophet." Shea commented, "Stephen is the last prophet to speak to the Jewish people of Judea as the elect people of God. But his voice is silenced in death by stoning. In silencing him they also silence the prophetic voice addressed to them with finality. . . .

"As far as Daniel's own people are concerned 'vision' and 'prophet' were sealed up or brought to an end with the rejection of this final prophet sent to them according to Acts 7."[7]

Line 6: "And to anoint the Most Holy." The key question here is the identity of "the Most Holy." During the first few centuries of Christianity, interpreters applied it to the anointing of Jesus as the Messiah at His baptism. However, the Hebrew words *qodesh qodashim* suggest a different interpretation. These words occur more than forty times in the Old Testament outside of the book of Daniel, and they always refer to the sanctuary, not to persons.* So far as I know, all Adventist interpreters today agree that *qodesh qodashim* in Daniel 9:24 refers to the sanctuary, not to Christ. And since the only valid sanctuary at the end of the seventy weeks was the one in heaven, the "anointing" of that sanctuary refers to its dedication or inauguration at the time Christ began His ministry after His ascension.

Twenty-five hundred years ago, God laid out a tremendous spiritual challenge to His people in the seventy-week prophecy. His vision for His people today is just as ambitious as it was then. Our challenge is, by the power of His Holy Spirit, to fulfill that vision today.

---

1. William Shea, "The Prophecy of Daniel 9:24–27," in *70 Weeks, Leviticus, Nature of Prophecy,* 78–84. My comments throughout this chapter are largely based on Shea's analysis.
2. Ibid., 78.
3. Ibid.
4. Ibid., 79.
5. Ibid., 81.
6. Ibid.
7. Ibid., 82.

---

*1 Chronicles 23:13 is a possible exception (for example, see the NASB), but most versions translate *qodesh qodashim* in this verse as "holy things," not a holy person, and Shea agrees (see *70 Weeks, Leviticus, and the Nature of Prophecy,* 83).

Chapter 25

The Beginning and End of the Sixty-Nine Weeks

What did Gabriel mean when he told Daniel that seventy weeks had been set aside, decreed, "cut off," for his people? The word *week* is a chronological statement. It means a period of seven days. When we multiply seventy weeks times the seven days in a week, we come up with 490 days. So how are we to understand these seventy weeks or 490 days? Did Gabriel have in mind a literal period of 490 days, which amounts to a little over a year and a third? And when was this period supposed to begin, and when was it supposed to end? Without answers to these questions, Gabriel's announcement to Daniel that seventy weeks had been set aside for his people is meaningless.

Fortunately, Gabriel went on to explain very specifically when the seventy weeks would begin and end. Here's what he said,

"Know therefore and understand,
That from the going forth of the command
To restore and build Jerusalem
Until Messiah the Prince
There shall be seven weeks and sixty-two weeks;
The street shall be built again and the wall,
Even in troublesome times."

Notice the very specific information Gabriel gave Daniel about the beginning and end of the seventy weeks: "*From* the going forth of the command to restore and build Jerusalem *until* the Messiah the Prince . . ." (emphasis added). In the remainder of this chapter, I'll analyze these words that Gabriel spoke to Daniel. I'll begin by sharing with you the traditional Adventist interpretation, which I hope this chapter will convince you is entirely biblical.

How Adventists interpret Daniel 9:25

Gabriel told Daniel that "from the going forth of the command to restore and build Jerusalem until Messiah the Prince" would be "seven weeks and sixty-two weeks." Simple mathematics tells us that seven plus sixty-two equals sixty-nine. Gabriel identified the beginning and ending points of these sixty-nine weeks very specifically. They were to begin with a command for the Jews to restore and build Jerusalem and end with Messiah the Prince. If we can figure out when a command or decree was issued to restore and build Jerusalem, then another simple mathematical calculation should take us to the date for the appearance of Messiah the Prince—who, for most of the past two thousand years, Christians have identified as Jesus Christ.* Seventh-day Ad-

ventists agree with this interpretation.

Three Persian emperors issued a total of four decrees that might be considered as qualifying as the beginning point of this prophecy, though not all of them were formal decrees. They are

- A decree by Cyrus in 538/537 B.C. (Ezra 1:2–4)
- A decree by Darius in about 520 B.C. (Ezra 6:3–12)
- A decree by Artaxerxes I in 457 B.C. (Ezra 7:12–26)
- A "decree" by the same Artaxerxes in 444 B.C.[2] (Nehemiah 2:1–8)

Seventh-day Adventists have consistently said the decree issued by Artaxerxes in 457 B.C. is the one that Gabriel referred to. Gabriel said that from that point to the appearance of Christ would be seven weeks plus sixty-two weeks, which is a total of sixty-nine weeks or 483 days. That's 483 years on the year-day principle. You are no doubt aware that in B.C. time, the numbers by which the years are identified decrease as one moves forward in time—457, 456, 455, etc. And since 457 is less than 483, we have to subtract 457 from 483 and add the remainder to A.D. time, like this:

---

*In fact, there is evidence that as early as the mid-second century B.C., the Essene sect at Qumran interpreted Daniel 9:25 as a reference to the coming Messiah.[1] The Essenes were an ultraconservative sect of Jews who lived in a community near the Dead Sea called Qumran for a couple centuries, till the Roman destruction of Jerusalem in A.D. 70. Their scribes wrote the scrolls that are now known as the Dead Sea Scrolls.

483   (7 weeks + 62 weeks x 7 days per week = 483 days/years)

– 457   (The date in B.C. time of the command to restore and build Jerusalem)

26   (The date in A.D. time for Messiah the Prince—Jesus—to appear)

However, we must make a minor adjustment to this calculation. Since there is no year 0 between 1 B.C. and A.D. 1, we have to add a year to our calculation. Thus, we should expect Jesus, the Messiah, to have appeared in A.D. 27.

You may be aware that the Hebrew word *messiah* means "anointed one." Jesus was anointed for His mission at His baptism, when the Holy Spirit descended on Him in the form of a dove. I find it extremely significant that the most detailed bit of chronological data in the New Testament, which is found in Luke 3:1–3, gives us very precise information about when Jesus was baptized. Luke wrote, "Now in the fifteenth year of the reign of Tiberius Caesar, Pontius Pilate being governor of Judea, Herod being tetrarch of Galilee, his brother Philip tetrarch of Iturea and the region of Trachonitis, and Lysanias tetrarch of Abilene, while Annas and Caiaphas were high priests, the word of God came to John the son of Zacharias in the wilderness. And he went into all the region around the Jordan, preaching a baptism of repentance for the remission of sins."

The fifteenth year of the reign of Tiberius Caesar was almost certainly A.D. 27.* Thus, according to the mathematical calculation I shared with you above, Jesus arrived precisely on time! This is how Seventh-day Adventists have traditionally interpreted Daniel 9:25. However, this interpretation has not gone without its challenges.

"From the . . . command"

The first challenge to this interpretation has to do with the meaning of the word that is translated *command* in the New King James Version: "From the going forth of the *command* to restore and build Jerusalem . . ." (emphasis added). The Hebrew word for "command" is *dabar,* which has the primary meaning of "word" but in some contexts can mean "decree," "matter,"

---

*I say "almost certainly," because there is some question as to whether Luke was using the Jewish or the Roman method of calculating the fifteenth year of Tiberius Caesar. In an article on New Testament chronology, the *Seventh-day Adventist Bible Commentary* concludes that it seems "most probable" that he used the Jewish method, which would date the fifteenth year of Tiberius Caesar as A.D. 27 (see *Seventh-day Adventist Bible Commentary,* 5:242–247, especially 247).

"thing," and even "cause."[3] It especially means "command" or "decree" when it is used in the sense of an order issued by God or an earthly king. The angel Gabriel used the word *dabar* when he said to Daniel, "At the beginning of your supplications the command [*dabar*] went out . . ." (verse 23). In this verse, it was clearly God who commanded Gabriel to interpret the vision to Daniel. Because of this, some interpreters have suggested that the "command [*dabar*] to restore and build Jerusalem" in verse 25 was simply a part of God's command to Gabriel in verse 23. Raymond Cottrell adopted this interpretation. He said, "Contextually, the 'word' that 'went out . . . to restore and rebuild Jerusalem' is the very 'word' that 'went out' . . . in response to Daniel's prayer. . . . Gabriel assures Daniel that *God Himself,* not some earthly monarch, had already answered his fervent prayer! Obviously that 'word' is one that only God Himself could possibly have issued, not some earthly monarch!"[4]

Where did Cottrell get the idea that God alone could issue a decree to restore and build Jerusalem? Who said that a human king couldn't issue such a decree? Far from the context *denying* that a human king could make this proclamation, the context suggests that a human king *would* issue such a decree. I have to agree with Brempong Owusu-Antwi, who in his dissertation, *The Chronology of Daniel 9:24–27,* said, "The context of the expression in Dan 9:25 involves a proclamation that would change the political and physical status of Jerusalem. . . . Thus *dabar* makes sense chronologically in the context of Dan 9:24–28 when it is regarded as a historical 'word,' that is, a pronouncement, command, or the like, which can be concretely marked out in a historical situation from which it goes forth."[5]

By a "historical 'word' . . . [that] can be concretely marked out in a historical situation," Owusu-Antwi means a human "word" or "decree" that we can date to a specific time in human history. Thus, the most logical conclusion is that a human king would and did issue the *dabar*—the "command [or decree] to restore and build Jerusalem." While Cottrell is not alone in his interpretation that the *dabar* in verse 25 is the same as God's *dabar* to Gabriel in verse 23, I believe I am correct in saying that the majority of scholars consider this *dabar* to refer to a command by an earthly king.

The decree "to restore and build Jerusalem"

A few pages back, I mentioned four decrees issued by Persian kings that might be considered the one Gabriel referred to. I will discuss the first two briefly and the third and fourth in greater detail.

The first decree was issued by Cyrus.

This decree is recorded in Ezra 1:2–4. It gave the Jews permission to return to their homeland and rebuild their temple, which they did under the leadership of Zerubbabel (Ezra 5:2). However, Adventists, along with many other scholars, recognize that the decree by Cyrus said nothing about restoring a measure of political independence to the Jews or about rebuilding Jerusalem, and therefore it doesn't qualify as the fulfillment of Gabriel's prediction.

The second decree was issued by Darius. When the Jews began their construction of the temple, the governor of the region, a man by the name of Tattenai, challenged them: "Who has commanded you to build this temple and finish this wall?" (verse 3). The Jews responded by citing the decree of Cyrus, but that wasn't enough for Tattenai. He wanted to *see* the decree. Today, a simple phone call, e-mail, or fax would suffice to verify such a decree, but our technology wasn't available to the Jews, and they didn't have a copy of the decree to show to Tattenai. So Tattenai wrote a letter to the emperor, who by this time was a man named Darius (verses 6–17), asking that a search be made in the royal archives to determine whether Cyrus had indeed issued such a decree.

Darius complied, and the decree was found. So Darius wrote back, informing Tattenai that Cyrus had indeed issued the decree in question (Ezra 6:3–12) and telling him to stay away from the temple construction project and let it go forward (verses 6, 7). In fact, he also ordered that the costs of the building project be paid from his own tax receipts (verse 8)! However, this decree by Darius was simply a reaffirmation of the original decree by Cyrus for the rebuilding of the temple. Since it wasn't a new decree, and since it again said nothing about Jewish independence or the rebuilding of the city of Jerusalem, Adventists, along with most other scholars, discount it as a fulfillment of Gabriel's prediction.

The first decree by Artaxerxes

Artaxerxes issued two decrees that scholars have suggested fulfill Gabriel's prediction. His first decree (which followed those by Cyrus and Darius) was issued in 457 B.C. You can read it in Ezra 7:12–26. This is the one that Adventists have historically considered to have fulfilled Gabriel's prediction. We need to examine two challenges that have been made to this conclusion.

The date 457 B.C. The first problem has to do with the date 457 B.C. Some scholars have suggested that Artaxerxes issued his first decree in 458 rather than 457. However, back in the mid-twentieth century, two Adventist archaeologists, Siegfried H. Horn and Lynn H. Wood, made a detailed study of the evidence from ancient sources, which they reported in a 160-page book titled, *The Chronology of Ezra 7.* They concluded that Ezra journeyed to Palestine in the spring and early summer of 457 B.C., and Artaxerxes' decree went into effect in late summer or early fall.[6] The Protestant scholar Walter R. Martin investigated Adventist teachings in detail during the mid-1950s, and after studying the evidence for the 457 date, he concluded that it is "the now verified time of the decree to rebuild Jerusalem."[7]

Also, a footnote to Daniel 9:24 in the *Harper Study Bible* says,

> The *terminus a quo* for the commencement of these sixty-nine weeks of years is stated to be *from the going forth of the word* (or decree) *to restore and build Jerusalem* (ver 25). This may refer to the divine decree, or one of three historical edicts: (1) the decree of King Cyrus in 538 B.C. (Ezra 1.1–4); (2) the order of Artaxerxes to Ezra in 457 B.C. (which apparently involved authority to erect the walls of Jerusalem, cf. Ezra 7.6, 7; 9.9); (3) the order to Nehemiah in 445 B.C. to carry through the rebuilding of the walls (which Ezra had not been able to accomplish). Of these choices, (1) must be ruled out as coming nowhere near to the time of Christ's ministry; (3) comes out too late, unless lunar years are used for the computation. Only (2) comes out right according to regular solar years, for it yields the result

of A.D. 27, or the commencement of Christ's ministry.[8]

My conclusion is that the Adventist dating of Artaxerxes' first decree to 457 B.C. is very reasonable.

No mention of the rebuilding of the temple. A second problem has to do with the event that was supposed to mark the beginning of the sixty-nine (and seventy) weeks: the issuing of a decree "to restore and build Jerusalem." Reading these words in English, one gets the impression that the words *restore* and *build* are synonyms, both of which refer to the same activity—something like saying "weep and cry." I think most students of Daniel 9 have assumed that the words *restore* and *build* both have to do with the reconstruction of Jerusalem.

The problem is that Artaxerxes' decree as recorded by Ezra in chapter 7 doesn't say anything about rebuilding Jerusalem. Construction on the temple had been completed more than fifty years earlier,[9] so Artaxerxes' decree was not about that. His decree authorized five things.

- It gave permission to any Jew who so desired to return to Jerusalem.
- It permitted those Jews who returned to take with them the money they would need to buy sacrificial animals and pay for other expenses related to the temple service.

- It ordered the officials of the Persian government in Palestine to provide the Jews with silver, wheat, wine, oil, and salt for the temple service.
- It forbade the taxation of the priests and other temple workers.
- It authorized the Jews to appoint "magistrates and judges who may judge all the people who are in the region beyond the River [Euphrates]" (Ezra 7:25).

Because there isn't a single word about rebuilding Jerusalem in the decree issued by Artaxerxes in 457 B.C., many scholars have concluded that it didn't fulfill the specifications of Gabriel's prediction about rebuilding Jerusalem. On the other hand, a decree by Artaxerxes in 444 B.C., which I will discuss below, gave specific authorization to Nehemiah to complete the construction of Jerusalem's walls. This is why some scholars look to that decree as the one that fulfilled Gabriel's statement that the seventy weeks would begin with a command to restore and build Jerusalem.

So what justification is there for considering Artaxerxes' 457 B.C. decree as the one that marked the beginning of the seventy weeks?

Restoring and building Jerusalem

The basic issue is whether Gabriel's words *restore* and *build* are synonyms, both referring to the reconstruction of Jerusalem, or whether they refer to two distinct aspects of the Jewish return to Palestine. Owusu-Antwi points out that the Hebrew words for *restore* and *build* aren't synonyms. They express "different ideas in the context of Dan 9:25 and apply to different aspects of Jerusalem."[10] I will discuss the word *restore* first and then the word *build*.

1. "Restore" Jerusalem. Nebuchadnezzar invaded Judea three times between 605 and 586 B.C. Two things happened as a result. First, the Jewish political system was dismantled, with the result that the Jews ceased to exist as a nation. Second, the Jews' temple and their city were destroyed. Gabriel's explanation to Daniel predicted that both of these situations would be reversed.

The word *restore* is a translation of the Hebrew word *l'hasib,* which is the infinitive form of the word *sub.* Owusu-Antwi made a detailed analysis of *sub* in the Hebrew Bible.[11] He concluded that in the Old Testament, when the causative form of *sub* (called the *Hiphil* in Hebrew grammar) is used with land, city, or nation as its object, it refers to the restoration of a people's political control over their city or nation, not to the rebuilding of the physical structures of those cities or nations. I will share with you enough of the evidence he cites to make his point clear. Note that in each instance a land or a city is the direct object of *sub*—that is, the thing being restored. (The italics in the Scripture quotations are all added.)

- Judges 11:13—When the Israelites first entered Canaan, they conquered the Amorites, who years earlier had conquered the Ammonites and taken over their land. Several centuries later, the king of the Ammonites demanded of Jephthah (one of the judges of Israel) that he "*restore* [*Hiphil* form of *sub*] those lands peaceably." In this case, *sub* clearly means the restoration of control, of governance, since no one could "rebuild" land.

- 2 Samuel 9:7—David was a close friend of King Saul's son Jonathan. When David became king over Israel, he wanted to show kindness to Jonathan's relatives, so he told Jonathan's son Mephibosheth that he would "*restore* [*Hiphil* form of *sub*] to you all the land of Saul your grandfather." Again, *sub* clearly means the restoration of control over the land, not the rebuilding of physical structures.

- 1 Kings 20:34—When the Israelites defeated the Syrians, Ben-Hadad, the Syrian king, proposed a treaty with the Israelites. He said to Ahab, king of Israel, "The cities which my father took from your father I will *restore* [*Hiphil* form of *sub*]." Again, the issue

is restoration of governance, not rebuilding anything.

- 2 Kings 16:6—"At that time Rezin king of Syria *captured* [*Hiphil* form of *sub*, "restored"] Elath for Syria, and drove the men of Judah from Elath." Again, the meaning of *sub* clearly has to do with the restoration of governance, not rebuilding.

Owusu-Antwi draws the following conclusion from his analysis of the biblical usage of the Hebrew word *sub* in Daniel 9:25: "All *Hiphil* forms of *sub* with 'land,' 'city,' or 'kingdom' as direct object . . . give evidence for a meaning of restoration of ownership or control (i.e., governance). Therefore, based on the analogy of the usage of *Hiphil* forms of *sub* surveyed in the Old Testament, I would suggest that the *Hiphil* infinitive 'to restore' in Dan 9:25 refers to the restoration of the control and governance of Jerusalem, before the rebuilding of physical structures can take place."[12]

Here's the point: *the restoration of governance to the Jews over Judea* **is** *mentioned in Artaxerxes' first decree, the 457* B.C. *decree.* Artaxerxes said, "And you, Ezra, according to your God-given wisdom, set magistrates and judges who may judge all the people who are in the region beyond the River [Euphrates], all such as know the laws of your God" (Ezra 7:25). In authorizing Ezra to appoint magistrates and judges, Artaxerxes was restoring a measure of autonomy, of self-governance, to the Jewish people. In verse 26, Artaxerxes also authorized the punishment of any who refused to observe the laws of God, even to the point of executing them! Thus, Artaxerxes was clearly giving the Jews the authority to govern themselves. And that is precisely what the word *restore*—the translation of the Hebrew word *sub*—means in Daniel 9:25. Thus, Artaxerxes' decree *did* fulfill the *restore* specification of Gabriel's statement, "From the going forth of the command to *restore* and build Jerusalem" (emphasis added).

2. "Build" Jerusalem. But what about the *building* part of Gabriel's statement? I will mention a couple of factors that need to be considered.

First, it's possible that Ezra's account of Artaxerxes' decree didn't include everything the decree said. I say this because Ezra gave two accounts of the first decree by Cyrus, and they are quite different from each other. Cyrus's decree as recorded in Ezra 1:2–4 authorized the Jews to return to Jerusalem and rebuild their temple, and it encouraged Jews who didn't return to donate money for the reconstruction project. However, his decree as it is recorded in chapter 6:3–5 says nothing about the return of the Jews. It focuses almost exclusively on the rebuilding of the temple—

even to specifying its dimensions! And it authorized the return of the gold and silver articles from the temple that Nebuchadnezzar had taken to Babylon years before. These two accounts of Cyrus's decree are not necessarily contradictory. What seems more likely is that neither one quotes the entire decree.

Similarly, Artaxerxes' decree as recorded in Ezra 7:12–26 may have mentioned the rebuilding of the city and Ezra simply didn't quote that part of the decree. There is significant evidence that this was indeed the case. Please follow carefully what I say next, because it's a bit complex. The evidence is found in Ezra 4, which I'll divide into four parts.

Part 1. The first five verses of Ezra 4 tell how the enemies of the Jews tried to prevent them from rebuilding the temple as it was authorized by Cyrus and *Darius.* I italicized the name *Darius,* because you need to remember it in order to make sense of my explanation in parts 2, 3, and 4—especially in part 4.

Part 2. This part begins with verses 6 and 7, which state that the Jews continued to experience opposition under the reigns of the Persian kings Ahasuerus and Artaxerxes, and verses 9–16 record a letter that the enemies of the Jews wrote to Artaxerxes. In part, that letter reads, "Let it be known to the king that the Jews who came up from you have come to us at Jerusalem, and *are* *building the rebellious and evil city, and are finishing its walls and repairing the foundation*" (verse 12; emphasis added). Please note that the enemies of the Jews accused the Jews of rebuilding their city, that is, Jerusalem. And they made this accusation to Artaxerxes, the king who issued the decree in 457.* The letter goes on to warn Artaxerxes that if the construction of Jerusalem is allowed to continue, his "treasury will be diminished" (verse 13), and it encourages him to check the records of past Jewish rebellion. It's significant to note that the letter doesn't suggest that the construction of the temple was illegal or that it was being done without royal consent. Had this been the case, the enemies of the Jews would surely have pointed out that fact. This is indirect evidence that Artaxerxes had in fact authorized the reconstruction of Jerusalem.

And there's more.

Part 3. Verses 17–22 state that Artaxerxes followed through on the recommendation of these enemies of the Jews. He checked the record in the royal archives and discovered that in the final years of the southern kingdom of Judah, the Jews had indeed been very rebellious against Nebuchadnezzar and the Babylonians. Ezra then quotes a letter that Artaxerxes wrote back to the enemies of the Jews. Verse 21 says, "Now give the command to make these men [the Jews] to cease, that this city may not be built until the command is given by me." Verse 23 says the enemies of the Jews "went up in haste to Jerusalem against the Jews, and by force of arms made them cease." Again, however, note that Artaxerxes never said the reconstruction was being done without his consent. And he didn't stop the reconstruction permanently; he only stopped it temporarily until he gave the order to resume reconstruction. It seems reasonable to conclude, then, that the reconstruction of Jerusalem *had* been authorized, and that both the enemies of the Jews and the king recognized this.

Part 4. The last verse in the chapter says something very interesting: "Thus the *work of the house of God* which is at Jerusalem ceased, and *it was discontinued until the second year of the reign of Darius* king of Persia" (verse 24; emphasis added). There are a couple of odd things about this verse. The previous eighteen verses had been about the Jews building their *city* under Artaxerxes and about Artaxerxes' order for them to stop. But verse 24 refers back to Darius, who preceded Artaxerxes as king of Persia, and it says that the work *on the house of God* ceased, not that the construc-

---

*This can't refer to Artaxerxes' decree in 444 B.C. because in that case the enemies of the Jews tried to stop the construction of Jerusalem's walls, but Nehemiah and his fellow Jews successfully resisted them and completed the project.

tion on the city ceased. What's the explanation for this oddity? A brief outline of the four parts of chapter 4 will help to clarify the problem and lead to a solution. Please note especially the two words *temple* and *Jerusalem,* which I have italicized, and notice the names of the kings, which I have bold-faced.

1. Verses 1–5: The enemies of the Jews try to stop them from rebuilding the *temple* during the reigns of Cyrus and **Darius.**
2. Verses 6–16: The enemies of the Jews write to **Artaxerxes** (who followed Darius by at least fifty years) stating that the Jews are rebuilding *Jerusalem* and urging him to stop them.
3. Verses 17–23: **Artaxerxes** authorizes the enemies of the Jews to stop the rebuilding of *Jerusalem.*
4. Verse 24: Work on the *temple* ceases until the second year of **Darius.**

Note the progression from the *temple* under Cyrus and **Darius** (part 1), to *Jerusalem* under **Artaxerxes** (parts 2 and 3), and back to the *temple* under **Darius** (part 4). Why this back and forth from Darius to Artaxerxes to Darius? Why the switch from the temple to the city Jerusalem and then back to the temple?

The best explanation seems to be that Ezra's primary purpose in chapter 4 was to show the opposition to all the Jewish reconstruction projects, both the temple and the city, and he inserted verses 6–23, about the reconstruction of *Jerusalem,* into his account of the reconstruction of the *temple.* Thus, the account of the work stoppage on the temple under Darius runs from verses 1–5, breaks to insert a parenthetical account in verses 6–23 about the work stoppage on rebuilding Jerusalem that had been authorized years later by Artaxerxes, and returns in verse 24 to the work stoppage on the temple years earlier under Darius. The New International Version recognizes this problem, placing a subhead at the beginning of verse 6 (the beginning of parts 2 and 3) that says, "Later Opposition Under Xerxes and Artaxerxes."

Thus, while the Bible doesn't actually *say* so, it seems most likely that Artaxerxes *did* authorize the reconstruction of Jerusalem in his 457 B.C. decree, and Ezra 4 records the reaction to that decree by the enemies of the Jews. William Shea said, "Why does the decree [to restore and build Jerusalem] appear in Ezra 7 when the rebuilding is referred to in Ezra 4? The book of Ezra is not arranged in a strictly chronological order. This is especially true of the material that appears in chapter 4. Its purpose was to record the on-going efforts of the enemies of the Jews to thwart both the rebuilding of the temple and the city."[13]

This of course raises the question of why

Artaxerxes would authorize the rebuilding of Jerusalem in 457 only to rescind it part way through the reconstruction project. Shea raises this question; his answer is that Artaxerxes is known from historical sources to have been a rather capricious individual who could be easily influenced to change his mind.[14] That appears to be what happened in the case of his authorization and then de-authorization of the rebuilding of Jerusalem.

In conclusion, the biblical evidence suggests that Artaxerxes *did indeed* authorize the Jews to rebuild their city at the time of his first decree in 457 B.C., and his decree as recorded in Ezra 7 simply omits that detail. He changed his mind when the enemies of the Jews protested, but, a few years later, he changed his mind again and allowed the Jews to continue rebuilding their city. That was the purpose of his second "decree," which we will now consider.

The second "decree" by Artaxerxes

Nehemiah was a Jew who served as a cupbearer for King Artaxerxes.* One day he received very disturbing news from some Jews who had come from Jerusalem: the walls of the city had been broken down and its gates burned. Nehemiah wept and fasted and prayed for several days. Apparently, the emperor was a perceptive individual because he recognized Nehemiah's

sadness and asked him about it. When Nehemiah explained what had happened to Jerusalem's walls and gates, the king inquired, "What do you request?" (Nehemiah 2:4). Nehemiah responded by asking for permission to go personally to Jerusalem and supervise the construction of its walls and gates. He also requested that Artaxerxes write two letters for him: one authorizing him to travel to Judea, and the second authorizing that the timber for the construction project be provided from the royal forest. The emperor granted Nehemiah's requests. He gave him time off from his job as cupbearer, and he wrote the letters Nehemiah requested. All this occurred in 444 B.C., thirteen years after the same King Artaxerxes had written his first decree that authorized the restoration of governance to the Jews and the rebuilding of Jerusalem.

Many conservative scholars consider Artaxerxes' second "decree" to be the one that fulfilled Gabriel's prediction about the rebuilding of Jerusalem because it specifically authorized Nehemiah to rebuild the city's walls. However, there are several problems with this conclusion.

First, you may have noticed that I've been putting the word *decree* in quotes when referring to the second decree by Artaxerxes. I did this because this so-called decree was actually just the two letters that

---

*The story I recount here is recorded in Nehemiah 1 and 2.

authorized Nehemiah to travel to Judea, build Jerusalem's walls, and obtain the building materials from the royal forests (Nehemiah 2:7, 8). It wasn't a royal decree such as that issued by Cyrus in 538, by Darius in 520, and by Artaxerxes in 457, each of which was called a decree (see Ezra 6:3, 8; 7:12, 13). Those by Cyrus and Artaxerxes authorized any Jew who wished to do so to return to Judea, and, in both cases, thousands responded. But Artaxerxes' letters for Nehemiah in 444 were never called decrees. They simply authorized Nehemiah as an individual to travel to Judea and lead out in the repair of Jerusalem's walls.

Second, the information about the broken-down walls and gates of Jerusalem came to Nehemiah as *news.* It would certainly not have been news to him—let alone *shocking news*—that Nebuchadnezzar had destroyed the walls of Jerusalem 150 years earlier. Nehemiah would have known that from his childhood. What seems much more likely is that reconstruction had already begun on Jerusalem's walls, and Nehemiah was shocked over the news that the enemies of the Jews had not only stopped the reconstruction but had actually torn down portions of the wall. This would, of course, have been the interference with the rebuilding of Jerusalem by the enemies of the Jews that is recorded in Ezra 4 and that I discussed a few pages back.

Third, Nehemiah didn't receive authorization to rebuild the *city* of Jerusalem. He requested and was granted permission only to rebuild its *walls.*

Fourth, Nehemiah and his fellow Jews completed their construction of the walls and gates of Jerusalem in just fifty-two days (see Nehemiah 6:15). They would hardly have completed the task in that short a time had they been rebuilding everything that Nebuchadnezzar had destroyed 150 years earlier. It seems much more likely that the only thing the Jews had to complete under Nehemiah's leadership was the part of the wall they had not finished at the time their enemies forced them to stop, plus whatever those same enemies had destroyed.

Fifth, a very convincing reason for rejecting Artaxerxes' authorization to Nehemiah as the fulfillment of Gabriel's prediction is that it doesn't fit the chronology of that prediction. Gabriel, you will recall, said that 483 years (sixty-nine weeks) would elapse from the issuing of the decree to restore and build Jerusalem until Messiah the Prince. I pointed out earlier in this chapter that 483 years reaches precisely from Artaxerxes' decree in 457 B.C. to A.D. 27, the very year of Christ's baptism. When those same 483 years are calculated from Artaxerxes' authorization for Nehemiah to rebuild Jerusalem's walls in 444 B.C., they stretch to A.D. 40—which was several years after Christ returned to heaven. The time period of 483 years simply doesn't work with the 444 date, but it fits perfectly with the 457 date.

Thus, evidence from both secular history and the Bible supports the conclusion that the decree fulfilling Gabriel's prediction about the "command to restore and build Jerusalem" as the starting point of the sixty-nine weeks (and the seventy weeks) is the one issued by Artaxerxes I in 457 B.C. So, I find the Adventist conclusion about the seventy weeks and their relationship to the 2,300 days of Daniel 8:14 to be very reasonable from a biblical perspective.

In conclusion, I will point out that Daniel 9:25, with its very specific prediction of the time of Christ's first coming, provides us with the assurance that the Bible truly is divinely inspired, for only a Being with divine foreknowledge could have made such an accurate chronological prediction hundreds of years in advance. I'm sure Daniel would have preferred that the Messiah arrive in his day, just as we wish Christ would hurry up and come again in our day. But our timetable isn't God's. Jesus will return "when the fullness of the time [has] come" (Galatians 4:4) in our day, just as He came at the right time two thousand years ago.

I will also point out that the same God who cared about Daniel's concerns cares about yours and mine too. He may not send His angel to us in person as He did to Daniel, but He will lead us to His answers to our questions and His solutions to our problems.

---

1. See Gerhard Hasel, "Interpretations of the Chronology of the Seventy Weeks," in *70 Weeks, Leviticus, Nature of Prophecy*, 47.

2. All of these dates are discussed by Arthur J. Ferch, "Commencement Date for the 70 Week Prophecy," in *70 Weeks, Leviticus, Nature of Prophecy*, 64–74.

3. See Owusu-Antwi, *The Chronology of Daniel 9:24–27*, 128.

4. Cottrell, "The 'Sanctuary Doctrine,' " 25; emphasis added.

5. Owusu-Antwi, *The Chronology of Daniel 9:24–27*, 130, 131.

6. Horn and Wood, *The Chronology of Ezra 7*, 117.

7. Martin, *The Truth About Seventh-day Adventism*, 174. Martin cited the book by Horn and Wood to support this statement. For a summary of the evidence supporting the 457 B.C. date, see Owusu-Antwi, *The Chronology of Daniel 9:24–27*, 295–299.

8. *Harper Study Bible*, 1313; emphasis in original.

9. See Ferch, "Commencement Date for the 70 Week Prophecy," 69.

10. Owusu-Antwi, *The Chronology of Daniel 9:24–27*, 132.

11. Ibid., 131–136.

12. Ibid., 135, 136.

13. William Shea, "The Prophecy of Daniel 9:24–27," in *70 Weeks, Leviticus, Nature of Prophecy*, 87; see also Owusu-Antwi, *The Chronology of Daniel 9:24–27*, 294, 295.

14. Ibid., 88.

Additional Note to Chapter 25

The Date for the End of the Seventy Weeks

If the seventy weeks (490 years) began in 457 B.C., then they ended in A.D. 34, which Adventists have said is the year when Stephen was stoned. In chapter 24, I shared with you the theological basis for identifying Stephen's martyrdom as the endpoint of the seventy weeks. The question here has to do with the chronological part of that conclusion. Is there any biblical evidence for A.D. 34 as the year of Stephen's death?

The answer is Yes, based on the available chronology that we have for the life of the apostle Paul. I am indebted to William Shea for the explanation that follows.

We know that Paul (who at that time went by the name Saul) was present when Stephen was stoned because Acts 7:58 says that he stood guard over the witnesses' clothes, and chapter 8:1 says he "was consenting to his death." The story in Acts doesn't give us enough chronological information to date Stephen's martyrdom. However, it is possible to arrive at an approximate date for Paul's conversion, which probably occurred no more than a few months after Stephen's death.

During Paul's second missionary journey, he spent a year and a half in Corinth. Partway through his stay there, the Jews hauled him before a Roman court because he "persuades men to worship God contrary to the law" (Acts 18:13). A man by the name of Gallio heard the case and promptly dismissed it on the grounds that it had to do only with Jewish law, not Roman law. Shea points out that "Gallio's proconsulship can be dated to A.D. 51–52 on the basis of an inscription found at Delphi which mentions him."[1] There is enough chronological data in the New Testament (see, for example, Galatians 1:18; 2:1) to work backwards from A.D. 51–52 to A.D. 34 as the year in which

Paul was converted and Stephen martyred. Shea concluded that "although the point may not be proved with finality, the most reasonable date available for the stoning of Stephen is sometime in A.D. 34."[2]

1. William Shea, "The Prophecy of Daniel 9:24–27," in *70 Weeks, Leviticus, Nature of Prophecy,* 104.

2. Ibid.

Chapter 26

The Seventieth Week and the Ultimate Fate of Jerusalem

Unfortunately, what seemed like such good news to Daniel when Gabriel began speaking (in chapter 9) became horribly bad news by the time he was through. While Jerusalem and the temple were to be restored during the 490 years, sometime after the conclusion of that period both would be destroyed. The question is not *whether* they would be destroyed but who would be responsible for their destruction. As we will see, the issue is the identification of "the prince" in verses 26 and 27.

These two verses are made up of twelve lines of poetry. Some of them I will analyze in detail while others, especially some that are rather obscure, I will comment on only briefly. Again, I have numbered them to facilitate the discussion.

1. "And after the sixty-two weeks
2. Messiah shall be cut off, but not for Himself;
3. And the people of the prince who is to come
4. Shall destroy the city and the sanctuary.
5. The end of it shall be with a flood,
6. And till the end of the war desolations are determined.
7. Then he shall confirm a covenant with many for one week;
8. But in the middle of the week
9. He shall bring an end to sacrifice and offering.
10. And on the wing of abominations shall be one who makes desolate,
11. Even until the consummation, which is determined,

12. Is poured out on the desolate."

Lines 1 and 2: "After the sixty-two weeks / Messiah shall be cut off, but not for Himself." The Messiah in this verse is Jesus Christ, who was referred to as "Messiah the Prince" in verse 25. The words *cut off* refer to His crucifixion. The Hebrew word is *karath,* and it suggests that the Messiah's death would be violent. *Karath* is in the passive voice, which means that the cutting off would be done *to* the Messiah by others. All of this is true of Jesus' death. Also, the text says that the Messiah would be cut off *after* the sixty-two weeks*—that is, *after* His anointing in A.D. 27. This also is true of Christ, since He was most likely crucified in either A.D. 30 or 31.[†]

The King James Version and the New King James Version say that the Messiah would be cut off, "but not for Himself." The New International Version, New American Standard Bible, and the Revised Standard Version say that He will "have nothing." Shea begins his discussion of these words by saying, "Whatever this statement means . . ."[1] The Hebrew words are *ein lo,* which Shea translates, "There shall not be to or for Him."[2] These words do not say who or what would be unavailable to the Messiah. Shea argues that the words mean that Jesus would have no one *for* Him; that is, He would be totally abandoned. This certainly was true of Christ—even His friends "forsook Him and fled" (Matthew 26:56; see also Mark 14:50). Raymond Cottrell argued that *ein lo* means that "the cut off prince would have no successor."[3] This, of course, would also be true of Christ.

Lines 3 and 4: "The people of the prince who is to come / Shall destroy the city and the sanctuary." The destruction of the city and the sanctuary almost certainly refers to the destruction of Jerusalem and the temple in A.D. 70. Who then is "the prince who is to come"? A very common interpretation is that he is an evil person because he would destroy Jerusalem and its temple. Raymond Cottrell adopted this view.[4] Dispensationalists, who push the last of the seventy weeks down to the end time, claim that this evil prince will be the antichrist during the Tribulation (what Adventists call "the time of trouble"). Since there is no exegetical basis for splitting the last of the seventy weeks from the first sixty-nine, I will dismiss that view without further comment.

However, two other interpretations do deserve our consideration. One is that the

---

*Gabriel spoke of "seven weeks and sixty-two weeks," a total of sixty-nine weeks. Thus, the statement "after the sixty-two weeks" means at the end of the sixty-nine weeks.

†The currently available data is insufficient to determine with finality the year when Christ was crucified. For a detailed discussion of this issue, see the *Seventh-day Adventist Bible Commentary,* 5:251–65; William Shea, "The Prophecy of Daniel 9:24–27," in *70 Weeks, Leviticus, Nature of Prophecy,* 102, 103.

"prince" in verse 26 is Titus, the Roman general who led in the attack against Jerusalem. By this interpretation, the people of this prince who is to come would be Titus's armies, who, of course, did destroy Jerusalem. The other interpretation is that "the prince" in this verse is the same Person as "Messiah the Prince" in verse 25, that is, Jesus. By this interpretation, the "people of the prince" would be the Jews, who, because of their rebellion, were the ultimate cause of the destruction of their own city.

So which is it? Notice that nothing in the text of verse 26 requires "the prince" to be an evil person. It's *the people* of the prince who is to come who will destroy the city and the temple, not the prince himself. The previous verse referred to "Messiah the Prince," which most Christian interpreters of the past two thousand years have interpreted as Jesus Christ. Line 2 of verse 26 speaks of "Messiah" being cut off after sixty-two weeks, and line 3 speaks of the "prince." In other words, verse 26 breaks apart these two titles for Jesus and uses each one separately. Thus, it seems to me that "the prince" in verse 26 is Jesus.*

Lines 5 and 6: "The end of it shall be with a flood, / And till the end of the war desolations are determined." The Roman armies did indeed invade Judea like "a flood."

And when they captured the city, they destroyed the temple and left scarcely any other building standing upright, making the word *desolations* an apt description of the city at that time.

Line 7: "He shall confirm a covenant with many for one week." One of the key issues with this line is the identification of "he." If "the prince" in line 3 is the Roman general Titus, then the word *he* refers to him. On the other hand, if "the prince" is Jesus, then the word *he* refers to Him.

Gabriel went on to say that the "he" in line 7 would "confirm a covenant with many *for one week*" (emphasis added). The word *week* here is an obvious reference to the last of the seventy weeks. If we identify the "he" as Titus, then an obvious question is how Titus confirmed a covenant with anyone for one week. There is no historical evidence that he did any such thing. Furthermore, Titus destroyed Jerusalem in A.D. 70, long after A.D. 34, when the "one week"—the seventieth and last week of the prophecy—had ended. On the other hand, if the "he" in line 7 is the Messiah, who is Jesus, and if the covenant is the same one that God had made with ancient Israel, then Jesus *did* try to confirm that covenant with the Jews. Their probationary time continued after His death until A.D. 34, and during this time God continued His effort to

---

*Jesus didn't destroy Jerusalem or the temple, but He predicted the destruction of both because of the rebellion of His people, the Jews (see Matthew 23:37–24:2; Luke 21:20).

get the Jewish people to accept Jesus as their Messiah through the preaching of the apostles. Unfortunately, every effort came to naught, and eventually, the Jews stoned Stephen, the last of the prophets that God sent to them, causing Him to reject them as His chosen people. This is how Adventists have always understood line 7, and I believe we have been correct in doing so.

Lines 8 and 9: "But in the middle of the week / He shall bring an end to sacrifice and offering." When we interpret the word *He* as Jesus, then it follows naturally that by His death Jesus brought an end to the Jewish sacrificial system. The Jews continued offering their sacrifices clear up to the destruction of the temple in A.D. 70; but following Christ's death, these sacrifices ceased to have any meaning in God's eyes. The torn veil in the temple signaled the end of those sacrifices (see Matthew 27:51; Mark 15:38; Luke 23:45). Again, this is standard Adventist interpretation, which I believe is correct.

Lines 10 to 12: "And on the wing of abominations shall be one who makes desolate, / Even until the consummation, which is determined, / Is poured out on the desolate."

The phrase, *on the wing of* is apparently an idiom that means "immediately thereafter" or "as an immediate consequence." In verse 25, Gabriel foretold the rebuilding of Jerusalem and the restoration of the Jews to a measure of political authority. However, this was not to last. In the final three lines of verse 27, Gabriel foretold the ultimate fate of Jerusalem: it would be desolated—that is, utterly destroyed. The one who caused that desolation—who made the city desolate—would, of course, be the Roman emperor and his forces.

Sadly, what began as a hopeful prediction of restoration for the Jews concluded with their final rebellion and destruction, from which there would be no more restoration. To this day, the Jews have clung to the belief that they are God's chosen people. How easy it is to think that one has God's favor when in fact he or she does not!

---

1. William Shea, "The Prophecy of Daniel 9:24–27," in *70 Weeks, Leviticus, Nature of Prophecy*, 92.
2. Ibid.
3. Cottrell, "The 'Sanctuary Doctrine,' " 25.
4. Ibid.

Chapter 27

The Year-Day Principle

I've referred to the year-day principle several times already in this book. According to this principle, in apocalyptic prophecy, a day symbolically represents one literal year. Thus, the 1,260 days of Daniel 7:25 and Revelation 12:6, 14 represent 1,260 years; the 2,300 days of Daniel 8:14 represent 2,300 years; and the seventy weeks of Daniel 9:24–27 represent 490 years.

Preterists think the year-day principle is flawed. So do futurists. I don't think, however, that they believe it to be flawed because there's anything wrong with the principle itself. I suspect the primary reason why they don't accept the year-day principle is that it doesn't fit their paradigm for interpreting apocalyptic prophecies. The idea of counting one prophetic day as a year of literal time makes sense only when the prophecies are interpreted according to the historicist paradigm.

Preterists believe that Daniel was fulfilled at about the time it was written. They interpret Daniel's anti-God figures—the little horns of Daniel 7 and 8—as representing Antiochus IV Epiphanes. Thus, preterists deny that these prophecies have anything to do with the long ages of history during the Christian era. Of course the year-day principle doesn't make sense to them—it's far too long to fit their scheme of interpretation!

Futurists generally recognize that the ferocious beasts of Daniel 7 represent the kingdoms of Babylon, Medo-Persia, Greece, and Rome. However, they identify the little horn as an end-time antichrist who will rule during the Tribulation, which is the final seven years of earth's history. And they interpret the time, times, and half a time of Daniel 7:25 as a literal three and a half years that make up the first part of this seven-year-long tribulation. According to this interpretation, there's a huge time gap in Daniel 7 between about the fifth century A.D. and the end-time tribulation, which the prophecy doesn't deal with. This is why futurists also don't see any need for a year-day principle.

On the other hand, for historicist interpreters of Daniel, the year-day principle is crucial. The prophecies that begin in 457 B.C. and A.D. 538 and that extend to our own day require the length of time this principle provides. In this chapter I will examine the biblical evidence that I believe supports the year-day principle as a valid method for interpreting the time periods in apocalyptic prophecy. I will begin with the scriptural evidence Adventists have offered throughout our history.

The traditional Adventist explanation

From the days of William Miller to the present, Adventists have pointed to two Bible texts in support of the year-day principle. The first is Numbers 14:34. The entire chapter is about the rebellion of the Israelites at the borders of Canaan, when the majority of the people yielded to the faithless report of the ten spies. God told Moses that because of Israel's refusal to cross over the Jordan River and conquer their new homeland, they would have to wander in the wilderness for forty years.

"According to the number of the days in which you spied out the land, forty days, for each day you shall bear your guilt one year, namely forty years, and you shall know My rejection." Notice the words "for each day you shall bear your guilt one year, namely forty years." This is the idea behind the year-day principle.

The second text we have used is in Ezekiel 4. In this chapter, God gave Ezekiel a message for the rebellious Israelites in the form of a parable that he was to act out. Ezekiel was to bear the people's iniquity by lying on his left side for 390 days and on his right side for forty days, a day for each year they had rebelled against God. Verse 6 says, "I have laid on you a day for each year." Again, notice the idea of a year for a day.*

These two texts—Numbers 14:34 and Ezekiel 4:6—constitute the primary biblical evidence that Seventh-day Adventists have traditionally given for the year-day principle of interpreting the time periods in Daniel and Revelation.

In centuries past, many Bible students interpreted the time prophecies of Daniel and Revelation according to the year-day principle. However, today, nearly all interpreters—conservative as well as liberal—deny the validity of this principle. Even some Seventh-day Adventists today deny the year-day principle. Desmond Ford af-

---

*Some critics object that, whereas in Numbers a day represents a year of literal time, in Ezekiel, a year represents a day of literal time. However, the year-day relationship is essentially the same either way.

firmed it in 1978 with a fairly lengthy appendix in his book *Daniel*.[1] But in the manuscript he presented two years later at Glacier View, he asked, *"Where is the proof for the year-day principle? Num. 14:34 and Eze. 4:6 and Dan. 9:24–27 are usually volunteered, but these certainly do not yield what is demanded of them.* (None of these passages state it as a rule for all symbolic prophecy that a day signifies a year.)"[2] And Raymond Cottrell called the year-day principle "a pseudo principle" for which "there is no Bible basis whatever."[3]

Are Ford and Cottrell correct? I will begin by agreeing that the Bible doesn't directly *state* the year-day principle anywhere. Neither of the texts I quoted above actually *states* it. Thus, Ford and Cottrell are correct in saying that the Bible doesn't *state* the year-day principle in so many words. However, I will also point out that nowhere does the Bible *state* the doctrine of the Trinity, yet most Christians, including Seventh-day Adventists, believe it to be one of the foundational teachings of Christianity. We believe that the Trinity can easily be *derived* from what the Bible says about God the Father, the Son, and the Holy Spirit. In a similar vein, I propose that the year-day principle can be *derived* from Scripture even though Scripture never *states* it as such.

So what is the biblical evidence from which we derive the year-day principle?

Daniel's long-outline prophecies

Keep in mind that the year-day principle goes hand in hand with the historicist method of interpreting Bible prophecy. Historicists understand Daniel's prophecies to cover thousands of years of history, beginning with the prophet's own time and continuing in an orderly flow to the end of the world, or, in the case of Daniel 8, to the time of the end. The time statements in both Daniel 7 and 8 are in this context. The 1,260 days in chapter 7:25 and the 2,300 days in chapter 8:14, if interpreted literally, amount to 3.5 and 6.3 years respectively, which is far too short to encompass the long periods that the historicist method requires. Obviously, then, by the historicist method, these time periods *have* to be interpreted symbolically. This shouldn't surprise us, since both Daniel 7 and 8 are highly symbolic, with beasts and horns representing great nations.

If we were starting to interpret these time periods for the first time, what unit of time would we think each day represents? We humans divide time in four primary ways: hours, days, months, and years. Hours are out of the question for the interpretation of these time periods, as are days. Even calculating them as months leaves us with too little time—42 months for the time, times, and half a time, and 76.7 months for the 2,300 evenings and mornings. Thus, if the symbolic time periods in Daniel 7 and 8 are to have any relevance to the historicist method of interpreting these prophecies, they have to be interpreted as years. And, as I pointed out in chapter 10, the Aramaic word for "time" in the expression "time and times and half a time" is 'iddan, the same word that appears in Daniel 4:16, and which many interpreters understand to mean "years."

I will also point out that when John repeated Daniel's 1,260-day time prophecy in Revelation 12, he also applied it to the persecution of God's people during a long stretch of time that would occur between Christ's ascension and the end-time crisis (see verses 6 and 14). Thus, the contexts in both Daniel and Revelation make it obvious that a literal three and a half years is totally inadequate to cover the vast period of history involved.

Some critics of the year-day principle have objected that neither Daniel 7:25, 8:14, nor 9:25 uses the Aramaic or Hebrew words for day. E. J. Waggoner of 1888 fame brought up this argument following his departure from the Adventist Church. He said, "Here [in Daniel 8:14] we are told to believe that we have for the figurative day a term that is never elsewhere used in the Bible for the word 'day.' . . . There is a Hebrew word that is everywhere rendered 'day,' and it is the only word for 'day' in the Hebrew Scriptures. Has it never occurred to you to wonder why an exception should be made here?"[4]

With respect to Waggoner's criticism, I will point out that if the angel who spoke about evenings and mornings in Daniel 8:14 had in mind a time period—and all interpreters agree that he did—then we have to understand those evenings and mornings to mean some *unit* of time. And everyone seems to agree that *days* are intended. Some interpreters understand 2,300 half days (1,150 full days); others understand 2,300 full days. However, one way or another, everyone comes up with a period of time marked by *days*. So what's wrong with Adventists interpreting "evening-morning twenty-three hundred" to mean 2,300 *days?*

Actually, the very absence of the literal word *day* in the original languages for the time prophecies of Daniel 7, 8, and 9 is one of the best evidences that the language is symbolic. William Shea comments, "The use of unusual time units that were not ordinarily employed for the computation of time, such as 'evening-mornings,' 'times,' and to some extent, even 'weeks,' lends support to the idea that something more than just literal time is involved here. Unusual units like these fit better with symbolic time and probably were chosen to emphasize that point."[5]

Gerhard Pfandl, one of the associate directors of the Biblical Research Institute,* points out that the "time and times and half a time" of Daniel 7:25 appears again

---

*The Biblical Research Institute is a department of the General Conference of Seventh-day Adventists.

in Revelation 12:6 as "one thousand two hundred and sixty days," in Revelation 12:14 as "a time and times and half a time," and in Revelation 13:5 as "forty-two months." On the other hand, he says, "the natural expression 'three years and six months' is not used once."[6] He then cites the nineteenth-century author Thomas R. Birks, who said, "The Holy Spirit seems, in a manner, to exhaust all the phrases by which the interval could be expressed, excluding always that one form which would be used of course in ordinary writing, and is used invariably in Scripture on other occasions, to denote a literal period. This variation is most significant if we accept the year-day system, but quite inexplicable on any other view."[7]

Someone might object that there is no consistency in the symbol employed for time units: time, times, and half a time in Daniel 7; evenings-mornings in Daniel 8; and weeks in Daniel 9. This should be no problem, however, in view of the fact that Daniel represented nations in chapter 2 as metals and clay, in chapter 7 as wild beasts and horns, and in chapter 8 as domesticated animals and horns. Thus, it shouldn't surprise us that Daniel used a variety of symbols to represent time.

When the year-day principle was first recognized

Some critics of the year-day principle claim that it wasn't known in Bible times, and, in fact, wasn't recognized by interpreters of prophecy for hundreds of years after the New Testament era. Thus, Raymond Cottrell said, "The day-for-a-year idea applied to Bible prophecy appears first in the ninth century Karaite Jewish scholar Nahawendi's attempt to relate the fulfillment of Daniel's prophecies to events of his day."[8]

However, William Shea has found significant evidence that the year-day principle was understood by Jewish interpreters of prophecy at least a thousand years before Nahawendi. He says, "On the basis of recent researches into the Jewish materials of the second century B.C., it has become evident that the year-day principle was known and applied by Jewish interpreters during the second century down to the post-Qumran period. It is no longer tenable to hold that the principle was a ninth century A.D. phenomenon."[9] Shea goes on to support this statement by citing evidence from Hellenistic literature, Qumran literature, and post-Qumran Jewish interpreters. I will mention two examples.

The Book of Jubilees was written sometime between 135 and 105 B.C., and it uses the word *weeks* more than eighty times. From his examination of the book, Shea says, "It is clear that these references to 'weeks' must be interpreted on the basis of the year-day principle."[10] He goes on to cite the example of Noah's age at the time

$$
\begin{array}{llll}
\text{19 jubilees} & = & 19 \times 49 \text{ years} & = & 931 \text{ years} \\
\text{2 weeks} & = & 2 \times 7 \text{ years} & = & 14 \text{ years} \\
\text{5 years} & = & 5 \text{ years} & = & 5 \text{ years} \\
\hline
\text{Total} & & & & 950 \text{ years}^{11}
\end{array}
$$

of his death, which was 950 years (see Genesis 7:6; 9:28). The Book of Jubilees gives this period as nineteen jubilees, *two weeks,* and five years. A jubilee equaled forty-nine years. Here is how this scheme works out.

Notice that the first and third of these elements are both stated in terms of years, but the second is stated as "weeks" and then applied as years based on the year-day principle. This is a clear example of the use of this principle at least one hundred years before Christ's birth.

The book of 4 Ezra (2 Edras) from about A.D. 100 (the post-Qumran period) applies the year-day principle twice. One instance has to do with a seven-year judgment prior to the Messianic kingdom. The author of 4 Ezra says, "Its duration shall be as it were a week of years. Such is my judgment and its prescribed order" (4 Ezra 7:43, 44). Shea points out that "this apocalypse employs the word for 'week' as representing (by means of the seven days of the week) a period of seven years. The year-day principle is thus made explicit here since the 'week' is identified as one 'of years.' "[12]

Thus, the year-day principle did not originate with the Jewish scholar Nahawendi in the ninth century A.D. Jewish commentators as far back as the second century B.C. explicitly stated it!

Actually, this principle existed even before that.

Old Testament use of *day* to mean *years*

As was previously mentioned, the Hebrew word for "day" is *yom,* as in "*Yom* Kippur" (*Day* of Atonement). Sometimes, however, *yom* is used in the Old Testament with the obvious meaning of "year." This happens even in the book of Daniel. For example, Daniel 1:18 says that when Daniel and his three friends had completed their training at the "University of Babylon," they appeared before King Nebuchadnezzar "at the end of the *days*."* However, verse 5 says that their education was to last three *years*. Thus, the word *days* in verse 18 has to mean "years" (see also Daniel 4:16, 34).

The word for "days" was also used in the sense of "years" elsewhere in the Old

---

*In the Bible texts quoted in this section, I have italicized the words *day* and *year*. They aren't italicized in English Bibles.

Testament. For example, Exodus 13:10 says that the Passover was to be celebrated "from *year* to *year*." However, the Hebrew literally says "from *days* to *days*," with the meaning of "yearly." The Hebrew behind , a "yearly sacrifice" in 1 Samuel 20:6 is literally, a "sacrifice of the *days*." Similarly, the original Hebrew of 1 Samuel 27:7 says that David lived among the Philistines for "*days* and four months," which means "a *year* and four months." And 1 Kings 1:1 reads that David was "old, advanced in *years*" even though the Hebrew actually says that he was "old, advanced in *days*."

Sometimes in the Old Testament, "days" and "years" appear parallel to each other, clearly indicating that they mean the same thing. For example, Genesis 5:5 says, "So all the *days* that Adam lived were nine hundred and thirty *years*; and he died." This formula is repeated ten times in Genesis 5. And we find this same pattern in Old Testament poetry. For example, Job 10:5 asks, "Are Your *years* like the *days* of a mighty man?" And Deuteronomy 32:7, which is written in poetic format, says, "Remember the *days* of old, / Consider the *years* of many generations."

Finally, in Leviticus 25:2, God commanded the Israelites, "When you come into the land which I give you, then the *land* shall keep a *sabbath* to the LORD" (emphasis added). How is the *land* supposed to

observe the *Sabbath*? How is a farmer supposed to give his land a Sabbath *day's* rest? He can't, if the weekly day of rest is meant by "sabbath." However, the text means that every seventh *year* the Israelite farmer was to allow his land to remain uncultivated and his vineyards and orchards to remain unpruned for the whole year (see Exodus 23:10, 11). William Shea calls this "the earliest biblical text in which the year-day principle is reflected."[13] He says, "[Thus] the relationship that came to be established between the terms for 'day' and 'year' forms the general linguistic usage and thought pattern from which a later, more specific quantitative relationship in prophetic texts will spring. It is evident that the year-day principle did not crop up suddenly in prophecy *sui generis.** When it came upon the scene of action, it was drawn from a more general relationship that was already a part of Hebrew thought."[14]

This is just some of the biblical evidence that Shea cites for the use in the Old Testament of the words *day* and *days* when *years* was actually intended. These examples do not, of course, state that the year-principle should be used for the interpretation of apocalyptic prophecy. They're simply evidence that the Hebrew mind often thought in these terms.

Earlier, I commented at some length about the traditional Adventist use of

---

*That is, without precedent, or, as we might say in English, "out of thin air."

Numbers 14:34 and Ezekiel 4:6 as evidence of the year-day principle. These texts also don't state that the year-day principle should be used to interpret apocalyptic time prophecies. However, they are further evidence that the Hebrew mind often thought in year-day terms. The point for our discussion is that it shouldn't surprise us to see in the apocalyptic time prophecies of Daniel and Revelation that same Hebrew way of thinking. The prophets would probably themselves be surprised that we even questioned it.

Daniel 9:25

One of the strongest evidences for the year-day principle is the seventy weeks of Daniel 9:24, 25. Verse 24 says, "Seventy *weeks* are determined for your people and for your holy city," and verse 25 speaks of "seven *weeks* and sixty-two *weeks*" (emphasis added).

William Shea makes the key point that "all commentators on Daniel agree that the events prophesied in Daniel 9:24–27 could not have been completed within a literal 70 weeks or one year and five months."[15] Writing in the *Harper Study Bible*, Harold Lindsell said, "One conclusion seems self-evident. Each *week* or 'heptad' must be a period of seven years or a total of 490 years."[16]

The reason that scholars generally agree on interpreting Daniel's "weeks" as years is simple: whether one is a preterist, a futurist, or a historicist, sixty-nine or seventy literal weeks simply do not constitute enough time for the rebuilding of the temple and the city of Jerusalem. Thus, in Daniel 9, even preterists, who see the primary fulfillment of Daniel's prophecies occurring in the second century B.C., have to deal with the same issue that historicists are faced with in the time prophecies of Daniel 7 and 8—namely, applying a prophetic statement about time to a long-term historical reality. When the time period as understood literally is too short to fit into our interpretive paradigm, then we all—preterists, futurists, and historicists—have no choice but to interpret *days* to be symbolic of *years*.

However, interpreters have arrived at these years in Daniel 9:24, 25 in a couple of ways. The Hebrew word for "weeks" in these verses is *shabua*. Some preterists and futurists prefer to translate *shabua* as "sevens" (NIV), "heptads," or "hebdomads." (Both of the latter words mean "groups of seven.") By avoiding the translation "week," which involves days, they can interpret "years" as the *literal* meaning of *shabua* rather than having to reach this conclusion through the symbolic year-day process. This appeals to preterists and futurists because if they can arrive at the meaning "years" for the term *shabua* without having to interpret days as symbolic of years, then they don't have to apply the year-day principle to Daniel's previous time prophecies in chapters 7 and 8. Shea comments,

One reason for this approach in translation [translating *shabua* as "sevens," "heptads," or "hebdomads"] is to separate the 70-week prophecy of Daniel 9 from the other time prophecies of the book and to place it in a distinct class by itself. The effect of this is to blunt the implications of the year-day principle advocated by the historicist system of interpretation.

If the year-day principle is thus denied its function in the interpretation of Daniel 9:24–27, then preterists and futurists alike are at liberty to deny its application to the other time prophecies. On the other hand, if it is valid to apply the year-day principle to the "days" of the "weeks" in Daniel 9, then it is logical to apply the same principle to the "days" in the time prophecies found elsewhere in Daniel.[17]

So, should *shabua* in Daniel 9:24–26 be translated as "weeks," or should it be translated as "sevens"?

The word *shabua* occurs thirteen times in the Old Testament outside the book of Daniel. The problem with translating it as "sevens," "heptads," or "hebdomads" in Daniel 9 is that nearly all English versions translate *shabua* as "weeks" in each of these other thirteen occurrences. In fact, *shabua* appears in Daniel 10:2, 3, and there it is translated "weeks." Seven of the thirteen occurrences of *shabua* outside the book of Daniel are in connection with the Israelite Feast of Weeks (*shabua*) (see Exodus 34:22; Numbers 28:26; Deuteronomy 16:10).* It would hardly make sense to translate this as "Feast of Sevens"!

Shea concludes that "usages [of *shabua*] elsewhere in Daniel, elsewhere in the OT, in extrabiblical Hebrew, and in cognate Semitic languages all indicate that this word should be translated as 'weeks.' *No support can be obtained from any of these sources for translating this word any other way than as 'weeks.' "*[18]

Some critics have noted that the word *shabua* has a masculine ending in Daniel 9:24, 25, whereas everywhere else in the Old Testament it has a feminine ending. Shea's comment on this fact is quite simple: "The masculine plural ending on this word in Daniel 9, in contrast to its feminine plural ending elsewhere in the OT, is of significance only in indicating that it is one of many Hebrew nouns with dual gender."[19]

It works!

I will conclude this discussion about the year-day principle by pointing out its very accurate fulfillment in Daniel 9:24, 25. I explained this in detail in chapter 25, so will only summarize that discussion here.

Artaxerxes' decree to "restore and build

---

*Called "Pentecost" in the New Testament (see Acts 2:1).

Jerusalem" was issued in 457 B.C. That date seems to be fixed in cement about as firmly as any date in ancient history. Exactly sixty-nine weeks later (483 years on the year-day principle) in A.D. 27, Jesus was baptized. There is no prophecy in Scripture with a more exact fulfillment than that. This confirms the validity of the year-day principle, giving us confidence to use it with other apocalyptic time prophecies.

Some critics have objected to transferring the year-day principle from Daniel 9 to the time prophecies of chapters 7 and 8 on the grounds that the prophecies of Daniel 7 and 8 are highly symbolic, whereas chapter 9, including Gabriel's comments to Daniel, are quite literal. Therefore, so the argument goes, it is inappropriate to apply a principle of interpretation from a literal passage to a symbolic one.

I ask, Who says? Why can't a method of interpretation in a literal context be applied to a symbolic one if it helps us to understand the symbolic one?

And while it's true that Daniel 7 and 8 are highly symbolic, they aren't entirely so. The saints in chapter 7 are literal, as is the Ancient of Days, as are the angels surrounding His throne, as is the judgment they're all attending. In chapter 8, the Prince of the host is literal, as are His sanctuary and the truth that are cast to the ground. All symbolic prophecy needs some literal aspects in order to make sense. A prophetic passage that is 100 percent symbolic can be extremely difficult to interpret. A case in point is Revelation 8:6–12, the first four trumpets, which most Adventist interpreters understand to be symbolic. This passage is, in fact, so symbolic that one can scarcely find two Adventist interpreters who agree on its meaning.

My point is that just as most symbolic prophecies include some literal terms, so Gabriel's explanation to Daniel in chapter 9:24–27, which is mostly literal, also includes some symbolic terms. Who's to say, then, that a principle of interpretation that works in one type of prophecy can't work in another?

Numerous other arguments have been advanced both for and against the year-day principle, but what I have shared with you in this chapter is enough to persuade me that it has a solid biblical basis.[20]

---

1. Ford, appendix F in *Daniel,* 300–305.
2. Ford, "Daniel 8:14," 295; emphasis in the original.
3. Cottrell, "The 'Sanctuary Doctrine,' " 23.
4. Quoted in Ford, "Daniel 8:14," 60.
5. Shea, *Selected Studies in Prophetic Interpretation,* 74.
6. Pfandl, "The Year-Day Principle," *Reflections,* 1–3.
7. Thomas R. Birks, *First Elements of Sacred Prophecy* (London: William E. Painter, 1843), 352, quoted in Pfandl, "The Year-Day Principle," 2.
8. Cottrell, "The 'Sanctuary Doctrine,' " 26.

9. Shea, *Selected Studies in Prophetic Interpretation,* 105.

10. Ibid., 106.

11. Ibid.

12. Ibid., 110.

13. Ibid., 83.

14. Ibid., 81.

15. Ibid., 89.

16. *Harper Study Bible,* 1312; emphasis in the original.

17. Shea, *Selected Studies in Prophetic Interpretation,* 89.

18. Ibid., 91; emphasis added.

19. Ibid., 90.

20. For a much more complete presentation of the evidence in favor of the year-day principle, see Shea, *Selected Studies in Prophetic Interpretation,* 67–110.

Issues in Hebrews

Chapter 28

Jesus' Entrance "Behind the Veil"

Back in January 2008, I received the following letter at our *Signs of the Times®* office from a person who shall remain unnamed in this book:

> "The B-I-B-L-E, now that's the book for me! I stand alone on the word of God! The B-I-B-L-E."
>
> I grew up singing this in Sabbath School. I believed it. Imagine my shock when I read the book of Hebrews. Using the *SDA Bible Commentary,* I learned that when Christ went within the veil, the "veil" *always* refers to the veil separating the Holy and Most Holy Place.* Hebrews absolutely teaches He went into the Most Holy Place at His ascension. Hebrews 9 compares and contrasts the earthly high priest—who went into the Most Holy Place (Hebrews 9:7) with blood to atone. If Jesus atoned with His blood at His ascension (read *all* of chapter 9! And the whole book!)—then it *has* to follow He did *not* wait till 1844 to go into the Most Holy Place in heaven! . . .
>
> So—when the SDA Church renounces this simply unbiblical doctrine, I may return—but I'm not holding my breath! I'm fourth generation and educated and can read Hebrews for myself!

This letter highlights an important issue in the Adventist interpretation of the sanctuary: Hebrews appears to contradict our interpretation. For more than one hundred years,

---

*This is not what the commentary says. See *Seventh-day Adventist Bible Commentary,* 7:437, 438.

those who dispute our interpretation of the sanctuary and the investigative judgment have based much of their criticism on the book of Hebrews. Thus, it's very important that we pay careful attention to Hebrews. To bring up every argument on both sides along with each side's response would fill this entire book. However, in this chapter and the five that follow, I will bring up some of the more significant arguments on both sides. At the conclusion, I hope you will agree with me that the arguments in support of our traditional Adventist view of the sanctuary and the investigative judgment have strong biblical support.

Let me introduce some of the people in the current debate. I have cited Desmond Ford often in this book and will do so frequently in our examination of Hebrews. Norman Young, now retired, was, for many years, a professor in the theology department of Avondale College, Cooranbong, Australia. He also believes that Hebrews contradicts much of our traditional Adventist teaching. Young has written two significant articles on this issue for *Andrews University Seminary Studies.* Richard Davidson is chairman of the Old Testament Department at the Andrews University Theological Seminary. He has written two articles on Hebrews for *Andrews University Seminary Studies* that I have found very helpful. Felix Cortez is a professor in the theology department at Montemorelos

University in Mexico. He wrote his doctoral dissertation at Andrews University on Hebrews. Finally, Carl Cosaert, a professor in the school of religion at Walla Walla University, wrote his master's thesis on the term *ta hagia* ("the sanctuary") in the Septuagint, the Pseudepigrapha, and the writings of Philo and Josephus. His thesis and an article by him on the same topic in *Andrews University Seminary Studies* have been helpful. I may not always cite these authors directly, but I will bring up some of their more cogent arguments and comment on them.

Now to the issues in Hebrews!

The problem texts

Hiram Edson had his "cornfield vision" the morning of October 23, 1844. From that "vision," he concluded that "instead of our High Priest *coming out* of the Most Holy of the heavenly sanctuary to come to this earth on the tenth day of the seventh month, at the end of the 2300 days, he for the first time *entered* on that day the second apartment of that sanctuary."[1] Adventists have maintained this view of the sanctuary ever since. However, critics of our interpretation have pointed to several texts in Hebrews that make it very clear that Jesus entered the Most Holy Place of the heavenly sanctuary in A.D. 31. Consider the following texts, noting especially the words I have italicized.

Hebrews 1:3—"[Jesus] being the brightness of His [God's] glory and the express image of His person, and upholding all things by the word of His power, when He had by Himself purged our sins, *sat down at the right hand of the Majesty on high.*"

Hebrews 8:1—"This is the main point of the things we are saying: We have such a High Priest, *who is seated at the right hand of the throne of the Majesty in the heavens.*"

Hebrews 9:24—"Christ has not entered the holy places made with hands, which are copies of the true, but into heaven itself, *now to appear in the presence of God for us.*"

Hebrews 10:19, 20, 22—"Therefore, brethren, *having boldness to enter the Holiest* by the blood of Jesus, by a new and living way which He consecrated for us, *through the veil,* that is, His flesh, . . . let us draw near with a true heart in full assurance of faith."

One other text in Hebrews has especially been used against our Adventist teaching that Jesus waited until 1844 to enter the Most Holy Place of the heavenly sanctuary:

Hebrews 6:19, 20—"This hope we have as an anchor of the soul, both sure and steadfast, and *which enters the Presence behind the veil, where the forerunner has entered for us, even Jesus,* having become High Priest forever according to the order of Melchizedek."

This text says that Jesus is our High Priest and that He has entered into God's presence "behind the veil." The words *behind the veil* are significant because the Most Holy Place of the earthly sanctuary was behind a veil, a curtain. Thus, the author of Hebrews* seems to be saying that at the time he wrote his document, Jesus had already entered the Most Holy Place. The problem is obvious: Adventists have historically maintained that Jesus did not enter the Most Holy Place of the heavenly sanctuary until 1844. On the other hand, a number of texts in the New Testament make it very clear that even in the New Testament era, Jesus was either standing or sitting at God's right hand—*which would suggest that He was in the Most Holy Place of the heavenly sanctuary.* Hebrews 6:19 even puts Him "behind the veil"!

Desmond Ford took strong exception to the idea that Jesus waited until 1844 to enter the Most Holy Place of the heavenly sanctuary. Chapter 2 of his Glacier View

---

*Tradition says that Paul wrote Hebrews. Most scholars today doubt this to be the case. Rather than enter the debate, in my chapters on Hebrews I will refer to whoever wrote this book as "the author."

manuscript consists of more than one hundred pages in which he discusses his understanding of the sanctuary in Hebrews. At the beginning of the chapter, he states what he considers to be his central thesis: "Hebrews clearly affirms that in fulfillment of the Day of Atonement type, Christ by the cross-resurrection-ascension event entered upon the ministry prefigured by the sanctuary's *second* apartment."[2] Ford's logic can be reduced to a simple syllogism:

- Jesus entered heaven's Most Holy Place "behind the veil" in A.D. 31.
- The only service in the Levitical year when the high priest went "behind the veil" was the Day of Atonement.
- Therefore, Hebrews 6:19, 20 is about Christ's Day of Atonement ministry in the Most Holy Place of the heavenly sanctuary, which began in A.D. 31, not 1844.

Ford cites several similar texts from other parts of the New Testament that state that immediately upon Christ's ascension He sat down with God on His throne and/or was at God's right hand.* Ford says that these statements are clear evidence that Jesus entered upon His Day of Atonement ministry in A.D. 31.[3] Commenting specifically on Hebrews 6:19, 20, Ford says that

this passage "unambiguously affirms that the antitype of the Day of Atonement came with the death and ascension of Christ."[4] Because Hebrews 6:19 is one of the texts cited most frequently by our critics, I will restrict my comments in this chapter mostly to an analysis of these two verses.

The Adventist response

One of the early Adventist responses to the problem posed by Hebrews 6:19, 20 was that of Elmer E. Andross, who served the church for many years as a Bible teacher, evangelist, missionary, and administrator. In 1911, Andross published a book, *A More Excellent Ministry,* in which he took the position that Jesus' entrance "within the veil" (KJV) was comparable to Moses' entrance into the Most Holy Place of the earthly sanctuary at the time of the sanctuary's inauguration rather than Aaron's entrance into the sanctuary at the time of the Day of Atonement (see Exodus 30:22–30; 40:1–16; Leviticus 8:10–13; Numbers 7:1–88). From this, Andross concluded that "in like manner, Christ, after making His offering on Calvary, passed 'within the veil' of the heavenly sanctuary and anointed the ark of the testament, and with His own blood performed the service of *consecration.*"[5] Note the italicized word, *consecration.* Andross argued that Hebrews 6:19,

---

*See Mark 16:19; Luke 22:69; Romans 8:34; Ephesians 1:20; Colossians 3:1; Hebrews 10:12; 12:2; and 1 Peter 3:22.

20 is about Christ's consecration/inauguration of the heavenly sanctuary, not His heavenly Day of Atonement ministry. Andross also concluded that, after inaugurating the heavenly sanctuary, including the Most Holy Place, Christ left that apartment and sat down with God on a throne in the Holy Place.[6]

More recently, some Adventists have pointed out that there were three veils in the earthly sanctuary: one at the entrance to the courtyard (Numbers 3:26), another between the courtyard and the Holy Place (Exodus 26:36), and a third separating the Holy Place from the Most Holy Place (Exodus 26:31, 33). They argue that the veil referred to in Hebrews 6:19, 20 isn't necessarily the one separating the Holy Place from the Most Holy Place. The *Handbook of Seventh-day Adventist Theology* says, "By itself the term cannot be used to determine which of the veils is intended."[7] After a rather complex line of reasoning, the *Handbook* states, "The text does not discuss the specific place within the heavenly sanctuary where Christ entered after His ascension. That Christ entered the sanctuary means that He has full access to God."[8]

On the other hand, a number of Adventist scholars have concluded that, by the words "behind the veil" the author of Hebrews *did* mean the veil between the Holy Place and the Most Holy Place. Richard Davidson, the chairman of the Old Testament Department at the Andrews University Theological Seminary, said, "Reference by the author of Hebrews to the veil in Heb 6:19, 20, following LXX [Septuagint] usage, most probably has in view the 'second' veil, i.e., the veil before the Most Holy Place."[9]

The books of Exodus, Leviticus, and Numbers constitute our primary source of information about the earthly sanctuary, its furnishings, and its services. These books mention only two occasions when anyone entered the Most Holy Place. One was when Moses placed the ark of the covenant in the Most Holy Place and dedicated it with oil, and the other was on the yearly Day of Atonement. Therefore, Hebrews 6:19, 20, which speaks of Jesus entering the Most Holy Place of the heavenly sanctuary "behind the veil," is about either the inauguration of the heavenly sanctuary or the heavenly Day of Atonement. The question is, Which of these did the author of Hebrews have in mind?

The immediate context of Hebrews 6:19, 20

Because of our conviction that the heavenly Day of Atonement didn't begin until 1844, Adventists have always said that chapter 6:19, 20 does *not* refer to the Day of Atonement. The *Handbook of Seventh-day Adventist Theology* says, "Contextual considerations rule out the discussion of the antitypical day of atonement in Hebrews 6:19."[10] I believe this statement in the *Handbook* is correct, and I disagree with Ford's statement that Hebrews 6:19 "unambiguously" refers to the Day of Atonement. Ford assumes that Christ's standing at God's right hand *has* to mean that He was performing the Day of Atonement ministry. However, there are two reasons for questioning that conclusion.

First, Day of Atonement language is missing. The first thing to notice is that nothing in the immediate context of Hebrews 6:19, 20 suggests a Day of Atonement interpretation. From beginning to end, chapter 6 is an encouragement for readers to make sure they don't give up their faith in Jesus. In verses 1–8, the author says that it is impossible for those who once had faith and then gave it up to renew it again. In verses 9–12, he tells his readers that he is sure they won't give up their faith. In verses 13–18, he holds up Abraham as one who patiently clung to his faith even when God seemed not to have kept His promise. And the author begins chapter 7—which immediately follows 6:19, 20—with the story about Abraham giving tithe to Melchizedek. From this, it's evident that the context both before and after 6:19, 20 has nothing to do with the Day of Atonement, and this casts doubt on whether the verses themselves are about Christ's heavenly Day of Atonement ministry.

Second, inauguration language is present. On the other hand, the immediate context supports the conclusion of Elmer Andross that the subject of Hebrews 6:19, 20 is the inauguration of the heavenly sanctuary. As an introduction to this line of reasoning, I will call your attention to Exodus 40. Verses 1–11 tell how Moses put the various articles of furniture in place and anointed each with oil, and verses 12–16 describe the ordination of Aaron and his sons to the priesthood. The point for our discussion is that *the inauguration of the sanctuary and the ordination of Aaron and his sons as priests were all part of the same ceremony.*

The reasoning by the author of Hebrews is fairly simple. In Hebrews 5:5, 6, he said, "Christ did not glorify Himself to become High Priest, but it was He [God] who said to Him: . . . 'You are a priest forever according to the order of Melchizedek.' " The author was referring to the time when God appointed Jesus to be a High Priest. In verse 10 of the same chapter, he said even more specifically that Jesus was "*called by God as High Priest* 'according to the order of Melchizedek' " (emphasis added). God's call for Jesus to be a High Priest is analogous to the appointment and ordination of Aaron as high priest. And in Exodus, the ordination of the first priests, including the first high priest, was part of the same ceremony as the inauguration of the sanctuary.

Next notice that in Hebrews 6:19, 20, the author again speaks of Jesus "*having become* High Priest forever according to the order of Melchizedek" (verse 20; emphasis added). This is an unambiguous reference to the time when Jesus began His high priestly ministry, which in the earthly sanctuary coincided with the time when the sanctuary was inaugurated. Thus, the context of statement in Hebrews 6:19, 20 that Jesus went "behind the veil" *does* support the idea of inauguration.

Given the fact that there is no specific reference whatsoever to the Day of Atonement anywhere in Hebrews 5, 6, or 7, and in view of the repeated references throughout these chapters to Jesus' appointment as High Priest "according to the order of Melchizedek," it seems much more reasonable to understand 6:19, 20 as an antitype of the inauguration of the earthly sanctuary and the ordination of its priests rather than as an antitype of the earthly Day of Atonement services. Felix Cortez comments, "Heb 6:19–20 . . . should be understood in the context of an analogy to Moses' inauguration of the sanctuary and not to the annual ritual of the Day of Atonement."[11]

Thus, while neither the Day of Atonement nor the inauguration of the heavenly sanctuary is specifically named in Hebrews 6:19, 20, the immediate context of these verses *does* indicate a heavenly inauguration/ordination event rather than a heavenly Day of Atonement event. This conclusion is supported by a careful analysis of Hebrews 9 and 10, which we will consider in two later chapters of this book.

Was Moses a priest?

Some people have objected to the explanation of Hebrews 6:19, 20 that I have given here. They say that Moses dedicated the sanctuary, but he was never ordained as a priest; but Hebrews speaks of Christ being made a priest. How then could Moses be a type of Christ's heavenly priesthood? I'll suggest a couple of reasons why this actually is not as much of a problem as it appears to be at first glance.

Moses as priest—a type of Christ. First, prior to the ordination of Aaron and his sons as priests, Moses carried out the priestly functions for Israel. For example, shortly after the giving of the Ten Commandments on Mount Sinai, Moses called the people together to establish a covenant between them and God (see Exodus 24:1–8). He authorized some young men to sacrifice oxen as peace offerings (verse 5), and then he took some of the blood, put some of it in basins, and sprinkled it on an altar that he had built for the occasion.* He also sprinkled the blood on the people (verse 8). All of these are functions the priests

---

*See verse 4. The sanctuary altar hadn't been built yet.

would carry out once they were ordained and the sanctuary was inaugurated. But at this point, there was no sanctuary and there were no priests, so Moses fulfilled the priestly functions.

The same thing is true of the inauguration of the sanctuary that is recorded in Exodus 40 (see also Numbers 7). Moses put all the sanctuary's furnishings in place (verses 1–8), and then he anointed each one (verses 9–16). Thus, at this point, Moses was filling a priestly role.

Numbers 7 gives a very detailed account of the inauguration of the sanctuary. Verse 1 says that after Moses had set up the sanctuary, he "consecrated it and all its furnishings, and the altar and all its utensils; so he anointed them and consecrated them." The rest of the chapter—eighty-eight verses!—tells how, over a period of twelve days, representatives from each of the tribes of Israel brought gifts to the tabernacle and sacrificed animals as burnt offerings. The text doesn't say that Moses did the actual sacrificing of the animals, but it says he supervised the entire operation, acting in essence as high priest. Exodus 40 also tells how Moses ordained Aaron and his sons as priests by anointing them with oil (see verses 12–16), which was also a priestly function.

The author of Hebrews recognized that Moses had a priestly function. In Hebrews 3:1, 2, he said, "Therefore, holy brethren, partakers of the heavenly calling, consider the Apostle and High Priest of our confession, Jesus Christ, who was faithful to Him who appointed Him, as Moses also was faithful in all His house." The author compared Jesus' role as High Priest with Moses, in essence affirming that Moses had a priestly role.

Moses as chief administrator—a type of God. As additional confirmation of the appropriateness of comparing Moses' priestly functions with those of Christ, note that when Moses inaugurated the sanctuary and ordained its priests, he was acting in his role as the chief administrator of the Israelite people. Similarly, Hebrews makes it clear that God, the Chief Administrator of the universe, is the One who appointed Christ as High Priest in the heavenly sanctuary (see chapter 5:1–6). Thus, we can also say that in ordaining Aaron and his sons as priests, Moses was acting as a type of God, who appointed Christ as High Priest in the heavenly sanctuary. This conclusion is borne out by several texts in Hebrews that refer to Jesus as a High Priest "according to the order of Melchizedek" (see Hebrews 5:6, 10; 6:20; 7:11, 17, 21). Melchizedek was both a king (an administrator, like Moses) and a priest (see Hebrews 7), making him a fit representation of Jesus, who also was both a king (administrator) and a priest.

The point is that whichever way we choose to view Moses, whether as a type of

Christ in His role as Priest or as a type of God in His role as Chief Administrator of the universe, the end result is the same: Hebrews 6:19, 20 is about the inauguration of the heavenly sanctuary and Christ's ordination as our heavenly High Priest, not about the heavenly Day of Atonement.

One matter that I have only mentioned in this chapter is the Bible's description of Jesus standing beside God or sitting beside Him on His throne. That will be the topic of the next chapter.

1. Quoted in the *Seventh-day Adventist Encyclopedia,* s.v. "Edson, Hiram"; emphasis in the original.

2. Ford, "Daniel 8:14," 160; emphasis in the original.

3. Ibid., 161.

4. Ibid., 201.

5. Andross, *A More Excellent Ministry,* 52; emphasis added.

6. Ibid., 53.

7. *Handbook,* 416.

8. Ibid., 417.

9. Davidson, "Inauguration or Day of Atonement?" 1, 69.

10. *Handbook,* 417.

11. Cortez, " 'The Anchor of the Soul That Enters Within the Veil,' " 34.

Chapter 29

Seated on God's Throne

In the previous chapter, I quoted five texts in Hebrews that state that Jesus is seated with God on His throne. As I've already noted, the ark of the covenant in the earthly sanctuary was a type of God's throne in heaven. Therefore, the statement that Jesus is seated on God's throne in heaven suggests that He had already entered the Most Holy Place of the heavenly sanctuary at the time Hebrews was written.

Hebrews isn't the only place in the New Testament that tells us that Jesus was either standing beside God or sitting beside Him on His throne. In Revelation 3:21, John quotes Jesus as saying, "To him who overcomes I will grant to sit with Me on My throne, as I also overcame and sat down with My Father on His throne." Revelation was probably written in the last decade of the first century, but Jesus' place on or beside God's throne dates back to only a few days after He ascended to heaven. Peter told his audience on the Day of Pentecost that Jesus had been "exalted to the right hand of God" (Acts 2:33). And at least ten other texts in the New Testament say the same thing.

So how do we deal with the obvious fact that Jesus sat down at the right hand of God on His throne in the Most Holy Place of the heavenly sanctuary at His ascension? How can Adventists say that He didn't enter heaven's Most Holy Place until 1844?

Location or status?

As a start to answering this question, we need to ask the meaning of the statement about Jesus sitting at God's right hand. Here's what I propose, while "the right hand of God" sounds very much like a statement about *location,* it actually has more to do with *status.* The Old Testament passage that the author of Hebrews cites in support of his statement about Jesus sitting at God's right hand is Psalm 110:1, which says, "The LORD said to my Lord, 'Sit at My right hand, till I make Your enemies Your footstool.' " About this text, the *Seventh-day Adventist Bible Commentary* says, "According to Jesus' statement the conversation occurred between God the Father and God the Son. Christ is seated in the place of highest honor in the universe, the right hand of His Father."[1] Thus, location is not the primary emphasis of the text. The point is Christ's kingly status.

Elsewhere in the Old Testament we see the same emphasis on *status* as the primary meaning of sitting at someone's right hand. You will perhaps recall that as David approached the end of his life, there was a contest over who would succeed him. David had promised Bathsheba that her son Solomon would be the next king, but Solomon's half brother Adonijah also wanted to be king and began conspiring to fulfill his desire. When Bathsheba became aware of Adonijah's scheme, she went to David and "said to him, 'My Lord, you swore by the LORD your God to your maidservant, saying, "Assuredly Solomon your son shall reign after me, and he shall sit on my throne" ' " (1 Kings 1:17). Notice that the words *sit on my throne* are juxtaposed with *reign after me.* In this case, sitting on the

throne means reigning as king. First Kings 2:12 says, "Then Solomon sat on the throne of his father David; and his kingdom was firmly established." It isn't likely that Solomon never left the throne for even a moment, so again, the primary meaning of sitting on the throne is status, not location.

This emphasis is particularly evident in 2 Chronicles 6:3, 10. The entire chapter is about the dedication of Solomon's temple. In verse 3, Solomon, no doubt standing on a platform, "turned around and blessed the whole assembly of Israel." Obviously, Solomon wasn't sitting on his throne at that time. Nevertheless, in verse 10, Solomon said, "So the LORD has fulfilled His word which He spoke, and I have filled the position of my father David, and sit on the throne of Israel, as the LORD promised." Since Solomon wasn't literally seated on his throne when he spoke these words, the expression to "sit on the throne of Israel" had to refer to his status as king over Israel. Solomon himself understood it this way, as is evident from his statement "I have filled the position of my father David, and sit on the throne of Israel." To "sit on the throne" meant to "fill the position of king."

In the same way, the New Testament statements—including those in Hebrews—that following Christ's ascension He "sat down at the right hand of God" or "sat down with God on His throne" may carry implications of location. But the evidence from the Old Testament suggests that the primary point is Christ's exalted status as King, not just *where* He sat.

The New Testament view of the heavenly sanctuary

The issue we've been dealing with in both the previous chapter and this chapter is whether Jesus went into the Holy Place or the Most Holy Place of the heavenly sanctuary at His ascension. It seems to me that before we can answer that question definitively, we have to ask, What *is* the Holy Place in the heavenly sanctuary? What *is* the Most Holy Place? What are they like?

I will begin my discussion of these questions by stating my conclusion, and then I will share with you my reasons for it. My conclusion is that the throne room Jesus entered at His ascension includes both the Holy Place and the Most Holy Place. You may question that idea, but please read to the end of this chapter before you reject it. I will share with you four reasons for my suggestion.

1. All Three Members of the Godhead are represented in the two apartments of the earthly sanctuary. God the Father is represented by the ark of the covenant in the Most Holy Place; Jesus Christ, the Bread of Life, is represented by the table of shewbread in the Holy Place; and the Holy Spirit is represented by the seven-branched lamp stand, also in the Holy Place. We know, of course, that the Father, Son, and Holy Spirit are all Deity. Thus, it seems reasonable to conclude that They are together in the heavenly sanctuary, not divided by being placed in two separate rooms. This is particularly evident given the fact that in the earthly sanctuary, Jesus is represented by the table of shewbread in one room while the Father is represented by the ark of the covenant in another room, but in heaven They are seated together on God's throne.

2. There is no veil in the heavenly sanctuary. Without the veil in the earthly sanctuary, there would have been only one apartment. Why the veil? Its purpose was to shield the priests from entering directly into God's presence on a daily basis (see Leviticus 16:3). But there is no need for Jesus, our High Priest, to be shielded from exposure to God's presence, and, thus, there is no need of a veil. This is the second reason for my suggestion that the heavenly sanctuary Jesus entered following His ascension consists of one "room," not two.

My suggestion that there is no veil in the heavenly sanctuary does appear to contradict Hebrews 6:19, which says that in New Testament times, Christ "enter[ed] the Presence behind the veil." Why would the author of Hebrews say that Christ entered "behind the veil" if there is no veil in the heavenly sanctuary? The issue is whether the author intended his readers to understand these words as a literal description of the architecture of the heavenly sanctuary or whether he was using the reader's understanding of the architecture of the earthly sanctuary to make a point about Christ's ministry in the heavenly sanctuary. His main point—which appears several times both in Hebrews and elsewhere in the New Testament—is that Jesus entered into God's presence immediately upon His ascension, and the words *behind the veil* are his way of saying that.

3. Though in the earthly sanctuary the altar of incense was in the Holy Place, that altar was considered to be a furnishing of the Most Holy Place. In fact, Hebrews *locates* the altar of incense in the Most Holy Place. Hebrews 9:3, 4 says, "Behind the second veil [was] the part of the tabernacle which is called the Holiest of All, which had the golden censer [altar of incense] and the ark of the covenant."

Why did the author of Hebrews say that the altar of incense was in the Most Holy Place when in the earthly sanctuary it was located in the Holy Place? He doesn't explain this apparent inaccuracy.* However, I suspect the reason is that the altar pertained to a Most Holy Place form of priestly ministry. The earthly sanctuary located

it in the Holy Place simply because the priests needed to be shielded from appearing in God's visible presence on a daily basis. But because their ministry at the altar was actually a Most Holy Place form of ministry, the altar was placed as close to that apartment as possible without actually being in it. I say this for four reasons.

First, God's instruction to Moses suggests that the altar of incense served a Most Holy Place function. God told Moses that he was to "put it [the altar of incense] before the veil that is before the ark of the Testimony, before the mercy seat that is over the Testimony, where I will meet with you" (Exodus 30:6; see also 40:5). Commenting on this text, Harold S. Camacho, in an article in *Andrews University Seminary Studies,* said, "It is most significant that the location of this altar is given, not in conjunction with the Holy Place or its furnishings, but rather in connection with the Holy of Holies and its articles. . . . This would seem to imply that the altar of incense is very closely related to the Most Holy Place and to the communication with God spoken of in connection with that room."[2]

Second, 1 Kings 6:22 says that in constructing the temple of the Lord, Solomon "overlaid with gold the altar that belonged

---

*William G. Johnsson says he considers the author's placing the altar of incense in the Most Holy Place "a slip." See his book *Hebrews,* Bible Amplifier series (Nampa, Idaho: Pacific Press® Publishing Association, 1994), 157.

to the inner sanctuary" (NIV; see also the RSV). Notice that the writer of 1 Kings understood that though the altar of incense was located in the Holy Place, it "belonged to"* the Most Holy Place. That is, its function was a Most Holy Place function.

Third, the very same thing is suggested by the author's choice of words in Hebrews 9:2–4. Note especially the italics, which are mine, in the following texts. In verse 2, the author said, "A tabernacle was prepared: the first part, *in which* [Greek: *in hē*] was the lampstand, the table, and the showbread." On the other hand, verses 3 and 4 say, "Behind the second veil, the part of the tabernacle which is called the Holiest of All, *which had* [Greek: *echousa*] the golden censer [altar of incense] and the ark of the covenant." The Greek *in hē* in verse 2 clearly refers to the *location* of the various articles of furniture within the Holy Place. However, *echousa* is more properly translated "having" (or the NKJV, "which had").

Richard Davidson has noted—correctly, I believe—that "by using the term *echousa* ('having'), the writer of Hebrews seems to indicate that the altar of incense is 'properly belonging to' the Most Holy Place in *function,* although not actually located in the Most Holy Place."[3] Davidson's translation of *echousa* as "properly belonging to" is basically identical to the New International Version translation of 1 Kings

6:22, which says that the altar of incense *"belonged to"* the inner sanctuary."

Finally, the conclusion that the altar of incense, while located in the Holy Place of the earthly sanctuary, actually pertained to Most Holy Place ministry, is supported by a scene in Revelation—which also introduces the fourth reason for my suggestion that the heavenly sanctuary consists of one room, not two.

4. Revelation's description of the heavenly sanctuary places the altar of incense "before the throne." In Revelation 8:3, John saw an angel offering incense "upon the golden altar which was before the throne." Please notice that the altar of incense was located *before God's throne,* which is the antitype of the ark of the covenant in the earthly sanctuary. Notice also that Revelation gives no hint that there was a veil between the altar and the throne. They are all in the same "room," just as they are in Hebrews 9:3.

Revelation 4:5 also supports my suggestion that the heavenly sanctuary is one room, not two. In Revelation 4, John gives us the Bible's most complete description of God's throne room. Among other things, he says that "before the throne, seven lamps were blazing" (verse 5, NIV). These seven lamps seem obviously to be the heavenly antitype of the seven-branched lamp stand in the earthly sanctuary. In the earthly sanctuary, this lamp stand was located in

---

*The Hebrew preposition can mean "to," "for," "towards," "belonging to," and so forth.

the Holy Place, but in heaven it is located "before the throne"—heaven's antitype of the ark of the covenant.

Thus, in vision, John saw both the altar of incense and the lamp stand located in heaven's Most Holy Place—"before the throne"—rather than in the Holy Place. Again, this suggests that God's throne room in heaven includes everything that was symbolized by the furnishings in both apartments of the earthly sanctuary.

Another significant factor to consider in the question of whether there is a veil in the heavenly sanctuary is the fact that when Jesus died, the veil in the temple was torn in two—from top to bottom. Adventists have always interpreted this to mean that the services in the earthly sanctuary had come to their end and Jesus' ministry as our High Priest in the heavenly sanctuary had begun. I agree with that interpretation.

However, I believe there is an additional meaning that can be attached to this event. The veil separated the people from God. Even the regular priests were forbidden to pass through that veil, on pain of death. Only the high priest could enter the Most Holy Place, and he only once a year. In other words, the veil represented limited access to God. But Christ's death brought an end to that system. Now every believer has unlimited access to God. I suggest that the rending of the veil in the temple was symbolic of this new reality. And that is

precisely the lesson that Hebrews teaches. Because Christ has died and is now our High Priest in the heavenly sanctuary, every Christian can "come boldly to the throne of grace" (Hebrews 4:16). The rending of the veil in the earthly sanctuary symbolized both the end of that limited system for approaching God and the beginning of a new system in which there would be no "veil" separating the people from God.

Desmond Ford more or less agrees with the idea that the heavenly sanctuary has one room, not two. He said, "Most commentators refer to the absence of a veil in the heavenly sanctuary because since the cross the two apartments have become one." I would agree with that statement. However, Ford also said that "the term 'sanctuary' once used for a bipartite structure now applies to the single 'throne room' of heaven."[4] In other words, Ford views the entire heavenly sanctuary as an antitype of the earthly Most Holy Place only. I, on the other hand, understand the removal of the veil to mean that both apartments are now joined into one "room," which is the antitype of both the Holy Place and the Most Holy Place.

From Ford's perspective, the ministry that Christ carried out following His ascension in A.D. 31 must have been exclusively a Most Holy Place ministry since, as he understands it, the sanctuary Christ entered was exclusively the Most Holy Place.

And since the only ministry that was ever carried out in the Most Holy Place of the earthly sanctuary took place on the Day of Atonement, the ministry of Christ in heaven's Most Holy Place that began in A.D. 31 must also have been a Day of Atonement ministry. Therefore, Christ couldn't have *begun* His Most Holy Place Day of Atonement ministry in 1844.

However, from my perspective, the absence of a veil in the heavenly sanctuary means that in A.D. 31, Jesus entered the Holy Place as much as He did the Most Holy Place. Or, to put it another way, the heavenly sanctuary incorporates both the Holy Place and the Most Holy Place of its earthly type. This means that the ministry Jesus carried out after His ascension is as likely to have been a Holy Place ministry as a Most Holy Place ministry.

Does this mean that heaven's sanctuary has only one location rather than two, as in the type? Not necessarily. The biblical evidence suggests that it *does* have two locations.

A "Most Holy Place" in heaven

I will begin by reminding you of what I said in chapter 21: the heavenly judgment described in Daniel 7—including the Son of man's approach to God's throne—is an eschatological Day of Atonement. By the historicist method of interpreting Daniel's prophecies, chronologically, this judgment fits the same period of earth's history as does the cleansing/restoration/vindication of the sanctuary in Daniel 8:14.*

Here is how Daniel introduces that judgment/Day of Atonement scene in Daniel 7:9, 10: "As I looked, 'thrones were set in place, and the Ancient of Days took his seat' " (verse 9, NIV). Notice that Daniel saw thrones (plural) "set in place." In other words, these thrones, including God's throne, had not been in this particular location before. Rather, they were moved here and set in place. This idea is reinforced by the last part of verse 9, which says that God's throne "was a fiery flame, its *wheels* a burning fire" (emphasis added). Why does God's throne have "wheels"? William Shea makes an interesting comment: "The implication is that it was through some kind of locomotion related to these wheels that, riding upon His throne, *God came into the audience chamber* where He met with His angelic host."[5]

So, if we take Daniel's vision in its most literal sense, then we have to conclude that for the purpose of the investigative judgment, God's throne, the antitype of the ark of the covenant, was moved to a new location. And

---

*Interestingly, though Ford understands Christ's Day of Atonement ministry in heaven to have begun at His ascension, he makes it very clear in his Glacier View manuscript that Daniel 8:14 does point to an eschatological Day of Atonement. (See pages 205, 206 of this book.)

since Jesus, the Son of man, appeared before God's throne in Daniel's vision (see verses 13, 14), Jesus also moved to this new location.

I propose that in showing God's throne moving to a new "place," Daniel 7:9, 10 implies that heaven's throne room does indeed have two parts. The first part is the "place" where Jesus sat down with His Father in A.D. 31, and the second part is the "place" where the judgment in Daniel 7 occurs. Each one can be considered heaven's Holy Place, and each can also be considered heaven's Most Holy Place. We can consider the location where Jesus sat down with His Father in A.D. 31 to be heaven's Holy Place because, even though God's throne is located there, the two apartments are now in one "room." Thus, it's reasonable to understand that for eighteen hundred years Christ carried out the type of ministry in the heavenly sanctuary that is represented by the activity of the priests throughout the year in the Holy Place of the earthly sanctuary. At the same time, we can consider Daniel 7 to describe a second location in the heavenly sanctuary where heaven's Day of Atonement and the investigative judgment take place. This would be the antitype of heaven's Most Holy Place, but at the same time it would contain everything from the first location, including heaven's Holy Place.

Is this what heaven is really like? I don't know; it's just a suggestion. What I do know is that heaven is vastly different from anything we've ever experienced on this earth, and that in explaining it to us, God is limited to using language and images that are familiar to us. Thus, I think it's a mistake for us to argue overly much about heavenly architecture. It's enough for us to know that Jesus entered into God's immediate presence when He returned to heaven two thousand years ago. It's enough for us to know that an important judgment began in heaven in 1844, and that this judgment is heaven's counterpart of the earthly Day of Atonement, which will forever solve the problem of evil. It's enough for us to know that Jesus, the Son of man, is involved in every aspect of our salvation, including heaven's eschatological Day of Atonement. And it's enough for us to know that at every step of the way, whichever "room" they are in, Father and Son are working side by side to ensure that all sincere believers find their way to their heavenly home.

---

1. *Seventh-day Adventist Bible Commentary,* 3:880.

2. Camacho, "The Altar of Incense in Hebrews 9:3–4," 8, 9.

3. Davidson, "Typology in the Book of Hebrews," in *Issues in the Book of Hebrews,* 178, 179; emphasis in the original.

4. Ford, "Daniel 8:14," 235, 239.

5. Shea, *Selected Studies on Prophetic Interpretation,* 119; emphasis added.

Chapter 30

The Theme of Hebrews

Imagine for a moment that you are a sixty-year-old Jewish Christian living in or near Jerusalem in A.D. 65. When you became a Christian about twenty-five years ago, you fully expected that Jesus would return within the next few years. After all, He Himself promised that, after building a place for His people, He would return "and receive you to Myself; that where I am, there you may be also" (John 14:3). And the angels who spoke to the disciples immediately following His ascension assured them that He would return "in like manner as you saw Him go into heaven" (Acts 1:11).

However, after twenty-five years with no Jesus showing up, your faith is wavering, and you're wondering if perhaps the Christians have been wrong all along. The rituals associated with the temple in Jerusalem had been profoundly meaningful to you in your youth; in fact, you still participate in them occasionally, as do many of your Christian friends. And, unfortunately, the prejudice against Christians in Jerusalem and Judea is oppressive. Ridicule is common, many economic opportunities are unavailable to you, and your situation is precarious—it seems like every Jew is constantly watching for an excuse to press legal charges against Christians. So, one day, you mention to some of your Christian friends your thought of maybe returning to Judaism, and you discover that their feelings are similar to yours.

The New Testament book of Hebrews seems quite clearly to have been addressed to Jewish Christians such as these, those who were wavering in their faith in Jesus and who were considering a return to Judaism, which still held a strong appeal to them. A mature Jewish Christian wrote Hebrews to explain to these wavering fellow-believers the real significance of the rituals that had been so meaningful to them in the past. His purpose was to encourage them to hold fast to their faith in Jesus.

Of course, the most important observance in the Hebrew religious year was the Day of Atonement. This was the day on which all the sins that had been committed during the previous year were removed forever from the camp of Israel, and the people could feel that both they and their sanctuary had been fully cleansed spiritually. Thus, it should come as no surprise that, in his effort to encourage wavering Jewish Christians, the author of Hebrews made several references to the Day of Atonement. Some interpreters see so many references to the Day of Atonement in Hebrews that they consider it to be the major theme of the book—the backbone of the author's line of reasoning. Desmond Ford, for example, says, "Christ's high priestly work is the main theme of Hebrews, and the only distinctive work of the high priest was that of the Day of Atonement."[1] "Never is the Day of Atonement absent from the mind of the apostle."[2] Thus, the issue I wish to consider with you in this chapter is the theme of Hebrews, especially of chapters 8–10.

As I understand it, Ford's basis for considering the Day of Atonement to be the major theme of Hebrews is twofold. First, throughout the book, the author stressed Christ's entrance into the very presence of God—into His throne room, which Ford views as exclusively the antitype of the Most Holy Place of the earthly sanctuary. And since the only activity in the Most Holy Place of the earthly sanctuary was the high priest's rituals on the Day of Atonement, Ford assumes that every mention of Christ standing in the Father's presence or sitting with Him on His throne is a reference to the Day of Atonement. In chapter 2 of his Glacier View manuscript, in which he dealt with Hebrews, he said that the central thesis of the chapter was that "Hebrews clearly affirms that in fulfillment of the Day of Atonement type, Christ by the cross-resurrection-ascension event entered upon the ministry prefigured by the sanctuary's *second* apartment."[3] Ford then quoted each of the references in Hebrews to Christ's presence with God and also Hebrews 6:19, 20, which speaks of Christ's entrance "behind the veil." I dealt with these texts in the previous two chapters, so I won't repeat that discussion here.

Ford's second reason for considering the Day of Atonement to be the theme of Hebrews is the references to the Day of Atonement in Hebrews 8–10. We'll address that question now—is the Day of Atonement indeed the major theme of Hebrews 8–10? I will argue instead that the theme of these chapters is the old and new covenants, and throughout them, the author of Hebrews stresses the superiority of the new covenant over the old covenant. Since each covenant had a sanctuary, the author also stresses the superiority of Christ's sacrifice and His ministry in the heavenly sanctuary over the sacrifices and ministry performed by the priests in the earthly sanctuary.

Because a detailed examination of Hebrews 8–10 would go beyond the scope of the present chapter in this book, I'll give you a summary of their content, quoting only the most relevant words, phrases, and sentences. Among other things, I will point out four indisputable references to the Day of Atonement and one about which commentators disagree. Readers who are familiar with the contents of Hebrews 8–10 will easily follow my summary. Those who aren't familiar with these chapters may find it helpful to read them first so they can understand my comments.

Hebrews 8

The eighth chapter of Hebrews divides nicely into two parts.

Part 1, verses 1–6. In these verses, the author explains that Jesus is the High Priest in the heavenly sanctuary, of which the earthly sanctuary is a copy. The earthly sanctuary had priests who offered sacrifices, and therefore Christ, the High Priest in the heavenly sanctuary, must also "have something to offer" (verse 3). This part of

chapter 8 concludes with these words: "But now He [Jesus] has obtained a more excellent ministry, inasmuch as He is also Mediator of a better covenant, which was established on better promises" (verse 6). The key word in this verse is *covenant*.

Part 2, verses 7–13. In verse 7, the author said, "If that first covenant had been faultless, then no place would have been sought for a second," and, in the next several verses, he quotes a long passage from Jeremiah in which the prophet predicted that God would institute a new covenant "with the house of Israel and with the house of Judah" (verse 8). This covenant wouldn't be like the one He made with the Israelites when they left Egypt (verse 9). In this new covenant, He would "put [His] laws in their mind and write them on their hearts" (verse 10). The concluding verse in the chapter says, "In that He says, 'A new covenant,' He has made the first [covenant] obsolete. Now what is becoming obsolete and growing old is ready to vanish away."

My suggestion, as I said earlier, is that the theme of chapters 8–10 is the contrast between the old and new covenants, and the author's point is that the old covenant is ineffective for bringing about real spiritual change in the minds and hearts of God's people, but the new covenant *can* bring about this change. The author used the Old Testament sanctuary services, including its Day of Atonement, as an example of the ineffective nature of the old covenant. By way of contrast, he pointed out that Christ's ministry in the heavenly sanctuary is effective at changing minds and hearts.

Hebrews 9

Chapter 9 divides into four parts.

Part 1, verses 1–10. In verses 1–10, the author described the Old Testament sanctuary. Verse 1 says, "Even the first covenant had ordinances of divine service and the earthly sanctuary," and in the next nine verses the author describes the furnishings in both apartments of the sanctuary (verses 2–5) and the ministry performed by its priests in both apartments (verses 6, 7). Verse 7 contains one of the indisputable references to the Day of Atonement in Hebrews 8–10. The author said that "into the second part [the Most Holy Place of the earthly sanctuary] the high priest went alone once a year." The statement about the high priest's ministry "once a year" clearly points to the Day of Atonement.

In verse 8, the author refers to the heavenly sanctuary: "The Holy Spirit indicating this, that the way into the Holiest of All was not yet made manifest while the first tabernacle was still standing." The Greek term translated "Holiest of All" in the New King James Version is *tōn hagiōn*,

which is the plural form of the singular *ta hagia*.* Interpreters of Hebrews differ on whether the author meant the "sanctuary" or "Most Holy Place." This is a significant issue that I will comment on in the next chapter.

Part 2, verses 11–15. In the second section of chapter 9, the author describes Christ's ministry in the heavenly sanctuary services under the new covenant. The most controversial text in this section is verse 12, which says, "Not with the blood of goats and calves, but with His own blood He [Christ] entered the Most Holy Place once for all, having obtained eternal redemption." Many Bible versions, including the New King James, say "Most Holy Place" or some variation thereof, an indication that many interpreters consider it to be another reference to the Day of Atonement in Hebrews 8–10. I will examine this verse in detail in the next chapter.

The author went on to point out that "if the blood of bulls and goats and the ashes of a heifer, sprinkling the unclean, sanctifies for the purifying of the flesh [under the old covenant], how much more shall the blood of Christ . . . cleanse [purge] your conscience from dead works to serve the living God [under the new covenant]?" Notice the contrast between the ineffective earthly sanctuary ministry and Christ's ef-

---

*Throughout the rest of my discussion of Hebrews, I will use the singular *ta hagia*, even when the Greek is the plural *tōn hagiōn*.

fective ministry in the heavenly sanctuary.

In verse 15, the last verse of this section, the author said, "For this reason He [Jesus] is the Mediator of a new covenant, . . . for the redemption of the transgressions under the first covenant." Notice the stress on the covenants and the superiority of the new covenant over the old covenant.

Part 3, verses 16–22. The third section of chapter 9 points out that the ratification of a covenant requires blood. In verse 18, the author said that "not even the first covenant was dedicated without blood," and in the next several verses, he commented on the ritual by which Moses ratified the first covenant. Among other things, he said that Moses sprinkled with blood "both the tabernacle and all the vessels of the ministry" (verse 21; the entire ritual is described in verses 19–21). Commenting on the sprinkling of blood by which Moses ratified the old covenant, the author said, "According to the law almost all things are purged with blood, and without shedding of blood there is no remission" (verse 22).

Part 4, verses 23–28. Having commented on the ritual by which the old covenant was ratified, the author turned in the last section of chapter 9 to the heavenly sanctuary. He said, "It was necessary that the copies of the things in the heavens should be purified with these, but the heavenly things themselves with better sacrifices than these" (verse 23). His point is that

Moses ratified the old covenant by sprinkling the sanctuary and its furnishings with animal blood, but Jesus cleansed the heavenly sanctuary with His own blood, which comes from a much better sacrifice than that of mere animals. Notice the emphasis on the cleansing function of blood. I will return to this detail in the next chapter.

In the remainder of this section, the author commented on Christ's ministry in the heavenly sanctuary and how much superior it is to the ministry of the high priests in the sanctuary under the old covenant. Christ didn't enter into a sanctuary constructed by human hands but into heaven itself. Nor does He need to "offer Himself often, as the high priest enters the Most Holy Place every year with blood of another" (verse 25). Christ's sacrifice was once for all time. Notice the clear reference to the Day of Atonement. The author actually refers to the earthly Day of Atonement, but it's obvious that he applies it to Christ's heavenly Day of Atonement ministry. The author's point in 9:25 is that Christ's one sacrifice is an example of the superiority of His ministry over that of the high priest on the earthly Day of Atonement because that ritual had to be repeated every year. This is another example of the superiority of the new covenant over the old covenant.

Hebrews 10

Chapter 10 is divided into five sections,

but I will comment only on the first four.

Part 1, verses 1–4. In the first section, the author made two obvious references to the earthly Day of Atonement. In verse 1, he said, "The law, having a shadow of the good things to come, and not the very image of the things, can never with these same sacrifices, which they offer continually *year by year,* make those who approach perfect." And in verse 3, he said, "In those sacrifices there is a reminder of sins *every year.*" His point is that the sacrifices under the old covenant—especially those on the Day of Atonement—were ineffective for bringing about a real change in people. The words I've italicized in these verses are two more obvious references to the Day of Atonement.

Part 2, verses 5–10. In the second section, the author pointed out that Jesus' sacrifice of His body was by an act of obedience to God's will, and in verse 9, the author applied the words of Psalm 40:8 to Jesus: "Behold, I have come to do Your will, O God." He concludes verse 9 by saying, "He [God] takes away the first that He may establish the second." The author didn't say what "the first" and "the second" are, but it seems most likely that he meant that the old covenant and its earthly sanctuary had become obsolete, which is why God took both away and replaced them with the new covenant with Jesus' ministry in the heavenly sanctuary.

Part 3, verses 11–18. In the third section, the author once again contrasts the old covenant sanctuary service with the new covenant sanctuary service. "Every priest stands ministering daily and offering repeatedly the same sacrifices, which can never take away sins. But this Man [Jesus], after He had offered one sacrifice for sins forever, sat down at the right hand of God" (verses 11, 12). The point is that "by one offering He [Jesus] has perfected forever those who are being sanctified" (verse 14). In other words, Jesus' sacrifice *is* effective for bringing about a permanent change in human lives. Then the author quotes Jeremiah's famous statement, "This is the covenant that I will make with them after those days, says the LORD: I will put My laws into their hearts, and in their minds I will write them" (verse 16).

So we have come full circle. The author began his discussion of the covenants in chapter 8 by quoting Jeremiah's statement that under the new covenant God would write His laws on His peoples' minds and hearts. In all of chapter 9 and the first part of chapter 10, he explains how Christ's one sacrifice and His high priestly ministry in heaven made this possible. And he concludes by quoting once again Jeremiah's famous statement about God writing His law in human minds and hearts through the new covenant.

Part 4, verses 19–25. In section four, the

author appeals to his readers to take advantage of this new covenant. "Therefore, brethren," he says, "having boldness to enter the Holiest by the blood of Jesus, . . . let us draw near with a true heart in full assurance of faith, having our hearts sprinkled from an evil conscience and our bodies washed with pure water" (verses 19, 22).

Summing up what we have seen in this chapter, while the author of Hebrews did speak about the Day of Atonement in chapters 9 and 10, that was not his primary burden. His theme in Hebrews 8–10 was the covenants, and he used the Day of Atonement as one way to show how much superior Christ's high priestly ministry under the new covenant is to that of the earthly high priests under the old covenant.

However, we still aren't ready to draw a final conclusion about the Day of Atonement in Hebrews 9 and 10. In order to do that, we need to consider several other issues.

---

1. Ford, "Daniel 8:14," 182.
2. Ibid., 253.
3. Ibid., 160; emphasis in the original.

Chapter 31

The Day of Atonement in Hebrews 9 and 10—Part 1

I have been aware for many years of the problems that Hebrews poses for our historic Adventist teaching about the investigative judgment. Because of this, I embarked on a detailed study of the book of Hebrews several years ago. I began with chapter 1, verse 1, and progressed slowly and prayerfully through to chapter 10, writing my own detailed, verse-by-verse commentary as I went along. By the time I was through, I had reached certain definite conclusions, some of which you will read in this chapter.

I pointed out at the end of the previous chapter that we still need to consider several issues before we draw a final conclusion about the Day of Atonement in Hebrews 9 and 10. This chapter and the next are about those other issues, which are quite technical. My reason for bringing them up here is that these issues have for more than a hundred years been among the chief arguments of our critics against our teaching about a pre-Advent investigative judgment in the heavenly sanctuary. Thus, technical or not, it's imperative that we deal with them.

Several times in the pages that follow I refer to the Septuagint. Scholars recognize that the author of Hebrews relied heavily on the Septuagint version—a fact that is often significant in the interpretation of his meaning.

Hebrews 9:8

In the verses preceding Hebrews 9:8, the author described the furnishings in the earthly sanctuary (verses 2–5) and the ministry of its priests (verses 6, 7). Then he said, "The Holy Spirit [was] indicating [by] this, that the way into the Holiest of All [Greek: *ta hagia*] was not yet made manifest while the first tabernacle [Greek: *protēs skēnēs*] was still standing." Both of the Greek terms I noted, *ta hagia* and *protēs skēnēs,* are critical to interpreting verse 8.

Everyone agrees that the words *ta hagia* refer to the heavenly sanctuary. The question is whether they refer to the heavenly sanctuary as a whole or only to its Most Holy Place. Commentators are divided on this issue, though I think I'm safe in saying that most prefer "Most Holy Place." In the New King James Version, *ta hagia* is translated as "Holiest of All"—that is, the Most Holy Place.

This issue is, in fact, quite critical. If by *ta hagia* the author of Hebrews meant the sanctuary as a whole, that would allow for the possibility of Jesus having begun a Holy Place type of ministry in the heavenly sanctuary in A.D. 31, which could then have been followed by a Most Holy Place ministry. However, if by *ta hagia* the author meant exclusively the Most Holy Place of the heavenly sanctuary, then obviously Jesus must have begun just a Most Holy Place/Day of Atonement ministry in the heavenly sanctuary in A.D. 31. We'll look at both *protēs skēnēs* and *ta hagia* to determine whether by the latter Greek term the author of Hebrews meant the entire Old Testament sanctuary or only its Most Holy Place.

Protēs skēnēs means "first tabernacle." Prior to using this term in verse 8, the au-

thor used it in verses 2 and 6, where in both instances it clearly refers to the Holy Place of the earthly sanctuary. Thus, at first glance, it would seem reasonable to understand it to mean the same thing in verse 8. If that is the case, then verse 8 can be paraphrased as saying that "the way into the Most Holy Place of the heavenly sanctuary had not been opened up as long as the Holy Place in the earthly sanctuary was still in operation." But that seems a bit odd. Why should Christ's entrance into heaven's *Most Holy Place* depend on whether the *Holy Place* of the earthly sanctuary was still functioning? Didn't ministry in both apartments end at the same time in A.D. 31?* It seems more reasonable to say that Christ's entrance into the heavenly sanctuary as a whole could not have occurred as long as *any part* of the entire earthly sanctuary was still in operation.

And, in fact, there is a strong contextual basis for this conclusion. As I pointed out in chapter 30, the theme of Hebrews 8–10 is the superiority of the new covenant, with its heavenly sanctuary, over the old covenant, with its earthly sanctuary. The author of Hebrews devoted the last half of chapter 8 to an explanation of the old covenant, and he began chapter 9 with the statement that "even the first covenant had ordinances of divine

---

*The Jews continued carrying out the services in the earthly sanctuary (the temple in Jerusalem) until its destruction in A.D. 70. However, from God's perspective, those sacrifices no longer had meaning after Christ had made the once-for-all, ultimate sacrifice for sin.

service and the earthly sanctuary" (Hebrews 9:1). In the next several verses, he described both the furnishings and the ministry of the priests in that earthly sanctuary. Verse 8 then comes back to a consideration of the entire earthly sanctuary and its antitype in heaven.

Thus, in spite of the previous uses in chapter 9 of the term *protēs skēnēs* with the meaning of "Holy Place," it seems reasonable to conclude that in verse 8 this term means the sanctuary as a whole. Paraphrased this way, Hebrews 9:8 reads, "The Holy Spirit was indicating by this, that the way into the heavenly sanctuary as a whole was not yet made manifest while the earthly sanctuary as a whole was still operating." This appears to me to be the more logical way to understand Hebrews 9:8.

Now, what about *ta hagia?* When the author of Hebrews used this term, did he mean the heavenly sanctuary as a whole or only its Most Holy Place, as most commentators believe?

I will begin my answer by pointing out that the author of Hebrews was a very astute Jewish Christian who understood both Judaism and Christianity very well. We can assume that he would have used the plural of *ta hagia* in harmony with the general Jewish understanding of the time. Carl Cosaert, a professor in the School of Theology at Walla Walla University, wrote his master's thesis on this topic. He investigated the use of the Greek words *ta hagia* in both their singular and plural forms in the Septuagint, in the Old Testament Pseudepigrapha, and in the writings of Philo and Josephus, both of whom were contemporaries or near contemporaries of the author of Hebrews.*

Cosaert found that the plural form of *ta hagia* is never used in any of these sources in reference to the Most Holy Place. Rather, he found that "whenever the plural form by itself is used [in these sources], it exclusively describes the whole sanctuary in general. Moreover, whenever specific reference is made to the Most Holy Place, the plural form by itself is never used. Instead, the Most Holy Place is referred to by either the use of the singular form of *hagios*, . . . some qualifying term, . . . or, more typically, a form of the phrase *hagion tōn hagiōn*."[1]

The point is that the author of Hebrews would most likely have used the plural of *ta hagia* in harmony with its use in the Septuagint and other contemporary sources. This supports the translation of *ta hagia* in verse 8 as "sanctuary" rather than "Most Holy Place."

My conclusion from this discussion of Hebrews 9:8 is that there are excellent contextual and cultural reasons for translating *ta hagia* in Hebrews 9:8 as "sanctuary" rather than "Most Holy Place." And with that

---

*Hebrews was almost certainly written before A.D. 70. Philo was a Jewish philosopher who lived from 20 B.C. to A.D. 50, and the historian Josephus, who was of priestly descent, lived from A.D. 37 to about A.D. 100.

translation, it's entirely biblical to consider that Christ began a Holy Place ministry in the heavenly sanctuary when He ascended in A.D. 31, not an exclusively Most Holy Place ministry. We'll consider additional issues in Hebrews 9:8, 9 in chapter 33.

Hebrews 9:12

Hebrews 9:12 has also been widely interpreted to mean that Christ began a Most Holy Place form of ministry upon His ascension. This verse says, "Not with the blood of goats and calves, but with His own blood He entered the Most Holy Place [Greek: plural of *ta hagia*] once for all, having obtained eternal redemption." The majority of commentators and translators understand the author of Hebrews to have meant the Most Holy Place. They do this for at least two reasons.

First, the plural of *ta hagia* in verse 12 probably means whatever it meant in verse 8, and since most scholars understand this expression in verse 8 to mean the Most Holy Place, they carry that meaning to verse 12. However, as I just pointed out, "sanctuary" seems to be a more appropriate translation of *ta hagia* in verse 8, and thus also in verse 12.

Second, scholars note that verse 12 says Christ did not enter the heavenly sanctuary "with the blood of goats and calves, but with His own blood." A bull and a goat were sacrificed on the Day of Atonement

in the earthly sanctuary, which leads people to think that the author had in mind Christ's Day of Atonement ministry in the heavenly sanctuary. From this perspective also, "Most Holy Place" appears to be the preferred translation of *ta hagia*.

In response, I will point out what I already noted above—that the plural form of *ta hagia* is *never* used to refer to the Most Holy Place in the Septuagint, the Old Testament Pseudepigrapha, or the works of Philo or Josephus. While this is not conclusive evidence for its meaning in Hebrews 9:12, it is highly suggestive. And while the reference to goats, calves, and bulls in verses 12 and 13 does appear to suggest a Most Holy Place ritual, an examination of the Greek words for these animals in both Hebrews and Leviticus 16—the passage containing Scripture's primary description of the Day of Atonement—casts doubt on that conclusion.

The Greek word for "calves" in verse 12 is *moschōn,* which is the same word the Septuagint uses in Leviticus 16:3 for the young bull that was sacrificed on the Day of Atonement. However, the word for "goats" in Hebrews 9:12 is *tragōn,* whereas in the Septuagintal version of Leviticus 16, the word for both the Lord's goat and the scapegoat is *chimaros,* and the word *tragos* (the singular form) doesn't appear even once in that Day of Atonement chapter. Nor are the words *tragos* and *tragōn* used anywhere else in the chapters of the Pentateuch that deal with the sanctuary—with the exception of Numbers 7, where it appears thirteen times. Significantly, Numbers 7 is one of the major passages in the Pentateuch dealing with the *inauguration* of the earthly sanctuary—which is additional evidence in support of the conclusion I've drawn in chapter 28 that Christ's entrance "behind the veil" in Hebrews 6:19, 20 is connected with the inauguration of the Most Holy Place, not with the Day of Atonement.*

The author of Hebrews mentions goats and calves again in chapter 9:19, albeit in reverse order: "calves and goats." This time the ratification and inauguration of the covenant are unquestionably the context. Davidson comments that "the author of Hebrews unmistakably links the conjoining of these two animals with the background of inauguration, not the Day of Atonement."[2]

Thus, the conclusion that the plural of *ta hagia* in Hebrews 9:12 should be translated "sanctuary" rather than "Most Holy Place" has significant biblical support.

Hebrews 10:19, 20

In the New King James Version, Hebrews 10:19, 20, along with the first part of verse 22 (to complete the sentence), says, "Therefore, brethren, having boldness to enter the Holiest [Greek: plural of *ta hagia*] by the blood of Jesus, by a new and living way which He consecrated for us, through the veil, that is, His flesh, . . . let us draw near with a true heart in full assurance of faith." Again, the word *Holiest* in the New King James Version suggests that the translators understood *ta hagia* to refer to the Most Holy Place. However, as I've already pointed out, the plural of *ta hagia*—which the author used here—didn't refer exclusively to the Most Holy Place in Jewish literature of the time. This immediately casts doubt on the idea that the author of Hebrews meant the Most Holy Place in chapter 10:19, 20.

This conclusion is supported by a comparison of these verses with Hebrews 6:19, 20, which I analyzed in chapter 28 of this book. Please notice the similarity between these two passages:

Hebrews 6:19, 20—"This hope we have as an anchor of the soul, both sure and steadfast, and which enters the Presence behind the veil, where the forerunner has entered for us, even Jesus, having become High Priest forever according to the order of Melchizedek."

Hebrews 10:19, 20—"Therefore, brethren, having boldness to enter the Holiest

---

*However, Norman Young points out that "Philo, the first century [A.D.] Jewish philosopher, uses *tragos* more frequently than *chimaros* for the sin-offering goat of the Day of Atonement." "The Day of Dedication or the Day of Atonement? The Old Testament Background to Hebrews 6:19-20 Revisited," *Andrews University Seminary Studies* 40, no. 1 (Spring 2002): 65.

by the blood of Jesus, by a new and living way which He consecrated for us, through the veil, that is, His flesh . . ."

Jesus and His high priestly ministry are the subjects of both of these passages. Both say that Jesus has gone "behind" or "through the veil." And both encourage believers to take hold of this hope. In my discussion of Hebrews 6:19, 20, I explained why "behind the veil" should be understood as a reference to the inauguration of the heavenly sanctuary and Christ's appointment as High Priest in that sanctuary, rather than as a reference to the heavenly Day of Atonement. The parallel nature of these verses suggests that Hebrews 10:19, 20 should also be understood as inauguration.

This conclusion is supported by the use of the Greek word *egkainizō* in verse 20, which the New King James Version translates as "consecrated." I find it significant that in the part of the Pentateuch dealing with the sanctuary rituals as translated in the Septuagint, a form of the noun *egkainizō* appears only four times—again, all of them in Numbers 7.* And as I pointed out above, Numbers 7—the entire chapter—describes in detail the rituals that were performed in connection with the inauguration of the sanctuary. Thus, the word *consecrated* (*egkainizō*) in Hebrews 10:20 should be understood as a reference to the

inauguration of the heavenly sanctuary, not to the Day of Atonement.

There is additional evidence in support of this conclusion within Hebrews itself. The word *egkainizō* also appears in Hebrews 9:18, "Therefore not even the first covenant was dedicated [*egkainizō*] without blood." I will point out in chapter 32 of this book that Hebrews 9:16–22 merges the rituals associated with the ratification of the covenant and the inauguration of the sanctuary. Thus, the use of *egkainizō* in Hebrews 9:18 in connection with the inauguration of the sanctuary supports the interpretation that Hebrews 10:20 is also a reference to the inauguration of the sanctuary. Therefore, even if the words *ta hagia* in Hebrews 10:20 do refer to the Most Holy Place (a conclusion that the typical use of the word in the first century A.D. contradicts), then it should be understood as a reference to the inauguration of the sanctuary, not the Day of Atonement. This is further support for the same conclusion with respect to Hebrews 6:19, 20 that I drew in chapter 28 of this book.

We still need to investigate several other issues related to the Day of Atonement in Hebrews. That will be the subject of the next chapter.

_____

1. Cosaert, "The Use of *Hagios* for the Sanctuary," 102, 103.

2. Davidson, "Inauguration or Day of Atonement?" 79.

_____

*Numbers 7:10, 11, 84, 88.

Chapter 32

The Day of Atonement in Hebrews 9 and 10—Part 2

I pointed out in chapter 30 that many commentators consider the Day of Atonement to be the major theme of Hebrews. In the previous chapters, we've been examining that claim, and we've found that two other themes predominate—inauguration and covenants. In this chapter, we will examine four other issues that are related to the discussion about the Day of Atonement in Hebrews.

Cleansing in Hebrews

The objective of the earthly Day of Atonement was to cleanse the sanctuary of the sins that had accumulated there during the previous year and to remove them entirely from the camp of Israel. The Hebrew word translated "cleanse" in Leviticus 16:19, 30 is *taher.* The Septuagint uses the Greek word *katharizō,* which also means "to cleanse." This word is also used in Hebrews 9:14, 22, 23, and 10:2.

Since *katharizō* is the Greek word that the Septuagint uses in Leviticus 16 for the cleansing of the sanctuary, we are naturally interested in how the author of Hebrews used this word, for it can give us some clues about his interpretation of the Day of Atonement. Examining the four texts above, we discover that he used the word in two ways.

The first kind of usage: cleansing the sanctuary. The author of Hebrews used the word *katharizō* in contexts having to do with the cleansing of the sanctuary. We find this in chapter 9:22, 23, where he said, "According to the law almost all things are purified [*katharizō*] with blood, and without shedding of blood there is no remission. Therefore it was necessary that the copies of the things in the heavens should be purified [*katharizō*] with these, but the heavenly things themselves with better sacrifices than these."

Many commentators see this cleansing of the heavenly sanctuary as a reference to the heavenly Day of Atonement. They make this connection because in the next two verses the author speaks about the Day of Atonement: "Christ has not entered the holy places made with hands, which are copies of the true, but into heaven itself, now to appear in the presence of God for us; not that He should offer Himself often, as the high priest enters the Most Holy Place every year with blood of another" (verses 24, 25).

Since the author spoke of Christ's heavenly Day of Atonement ministry immediately after he referred to the cleansing of the heavenly sanctuary, the context seems to suggest that in verse 22 he was speaking about Christ's Day of Atonement cleansing of the heavenly sanctuary. However, context has to do not just with what comes *after* a particular text; it also has to do with what comes *before*. And in this case, what comes before is actually a more relevant part of the context than what comes after. In verses 19 to 22, the author explained—somewhat imprecisely (see the next section of this chapter)—how Moses ratified the old covenant by sprinkling the people and the sanctuary with blood (see Exodus 24:1–8). Then, in verse 23, he began his application to the new covenant and Christ's ministry in the heavenly sanctuary, saying that "the copies of the things in the heavens should be purified with these [the blood of animals], but the heavenly things themselves with better sacrifices than these."

Obviously, the author had in mind the ratification ritual he had just described. This is particularly apparent from his use of the word *these*: "It was necessary that the copies of the things in the heavens should be purified [*katharizō*] with *these,* but the heavenly things themselves with better sacrifices than *these*" (emphasis added). The word *these* refers *back* to the blood sprinkled when Moses ratified the covenant, not *forward* to the author's comment about the Day of Atonement. This leads to the conclusion that the author was relating this particular cleansing aspect of the heavenly sanctuary to the time that the covenant was ratified, not to the cleansing that took place on the Day of Atonement.

The second kind of usage: cleansing the conscience. In Hebrews 9:14 and 10:2, the author used the word *katharizō* to describe the effect of Christ's sacrifice on the minds and hearts of his readers. In 9:14, he said that the blood of Christ would "cleanse [*katharizō*] your conscience from dead works to serve the living God," and in

10:2, he said that those who were "once purified [*katharizō*], would have had no more consciousness of sins." And, of course, Leviticus 16:30 plainly says that one purpose of the Day of Atonement was to "make atonement for *you,* to cleanse [Greek: *katharizō*] *you,* that *you* may be clean [*katharos,* the adjectival form of *katharizō*] from all your sins before the LORD" (emphasis added). The question is whether the author of Hebrews was speaking of the cleansing the Day of Atonement provided.

There's a significant difference between the cleansing of Israel accomplished by the Day of Atonement and the cleansing the author of Hebrews desired his readers to experience. In the Levitical system of rituals, the people were purged of their sins individually throughout the year each time they brought a sacrifice for their sins. The cleansing on the Day of Atonement, on the other hand, was for the entire camp. It was a collective removal of all their sins from the sanctuary—a corporate cleansing that happened for everyone at the same time at the end of their religious year.

In contrast, the cleansing spoken of in Hebrews 9:14 and 10:2 was applied to the consciences of the individual readers of the book, and Hebrews assured them that this spiritual benefit was immediately available to them or any other Christian. Thus, this cleansing is more like the purging from sin that was available to the Israelites throughout the year rather than the collective cleansing from sin that they received on the Day of Atonement. Furthermore, in the author's description of the ritual for ratifying the covenant, he said Moses "sprinkled both the book itself *and all the people*" (Hebrews 9:19; emphasis added), and he says this New Testament era cleansing is superior because it cleanses the conscience.

Nevertheless, there is a way to apply this cleansing to the Day of Atonement in verse 25. Cortez points out that after the high priest had cleansed the Most Holy Place and the Holy Place on the Day of Atonement, he went out to the altar and sprinkled blood on it to "*cleanse* it, and *consecrate* it from the uncleanness of the children of Israel" (Leviticus 16:19; emphasis added). Notice that the Day of Atonement provided both a *cleansing* of the sanctuary and a *consecration* of the sanctuary. Cortez says that "this act of cleansing and consecration of the altar was, in fact, an act of *re-consecration.* . . .

"Thus, the Day of Atonement brings the tabernacle back to its original state of purity and, in this sense, re-founds it or re-inaugurates it."[1]

If this is correct, then even if the author meant to apply the cleansing in verse 22 to the Day of Atonement, it would have been the re-inauguration aspect of the Day of Atonement that he had in mind.

Imprecise descriptions of earthly sanctuary rituals

When we examine the descriptions that the author of Hebrews gives of the Levitical sanctuary rituals, we discover a number of differences between what he says and what we read in the Old Testament. One of the most notable instances where this occurs is in his description of the ratification of the old covenant in chapter 9:19–22 (compare with Exodus 24:1–8). Cortez says, "It is important to note in this connection that Hebrews' description of the inauguration of the first covenant deviates from the account of Exod 24:1–11 in several respects."[2] I've listed below some of the ways in which the Old Testament account and the account in Hebrews differ from each other:

- Hebrews speaks of the sacrifice of *moschōn* (calves) and *tragōn* (goats), whereas the account in Exodus 24 speaks only of the sacrifice of "young bulls" (Greek: *moscharia;* Hebrew: *parim*).
- Hebrews says that Moses used "water, scarlet wool, and hyssop" to sprinkle the book (of the law) and the people (verse 19), whereas the account in Exodus says nothing about the use of water, scarlet wool, and hyssop. However, scarlet and hyssop are mentioned in connection with other rituals (see Leviticus 14:6; Numbers 19:6). The author of Hebrews apparently merged these rituals.
- Exodus 24:8 quotes Moses as saying, "Behold, the blood of the covenant," whereas Hebrews quotes him as saying, "This is the blood of the covenant" (verse 20).
- Hebrews says that Moses sprinkled blood on the book, the people, the tabernacle, and "all the vessels of the ministry" (verses 19, 21). Exodus, however, mentions only the people and the altar being sprinkled with blood (verses 6, 8).
- Exodus 40:9, 10; Leviticus 8:10, 11; and Numbers 7:1 all speak of Moses anointing the tabernacle and all that was in it as part of the ritual for consecrating the sanctuary. Thus, Hebrews combines the ritual for the ratification of the covenant with the ritual for consecrating the sanctuary.
- Hebrews speaks of Moses using blood to consecrate the sanctuary and its furnishings, but the accounts in Exodus (40:9, 10) and Leviticus (8:10, 11) say that Moses used oil.

Why does the account of the ratification of the covenant in Hebrews differ so significantly from the accounts in the Old Testament? Why does the author of Hebrews combine the rituals for the ratification of the covenant and the consecration of the sanctuary? Cortez comments, "These deviations . . . are important for the argument of Hebrews. They make possible the description of the sacrifice of Christ as a complex event that included . . . the consecration of the heavenly sanctuary (9:23) and the inauguration of the believers' priestly access to the presence of God (10:19–23)."[3]

The point is this: The author of Hebrews wasn't necessarily giving his readers a detailed, point-by-point analysis of the Old Testament rituals. Rather, he adapted these rituals to fit the point he was making. So, while we can draw some conclusions about the antitypical meaning of these rituals from what he said, his imprecise use of the rituals suggests that we should avoid being too dogmatic.

No scapegoat in Hebrews

The most glaring omission in the author's explanation of the Day of Atonement is the lack of any reference whatsoever to the crucial scapegoat ritual. The earthly Day of Atonement wasn't completed until the sins of the people had been removed from the sanctuary and the scapegoat had borne them away from the camp of Israel forever. Leviticus withholds the pronouncement of the people's cleansing till *after* the goat had departed the camp (see Leviticus 16:21, 22, 30). Thus, I find it very significant that in

his discussion of the Day of Atonement, *the author of Hebrews made absolutely no reference to the scapegoat.* He was utterly silent about this crucial aspect of the Day of Atonement. Why?

There is another omission in Hebrews that is significant if the Day of Atonement is its primary theme. I pointed out in chapter 20 that theodicy—God's plan to solve the problem of evil—is a major theme of both the Levitical rituals and the prophecies of Daniel 7 and 8. In Daniel 7, the beast powers and the little horn are defeated, and dominion over the world is given to the Son of man and His saints. In Daniel 8, the sanctuary is "cleansed" of the little horn's attack and restored to its rightful state. In Leviticus 16, the Day of Atonement illustrates a similar solution to the problem of evil: eliminating it from the camp of God's people, which in the antitype means eliminating it from the entire universe.

However, as important as God's plan to rid the universe of evil is, Hebrews basically says nothing about it. If the theme of Hebrews 8–10 is the Day of Atonement, I find it very strange that the scapegoat and God's plan for ending evil, which the Day of Atonement so clearly illustrates, are so totally ignored. I don't say this to fault the author of Hebrews. The point is that he wasn't writing about those matters. Instead, his concern was with the new covenant, the writing of God's laws on the minds and hearts of Christians, and the transformation of their lives through the sacrifice of Christ and His mediatorial ministry in the heavenly sanctuary. I'm sure if we could ask the author, he would affirm the importance of the elimination of evil from the universe. He might even tell us that he intended to emphasize this aspect of the Day of Atonement in the next book he wrote. But he would also explain that it wasn't his concern in Hebrews.

In the earthly sanctuary, the people weren't cleansed of their sins until after the high priest had emerged from the sanctuary on the Day of Atonement. Cortez makes a significant observation about the difference between the Levitical account of the high priest leaving the sanctuary and the account in Hebrews: "If Hebrews follows a Day of Atonement typology relating the cleansing of the conscience (9:14) with the purification of the sanctuary (vs. 23), we have the problem that Jesus has not come out of the most holy place yet (heaven). . . . Several scholars believe that this exit of the most holy place is described in Heb 9:28, which lies still in the future, . . . and the purification of sins has not been accomplished yet; but, for Hebrews purification of sin *has* been accomplished (Heb 10:10–13, 18)."[4]

Cortez is saying that in the Old Testament description of the Day of Atonement, the people weren't declared cleansed of their sins until after the high priest had completed the day's rituals, including the scapegoat ritual, and he had emerged from the sanctuary—from both the Most Holy Place and the Holy Place. But Hebrews says nothing about Christ leaving the heavenly sanctuary. The whole point of the book is that *Christ was in the heavenly sanctuary at that time.* How, then, could the author of Hebrews assure his readers that their consciences had been cleansed of sin when Jesus had not yet emerged from the heavenly sanctuary?

I resolve this issue with a principle I referred to in chapter 22—that God always assures His people that they have already received all the spiritual benefits that His plan of salvation provides, even though the legal transaction that validates those spiritual benefits is still in the future. Thus, through Isaiah, God could assure ancient Israel with the words "I *have* redeemed you" (Isaiah 44:22; emphasis added) even though the legal transaction of the Crucifixion that secured their redemption was still hundreds of years in the future. Similarly, I propose that the author of Hebrews could assure his readers that their consciences had been cleansed of sin even though the legal transaction of the investigative judgment by which those sins would be cleansed (or blotted) from heaven's records was still thousands of years in the future.

Future judgment/Day of Atonement in Hebrews

Adventists teach that the Day of Atonement is a type of the judgment that will take place in the heavenly sanctuary shortly before Christ returns to this earth. One of the criticisms of our teaching is that Hebrews knows nothing about that.

It's true, of course, that the author of Hebrews didn't have our more complete understanding of the end-time application of the Day of Atonement. However, two passages in Hebrews indicate that he understood it to apply to a future judgment.

The first passage is Hebrews 9:27. In verse 25, the author said that Christ appeared in the presence of God, "not that He should offer Himself often, as the high priest enters the Most Holy Place every year with blood of another." This text makes a direct reference to the high priest's entrance into the Most Holy Place in the earthly sanctuary on the Day of Atonement, and in verse 26, the author applies this to Christ, who "once at the end of the ages, . . . has appeared to put away sin by the sacrifice of Himself."

Notice that the author applied Christ's heavenly Day of Atonement to His "sacrifice of Himself." Seventh-day Adventists agree fully that the *sacrifices* that were offered on the earthly Day of Atonement were fulfilled by Christ's death on the cross. It's the rest of the activities of that day that we say have an end-time fulfillment in the form of judgment. And that is what the author of Hebrews referred to in the very next verse, where he wrote, "As it is appointed for men to die once, but after this the judgment" (verse 27). Then, in verse 28, he spoke about Christ's second coming: "To those who eagerly wait for Him He will appear a second time, apart from sin, for salvation." This is precisely the Adventist understanding of final events: an investigative judgment followed by Christ's second coming.

Chapter 10 has another reference to a future judgment. In verses 24 and 25, the author wrote, "Let us consider one another in order to stir up love and good works, not forsaking the assembling of ourselves together, as is the manner of some, but exhorting one another, and so much the more as you see the Day approaching." Notice that the New King James Version translators have capitalized the word *Day*. I think the majority of interpreters would interpret this "Day" to refer to Christ's second coming. However, Richard Davidson points out that "the term 'The Day' (Aramaic *yoma'*) was a technical term for the Day of Atonement in the Mishnah (see the whole tractate entitled *Yoma* describing the Day of Atonement services of the Second Temple), and very well may be a reference to the Day of Atonement here in [Hebrews 10:25]."[5]

Davidson goes on to point out that

"such a conclusion seems confirmed by the verses that follow, which describe a future judgment (from the time perspective of the author of Hebrews)."[6] And judgment is indeed what the author of Hebrews speaks about in the next two verses: "For if we sin willfully after we have received the knowledge of the truth, there no longer remains a sacrifice for sins, but a certain fearful expectation of judgment, and fiery indignation which will devour the adversaries" (Hebrews 10:26, 27).

Also, in verse 28, the author says, "Anyone who has rejected Moses' law dies without mercy on the testimony of two or three witnesses"—which suggests that he had an understanding of God's final judgment as "investigative." And in verses 29 and 30, he speaks of the "much worse punishment" that will come on those who "trampled the Son of God underfoot, counted the blood of the covenant by which he was sanctified a common thing, and insulted the Spirit of grace." This is a clear reference to the day of executive judgment at the end of the millennium.

Thus, the key points of the Adventist understanding of the investigative judgment all appear in Hebrews, albeit in abbreviated form:

- The author recognized that the judgment was future to his day (9:27).
- He understood that it would have an investigative phase "on the testimony of two or three witnesses" (10:28).
- He recognized that it would conclude with an executive phase (10:26–30).
- He put this judgment in the context of Christ's ministry in the Most Holy Place of the heavenly sanctuary and the Day of Atonement (9:25–27).

Conclusion

To sum up the discussion in this chapter and the two previous ones: the author of Hebrews was making the specific point that Jesus had entered into God's very presence, and therefore, through Him, every one of his readers could also enter into God's presence and obtain forgiveness and cleansing from their sins. They could be assured of this personal cleansing even in the sense of the cleansing the Day of Atonement would provide.

However, this doesn't mean that the author of Hebrews was giving his readers the last word on the antitypical meaning of the Day of Atonement. The primary theme of Hebrews 8–10 is the covenants, with the Day of Atonement simply an illustration of the superiority of Christ's sacrifice and mediatorial ministry under the new covenant. The fact that in his description the author merged several Levitical rituals together is a clear indication that he wasn't giving his readers a precise, point-by-point analysis of any of them, including the Day of Atonement. But the most glaring evidence that the author wasn't attempting a detailed application of the earthly Day of Atonement ritual to Christ's heavenly ministry is the fact that he was utterly silent about the crucial scapegoat ritual and God's plan for ending evil that it so clearly illustrated.

My conclusion, then, is this: *Hebrews doesn't give us the final word on the heavenly Day of Atonement.* If we today find evidence elsewhere in the Bible for an antitypical Day of Atonement, we can feel perfectly free to analyze it and apply it to the fullest extent possible without fearing that what Hebrews says will somehow invalidate our conclusions. And that evidence *is* present elsewhere in Scripture, as we have seen from our analysis of Daniel 7 and 8. Desmond Ford himself recognized this. In his Glacier View manuscript, he said,

> *Now we wish to emphasize that what is true on the apotelesmatic principle of the kingdom of God, the Jubilee, the Passover, the Feast of Tabernacles is also true of the Day of Atonement. Hebrews 9 applies that type especially to the cross, but the Apocalypse and Paul apply it to consummated eschatology—to the last judgment.*[7]

Forensically, this [the cleansing of the sanctuary] took place at the cross, but its consummation is the last judgment which will cleanse the universe from sin and sinners. Here is the inspired Scriptural interpretation of Dan. 8:14. It does indeed point to the Day of Atonement fulfilled at Calvary; and soon to be "filled full" by the final judgment of God.[8]

Several times in his Glacier View manuscript, Ford spoke about the Day of Atonement being *fulfilled* at the cross but *consummated* in the end time, as though somehow the end-time *consummation* cannot be considered a *fulfillment.* This, to me, is simply playing with words. If the Day of Atonement is *consummated* in the end time, then at least that aspect of the Day of Atonement is *fulfilled* in the end time.

It seems almost certain to me that the author of Hebrews wasn't aware of everything we know about the end-time application of the Day of Atonement. We understand this aspect of the Day of Atonement from our study of Daniel, but Daniel's angel guide told him very specifically that certain aspects of his prophecies were "shut up" and sealed until the time of the end (Daniel 12:4). Thus, the author of Hebrews wasn't *supposed* to understand all the end-time applications of the Day of Atonement that we find in Daniel. I agree with a couple of Alwyn Salom's comments on Hebrews:

Although Hebrews provides valuable insights into the doctrine of the sanctuary, it does not speak directly to the subject of Christ's two-phased priestly ministry or to the prophetic time for the commencement of the final judgment.[9]

Hebrews is silent on some matters which intensely interest Adventists. These matters are part of our concerns as we look at the eschatological scene. But they were not concerns of the writer of Hebrews. They are our questions, not the apostle's. We must be careful in the interpretation of this book—as of all Scripture—that we do not seek answers for questions which are irrelevant to the writer's concerns.[10]

I couldn't have said it better.

---

1. Cortez, " 'The Anchor of the Soul,' " 415.

2. Ibid., 377.

3. Ibid., 378, 379.

4. Ibid., 23; emphasis added.

5. Davidson, "Christ's Entry 'Within the Veil,' " 188. The article as printed in the *Andrews University Seminary Studies* gave "Heb 9:25" as the last item in the quote, but I believe this is a misprint. I believe it should say 10:25, and that is how I quoted it.

6. Ibid., 188.

7. Ford, "Daniel 8:14," 517; emphasis in the original.

8. Ibid., 417.

9. Alwyn Salom, "Sanctuary Theology," in *Issues in the Book of Hebrews,* 200, 201.

10. Ibid., 218.

Chapter 33

The Daily Service in Hebrews

Our study of Hebrews wouldn't be complete if we didn't consider the distinction that Seventh-day Adventists have traditionally made between the daily and the yearly services in both the earthly and the heavenly sanctuaries. We compare the services that the Israelite priests performed each day throughout the year to Christ's ministry in the heavenly sanctuary between A.D. 31 and 1844, and we compare the earthly Second Apartment ministry to that of Christ in heaven from 1844 to the close of probation.

This distinction, Ford says, is foreign to Hebrews. He offers at least three reasons for this conclusion: (1) There is no "First Apartment" in heaven; (2) Hebrews knows nothing of a "daily service" in the heavenly sanctuary; and (3) the First Apartment ministry in the earthly sanctuary was a type of the ineffective ministry of the Levitical sanctuary system. I'll examine Ford's reasons in the order I've given them here.

No "First Apartment" in heaven

I dealt with the issue of two apartments in chapter 29, and my conclusion was that the two apartments have been merged into one. Ford understands this. He said, "Most commentators refer to the absence of a veil in the heavenly sanctuary because since the cross the two apartments have become one, there being now no separation from the presence of God."[1] "The fact that the veil had been torn down by God meant that the heavenly sanctuary knew no divisions, and that henceforth the term 'sanctuary' once usable for a bipartite structure now applies to the single 'throne room' of heaven."[2] As I pointed out in chapter 29, I differ from Ford in that he views the entire room in the heavenly sanctuary as exclusively "the single 'throne room' of heaven"—in other words, the Most Holy Place—whereas I view it as a combined Holy Place and Most Holy Place.

The key question is this: Is there a First Apartment *ministry* in the heavenly sanctuary? Ford assumes that because the entire heavenly sanctuary must be the antitype of the Most Holy Place alone, everything that happens in the heavenly sanctuary must exclusively be an antitype of what the high priest did in the Most Holy Place. And since the only activity in the earthly Most Holy Place occurred once a year on the Day of Atonement, any mention of the heavenly sanctuary must by default be a Most Holy Place/Day of Atonement ministry. This would mean that any reference to Christ standing or sitting in the immediate presence of His Father is a Second Apartment, Day of Atonement ministry.

I disagree. If there is no First Apartment *as such* in the heavenly sanctuary, then neither does that sanctuary have a Second Apartment *as such*. There is instead a single throne room that was represented in the earthly sanctuary by both apartments.* This will become clear as we proceed.

No "daily service" in Hebrews

Ford was very emphatic that Hebrews says nothing about a "daily service" type of ministry in the heavenly sanctuary. He said, for example, "Never in Hebrews do we find a setting forth of a first apartment ministry in heaven."[3] "To represent Him [Christ] as engaged in that done by the lower priests who only rarely were concerned with blood in the first apartment is to degrade Him and to turn Hebrews on its head."[4] "Hebrews does not teach the existence of a special holy place ministry in the heavenly sanctuary. It denies such repeatedly by affirming Christ's presence in 'the Most Holy' since His ascension."[5]

Ford says that Hebrews knows nothing of a First Apartment ministry. However, the author of Hebrews did understand the distinction between the daily and yearly services in the *earthly* sanctuary. In chapter 9:6, 7, he said, "The priests always [that is, daily] went into the first part of the tabernacle, performing the services. But into the second part the high priest went alone once a year." In Hebrews 7:27, he said that Christ "does not need daily, as those high priests, to offer up sacrifices," for the simple reason that Christ "did [this] once for all when He offered up Himself."

And in Hebrews 10:11, 12, the author of this epistle referred to the daily service both by the high priests in the earthly sanctuary and by Christ in His heavenly sanc-

---

*However, see chapter 28, where I point out biblical evidence that the heavenly sanctuary does in a sense have two "rooms."

tuary. In verse 11, he said, "Every priest stands ministering daily and offering repeatedly the same sacrifices, which can never take away sins." Then, in verse 12, he said, "But this Man, after He had offered one sacrifice for sins forever, sat down at the right hand of God." The immediate context of Christ sitting down at the right hand of God is the earthly sanctuary's daily service, not its yearly service.

I agree that Christ has been in heaven's Most Holy Place since His ascension. But I also propose that since in the heavenly sanctuary the two rooms have been merged, Christ has been in heaven's Holy Place as well, and He has been carrying out all the ministries that are the antitype of the earthly priests' ministry in the earthly Holy Place.

I find it very strange to say that it is degrading to Christ to suggest that He is carrying out the ministry represented by the so-called lower priests. When these "lower priests" officiated in the morning and evening sacrifice, were they representing Gabriel? Of course not! When they assisted a sinner in slaughtering a lamb and sprinkling its blood on the altar in the courtyard or the Holy Place, were they representing one of the other angels in heaven? Of course not! The sacrifice of the lamb represented Christ's death on the cross, and any additional ministry the priests performed on the sinner's behalf beyond that represented Christ's ministry in the heavenly sanctuary. How can that degrade Christ, His sacrifice, or His mediatorial ministry?

The antitype of the daily service

As Ford understands it, the daily service in the earthly sanctuary wasn't a type of anything in the heavenly sanctuary. It was a type of all the ineffective services in the earthly sanctuary throughout the entire period of that sanctuary's existence. On the other hand, the high priest's ministry once a year in the Most Holy Place was a type of Christ's effective ministry in the heavenly sanctuary from A.D. 31 till His second coming (or till the close of probation). Ford bases this conclusion on Hebrews 9:8, 9. After describing the furnishings and the ministry of the priests in the two apartments of the earthly sanctuary in verses 2–7, the author of Hebrews said that the Holy Spirit was "indicating [by] this, that the way into the Holiest of All was not yet made manifest while the first tabernacle was still standing. It [the first "tabernacle"] was symbolic for the present time in which both gifts and sacrifices are offered which cannot make him who performed the service perfect in regard to the conscience" (verses 8, 9).

In chapter 31, I pointed out two ways to understand verse 8, which I will explain in greater detail here. Ford understands *protēs skēnēs* ("first tabernacle") in verse 8 to mean the earthly Holy Place only, and he understands *ta hagia* to refer to the heavenly Most Holy Place only. He does this because *protēs skēnēs* in verses 2 and 6 clearly does refer to the earthly Holy Place. However, if *protēs skēnēs* in verse 8 means exactly the same thing as it does in verses 2 and 6, then we would have to translate verse 8 to mean something to the effect that the way into the Most Holy Place of the heavenly sanctuary could not be opened as long as the Holy Place in the earthly sanctuary was still in operation, which, as I noted in chapter 31, seems unlikely.

This is why conservative Adventist scholars say that *protēs skēnēs* ("first tabernacle") in verse 8 refers to the entire earthly sanctuary, and *ta hagia* refers to the entire heavenly sanctuary. That is, the entire earthly sanctuary and its ministries are a type of the entire heavenly sanctuary and Christ's more effective ministry therein, and the author of Hebrews means that the entire heavenly sanctuary ministry cannot begin until the entire earthly sanctuary ministry has ended. This is very consistent with Hebrews 9:1, where the author stated that "the first covenant had ordinances of divine service and the earthly sanctuary." The author equated the entire earthly sanctuary with the old covenant. Logically, then, the entire heavenly sanctuary should be associated with the new covenant. And the entire earthly sanctuary under the old

covenant is a type of Christ's superior ministry in the heavenly sanctuary under the new covenant.

One's interpretation of verse 9 depends on how one understands these issues in verse 8. Verse 9 says, "It [the first tabernacle] was symbolic for the present time in which both gifts and sacrifices are offered which cannot make him who performed the service perfect in regard to the conscience." The Greek word translated "symbolic" in this verse is *parabolē*, which you no doubt recognize is rendered "parable" in English. Thus, "symbolic" is a good translation.

Ford resolves the oddity I described above by concluding that *protēs skēnēs* refers, not to the Holy Place in the earthly sanctuary, but to the entire Old Testament sanctuary *era*. He says, *"A first apartment ministry would only be relevant until the cross and never after, and it represented the limited blessings of the typical era."*[6] "The first apartment stands for the entire Mosaic sanctuary, and the second apartment represents the entire heavenly sanctuary."[7] And, "we think the evidence is clear that [in Hebrews 9:8 the author] is saying that the first apartment was symbolic of the whole earthly sanctuary during the Jewish age."[8]

Conservative Adventist scholars, on the other hand, understand *protēs skēnēs* and *ta hagia* to represent the entire earthly sanctuary and the entire heavenly sanctuary respectively; with the rituals in the entire earthly sanctuary, both Holy Place and Most Holy Place, being a type of Christ's greater ministry in the entire heavenly sanctuary, both Holy Place and Most Holy Place.

Ford's view differs only slightly—though it is an important "slightly"—from what conservative Adventist scholars are saying. Both Ford and conservative Adventist scholars are changing the meaning of *protēs skēnēs* in verse 8 from what it means in verses 2 and 6, where it clearly refers to the earthly Holy Place only. Both are changing *protēs skēnēs* to mean something much broader—which of course is reasonable, since the author of Hebrews said that the earthly sanctuary should be understood symbolically, as a "parable." Conservative Adventists interpret *protēs skēnēs* to refer to the entire earthly *sanctuary* while Ford interprets it to mean the entire earthly sanctuary *era.*

Ford justifies this on the basis of verse 9, which says that the *protēs skēnēs*—the Holy Place in the earthly sanctuary—was a parable, a type, of the ineffective ministry of the Old Testament sanctuary *era,* and thus it isn't a type of anything in the heavenly sanctuary during the Christian era. But it seems to me much more consistent with the covenants theme of Hebrews 8–10 to say that the earthly sanctuary and its rituals—both Holy Place and Most Holy Place—are a parable, a symbol, of Christ's entire ministry in the heavenly sanctuary, both Holy Place and Most Holy Place.

Let's assume for the moment that Ford is correct, that the First Apartment of the earthly sanctuary is a type of the ineffective ministry in the earthly sanctuary, representing the entire era before the cross. We have then the odd situation that the First Apartment ministry in the earthly sanctuary was a type of itself! The type is a type of the type. Somehow, that doesn't sound quite right.

We also need to ask whether the sacrifice of the lambs and other animals in the daily service represented Christ's death on the cross. And we need to ask whether the priest's application of the animals' blood to either the altar of sacrifice in the courtyard or the altar of incense in the Holy Place represented anything that Christ has been doing as our Mediator in the heavenly sanctuary since Calvary. If so—and I hardly see how anyone can argue otherwise—then the services in the First Apartment of the earthly sanctuary did not represent the earthly pre-cross *era* at all. They represented an important part of God's *real* plan of salvation that would take place when the services in the earthly sanctuary reached their end. They were a type of something in the heavenly sanctuary—the slaughter of the lamb represents Christ's death on the cross, and the mediatorial ministry of the priests at the altar of sacrifice in the courtyard and the altar of incense in the Holy Place represents Christ's ministry in the heavenly sanctuary for the forgiveness of ours sins during the New Testament era (see 1 John 1:9; 2:1).

I argued in chapter 29 that God's throne room in the heavenly sanctuary is a combined "First Apartment" and "Second Apartment." Thus, it's reasonable to assume that Christ's ministry in the heavenly sanctuary since A.D. 31 includes the antitype of the ministry carried out by the priests in the daily services of the earthly sanctuary. When you and I confess our sins and seek God's forgiveness, Jesus responds from God's great throne room with His First Apartment ministry. It seems to me that Hebrews 4:14–16 is an excellent representation of Christ's First Apartment ministry in the heavenly sanctuary: "Seeing then that we have a great High Priest who has passed through the heavens, Jesus the Son of God, let us hold fast our confession. For we do not have a High Priest who cannot sympathize with our weaknesses, but was in all points tempted as we are, yet without sin. Let us therefore come boldly to the throne of grace, that we may obtain mercy and find grace to help in time of need."

In conclusion

My conclusion from the discussion in this chapter and the five preceding ones is that the author of Hebrews is particularly anxious for his readers to understand that, whereas God's people who lived prior to the cross had very limited access to God through the earthly sanctuary, now every believer has direct access to God through Christ, who is seated at His Father's right hand in heaven's great throne room. There is no longer any veil to shield priests and people from God's presence. The great temple in heaven includes both the Holy Place and the Most Holy Place of the earthly sanctuary, and Christ is performing the ministries that were represented by both. The author of Hebrews illustrated his point several times with references to Christ's yearly Day of Atonement ministry, but even here he was imprecise, combining certain rituals and leaving out major details. Most notably, he made no reference whatsoever to the crucial scapegoat ritual on the earthly Day of Atonement.

We should understand that the author's primary burden was to assure his wavering fellow Jewish Christians that Christ's heavenly ministry was far superior to any rituals they might participate in at the temple in Jerusalem. Christ could truly cleanse their minds and hearts of sin in ways that the sacrifice of sheep and goats never could. However, we must not expect the author of Hebrews to have all the insights about the heavenly sanctuary and the final fulfillment of the Day of Atonement that we find so clearly expressed in Daniel, because that was largely sealed till the time of the end (see Daniel 12:4, 9).

Many critics of the Adventist teaching about an end-time investigative judgment in heaven, which is an antitype of the earthly Day of Atonement, have used Hebrews as one of their main supports. Hebrews, they say, absolutely contradicts and invalidates our traditional understanding. However, my analysis concludes otherwise. I believe there is strong biblical evidence to support the conclusion that there is an end-time investigative judgment in the heavenly sanctuary that is the antitype of the Day of Atonement in the earthly sanctuary. While Hebrews doesn't elaborate at length on this conclusion, it does suggest it and by no means contradicts it.

---

1. Ford, "Daniel 8:14," 235.
2. Ibid., 239.
3. Ibid., 221.
4. Ibid., 226.
5. Ibid., 227.
6. Ibid., 165; emphasis in the original.
7. Ibid., 167.
8. Ibid., 243.

Concluding Thoughts

Chapter 34

Ellen White and the Investigative Judgment

Seventh-day Adventists believe that Ellen White received the gift of prophecy in the same sense that the Bible writers did, that the Holy Spirit inspired her in the same way He inspired them. However, we also affirm that the Bible is the foundation of our faith and that our major teachings are based on Scripture, not on what Ellen White said. That's why in this book I have drawn the evidence for the various aspects of the investigative judgment from Scripture. Only here and there have I quoted Ellen White, and even in those instances, my purpose was not primarily to use her as proof of the correctness of the topic under consideration; rather, I quoted her as one point of evidence among others regarding what Adventists have historically believed about certain aspects of the investigative judgment.

However, because Adventists do consider her to have been inspired by God, she has naturally shaped our understanding of the investigative judgment to a considerable extent. Therefore, it's appropriate that we should devote a few pages of this book to a consideration of what she said. Please note that much more could be said about Ellen White and the investigative judgment than what I can say in this chapter.

In chapters 3 and 4, I dealt with Ellen White's understanding of the judgment as it relates to righteousness by faith and the great controversy, so I won't deal with those issues here. In this chapter I'll focus on four issues: (1) Raymond Cottrell's view of Ellen White as a doctrinal authority; (2) who Ellen White portrayed as making the decisions in the investigative judgment about who gets eternal life and who doesn't; (3) what Ellen White said about the relationship between the investigative judgment and atonement; and (4) the implications of a vision in which Ellen White saw the heavenly sanctuary.

Raymond Cottrell and Ellen White's doctrinal authority

Having just said that Ellen White is not the foundation for the Adventist teaching about the investigative judgment, I must point out that at least one individual in Adventist history claimed that she was. Raymond Cottrell, whose views I discussed briefly in chapter 7, didn't believe that the Adventist teaching about the investigative judgment and related topics could be sustained from Scripture. Nevertheless, he believed in the investigative judgment doctrine. I will briefly explain his reasoning.

Cottrell divided the history of God's people into three eras: the Israelite era from Abraham to Christ, the Christian era from A.D. 31 to 1844, and the Adventist era from 1844 to the Second Coming. He claimed that God gave a special revelation—through prophets—to each era that stated how His eternal kingdom would be established at the end of that era. However, when His people in an era rejected His plan for them, His statements about the events leading up to the establishment of His eternal kingdom at the end of that era closed, and God started over again with a new group in a new era and a new end-time scenario.

God's special revelation for each era was built on the *principles* stated in the revelation(s) of the previous era(s), but the way those principles worked out differed from how the principles of the previous era(s) would have worked out. Also, the prophets in each era quoted from the Scriptures of previous eras, but they often interpreted the previous era's prophets in ways that were quite inconsistent with what the original prophets actually meant in the context of their historical situation.*

Cottrell then reasoned that Ellen White was God's prophet for the Adventist era, and he believed that even though the cleansing of the sanctuary and the 2,300 days in Daniel 8:14 had absolutely nothing to do with an antitype of the Day of Atonement in 1844, these were valid interpretations for the Adventist era *simply because Ellen White said so.* Her interpretation of these prophecies didn't have to match what Daniel intended because as an inspired writer for our era, she was reinterpreting Daniel just as the New Testament writers reinterpreted the Old Testament prophecies in ways that their Old Testament authors never intended. Thus, Cottrell could affirm that he believed implicitly in the traditional Adventist interpretation of Daniel 8:14 simply because Ellen White affirmed it. For example, he said,

---

*This is indeed true of the New Testament writers. They often applied Old Testament prophecies in ways that had nothing to do with what the original prophet meant. See, for example, Matthew 2:18, where Matthew took the prophecy of Jeremiah 31:15 about Rachel weeping for her children and applied it to Herod's slaughter of the baby boys in Bethlehem. Jeremiah had no such thing in mind when he spoke those words.

Ellen White re-interprets Daniel for our time. And because I fully believe and am convinced that God spoke to and through Ellen White and I accept her writings 100%, I accept her reinterpretation, her approval of the Adventist interpretation of the heavenly sanctuary, the investigative judgment, 1844, because I accept her as an inspired writer. . . . And so we recognize both the contextual interpretation [what Daniel originally meant in the context of his times] and the reinterpretation by NT writers and Ellen White bringing to us what God would have us understand in our time.[1]

Ellen White was God's messenger to the remnant church. . . . A person needs to recognize the teaching authority of Ellen White it seems to me, in order to establish our interpretation of Daniel 8:14.[2]

I hold a different view of Ellen White's role in relationship to Scripture. Our Adventist teachings must always have their foundation in Scripture. However, once a particular teaching has been developed from Scripture, I'm quite willing for Ellen White to fill in some details that are not found in Scripture. For example, our basic teaching about the conflict between good and evil is clearly scriptural, but Ellen White fills in many details of that conflict that are not found in Scripture. The same is true of our understanding of end-time events; while the basic concepts are scriptural, Ellen White adds many insights of her own.

My objection to Cottrell's explanation of the investigative judgment is that he made her the *foundation* for our understanding of this doctrine. That I cannot accept— nor do I think we must accept it. In this book I have shown what I believe is a firm biblical basis for the doctrine of the investigative judgment as a Day of Atonement in the heavenly sanctuary that began in 1844.

Who makes the decisions in the judgment?

In chapter 2 I recounted a conversation I had a number of years ago with a Church of Christ Christian who told me that he objected to our Adventist teaching about the investigative judgment because "no one can ever have any assurance of salvation with a doctrine like that." As I pointed out in chapter 2 and also in chapter 4, the issue is who, in the investigative judgment, makes decisions about the salvation of God's people. If the purpose of that judgment is for God to make up His mind about the worthiness of His people for citizenship in His eternal kingdom, then, indeed, no one can have the assurance of salvation until the judgment takes place. However, I pointed out in chapter 2 and even more fully in chapter 4 that God's purpose in conducting an investigative judgment isn't to make up His own mind. It's to settle the sin problem forever by giving the angels an opportunity to review His decisions regarding the salvation of each saint. It's to give them the opportunity to examine Satan's charges against each saint and then to let them reach their own verdict. So, the question of who makes decisions in the investigative judgment—God or the angels—is a crucial one.

Ellen White devoted an entire chapter to the investigative judgment in her book *The Great Controversy*.[3] One of the questions that can be raised from that chapter is whether God or the angels make the decisions. The problem is highlighted by statements such as the following: "As the books of record are opened in the judgment, the lives of all who have believed on Jesus come in review before God. Beginning with those who first lived upon the earth, our Advocate presents the cases of each successive generation, and closes with the living. Every name is mentioned, every case closely investigated. Names are accepted, names rejected."[4]

Two thoughts in this paragraph appear to justify the conclusion that Ellen White understood God to be the one who makes decisions in the investigative judgment. First, "the lives of all who have believed on Jesus come in review before God," and second, "names are accepted, names rejected." This suggests that God is the One who will make the decisions, accepting and rejecting names. Also, several times in this chapter, Ellen White spoke of those who are "accounted worthy" to receive eternal life,[5] suggesting that the decision about whether they are accounted worthy is not made until the judgment. In what follows in this section, I will respond to this problem.

God presides. The first thing we need to keep in mind is that God will preside in the investigative judgment. This much is evident from the picture of the judgment in Daniel 7:9, 10, where the Ancient of Days is seated on His throne surrounded by millions of angels, and "the judgment was set, and the books were opened" (verse 10, KJV). However, as I pointed out in chapter 2, "even in our human court systems, there's a jury as well as a judge, and the jury has to reach a conclusion as to the guilt or innocence of the person on trial." That, I believe, is how we need to understand the decisions that are made in the investigative judgment.

So, who is the jury in that process?

The angels are involved. Throughout the chapter on the investigative judgment in *The Great Controversy*, Ellen White makes it clear that the angels are intimately involved in that judgment. She begins the chapter by quoting Daniel 7:9, 10, which shows millions of angels surrounding God's throne, and she concludes the second paragraph on that page with these words: "[God] is to preside in the judgment. And *holy angels* as ministers and witnesses . . . attend *this great tribunal.*"[6] Following are some of her other statements about the role of the angels in the investigative judgment:

- "Attended *by heavenly angels,* our great High Priest enters the holy of holies . . . to perform the work of investigative judgment."[7]
- "[Jesus] lifts His wounded hands before the Father *and the holy angels.*"[8]
- "Sin may be concealed [from friends and loved ones] . . . ; but it is laid bare *before the intelligences of heaven.*"[9]
- "How little solicitude is felt [by human beings] concerning that record which is to meet *the gaze of heavenly beings.*"[10]

These statements make it evident that Ellen White clearly understood that the angels have a role in the investigative judgment.

The passive voice. Throughout Ellen White's chapter on the investigative judgment, references to decisions being made are quite consistently in the passive voice. The passive voice states what was done but doesn't say who did it. Thus, the statement that "the ball was hit" is a complete sentence, but unless it goes on to say "by John," we can only assume who hit the ball. When writing about this judgment, Ellen White said, "Names are accepted, names rejected." That's a passive sentence, and Ellen White didn't go on to say who does the accepting and the rejecting. Also, when Ellen White wrote of "those who in the judgment are 'accounted worthy,' "[11] she didn't say by whom they are accounted worthy. There is no "by so-and-so" statement in these quotations. It's easy enough to assume that God is the One who makes the decisions, but the statements don't actually *say* this.

I find it significant that Daniel 7:21, 22 also uses the passive voice in connection with decisions in the judgment: "I beheld, and the same horn made war with the saints, and prevailed against them; until the Ancient of days came, and *judgment was given to* [or, "in favor of"] the saints of the most High" (KJV; emphasis added). It's easy to assume that it was the Ancient of Days who passed judgment in favor of the saints, but again, Daniel didn't say that, because his sentence is in the passive voice.

Similarly, it's easy to assume that in Ellen White's statement about names being accepted and rejected, God is the One who makes the decisions about each saint's worthiness to be saved. However, we need to keep these words in the context of Ellen White's repeated emphasis in the chapter that angels participate in the judgment. I propose that it's the angels who accept and reject names, and it's the angels who account the saints to be worthy of eternal life. Because God presides at the judgment, it's appropriate to link Him to the process, and it's in this context that we should interpret Ellen White's statements where it appears that He is the One who decides.

Of course, as I've said before, we must understand the angels' accepting and rejecting of names and their accounting the saints worthy of eternal life *in terms of their endorsing the decisions God has already made.* The angels don't determine who will be saved and who will be lost. God does that. In judging people's eternal salvation, the angels are merely confirming for themselves the righteousness of God's decisions. They're building their faith in His justice.

There is one exception to these passive sentences about decisions in the judgment. Near the end of her chapter on the investigative judgment, Ellen White wrote, "Though all nations are to pass in judgment before God, yet He will examine the case of each individual with as close and searching scrutiny as if there were not another being upon the earth."[12] This statement is in the active voice, which means that it names God as the One scrutinizing human lives, and the implication is that He is the One making decisions in the judgment.

I will respond by pointing out that God

actually does scrutinize the details of each human being's life at the time he or she lives and dies. This, of course, includes His examination of those who are alive now, during the time of the judgment. The question is whether it's even *necessary* for the omniscient God to scrutinize the lives of human beings who lived in ages past so that He can decide in the judgment who is worthy of salvation. I propose that, because He is omniscient, He doesn't need to do so, and it's a mistake to conclude from this statement by Ellen White that He is the One making the decisions in the judgment. In the paragraph where this statement appears, Ellen White comments at length on the seriousness with which each Christian should live in light of the judgment, and it seems to me that's her point in this statement—and not whether God is actually the One reviewing lives and making decisions.

A related issue that we need to deal with briefly is a statement by Ellen White in *The Great Controversy* that in the judgment "the divine Intercessor [Christ] presents the plea that all who have overcome through faith in His blood be forgiven their transgressions."[13] This seems to suggest that God's people must wait until the judgment for their sins to be forgiven, whereas the Bible promises immediate forgiveness as soon as our sins are confessed (see, for example, 1 John 1:9).

My response to this problem is very

simple: Ellen White was very well acquainted with the biblical teaching about righteousness by faith. Anyone who has read books such as *Steps to Christ, Christ's Object Lessons, The Desire of Ages,* and the chapters on righteousness by faith in *Selected Messages* (book 1, pages 350–400), knows that she had a very clear understanding of the gospel. She repeatedly assured her readers of Christ's forgiveness and acceptance of them the moment they repented and confessed their sins.* Every writer will sometimes say things that at first glance appear to contradict what he or she believes and has stated very clearly elsewhere. Paul himself did this now and then (compare Romans 3:20 with 2:13). Therefore, we have to take an author's primary belief system as the foundation for our interpretation of his or her writings and interpret apparently contradictory statements within that framework rather than using the isolated, apparently contradictory statement as if it represented the author's belief. We misrepresent Ellen White when we twist statements like the one I quoted above to make them contradict other statements in which she has stated in a very clear way her beliefs about righteousness by faith and the forgiveness of sin.

The paragraph in *The Great Controversy* that contains Ellen White's statement about forgiveness begins with these words:

"The deepest interest manifested among men in the decisions of earthly tribunals but faintly represents the interest evinced in the heavenly courts when the names entered in the book of life come up in review before the Judge of all the earth."[14] Then comes the statement that Jesus is asking for the forgiveness of His people. So who in "the heavenly courts" is manifesting "the deepest interest" in the proceedings? I propose that it's the angels. And Ellen White's point is that, in the face of Satan's charges against the saints, which the angels are considering, Jesus is asking *the angels* to accept His judgment of the saints' cases, which is forgiveness and "pardon and justification, full and complete."[15] And, of course, they will! While Ellen White doesn't actually *say* this, it's consistent with what she *does* say in this chapter.

The investigative judgment and the atonement

One of the major criticisms of the Adventist concept of the investigative judgment is that it includes the idea that Christ will make an atonement for His people at that time. Ellen White stated this idea very clearly: "Attended by heavenly angels, our great High Priest enters the holy of holies and there appears in the presence of God . . . *to make an atonement* for all who are shown to be entitled to its benefits."[16] Most

---

*See for example the last paragraph on page 41 of *Steps to Christ* and *Selected Messages,* 1:382, 392.

Christians understand that Christ made the atonement for sin on the cross, and the idea that there remains an atonement to be made during the investigative judgment is offensive to them.

The issue is whether the word *atonement* should be applied exclusively to Christ's sacrificial death on the cross or whether it is appropriate to use it in connection with His mediatorial ministry in the heavenly sanctuary as well. The only place where the word *atonement* appears in the New Testament is in the King James Version of Romans 5:11, "We also joy in God through our Lord Jesus Christ, by whom we have now received the atonement." In this verse, the word *atonement* is a translation of the Greek word *katallagē*. All modern versions of this verse translate *katallagē* as "reconciliation," and that's how it is translated everywhere else in the New Testament.

The word *atonement* is thus exclusively an Old Testament word, where it is a translation of the Hebrew word *kippur* that I discussed in detail in chapters 19 and 20. And in the Old Testament, *kippur* is used to describe the results during the daily service of both the sacrifice of the animal, which represented Christ's death, *and the priest's mediation on behalf of the sinner, which represented Christ's mediatorial ministry in heaven.** Also, the word *kippur* is used in connection with the yearly Day of Atonement, *and it clearly includes the priestly mediation in the tabernacle* and not just the sacrifices offered on that day. Thus, the Seventh-day Adventist use of *atonement* in connection with Christ's priestly mediation in the heavenly sanctuary is very much in harmony with the biblical use of the word. Indeed, our use of the word is closer to the biblical use than that of most evangelical Protestants.

During the 1950s, Walter Martin approached the General Conference with a number of questions about our Adventist beliefs, one of which was the issue of the atonement during the judgment. The church responded to Martin's questions with the book *Seventh-day Adventists Answer Questions on Doctrine.* The authors of that book stated unequivocally that Seventh-day Adventists "fully agree with those who stress a completed atonement on the cross in the sense of an all-sufficient, once-for-all, atoning sacrifice for sin. They believe that nothing less than this took place on the cross of Calvary."[17]

However, the authors pointed out that "when . . . one hears an Adventist say, or reads in Adventist literature—even in the writings of Ellen G. White—that Christ is making atonement now, it should be understood that we mean simply that Christ is now *making application of the benefits of the sacrificial atonement He made on the*

---

*See, for example, Leviticus 4:13–20.

cross; that He is making it efficacious for us individually, according to our needs and requests."[18] They followed this up with a statement by Ellen White that in His ministry in the heavenly sanctuary since Calvary, Christ is "shed[ding] upon His disciples the *benefits* of His atonement."[19]

Adventists think of the investigative judgment that began in 1844 as a special form of Christ's mediatorial atonement in the heavenly sanctuary, but He has been carrying out some form of mediatorial atonement continuously since His ascension. It's in this sense that we must understand Ellen White's statements like the one I quoted earlier from *The Great Controversy*. Ellen White even used the word *benefits* in the statement in *The Great Controversy:* "Attended by heavenly angels, our great High Priest enters the holy of holies and there appears in the presence of God . . . to make an atonement for all who are shown to be entitled to its *benefits*" (emphasis added).

People in some Adventist circles raised quite a furor over the explanation given in *Questions on Doctrine* about "atonement" during the investigative judgment. I don't care to enter that debate here. Suffice it to say that I believe the explanation in *Questions on Doctrine* is correct.

Ellen White's vision of the heavenly sanctuary

In her book *Early Writings,* Ellen White gave a rather detailed account of a vision she received in which she was taken into the heavenly sanctuary. I will quote parts of two paragraphs of her description:

In the city [New Jerusalem] I saw a temple, which I entered. I passed through a door before I came to the first veil. This veil was raised, and I passed into the holy place. Here I saw the altar of incense, the candlestick with seven lamps, and the table on which was the shewbread. After viewing the glory of the holy, Jesus raised the second veil and I passed into the holy of holies.

In the holiest I saw an ark; on the top and sides of it [*sic*] was purest gold. On each end of the ark was a lovely cherub, with its wings spread out over it. Their faces were turned toward each other, and they looked downward. Between the angels was a golden censer. Above the ark, where the angels stood, was an exceeding bright glory, that appeared like a throne where God dwelt. Jesus stood by the ark, and as the saints' prayers came up to Him, the incense in the censer would smoke, and He would offer up their prayers with the smoke of the incense to His Father. In the ark was the golden pot of manna, Aaron's rod that budded, and the tables of stone which folded together like a book.[20]

In chapter 28, "Jesus' Entrance 'Behind the Veil,' " I argued that, while there are probably two "places" in the heavenly sanctuary that are the antitype of the Holy Place and the Most Holy Place of the earthly sanctuary, both the Father and the Son are together in both places with no separation such as a veil between them. Some Adventists may wish to argue that the statement from *Early Writings* is evidence that there *are* two apartments in the heavenly sanctuary with a veil between them.

However, it seems to me rather obvious that Ellen White is describing the heavenly sanctuary with language drawn from the description of the earthly sanctuary in the Old Testament, and it would be a mistake to assume that the heavenly sanctuary is literally just as she pictures it in this statement. The ark of the covenant in the earthly sanctuary is a type of God's throne in heaven, and the two angels standing on the cover of the ark represent the myriad of angels standing around God's throne (see Daniel 7:9, 10; Revelation 5:11). But surely heaven's throne room is vastly superior to its miniature representation in the earthly sanctuary! Ellen White also said that inside the ark she saw the Ten Commandments that folded like a book, the pot of manna, and Aaron's rod that budded. One might argue for a literal Ten Commandments in heaven, but it seems to me very strange to suppose that the pot of manna and Aaron's rod that budded exist in the heavenly sanctuary!

My point again is that the heavenly sanctuary is far superior to the earthly sanctuary, and it can hardly be thought of as an exact replica of the earthly sanctuary. Therefore, Ellen White's statement in *Early Writings* is more symbolic than it is literal.

---

1. Cottrell, "1844, the Investigative Judgment, the Sanctuary," 35.
2. Ibid., 37.
3. White, "Facing Life's Record," in *The Great Controversy*, 479–491.
4. Ibid., 483.
5. Ibid.; three times on page 482 and once on page 483.
6. Ibid., 479; emphasis added.
7. Ibid., 480; emphasis added.
8. Ibid., 484; emphasis added.
9. Ibid., 486; emphasis added.
10. Ibid., 487; emphasis added.
11. Ibid., 482.
12. Ibid., 490.
13. Ibid., 484.
14. Ibid., 483, 484.
15. Ibid., 484.
16. Ibid., 480; emphasis added.
17. *Seventh-day Adventists Answer Questions on Doctrine*, 342, 343.
18. Ibid., 354, 355; emphasis in the original.
19. White, *Early Writings*, 260; emphasis added.
20. Ibid., 32.

Chapter 35

Putting It All Together

As you know from reading this book, the Adventist doctrine of the investigative judgment brings together a number of issues from the Old Testament books of Leviticus and Daniel, along with significant input from Revelation in the New Testament. In the previous chapters of this book, we've examined these various pieces of the Adventist teaching about the investigative judgment in some detail; and with each one, our chief question has been, Is it biblical? Can it be reasonably demonstrated from Scripture? I have concluded that, yes, each part of the Adventist teaching about the investigative judgment can be defended from the Bible. In this chapter, I want to bring everything together as a whole.

The great controversy theme

The great controversy is the underlying theme of Seventh-day Adventist theology. The *Handbook of Seventh-day Adventist Theology* calls it "a hallmark of Adventist thought."[1] For many Protestants, the Cross is the central focus of their theology, and this is understandable, since the Cross is God's supreme act for the salvation of human beings. It's important to understand that Adventists don't diminish the Cross when we make the great controversy the theme of our theology. To the contrary, we put the Cross in the broadest possible perspective. The great controversy theme helps us to understand that the full purpose of the Cross wasn't just the salvation of human beings, important as that is. Christ's death is also the basis for God's defeat of Satan, the banishment of sin and suffering from the universe, and the establishment of His eternal kingdom.

The great controversy is above all else a story. It's a story about God, the intelligent beings He has created, and their relationship to Him. Some have been loyal to Him and His laws. Others, including Satan, have rebelled, claiming that God is unjust and His laws are impossible to keep. This conflict began in heaven, but it moved to planet Earth when our first parents sided with the rebellion. However, because they weren't fully aware of the implications of their choice and because God loved them deeply and wanted to spare them the fate of their choice, He implemented the plan of salvation. The Cross became God's solution not only for the human sin problem, but also for Satan's rebellion against Him. After all, one of the results of the cross was that "the accuser of our brethren . . . has been cast down" (Revelation 12:10). My point is that the Adventist teaching about the investigative judgment makes sense only in the context of the story about the great controversy. Let's review why.

God respects the intelligence and free will of all His creatures. He doesn't force the angels to obey Him, and He won't require them to accept anyone into heaven whom they fear might reintroduce rebellion, suffering, and death. The purpose of the investigative judgment is to give these heavenly beings an opportunity to review the life of every human being who has ever claimed to be a follower of God. This judg-ment also gives Satan a chance to make his best case against us before God and the angels. However, you and I need have no fear of Satan's attacks because we can rest assured that, as our Mediator, Jesus will present our case accurately before the angels, pointing out our repentance, our confession of sin, and His death that atoned for those sins. He'll point to His righteousness that covered our sins, and He'll claim for us "pardon and justification, full and complete."[2]

At the conclusion of the investigative judgment, God will be vindicated in all of His decisions in dealing with sin and sinners. The angels will agree that all those who have trusted in Jesus and overcome in His name deserve to spend eternity with them in His kingdom, while those who are in rebellion against God must be forever banished from the universe.

The word for this is *theodicy,* justifying God for the way He has dealt with the problem of evil. The Adventist teaching about the investigative judgment must be understood according to this definition of theodicy, or it won't harmonize with the biblical teaching about righteousness by faith.

Theodicy in Leviticus

One of the clearest Old Testament expositions of God's dealing with sin is found in the rituals prescribed for Israel in Leviticus. Studying these rituals may seem boring to us, but they are a miniature representation of God's plan to save human beings from sin and of His plan to eliminate sin eventually from the whole world and even from the universe.

In the Levitical system, sinners had the opportunity every day of the year to bring their animals to the sanctuary as sacrifices for their sins. The sin was transferred from the sinner to the animal, and the animal was slaughtered in payment for the sin. Of course, the blood of animals couldn't atone for human sin (see Hebrews 10:1). This was only a miniature representation of Christ's ultimate sacrifice on the cross, by which He bore the sins of every human being.

After the animal was killed, the priest collected its blood and sprinkled it either on the altar of sacrifice in the courtyard or the altar of incense in the Holy Place. By this act of mediation following the sacrifice, the sin was transferred to the sanctuary, and the sinner was forgiven. This represented Christ's mediatorial ministry on behalf of sinners in the heavenly sanctuary after His ascension in A.D. 31. Christ's mediation in the heavenly sanctuary applies the benefits of His sacrifice to individual sinners as they repent of their sins, confess them, and seek forgiveness.

In the earthly sanctuary, the transfer of the sin to the sanctuary meant that God accepted temporary responsibility for it. However, He didn't deserve to be responsible for the sin; He assumed that responsibility only for the purpose of relieving the sinner of it in the immediate present. This represents the fact that in the heavenly sanctuary, God assumes the responsibility for our sins so that we can be forgiven. Jesus accepted that responsibility on behalf of the Godhead when He died on the cross (see Isaiah 53:4–6, 12; 1 Peter 2:24).

In the earthly sanctuary, all the sins of the entire congregation were removed from the sanctuary on the Day of Atonement and placed on a scapegoat. The goat then hauled the noxious load to Azazel, a representation of Satan. This illustrates the fact that God shouldn't be held responsible for our sins, and He won't assume the responsibility for them forever. That responsibility will eventually be rolled back onto Satan, the originator of sin, and by his death and the death of all his followers, the rebellion against God that he initiated will be banished forever from the universe. "Sin and sinners [will be] no more. The entire universe [will be] clean."[3]

It's important to understand that these Levitical rituals were an acted-out representation of theodicy—God's plan to rid the world and the universe of sin.

Theodicy in Daniel

Daniel's prophecies in chapters 2, 7,

and 8 of his book mirror this theodicy. Starting with chapter 2, each prophecy focuses on the conflict between good and evil with increasing detail. All three prophecies begin in Daniel's time, and all three of them give a snapshot of world history from that time to the end of the world. This is called the "historicist method" for interpreting Daniel's prophecies. I will summarize each one.

Daniel 2. King Nebuchadnezzar's dream in chapter 2 provides an excellent case for demonstrating the historicist method of interpretation. It outlines the secular political forces that would dominate the Middle East and Europe for the next twenty-five hundred years.

Nebuchadnezzar was a heathen king who had no understanding of the Hebrew God. Thus, only at the end did the dream introduce the God of heaven who would overthrow all other kingdoms in the world and establish His own eternal kingdom. This provided the king with a glimpse into God's plan to resolve the problem of evil in the world—theodicy.

Daniel 7. The major focus of Daniel 7 is a "little horn"—an evil religious power that would oppose God and persecute His people. Adventists understand this little horn to represent the medieval papacy. In Daniel's vision of chapter 7, the little horn's activities are restricted to this world, but the resolution to the conflict takes place in heaven in the form of a judgment in which God presides while surrounded by millions of angels. This judgment condemns the apostate religious power represented by the little horn. The judgment also vindicates God's people and hands over the kingdoms of this world to the "Son of Man" and His people. This is a miniature picture of the conflict between good and evil—the great controversy—and its resolution. It is also an example of theodicy.

Daniel 8. The little horn in Daniel 8 represents the same evil religious power. In addition to persecuting God's people on this earth, the horn's attack in chapter 8 reaches clear up to Christ, "the Prince of the host." And the horn's special attack is on the Prince's heavenly sanctuary and His plan to save human beings from sin. Adventists have traditionally interpreted this little horn as the papacy, which holds doctrines that undermine the biblical teaching about salvation. I agree with that interpretation. However, there's more.

In Revelation 12, we discover that the power behind the little horns of Daniel 7 and 8 is none other than Satan himself. God's people are the special focus of his attack, and one of his primary strategies is to charge before God and the angels that God's people don't deserve God's favor. That's why Revelation calls Satan "the accuser of our brethren" (Revelation 12:10).

Satan's charge that God's people don't deserve eternal life is a direct attack on the plan of salvation that Christ is ministering in the heavenly sanctuary, and thus it is an attack on the heavenly sanctuary itself—an attack that Daniel 8:11 prophesied would happen.

Daniel 8:14 points to the solution to this problem. It predicts that a time will come when God's heavenly sanctuary will be "cleansed," "vindicated," "justified"—depending on how one wishes to translate the Hebrew word *nitsdaq*. My preference is "vindicated" because it fits best with the judgment in Daniel 7, which also vindicates the saints. And since the horn's attack on the sanctuary includes Satan's accusation that God's people are unworthy of eternal life, the resolution must obviously vindicate God's people, showing them to be worthy of God's favor after all. Of course, vindication of God's people is precisely the purpose of the judgment in chapter 7. And since the judgment comes at the very same point in the prophecy of Daniel 7 as the cleansing of the sanctuary does in the prophecy of chapter 8, the two quite obviously describe different aspects of the same process.

This vindication of God and His people by the judgment—called a "cleansing" of the sanctuary in Daniel 8—is theodicy of the highest order, which was also the function of the Levitical Day of Atonement.

The Day of Atonement in Daniel

There is significant evidence that the cleansing/vindication of God's people and the sanctuary in Daniel are heaven's antitype of the Levitical Day of Atonement. I say this for several reasons. Theodicy is one of the primary lines of evidence linking Leviticus with Daniel, because both Leviticus 16 and Daniel 7, 8 describe God's plan to resolve the sin problem. Indeed, the picture of the judgment in chapter 7 has striking similarities to the Day of Atonement. The ark of the covenant in Leviticus represents God's throne, and in Daniel we see God seated on His throne. The two cherubim over the ark of the covenant in the earthly sanctuary can be understood to represent the myriad of angels surrounding God's throne in the judgment. And the Son of man, whom we understand to be Jesus, approaches the throne, which reminds us of the heavenly High Priest approaching the ark of the covenant in the Most Holy Place on the Day of Atonement.

There is also significant evidence for a Day of Atonement in Daniel 8. First, this chapter deals with the rebellion of the little horn, and Satan is the power behind the horn. Thus, Daniel 8 describes an important part of God's process for dealing with the problem of evil, which is theodicy, and the Day of Atonement in the earthly sanctuary is, above all else, about theodicy.

Also, the ram and the goat in verses 3–8 are sanctuary animals, in contrast to the wild beasts of chapter 7. In fact, two rams and two goats were used on the Day of Atonement. There is also the fact that the cleansing of the sanctuary in 8:14 comes at precisely the same point in this chapter's outline of history as does the judgment in the historical outline of chapter 7. Thus, if the judgment in chapter 7 is a heavenly Day of Atonement scene, then so is the cleansing or vindication of the sanctuary in 8:14. Also, the little horn's attack on the sanctuary in chapter 8 is called a *pesha'* sin of rebellion in verse 13, and the Day of Atonement was the only time in the Levitical round of services when *pesha'* sins were dealt with. Finally, while the Hebrew words translated "cleansed" in Daniel 8:14 and Leviticus 16 are different, the Greek translators of the Old Testament used a single Greek word to translate these two Hebrew words.

For these reasons, the cleansing or vindication of the sanctuary in Daniel 8:14 can be understood as a heavenly Day of Atonement.

The year-day principle

The prophecies of Daniel 7 and 8 each include a time period. In Daniel 7:25, the time is given as "a time and times and half a time," which Revelation 12:6 reinterprets as 1,260 days. In Daniel 8:14, the time period is 2,300 evenings and mornings, which, in one way or another, all interpreters understand to mean days. However, the way we interpret these "days" depends on how we interpret the visions as a whole. Those who understand the visions of Daniel 7 and 8 to have been fulfilled in ancient history interpret the 1,260 days and the 2,300 days as literal time. They must, since interpreting them as years would extend the prophecies many centuries beyond the time of their supposed fulfillment. However, Seventh-day Adventists interpret both the 1,260 days and the 2,300 days according to the year-day principle, in which one symbolic day represents a literal year. One of the primary reasons we do this is that it's the only way these time periods can fit our historicist method, which sees the prophecies extending over thousands of years of world history. Furthermore, students of prophecy have used the year-day principle for interpreting Daniel's prophecies for more than two thousand years, and the basic concept of using the word *day* to represent a year was a part of Jewish thinking for two thousand years before that. Thus, there's nothing particularly new or unusual about the year-day principle.

The 1,260 days. Seventh-day Adventists believe the 1,260 days began in A.D. 538 with the Roman Emperor Justinian's appointment of the pope as head over all the

Christian churches, and they extended to 1798, when the imprisonment of the pope ended hundreds of years of political power that the Vatican had held over the nations of Europe.

The 2,300 days. We base our calculation of the 2,300 years on Daniel 9. Chapter 8 tells us that Gabriel ceased his explanation of the vision of chapter 8 just as he was getting into the explanation of the 2,300 days because Daniel became ill. However, this didn't end Daniel's interest in that mysterious time period. So, Daniel 9 says that several years later, in response to Daniel's earnest inquiry about the time for the Jews to return to their homeland and rebuild their temple, Gabriel again appeared to Daniel. He told the prophet that seventy weeks had been "cut off" for the Jews, but he didn't say what they had been cut off from. Adventists have historically said that they were cut off from the 2,300 days of Daniel 8, since that was the part of that vision that hadn't been explained yet.

The seventy weeks. On the year-day principle, seventy weeks represents 490 years. And Gabriel gave Daniel a specific event for the beginning of that period. He said that "from the going forth of the command to restore and build Jerusalem until Messiah the Prince, there shall be seven weeks and sixty-two weeks" (Daniel 9:25). Simple mathematics tells us that seven weeks plus sixty-two weeks equals sixty-nine weeks—a total of 483 days, or 483 years on the year-day principle. And the amazing thing is that from Artaxerxes' command "to restore and rebuild Jerusalem" in 457 B.C. until Christ's baptism in A.D. 27 was exactly 483 years! The seventy-week prophecy, then, confirms the validity of the year-day principle, and it also provides a basis from which to calculate the 2,300 years of Daniel 8:14. Since the seventy weeks began in 457 B.C., the 2,300 years also began at that time, and they ended in A.D. 1844, less than fifty years after the end of the 1,260 years of Daniel 7:25! I propose that only the God of heaven could begin two time prophecies (the 2,300 days and the 1,260 days) a thousand years apart in ancient history and conclude them within fifty years of each other in our time.

This understanding of Daniel's prophecies, and the confirmation given by Jesus' baptism right on time, comprise the reason Seventh-day Adventists say that the cleansing or vindication of the sanctuary in Daniel 8:14 began in 1844. And because the cleansing of the sanctuary in Daniel 8:14 comes at the same point in the outline of history as the judgment in chapter 7:9, 10, we've concluded that this judgment—what we call the investigative judgment—also began in 1844. We even narrowed that date down to October 22, 1844, based on an analogy between the various annual feast days in the Levitical religious calendar and the time of their fulfillment in the antitype.

In conclusion

How a person understands the investigative judgment and related topics depends on how that person interprets the biblical evidence. Our critics interpret the evidence in ways that differ from ours, which is understandable. My point is that, given our methods of interpretation, our conclusions about the investigative judgment, the seventy weeks, the 2,300 days, and the Day of Atonement are all solidly based on the Bible.

The New Testament book of Hebrews comments at length on the earthly and heavenly sanctuaries, and much of what the author of Hebrews says helps us to understand the work of our High Priest in the heavenly sanctuary. Some interpreters believe that Hebrews contradicts our Adventist understanding of the sanctuary, and especially the heavenly Day of Atonement. In chapters 28–33 of this book, I suggested that the author of Hebrews didn't have our understanding of the Day of Atonement and the investigative judgment *because he wasn't supposed to have it yet!* After all, the prophecies of Daniel extended nearly two thousand years beyond his time. And following a careful analysis of what the author of Hebrews did say, I concluded that his comments don't negate our understanding. These are the reasons why I believe our Adventist teaching about an investigative judgment in heaven prior to Christ's second coming has a strong biblical foundation.

---

1. Frank B. Holbrook, "The Great Controversy," in *Handbook,* 1000.
2. White, *The Great Controversy,* 484.
3. Ibid., 678.

Chapter 36

What Difference Does It Make?

In preparation for this chapter, I conducted a brief survey among some of my friends at Pacific Press®, where I work. My question was quite simple: What difference does the Adventist teaching about the investigative judgment make in your personal life, your spiritual walk with God? Here are some of the responses I got.

- "Why have a religion if there's no judgment to separate good from evil?"
- "The investigative judgment is like the air: it's always there, and I don't think about it."
- "It's a little frightening, because God looks at every aspect of my life."
- "I've heard people arguing about it, but I wonder what's the big deal? It doesn't make any difference in my relationship with God."
- "When I look at myself, I don't feel ready to be judged."
- "What is the investigative judgment? I never heard about it."

This little survey is certainly not scientific, but I believe that even the half dozen responses I got point out a problem: Seventh-day Adventists are for the most part aware of our teaching about the investigative judgment, but it doesn't have much spiritual meaning for them. Before we get too alarmed at that, let's put it in perspective with another teaching that is quite widely accepted as a part of orthodox Christianity. What kinds of responses would I get if I were to conduct a survey asking people about the spiritual benefit they receive from the doctrine of the Trinity? This doctrine has profound spiritual implications, but for most people it is—to put it in the words of a couple of my respondents—like the air: It's important as a doctrine, but what's the big deal? We don't really think about it all that much.

I should hasten to point out that obviously, we can't go around all day, every day, thinking about the Trinity, the investigative judgment, and the twenty-six other fundamental beliefs. Most of the time, these teachings remain in the background of our minds, outside our conscious awareness. Nevertheless, they influence our attitudes about ourselves and God as we go through the day. For example, how do you feel when you know you've done something wrong? You feel guilty, of course! And you have that feeling because you're aware that God is judging you for what you just did. At that moment the point isn't *when* the judgment takes place. It's simply that you *feel* judged. After all, it was Jesus Himself who said that one of the Holy Spirit's functions in our lives is to convict us "of guilt in regard to sin and righteousness and judgment" (John 16:8, NIV). Awareness of God's judgment against sin helps us to avoid yielding to temptation. And these feelings about judgment are entirely appropriate, provided we keep them in the context of the gospel. They are one of the ways God leads us to live a better life.

My point is that the doctrine of the judgment *does* affect our day-to-day spiritual attitudes. Thus, we can't say that the biblical doctrine of judgment has no spiritual implications for our lives. It has profound spiritual implications!

I've already pointed out in this book some of the spiritually harmful ideas some people have had about the judgment, such as the fear of never being good enough and the totally false notion that they can never be sure of their acceptance by God. But my purpose in this book hasn't been simply to correct false and spiritually destructive ideas about the investigative judgment. My purpose has also been to provide the background you need in order to understand the positive aspects of the judgment. The purpose of this chapter is to examine these positive aspects, if only briefly.

A transparent God

Suppose that General Motors, Ford Motor Company, and the Chrysler Corporation were to open up all of their financial, marketing, and personnel records and invite any and all to inspect them. Suppose they said there'd be no time limit on anyone's stay at the company's offices and no records would be withheld—ask for a document, and one of their friendly employees would hurry to retrieve it and hand it to you. They would even provide you with a comfortable and very private place to carry on your inspection.

Of course, that will never happen. But that's precisely what the investigative judgment is all about! God is opening up heaven's most secret records and allowing the angels to inspect them. Nothing will be withheld. Why? Because God is sure that His decisions are right, and He isn't afraid to let the angels have full information about them.

The doctrine of the investigative judgment tells us that we serve a very transparent God.

A reasonable God

Closely related to this idea is the realization that we serve a very reasonable God. Speaking through Isaiah, God said, "Come now, and let us reason together" (Isaiah 1:18). God created human beings with intelligence, and He respects that intelligence. He expects that we will want to understand His actions, so He explains Himself to us. Granted, we should have faith in God, and for a good reason: He can see far beyond our limited scope. He understands things that would be impossible for us to understand. But to the extent that we can understand, He invites us, "*Come now,* and let us reason together."

God's reasonableness is to me one of the great spiritual lessons of the investigative judgment. It tells me that my God isn't arbitrary. He isn't simply a divine dictator. Indeed, part of the reason why I can trust Him is that I know He's reasonable. If I have questions, He'll do His best to answer them within my limited ability to understand.

How does the investigative judgment tell me this? Daniel 7:9, 10 says that God is opening His record books to inspection by all His intelligent creatures in heaven. If God is willing to open His record books so the millions of angels around His throne can inspect them, then surely He's also willing to explain His ways to me. At the present time, my ability to understand is limited by my earthbound circumstances. But I know that a day is coming when I, too, will be able to examine those records in heaven, and if that examination raises further questions in my mind, then God will see to it that I receive adequate answers. I may not know how all the pieces of my life fit together now, but a day is coming when I *will* understand. So it's OK to wonder, to doubt, and to ask why. This doesn't offend God. He is reasonable. He respects our questions, even if our limitations mean He can't always fully answer them now.

This is one of the great lessons that I learn from the investigative judgment. And while I may not run around thinking about it all day, every day, the understanding that my God is reasonable and that He respects my questions gives me peace of mind throughout the day, even when I'm not thinking about it.

The doctrine of the investigative judgment tells us that we have a reasonable God who treats us as reasonable people.

A just God

The investigative judgment tells me that God is fair. The eternal reward that each person receives will be in harmony with the kind of life he or she has lived. The primary issue is whether we have trusted Jesus. Those who trust Him experience a spiritual change of mind and heart called "conversion" that enables them to keep God's laws out of a genuine desire to obey Him. Their lives will increasingly reflect obedience to God's laws and moral principles. This obedience will demonstrate that their faith is genuine (see James 2:14–17) and that they are qualified to live in God's eternal kingdom.

On the other hand, those who refuse to live in harmony with God's laws are responsible for perpetuating the problems that evil causes in our world. They won't be permitted a place in God's eternal kingdom, for they would simply continue the same attitudes and practices there that have caused so much suffering on this earth.

And God is utterly fair in His decisions about whom to include and whom to exclude. To dispel any possible doubt about the justice of His decisions, He has invited a huge committee of our peers—created beings like ourselves—to verify the accuracy of His decisions. Thus, while you and I may be surprised someday about who we meet in God's kingdom and who we don't meet there, we can be sure that everyone who deserves to be there will be there, and no one will be there who doesn't deserve to be there.

The doctrine of the investigative judgment tells us that we can trust God to be fair.

Guarding our spiritual experience

In her book *The Great Controversy,* Ellen White made a statement that some people have found quite frightening.

All who would have their names retained in the book of life should now, in the few remaining days of their probation, afflict their souls before God by sorrow for sin and true repentance. There must be deep, faithful searching of heart. The light, frivolous spirit indulged by so many professed Christians must be put away. There is earnest warfare before all who would subdue the evil tendencies that strive for the mastery. . . . Though all nations are to pass in judgment before God, yet He will examine the case of each individual with as close and searching scrutiny as if there were not another being upon the earth. Everyone must be tested and found without spot or wrinkle or any such thing.[1]

These words make it sound as though we must be absolutely perfect in order to pass God's scrutiny in the judgment. Because of statements such as these, some people charge Ellen White with being legalistic and causing undue fear of the judgment. However, we have to keep in mind that the Bible gives equally stern warnings that our actions have consequences for the judgment. Some of the most sobering words are those spoken by Jesus Himself. He said, "For every idle word men may speak, they will give account of it in the day of judgment" (Matthew 12:36). Paul cautioned that "we must all appear before the judgment seat of Christ, that each one may receive the things done in the body, according to what he has done, whether good or bad" (2 Corinthians 5:10). And the author of Hebrews said, "If we sin willfully after we have received the knowledge of the truth, there no longer remains a sacrifice for sins, but a certain fearful expectation of judgment, and fiery indignation which will devour the adversaries" (10:26, 27), and, "It is a fearful thing to fall into the hands of the living God" (verse 31).

The point that both Ellen White and the Bible are making is that we must heed the Bible's moral instruction, and, with God's help, do our very best to overcome the sins in our life. We must not be careless Christians.

The doctrine of the investigative judgment *tells us that our lives will be evaluated, so we need to pay careful attention to what we do.*

God is on our side

However, we must balance this whole concept with the gospel. Those who meet the standards of the judgment will do so only because Christ's righteousness covers them, never because of their own achievements. So, when we discover a sin or character defect, we needn't fear that this makes us unacceptable to God. No one is perfect. None of us can ever count ourselves sinless this side of Christ's second coming. The apostle John said, "If we say that we have no sin, we deceive ourselves, and the truth is not in us" (1 John 1:8). Our perfection will always be based on Christ's righteousness covering us. In her book *Steps to Christ,* Ellen White said, "Christ's character stands in place of [our] character, and [we] are accepted before God just as if [we] had not sinned."[2] One of the greatest lessons Christians can learn is that we must always rest in the righteousness of Christ. That's why Paul said, "Having been justified by faith, we have peace with God through our Lord Jesus Christ" (Romans 5:1). There truly is great peace in knowing that God accepts us just as we are.

The key question in the judgment, then, is whether we have accepted Christ's righteousness to cover our sinfulness. All those who are loyal to God's laws—who want to obey Him and are doing their best to obey Him—are covered with Christ's righteousness, and they will pass the scrutiny of the judgment. *We must understand the investigative judgment in this context.*

In the judgment, it is Satan who accuses us of being unworthy of God's favor. He's the "accuser of our brethren" (Revelation 12:10). He's the one who stands before God in the investigative judgment, "point[ing] to the record of [our] lives, to the defects of character, the unlikeness to Christ, which has dishonored [our] Redeemer."[3] Satan is the ultimate perfectionist, insisting that unless we have a flawless record, we don't deserve God's favor. Jesus, on the other hand, "shows [our] penitence and faith, and, claiming for [us] forgiveness, He lifts His wounded hands before the Father and the holy angels, saying: I know them by name. I have graven them on the palms of My hands."[4] Our only hope in the judgment is Christ's righteousness, never our own.

The good news of the judgment is that it's linked with the good news of salvation. Revelation 14:6, 7 unites the gospel and the judgment into a single end-time proclamation for God's people. The angel who proclaims "the hour of His judgment has come" is the same angel who has "the everlasting gospel to preach to those who dwell on the earth."

The doctrine of the investigative judgment tells us that God is on our side in the judgment. He's provided Christ's righteousness to cover our sinfulness, therefore, we needn't fear the judgment.

Sin and suffering will end

God's people live in a hostile world. The one who fomented the original rebellion in heaven is angry that he can't bend to his will the small band of people on this earth who are loyal to God and His laws. In symbolic language, Daniel 7:25 describes the extension of his rebellion to this earth as a little horn that is attacking the saints. Revelation 12:17 tells us that the dragon is furious with God's people and is on the warpath against them. And Revelation 13:7 represents Daniel's little horn as a beast that was given power "to make war with the saints and to overcome them." This is the great controversy theme—the conflict between good and evil—that we have discussed in previous chapters of this book. However, Daniel assures us that the investigative judgment will render a sentence against the little horn and "in favor of the saints of the Most High" (Daniel 7:22). Revelation echoes that favorable judgment. It says, "You are righteous, O Lord, the One who is and who was and who is to be, because You have judged these things. For they have shed the blood of saints and prophets, and You have given them blood to drink. For it is their just due" (Revelation 16:5, 6).

Daniel says that someday, the control that the forces of evil have held over the world will be destroyed (see Daniel 7:11, 26). Revelation 20 describes a lake of fire that will destroy all sin and sinners. On the other hand, Daniel assures us that "the greatness of the kingdoms under the whole heaven, shall be given to the people, the saints of the Most High" (Daniel 7:27). And Revelation 21 and 22 describe in detail a kingdom in which "God will wipe away every tear from their eyes; there shall be no more death, nor sorrow, nor crying. There shall be no more pain, for the former things have passed away" (Revelation 21:4).

From Daniel and Revelation we learn that *the conflict between good and evil will end someday.* And the investigative judgment, which is transpiring in heaven even as you read these words, will play a crucial role in settling that conflict. The pain and suffering we experience in this world as a result of sin won't continue forever. So the next time you wonder why God is allowing you or someone close to you to suffer, let the thought of the investigative judgment give you peace of mind.

The doctrine of the investigative judgment tells us that we're drawing near to the end of evil.

The history of Adventism

In several of the early chapters of this book, I explained the origin of the investi-gative judgment doctrine in the history of the Seventh-day Adventist Church. The Millerite movement and its demise in the Great Disappointment of October 22, 1844, are a crucial part of our story. The world, including most of the Protestant world, scoffs and tells us that the investiga-tive judgment is little more than a clever face-saving device to explain away our em-barrassment about the Great Disappoint-ment. But a careful examination of the facts connected with William Miller's movement persuades me that God led him to preach the way he did, and God allowed the Great Disappointment because He knew that's what it would take to jump-start our movement. Throughout world history, crises have been great motivators for God's people—the Cross being a prime example—and the Great Disappointment was a massive crisis, to say the least.

So, it's imperative that we never forget our history. One of the tragedies in today's Adventism is that many of our members—perhaps a majority—are only faintly aware of this history, and many know nothing about it at all. Unfortunately, some of those who do know about it find it embar-rassing. However, I propose that without that history we would be merely another nice Christian denomination on the Amer-ican religious scene.

The doctrine of the investigative judgment tells us who we are and why we're here.

Our mission

On October 23, 1844, Hiram Edson gained the insight that the sanctuary that was said to be "cleansed," "vindicated," in Daniel 8:14 is in heaven. Adventists have held to this view ever since. This and other aspects of our teaching about the investigative judgment have been severely criticized over the years, causing many Adventists to question its validity. Some have left the church, and many who remain have questions. This invariably diminishes the effectiveness of our witness, for in order to proclaim a message boldly, we have to be convinced of its truth. And that's one of the most significant reasons why it's important to understand that the investigative judgment has a solid biblical basis.

Christ's Great Commission calls us to "make disciples of all the nations" (Matthew 28:19). Revelation 14:6, 7, which describes an angel who comes down from heaven with "the everlasting gospel to preach to those who dwell on the earth—to every nation, tribe, tongue, and people," gives His commission an end-time setting. The "first angel's message" is the Great Commission for our day. It includes three things:

- The gospel
- The judgment
- The Sabbath*

Notice that the judgment is an important part of the gospel message for our day. This means that *God wants us to proclaim it.* That isn't easy in a world that either laughs at or condemns the investigative judgment. However, as we've seen in this book, it's a thoroughly biblical message, so the fact that the world doesn't accept it is beside the point. Throughout history, God's people have endured the world's scorn for their biblical message, but they proclaimed it just the same. And so must we.

The doctrine of the investigative judgment is an important part of our message to the world.

The end is near

The biblical teaching about the investigative judgment also assures us that we live in the time of the end. This is different from the end of time, when Jesus will actually return. The time of the end is the period leading up to His second coming. Our pioneers believed Jesus would come in their day, and every generation since has believed the same thing. I still want to believe He will come in my day, but I don't know that. What I do know is that ever since 1844, we've been living in the time of the end. Why do I say this? Because the angel Gabriel told Daniel that the vision of

---

*The angel's command to "worship Him who made heaven and earth, the sea and springs of water" (verse 7) is practically a direct quote of Exodus 20:11, the concluding verse of the fourth commandment.

chapter 8—which includes the 2,300 days/ years—"refers to the time of the end" (Daniel 8:17). The 2,300 days/years ended in 1844, and ever since, the world has been living on borrowed time. The year 1844 marks the time when the investigative judgment began in heaven, and on earth, it's the time when the countdown to Christ's second coming began.

The doctrine of the investigative judgment tells us that we are living in the time of the end.

If the investigative judgment is simply another dry doctrine, then we might as well relegate it to the dustbin of history. But the meaning of the investigative judgment—what I have shared with you in this chapter and throughout this book—makes the investigative judgment powerful good news for God's people!

And it's biblical!

---

1. White, *The Great Controversy,* 490.
2. White, *Steps to Christ,* 62.
3. White, *The Great Controversy,* 484.
4. Ibid.

Epilogue

Why do people believe what they believe? Why is it that the same evidence can lead two people to two completely different conclusions?

This phenomenon doesn't happen just in theological circles. It happens in politics. Shortly after his inauguration, President Barack Obama proposed a major revision of the nation's health care system. Some members of Congress were all for it; others were strongly opposed. Everyone was looking at the same basic evidence and drawing opposite conclusions.

It happens in science. Some scientists are convinced that our current way of life is leading the world into horrible ecological devastation. Others assure us that our way of life has nothing to do with it—that it's all part of nature's normal ups and downs. Yet the data they are examining is the same.

The same thing happens in every field of human endeavor. Name your topic, study it a while, and you'll find people disagreeing on what the evidence means. Why is that? Why can the same evidence be interpreted in such widely differing ways?

It's because there is no such thing as total objectivity. We all come at the evidence with our biases, with our minds about half made up, and we set out to prove what we already think is right. And usually we can find evidence to support our presuppositions. We should all do our best to be as objective as possible, and then we should acknowledge that we are still human.

In the first chapter of this book I told you that I decided, back in early 2007, to make a thorough study of all aspects of our Adventist teaching about the investigative judgment in order to settle certain questions I'd had for several decades. I'll admit that I was predisposed to reaching a positive conclusion. I make no apology for that. I think we sometimes rush to change our minds too quickly. It would have been easy enough for me to look at the challenges of the critics and join them. Part of the reason why I didn't is that I believe in the historic mission of the Seventh-day Adventist Church. That was a major part of my predisposition to view the investigative judgment and related topics positively. So I decided to examine the very best and most recent thinking among the Adventist Church's biblical scholars, then reflect on what I learned, and draw my conclusions.

The book you've been reading is the result. I'm sure I haven't answered every question that can be raised, but I believe I've addressed the main ones. I've done my best to take seriously the objections of the critics and to examine the biblical evidence on both sides. The result is my conclusion that the basic framework of our historic teaching about the investigative judgment truly is biblical—and it makes sense.

Selected Bibliography

Books

Andross, Elmer E. *A More Excellent Ministry.* Mountain View, Calif.: Pacific Press® Publishing Association, 1912.

Ballenger, Albion F. *Cast Out for the Cross of Christ.* Tropico, Calif.: Self published, 1909.

Canright, Dudley M. *Seventh-day Adventism Renounced.* New York: Fleming H. Revell, 1889.

Damsteegt, P. Gerard. *Foundations of the Seventh-day Adventist Message and Mission.* Berrien Springs, Mich.: Andrews University Press, 1988.

Doukhan, Jacques B. *Secrets of Daniel: Wisdom and Dreams of a Jewish Prince in Exile.* Hagerstown, Md.: Review and Herald® Publishing Association, 2000.

Ford, Desmond. *Daniel.* Nashville: Southern Publishing Association, 1978.

Froom, Leroy Edwin. *The Prophetic Faith of Our Fathers.* 4 vols. Washington, D.C.: Review and Herald® Publishing Association, 1950–1954.

Gane, Roy. *Altar Call.* Berrien Springs, Mich.: Diadem, 1999.

_____. *Cult and Character: Purification Offerings, Day of Atonement, and Theodicy.* Winona Lake, Ind.: Eisenbrauns, 2005.

_____. *Leviticus, Numbers.* The New International Version Application Commentary. Grand Rapids, Mich.: Zondervan, 2004.

Goldingay, John E. *Daniel.* Word Biblical Commentary, vol. 30. Dallas: Word Books, 1989.

Goldstein, Clifford. *False Balances.* Nampa, Idaho: Pacific Press® Publishing Association, 1992.

Handbook of Seventh-day Adventist Theology. Hagerstown, Md.: Review and Herald® Publishing Association, 2000.

Harper Study Bible. 2nd ed. Grand Rapids, Mich.: Zondervan Bible Publishers, 1971.

Heppenstall, Edward. *Our High Priest: Jesus Christ in the Heavenly Sanctuary.* Washington, D.C.: Review and Herald® Publishing Association, 1972.

Holbrook, Frank B., ed. *70 Weeks, Leviticus, Nature of Prophecy.* Daniel and Revelation Committee Series, vol. 3. Washington, D.C.: Biblical Research Institute, 1986.

_____., ed. *Symposium on Daniel.* Daniel and Revelation Committee Series, vol. 2. Washington, D.C.: Biblical Research Institute, 1986.

_____., ed. *Issues in the Book of Hebrews.* Daniel and Revelation Committee Series, vol. 4. Silver Spring, Md.: Biblical Research Institute, 1989.

Horn, Siegfried H., and Lynn H. Wood. *The Chronology of Ezra 7: A Report of the Historical Research Committee of the General Conference of Seventh-day Adventists.* Washington, D.C.: Review and Herald® Publishing Association, 1953.

Martin, Malachi. *The Keys of This Blood: The Struggle for World Dominion Between Pope John Paul II, Mikhail Gorbachev, and the Capitalist West.* New York: Simon and Schuster, 1990.

Martin, Walter R. *The Truth About Seventh-day Adventism.* Grand Rapids, Mich.: Zondervan Publishing House, 1960.

Moore, Marvin. *Could It Really Happen?* Nampa, Idaho: Pacific Press® Publishing Association, 2007.

_____. *How to Think About the End Time.* Nampa, Idaho: Pacific Press® Publishing Association, 2001.

Owusu-Antwi, Brempong. *The Chronology of Daniel 9:24–27.* Berrien Springs, Mich.: Adventist Theological Society, 1995. (This is the published version of Owusu-Antwi's dissertation. At the time of the writing of this book, Brempong Owusu-Antwi was president of the Adventist University of Africa in Kenya.)

Seventh-day Adventist Bible Commentary, The. 7 volumes. Washington, D.C.: Review and Herald® Publishing Association, 1955.

Seventh-day Adventist Church Manual. 17th ed. Silver Spring, Md.: Secretariat of the General Conference of Seventh-day Adventists, 2005.

Seventh-day Adventist Encyclopedia. Washington, D.C.: Review and Herald® Publishing

Association, 1966.

Seventh-day Adventists Answer Questions on Doctrine: An Explanation of Certain Major Aspects of Seventh-day Adventist Belief. Washington, D.C.: Review and Herald® Publishing Association, 1957. (Also referred to as *Questions on Doctrine.*)

Shea, William. *Selected Studies in Prophetic Interpretation.* Rev. ed. Daniel and Revelation Committee Series, vol. 1. Silver Spring, Md.: Biblical Research Institute, 1992.

Wallenkampf, Arnold, and Richard Lesher, eds. *The Sanctuary and the Atonement: Biblical, Historical, and Theological Studies.* Washington, D.C.: Review and Herald® Publishing Association, 1981.

Whidden, Woodrow W. *E. J. Waggoner: From the Physician of Good News to Agent of Division.* Hagerstown, Md.: Review and Herald® Publishing Association, 2008.

White, Ellen G. *The Acts of the Apostles.* Nampa, Idaho: Pacific Press® Publishing Association, 1911.

_____. *Counsels to Writers and Editors.* Nashville: Southern Publishing Association, 1946.

_____. *Evangelism.* Hagerstown, Md.: Review and Herald® Publishing Association, 1946.

_____. *The Great Controversy.* Nampa, Idaho: Pacific Press® Publishing Association, 1911.

_____. *Patriarchs and Prophets.* Nampa, Idaho: Pacific Press® Publishing Association, 1958.

_____. *Selected Messages.* 3 volumes. Hagerstown, Md.: Review and Herald® Publishing Association, 1958–1980.

_____. *Steps to Christ.* Hagerstown, Md.: Review and Herald® Publishing Association, 1956.

Other Sources

Camacho, Harold S. "The Altar of Incense in Hebrews 9:3-4." *Andrews University Seminary Studies* 24, no. 1 (Spring 1986): 5–12.

Cortez, Felix. " 'The Anchor of the Soul That Enters Within the Veil': The Ascension of the 'Son' in the Letter to the Hebrews." PhD diss., Andrews University Theological Seminary, 2007.

Cosaert, Carl P. "The Use of *Hagios* for the Sanctuary in the Old Testament Pseudepigrapha,

Philo, and Josephus." *Andrews University Seminary Studies* 42, no. 1 (Spring 2004): 91–103.

Cottrell, Raymond F. "A Hermeneutic for Daniel 8:14." Document 024161 at the Center for Adventist Research, James White Library, Andrews University, Berrien Springs, Michigan.

_____. "The 'Sanctuary Doctrine'—Asset or Liability?" Paper presented at the San Diego Adventist Forum, San Diego, Calif., February 9, 2002. Also available as fourteen separate articles at http://www.atoday.com/view/all.

_____. "1844, the Investigative Judgment, the Sanctuary." Transcript of Adventist Forum presentation, Loma Linda, California, February 8, 1980. Also Document 024166 at the Center for Adventist Research, James White Library, Andrews University, Berrien Springs, Michigan.

Davidson, Richard. "Christ's Entry 'Within the Veil' in Hebrews 6:19-20: The Old Testament Background." *Andrews University Seminar Studies* 39, no. 2 (Autumn 2001): 175–190.

_____. "Inauguration or Day of Atonement? A Response to Norman Young's 'Old Testament Background to Hebrews 6:19–20 Revisited.' " *Andrews University Seminary Studies* 40, no. 1 (Spring 2002): 69–88.

_____. "The Meaning of *Nitsdaq* in Daniel 8:14." *Journal of the Adventist Theological Society* 7, no. 1 (1996): 107–119.

De Souza, Elias Brasil. "The Heavenly Sanctuary/Temple Motif in the Hebrew Bible: Function and Relationship to the Earthy [*sic*] Counterparts." PhD diss., Andrews University Theological Seminary, 2005.

Ford, Desmond. "Daniel 8:14, the Day of Atonement, and the Investigative Judgment." Manuscript presented at the Glacier View conference, Ward, Colorado, August 1980. (This manuscript has been published as a book by the same title [Casselberry, Fl.: Evangelion Press, 1980]. The pagination in the book differs from that in the manuscript. All page numbers in citations in this book, *The Case for the Investigative Judgment,* are from the manuscript Ford presented at Glacier View rather than the book.)

Pfandl, Gerhard. "The Year-Day Principle." *Reflections,* April 2007. (*Reflections* is the quarterly newsletter of the Biblical Research Institute.)

Proebstle, Martin. "Truth and Terror: A Text-Oriented Analysis of Daniel 8:9–14." PhD diss., Andrews University Theological Seminary, 2006.

Ratzlaff, Dale. "What Is the Meaning of the Cross?" *Proclamation!* 9 no. 3 (March–April 2008).

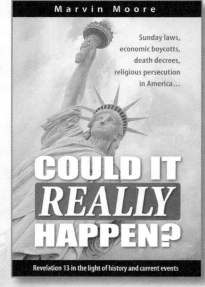